Arthur N. Howard

History of the French in America

With six Years of Life and Travel in the Province of Quebec

Arthur N. Howard

History of the French in America
With six Years of Life and Travel in the Province of Quebec

ISBN/EAN: 9783337216238

Printed in Europe, USA, Canada, Australia, Japan

Cover: Foto ©ninafisch / pixelio.de

More available books at **www.hansebooks.com**

CITY OF MONTREAL.

OF THE

FRENCH IN AMERICA,

WITH

SIX ✝ YEARS ✝ OF ✝ LIFE ✝ AND ✝ TRAVEL

IN THE

✳ PROVINCE ✳ OF ✳ QUEBEC. ✳

PUBLISHERS PREFACE.—The manuscript of part first of this work was written by a native of mine, and from my own personal experience of seven years in the Province of Quebec. I consider it an excellent and truthful portrayal of every day life in that province. Being also personally acquainted with most of the characters, many of the incidents of the book I can offer it to the public as a true picture of life without a word of fiction in it except the names which I have changed. Most of the characters in it are living.—R. A. N. HARVEY.

SALT LAKE CITY:
TIMES STEAM PRINT.
1885.

Chapter I.

In the year 1860 a family named Howard emigrated to the backwoods of Canada. The family consisted of father, mother and two sons. The husband was a thriftless being who had not sufficient energy to provide for his family, but allowed his wife's brother in London, named Goldsmith, to pay to his wife a yearly income of $400; after the wife's death the uncle of the children settled $300 a year on the two boys—whose names were Tom and Arthur—who had bought some property from another uncle in Montreal. The narrative commences on the 5th day of January, 1876, when the two brothers receive a letter from their uncle in London: "My dear boys I received your welcome letters and am happy to hear that you are comfortable with your father, at the same time I wish it to be understood that the money advanced to you must be laid out in the improvement of your new farm and I strongly advise you to try and make it at once produce the necessaries of life; get ready a portion of that ground and plant potatoes and wheat immediately, as you may lose the home farm so suddenly as to throw you into difficulties, your father is so uncertain both in his temper and management, he may either involve it in debt or sell it before you had time to prepare, on that account and for his interest as well as your own I again strongly recommend to make your farm the grand object of your exertions, so as not to have yourselves and father without the common necessaries of life; I am truly justified in being afraid of Mr. Howard's management, when I remember the sums of money he has wasted from his youth to this year and the charge, trouble and expense he has been to every one connected with him. I think for his sake and yours you ought to spend your income on your lots otherwise your time and money will be frittered away; as regards Mr. H's clearance I could put a boarding school girl, who could on uncleared land do three times as much as he did at half the cost. I expected to see at least 40 acres of good land cleared and fenced bearing good crops,

That property of yours will be a splendid place soon, although the labor is great the reward will be greater. Have you tried to get a contract for the wood at the mines? Have you seen any bears? How does my dear sister's tomb look? I hope the cedar hedge will thrive. Give my love to my niece; tell her I will write next week; she is a great pet of mine, also remember me to my brother Herbert and his wife. Everything here is dull and I am afaid trade will never revive in England; the tradesmen and mechanics have driven the trade into other countries by their strikes and short sighted foolish proceedings and now the wretched workhouses and open streets are full of half starved people, clerks and laborers as well as every kind of mechanics seeking in vain for employment at any wages, ever so little to keep them from starvation; there seems to be no hope of improvement; it is I fear permanent. I should like to live in your neighborhood. If I had possessed 13000 acres like your uncle Richard I should not have sold it but made it valuable property. Take care and do not rest in wet clothes or catch cold. I hope to hear good news about you all; tell uncle Herbert not to give up work or else he will fall sick. My dear Tom and Arthur, your loving uncle, J. Goldsmith." Saw the northern lights at midday, which are only seen in day time during the most severe winters; measured Joe Vincent's job of cord wood, cut him one cord on the 20 on account of the small branchwood in it, also because some of the piles were too loosely corded. Had a dispute with father and his hired boy Dodsley; Dodsley called me a liar for which I boxed his ears; father took Dodsley's part and said we had nothing to do with him; I told him that if we fed and clothed the boy he might at least render us some service occasionally, such as cleaning the stables, etc. On Sunday our cousins Sarah, Ethel, Philip, Walter and Jonathen Goldsmith, took tea with us and spent the evening in reading Chamber's miscellaneous and the British American magazine, full of interesting anecdotes and love stories. Next day Tom and I went to Richford and paid our accounts with storekeepers there; stayed all night at C. McMills, who keeps a hotel; next morning saw a span of colts valued at $100 which we thought too dear; on our way back Guertin told us he charged $2 a 1000 feet for sawing lumber; he offered to sell us a very fine horse for $100; next day Tom and father had a dispute about a gold watch and a bible that our dear mother left to Tom, which father did not want to let him have, he however came to terms and gave them to him. Andre L, to whom we gave a job of making shingles, said if we did not keep him supplied with cedar he would not finish the job; we promised to keep him better supplied and gave him an order on Bedard's store as part payment on the job. Went to Vincent's to hire them to draw saw logs, they could not as they had a large quantity of wood to draw for the R'wy Co. Magloire and is greatly captivated with Tetreault's daughter; she is very stout, frightfully pockmarked and has very ugly features, but I suppose it is a great blessing that many persons seem indifferent to the charms of beauty or a great many men and women would remain unmarried. I can understand a man marrying an ugly woman who is very talented, for intellectual beauty is of even more consequence than physical, but I do not admire a man's taste who marries a woman devoid of both these qualities. Jack Spencer came looking for work; gave him the job of drawing 100 saw logs to G's mill, 2 miles distance for $7 Louis Brodeur came to get us to go with our horses to snow-plow the roads; we went; there were 8 other teams whose owners had volunteered their services for the public good. In some parishes a man is given the contract of clearing the road in winter and keeping it in repair, getting $25 to keep 6 miles in order during the winter. Received a letter from Allan Robertson of New Brunswick, chiefly a letter of condolence on our dear mother's death, also events in his life at college and of his father's travels on the continent of Europe. Jan. 20, one of father's cows got strangled last night, got her foot in the yoke; went to Meredith's to buy another but the one he had for sale was nothing extra; was invited to stay to tea but declined with thanks and an excuse, Tom and I had a talk about our affairs, I wanted to build merely a log barn, Tom a frame one. I suggestsd that we might want to leave this place later on and it would be wiser to make what money we could out of the place and not spend all our income on it and keep a bank account in case of an emergency. Tom's idea however prevailed; a Frenchman wanted to sell us a horse and take a gun and revolver at $20 as part payment; we however declined. Derbue came looking for work; gave him 10 cords of wood to chop; father sold him the dead cow to make soap but we afterwards heard that he and his family actually eat it; Derbue wanted us to advance him money to get provisions but I did not like to trust him at which he was greatly offended. Next morning went to Aston with a double load of wood, had hard work starting the sleigh, it was frozen to the snow; had to chop the hard snow around the runners; only sold my load for $1.40 to the R'wy, it only passed for 3½ ft. wood, so I did not "cut" Vincent enough on it. We made a mistake in contracting our bark to Chelton, he gave me $6 for my last load while D. Doherty offered $9; in the evening went to G's; A. Larivere and his wife were there; they were only married this fall and are living on what was once Larivere's old homestead, on which his father settled in 1858, when he had to leave the east half of lot 30, on which he had squatted; uncle H having come to live on it from his other lot in the 6th range, which was too sandy to make farming a success. Larivere sen. although a hard worker, has been unsuccessful, partly through drink, he during the first few years went out west and made a considerable amount of money and returned to his wife who lived on the farm with the younger children; left his 3 oldest sons out west who often sent him sums of money but to no use; the crash came through unsuccessful lumbering operations and the homestead was sold; the family moved to another lot they bought from the British American Land Co. situated in the Point of Aston, which place he gave into the management of one of his sons on condition that he and his wife should receive their support from him, which is the usual way it is managed in this province. Andre is going to move in the Spring on 50 acres of land opposite to ours, which he has bought on credit; after a hard days work he and his wife make shingles to sell up-till 11 every night, so if frugality and industry is all that is required he ought to succeed. As it was a beautiful moonlight night I went out for a snow shoe tramp with Ethel and the two Miss Daytons to the top of Parker's hill; Parker, poor fellow, through drink has years ago been obliged to sell out and go west and has since had a village called after him and is its postmaster. F. Burke wanted to hire to us to drive our team, but even if we did want one I would never have him, for when his half starved oxen could not pull their load he placed a bundle of straw behind them and burnt them in a terrible manner, also another instance of his develish cruelty was the putting coal oil on a cat and setting her on fire till burnt to death, yet this scoundrel had the audacity to partake of the Holy Sacrament, a few days after this occurrence and that too with respectable members of the infallable church who were acquainted with all his villany. Mr. Meredith wrote to father saying he would sell a pure Ayrshire calf for $10; sent to Montreal for pork, where it is cheaper than here. Broke roads to the saw logs as it is a mild day, which is the best time for "breaking" roads as the snow packs better. We heard of pair of oxen for sale at $50 each but one pair was too old, 9 years and the other too young, 2½, which is too young for heavy work. Of late we are getting "cut" on our bark on account of its being considerably broken; at a tannery this is not objected to as it can be thrown into the mill and ground at once, but shipping such bark to the U. S. causes a great amount of extra work in loading and unloading it from the cars as well as waste; received a letter from uncle Richard: "My dear Arthur and Tom, I have to apologize for not writing sooner, but I have been exceedingly busy since I saw you last; I am attending Montreal general hospital at present, in fact that would occupy my time without anything else, I am happy to say through my son Richard's help I have got out all my accounts; things are frightful in town, going from bad to worse, but some of the sufferers really deserve what they are getting; sickness has been very prevalent this winter; when I was out I quite forgot to take out a cap Angelica sent to Tom, you can get it when you come in; we have no visitors at present and the sooner you come in the better, with love to your father, believe me to remain your affectionate uncle Richard I Goldsmith." Barclay brought 16 yards of cloth that his wife had wove for father; he invited us to a temperance meeting at East Hastings. Jonathan G. only made one load for us to-day; this is not fair, when i changed time with them last fall at plowing I worked from daylight till dark, they also want more than one bushel of oats per day for their horses. Feb. 6th, Tom and I went to Aston; he bought a cloth cap for $1 and a pair of kid mits for $1 30; paid 15 cents each for hair cutting; Tom went to Montreal; next day, Sunday, a beautiful day, put chloride of zinc on our mare's shoulder, which is sore, then went for a snow shoe tramp with Sarah, Ethel and Philip; in the evening young Kirwin came from Devlin's and asked us all to a dance there, aunt and uncle went and I spent the evening at G's.; Sarah read stories aloud till 10; roads next day bad to Guertin's mill, can only load on 2 logs a load; went to McDougall's at Aston for money he owed us, he was not at home, was at a school meeting, he is one of the village trustees for the village school; had a long chat with Mrs. McD, she is a French Canadian Roman Catholic, but has a fair education and speaks English as fluently as French; they seem to live very happily together notwithstanding their difference in religious belief, he being a Congregationalist, but there being no children may account for this; I believe from what I have heard that they had some trouble as regards the education of his daughter and only child by his first wife, who was a Protestant, and whom Mrs. McD tried to bring up as an R. C., but her father sent her to her grandmother, where she has always lived since, thus removing what is generally the cause of discord in married life between husband and wife when they hold opposite beliefs. On Friday, on returning in the evening from drawing saw logs to the saw mill uncle Herbert said his son had finished paying the time he owed us with his team; for peace sake I said nothing but knew from our account book he owed us still 4 days; Tom returned on Saturday; I made 4 loads of logs, the last upset 3 times; sold the "cut" of some birch and ash for square timber to Israel Dufresne at $1 per tree, he only takes the largest and best; the squared timber is bought by "buyers" and shipped to the U S and Europe. Dufresne is part lumberer, trapper and laborer; in autumn he shoots game, fishes and lays traps for fur bearing animals, chiefly mink, martin and otter, he also sells the skins of skunks after using a certain process to remove the disgusting odor and occasionally catches a bear in "dead falls" or steel traps; n winter he makes square timber, in spring makes sugar and in summer sometimes peels bark "by the cord," makes barrel hoops out of ash, but he never makes any attempt to clear or cultivate his lot of land. Spent Sunday at Doherty's, an Irish family, 3 miles from our place. Dennis Doherty offered me $800 for the cut of all the wood on our 2 lots, 34 and 35, which I refused; father wanted us to go and hear Chief Joseph of the Oka Indians speak of the illtreatment that his tribe received from the Seminary brothers; we went however to a lecture at Richford town hall, the audience consisted of about 40 persons; the lecturer was once a chaplain in the U. S. army; he commenced with a description of the horrors of war, on being captured by the Southerners he said "why do you take my horse for I do not fight against you and I attend to the spiritual wants of Southerners as well as Northerners, but the remonstrance was of no avail and I was sent with my comrades to Libby prison; the forced marches under a burning sun were of course harder on us than our guards, encumbered as we were with our cavalry boots; on arrival the jailor searched us all and took away all the greenbacks any of the soldiers had, but left them in possession of Southern money when they had any; some of the soldiers hid their money by removing the brass covering off their buttons and hiding a bill inside, another way was to put a $20 bill in a quid of tobacco in their mouths and when out of sight remove it; our rations were barely sufficient to keep life in us; the way we cooked our bread was to mix the flour in an old rubber coat and cook the dough on a flat stone; that bread would have been better for paving a road than the human stomach; after a time it was given cooked to us, a piece about the size of my hand and a piece of meat as large as my two fingers; sometimes we had a little soup that had a horrible taste, but it was too dark to see what it was composed of, one morning while taking some I discovered a large white maggot in it; the meat they gave us was so lively that I actually think if it was left on the ground it would have walked away. We used to have regular markets among ourselves; the way we got our provisions was to attach a piece of bone to a string and throw it out through the bars of the window with a bank note attached; the people outside would attach to the string an egg or potatoes, &c.; we had to pay $1 for either a potatoe or an egg. One of our greatest torments was vermin, the best blood in Libby prison flowed in their veins." The boss of McDougalls cordwood shanty wanted to buy the cut of the wood on 20 acres of land at 10 cents a cord, which we refused; sold the cut of the hemlock bark on both our lots for $700, $400 cash and a half lot of land equivalent to the $300; went by the 2 o'clock train to Montreal with Doherty; paid 30 cents for breakfast on arrival. At uncle Richard's the family were not up, Doherty left saying he would call in the evening; drove about the city with uncle during the day; the bargain was concluded in the evening, but found that the 100 acres in question could not be purchased, so the full $700 was to be paid instead. On returning bought the cut of fathers hemlock bark and pine lumber for $150. Of late D. Doherty has been buying lots of land sold at auction at St. Lengene, the capital of the Co. of Bradford, which are sold for the amount of taxes due on them; sometimes one can make 1000 per cent interest on the investment. I gave back to father the right of keeping his pine timber; he is indignant with me for buying his bark; I told him he had no right to be, seeing that I gave him $5 more than another man offered him, to whom he was going to sell. Father sold the cut of the basswood timber on 60 acres for $35 to a man who owns a steam saw mill at the end of this "Range." Had several very cold and stormy days during which we only attended to the animals and cut firewood for the house; passed these days in reading at home or in conversation at our neighbors. I take pleasure in listening to Philip when he plays on his violin, on which he is very skilful. I have always thought that good music has an elevating influence on man. I have been thinking that father, even at his present age, ought to succeed on his farm. He has over $200, very fair buildings, over 25 acres fit for the plow, a good wardrobe full of clothing, sufficient for a lifetime, 12 sheep, a horse and cow besides wheat, money he can make from the valuable timber his 100 acre lot contains, as well as a fine sugar bush of 700 trees. Received a letter from uncle Jerrold: "My dear Tom and Arthur, how does the barn get on? make it so that it can be enlarged and see that it is strong and water tight; if once well done always comfortable, but if rickety ever a nuisance. I dare say you will have cellars to keep your winter stores in

In Ireland they dig deep pits and cover the potatoes with large heaps of earth to keep out the frost, probably this would not do for your severe climate. Have you cleared out the brook and made it deeper, so as to drain the Beaver meadow? that land is worth all the labor you can spend on it as it will turn out rich and fertile. I suppose you will live in the barn until you are able to get up a nice house at your leisure. Uncle Richard has a capital plan of a house with a veranda and balcony. I hope he will often go and see you; as long as you take his advice and are guided by his counsel and assistance you are safe. He is wise, steady, good and experienced alike, and you are both thrice, even ten fold happy in having him as a staunch and loving friend; he has by his ability, prudence and good conduct realized, without one mortal to aid him, a fortune in a career of virtue and honor, by the blessing of God, escaping from calumny and disgrace, steering clear from the traps and assaults of the wicked jealous people that are always ready to lie in wait for every good and prosperous man. It is a well known and admitted fact that rom the very days of our blessed Lord down to this hour, scarcely can a truly generous and good man escape the slanders of the truly idle and wicked, and clever and cautious indeed must be the upright man who can so walk as to escape the pitfalls and illwill of the vicious and the bad, and so much do they outnumber the good men of the world it will behave in proportion as you are happy and prosperous, to avoid giving them the slightest pretence either by look or word for attacking your character. Your aunt is sitting by the fire with her sister reading texts from the Bible. The weather is warm and so mild that flowers and leaves are springing up in our garden. We went yesterday to our church and heard our American Church of Engiand pastor preach a most clever and edifying sermon extemporaneously without note or book; a pious man, he knew the Bible well and quoted it often from memory; the people were most attentive and you could see at once the effect of a good and sincere man. Rupert is in his own room reading hard for Oxford; we are sometimes obliged to drive him from it as it gives him a headache. The course of study here now is very hard, if you do not work 10 or 15 hours a day you are most likely rejected; the labor is

much greater than any mechanic or laborers work and much
more worrying and injurious to the health, so that we are obliged
to be very watchful and not let Rupert damage his constitution
by incessant study. It has just commenced to pour down rain
again; we have not had such a season for 33 years and as far
trade and business it seems to have fled away; we were grieved
to hear it is as bad in Canada and the U. S. so that a time of war
and trouble is dreaded in Europe, which however you will escape
in your happy Canada. How glad you must be in your pleasant
fields and woods with the fine open air of heaven and not shut
up in dusty smoky cities, hemmed in by smothering walls drains
and cesspools and every breath and breeze laden with foul con-
tagion and bad smells. Small pox is raging in England; our parliament is sitting and there is a great conflict raging between the
Conservatives who are in the ministry and the Liberals who are
out upon the Turkish or Eastern question. It is generally supposed that Russia intends to make war on Turkey and that in
the end we also shall declare war on Russia and help the Turks,
with love to uncle Herbert and all his family, and with best prayers to God for you both and much love, your affectionate
uncle Jerrold. P. S.—What are you going to call your lots?"
Received $27 from McDougall for cordwood. Tom gave me a
note for $83 payable in 1880, for money I advanced the firm that
I possessed when we first entered partnership. Went to church
on foot; met Andre L. and Louis B. returning from mass and they
advised me to take a short cut by a bush road through Fancher's
farm, did so and regretted it; I often sunk through treacherous
ice up to my knees in water; when ¾ the way spied Christie's
snow-capped hill with barn upon it through the tree tops, decided
to take a bee line for it but the crust on the snow was not strong
enough to support my weight and every few footsteps I sank over
knee deep in the snow; no one can imagine how wearisome or
aggravating it is to walk a mile in this manner, at the same time
I easily imagined how the poor English felt when they staggered
about in the snow as they resisted the French who attacked them
on snow shoes in one of their earliest contests on this continent.
On entering Christie's clearance my difficulties were over, for
here the frost had taken greater effect on the snow than where it

was sheltered by the forest; Mr. Willoughby had not arrived from Preston when I arrived, where he also holds services as well as at Richford and Davenport, the latter place he goes to on a week day. Maud and Florence Meredith were at church, the church was full for a wonder as generally there are not more than 15 or 20. Several persons during the week have applied for the contract of building us a house and barn; we had put up a notice on the station house asking for tenders. John Blake was the lowest bidder, $85 to finish a frame barn 40x30 feet, with a stable in it, he to square the timber and do all the work except the building of a stone foundation and the hauling of the materials on the spot, we of course furnishing the nails, shingles, hinges, &c.; the house to be of hewn logs 6 inches thick, 20 x 22 feet, he to hew the timber and merely erect the house and put in the doors and windows. Uncle Richard sent us an excellent plan for a barn with a stone stable, 7 feet high underneath, but it was too expensive for us in our present circumstances; one good feature I saw in it was that of having the floors of the stables so arranged as to save the liquid manure. J. Blake is an unfortunate man, for which he himself is to blame; he lost 2 farms by extravagantly going into debt with a storekeeper named Delage, who took his farm from him for a small debt he owed him by making a great amount of law costs and forcing the sale of the farm at a small figure. Delage has since cleared $1500 on the wood alone and has had the farm cleared from end to end. This same man is one of the largest land proprietors in the country and is the largest farmer; he has 27 farms. Several farmers have had auctions lately and sold out their stock, fodder, animals and implements; all amounts under $5 cash down, under $10 credit 6 monts, over $10 one year. For several days I was laid up in the house from a severe cold. I really think great benefit is derived from exercising one's will-power when sick and not giving way to every slight sickness as some people do; of all things a doctor detests most is to treat a desponding or dispairing patient. While in Aston a few days ago there was an election for Mayor. Roussin the "rouge" candidate was elected amid great enthusiasm; there was a triumphant procession of 70 sleighs headed by a brass band, after which many speeches were made from the balcony of the

hotel Phaneuf wanted to sell me an enormous pair of oxen for
$90; his wife is suffering from a cancer and her face is frightfully
eaten away by it; she appeared perfectly unconscious, it was a
sight I shall never forget; he wanted me to take some whiskey
with him but I told him I was a total abstainer. Carmichael boys
are great novel readers; I often ridicule to them their trashy and
sensational reading, in which the characters are all overdrawn,
the villain is painted too black, the hero too perfect and the lovers
too ridiculously sentimental; all sensible people should try and
avoid becoming fascinated with this worthless style of literature,
and any man who says I do this or that to "kill time" should not
receive the respect of any good man or woman; man on this
earth has such a short time to perform the great duties of life
that every hour and even second should be regarded by him as
precious and sacred and no book should be read or word uttered,
or action performed that would not benefit the man himself or
the rest of mankind. Several of the lamb's of father's sheep have
died and no wonder, the sheep were only fed on hay and straw,
they should have received additional nourishment and been kept
in a warmer building; animals badly kept are only a loss. Gave
L. Brodeur $15 for drawing the squared timber of the barn and
house; conversed with Tom how we should have our logging
done this spring, he thought we ought to buy a yoke of cattle, I
thought it would be cheaper to give it out by the job than to pay
a man $1 a day to help us, but to tell the truth I do not know
where all the money is to come from; there is $85 for building
the barn and house,about $25 for the stone foundations,$30 for the
sawing of lumber, $10 still due Andre for shingles, $15 to Louis
for hauling squared timber, $20 for seed, oats and potatoes, and at
least $12 for provisions from this to May, in all $167; all we have
to meet this is $78.62; my uncle Jerrold's quarterly allowance and
$100 cash in hand. One thing is certain father will have to buy
his provisions in future as he is going to get another boy from
Norfolk Home; this sheltering home is managed by charitable
ladies who gather helpless orphans in England and find homes
for them in Canada; at any rate we cannot possibly board both
boys for him. On Saturday went early to Aston market to buy
seed potatoes, father and 2 Frenchmen were with us; on our way

to the village we caught up to a Frenchwoman from France, her first husband was an officer in the French army; she first came to Montreal and swindled one of its leading citizens out of a large sum of money by threatening blackmail, then came out here with a man said to be her cousin, he was found dead a short time after their arrival and she has taken another partner, Francis Burke, the cruel wretch who burned a cat alive; at present she is cutting a great dash on the money she obtained in Montreal; she is the cause of great scandal in our neighborhood. She is well educated and a wonderfully fluent conversationalist; father advised me not to take her on our double sleigh but I told him that it would be a greater disgrace to pass a poor woman with a six mile walk before her on a frosty morning; of course if the others had not been with me I should have been under the painful necessity of passing her; bought 10 bushels of potatoes at 35 cts. a bushel. We have great difficulty with Blake, who keeps continually asking for money on the contract; we however adhere chiefly to the contract and only pay in proportion as the work advances; father told us if we continued living on farinaceous food only, we would get consumptive and that he had written to uncle Richard and was determined to investigate our accounts; told him we had no objection to show him or any one else our accounts and that the more economical we could live the better as long as we did not lose our health, which was never better than at present. Mr. Brodeur returned from mass with a sprig of blessed palm which French Catholics keep hanging up from the ceiling throughout the year, all Canadians regard it with veneration and will not remove it from its place in a deserted house. Saw the first flock of crows this season; Cousin Ethel is going to the French school and is getting quite proficient in French. It is quite amusing to see my aunt and Miss Dupont trying to carry on conversation as neither of them can converse in any other language than their own. To-day the 25th March is my birthday, I am 18 years of age. There has been sufficient mild weather to enable Guertin to start his saw mill which works by water; chose a site for our new house which will be rather too close to the road but this could not be avoided on account of the small size of the clearance; 30th March raining hard, dense fog, the snow will soon be gone. Mrs. C. asked me what became of our dear mother's personal effects. I am sure it is none of her business, father acted mean in not giving me some trifling article that my mother wore as a momento. 31st went to Guertin's gave him a list of the different sizes' of lumber we needed, 20 pieces of scantling 4 inches x 4 for braces for the barn, 13.00 ft. of lumber, 15 ft. long for boarding up the sides of the buildings and 800 ft. 13 ft long, also 1,000 ft 12 ft long for roofing, &c. Napoleon wanted to rent a sugar kettle, the rent is 1 lb of sugar for the season for every bucket of sap the kettle will contain. In coming back from Guertin's I had 600 ft. of lumber on; the road was flooded and frozen over but broke through and the sleighs became immerged. I was afraid the horses would get drowned but I succeeded in unhitching the traces; came home on horseback at full gallop nigh half frozen. Dufresne offered father 100 lbs of sugar as rent for his sugar bush, father accepted it as a good offer, as half the trees have not been supplied with troughs; we got out our sleighs with difficulty, we should not use them any more this winter as the roads are bare in many places, which quickly wears ont the shoeing of a sleigh; the wetting I got gave me a bad cold and sore throat. Andrie L. has a hired man one of the smallest and most crabbed specimens of humanity I have seen, not quite 4 ft. high and in his face can be seen the misery he has endured; he told me he has been hard at work at manual labor since he was 6 yrs old, which no doubt partially accounts for his being a dwarf; he was married at 14 yrs of age but is very industrious and can do very nearly as much work as an ordinary man. Tom sold hay to Andre at $7 per 100 bundles of 15 lbs each. Our letters to our friend Mr. Hogarth have been returned, I suppose he has gone to some new place. Was terribly pestered by Blake for more money than work was done for on the buildings; spent the evening at Mr. Wheeler's; Mrs. W. is of the opinion that farming is a very slow means of making money, says that Mr. Meredith is sick of it already and that he pays out four times more than he receives, and that were it not for the $4000 a yr. that he earns as mineralogist his scientific farming and farm would be a complete failure. I said of course his farm could not pay expenses for the first few years on account

of his doing every improvement in such first class style and
making so many permanent improvements on his place, such as
adding another story to his brick house, covering it with slate,
building new barns and stables, fencing his place anew, pulling
out stones and making underground drains, but that no doubt it
would in after yrs. for a Scotchman is the last man in the world to
spend his money unwisely. Louis' wife asked me if I saw him;
told her I saw him at Aston House, poor thing she knew well
that very little of his weeks earnings would come back home;
the father and mother encouraged him to marry her and settle
down for they feared he would return to the U. S. and remain
there; Canadian priests discourage emigration to the U. S. as
much as they can fearing I suppose the enlightning effect of
American institutions on their followers. The wife of Maurice
Dufresne works with him in the sugar bush and actually chops
wood and hauls sap, wading through the snow in masculine at-
tire with two heavy buckets full of sap in either hand; Maurice
said to me you ought to get married, you see you could make
your wife earn her living like mine, I replied I would sooner die
than make a slave of the woman I loved, and that I would consider myself worse than a brute if I allowed the object of my
affections to suffer the slightest hardship whatever; alas nature
has dealt hardly with this woman in depriving her completely of
all physical beauty and at the same time giving her a poor and
lazy husband. Went to Beniots to buy some syrup, his wife
was watching the boiling pots while her husband was gathering
the sap; she is the best looking Frenchwoman I ever saw, even
as she sat on the rough blocks of wood dressed in the poorest of
clothes the beauty of her face and the symmetry of her figure
would have attracted the attention of the most unobserving, however as I am not a connoisseur, I cannot attempt a minute
description, I was greatly surprised with her beantiful complexion,
which in my experience is a rarity among Frenchwomen; but
to use a novelist's expression, what struck me most was the happy combination of every line and feature,not one of which detract-
ed from the beauty of the others; how often do we see a beautiful
face spoiled by an unsightly nose or badly shaped mouth, or a
beautiful figure spoiled by an ugly face; as the wind blew the

smoke into her face causing the tears to start into her eyes I could not help thinking at the time how much I should like to see her change places with some fat old dowager for a week or so. If ruling children with a rod of iron makes good men and women, my cousins ought to be, for their parents now treat them as if they were little children though in reality they ought to be considered young men and women, and their parents still dictate to them in every thing; uncle and aunt have become more religious of late and have prayers occasionally in the evening; it is wonderful what a change takes place in some people as old age advances upon them. Called at Israel's house, only his wife was at home; said she could not pay what was owed us for cut of square timber; this woman is very masculine in some ways; she can chop wood as good as any man; she cleared over two acres of brush wood on father's lot by herself as her father was unable to perform the job after he had taken it; although this woman has the strength of a man she has not the courage of many women, and allows her insignificant husband to beat her out of the house when he is drunk. The stars can be seen through the roof of the shanty they live in and the floor is hewn logs; it is the oldest house about here and is in such a state of decay that if they do not leave it it will fall down upon them. Napoleon told me he is engaged in a lawsuit with J. Murphy and would have to sell all the sugar and syrup he made to pay his lawyers fee, and that he had the misfortune to lose 50 pails of sap by getting it in an old trough which burst; the lawsuit is about a $25 horse Murphy sold to Gilbert Miguault; Napoleon says he signed as witness; Murphy asserts that it was as security; strange Murphy does not leave law alone, seeing he burnt his fingers at it once. Had a dispute with some Frenchmen about some land; the time the division lines were changed Murphy ordered the two men off the land, (that they gained by the change) till they paid for the improvements, they had axes in their hands and advanced towards him, he attacked them, wrenching the axe from one of them and cut him sorely with it, a lawsuit was the result, in which Murphy lost $600 which crippled him financially for years. During the week we piled our lumber at Guertin's leaving spaces between each board to let the air through it to dry it. Received a letter from uncle Richard, "my dear Tom and Arthur I would have written long ere this but have been occupied in many ways so that I could not write; Doherty has paid another $150 which I duly credited to your account, he did not say one word about the lot and asked me to give him till July for the $100; it is for you to say wether I shall do it or not; you will oblige by letting me know your wish on this matter, I also want to know whether you will require the mare; my little mare is quite well again and I think she will be quite sufficient for my work during the summer; the mare is in fine condition just now and has improved much since you saw her, whatever you require for yourselves or the house let me know and I will send your order out to you. Has the man begun the house yet? I must conclude, believe me to remain your affectionate uncle Richard." "St. Augustian April 1st, Mr. J. Howard, dear sir, you wrote to me some time ago requesting me to get the line drawn between my lot and yours, I think it would be best to do it before the bark peeling season commences, as Doherty might peel some trees on my lot; hoping you are all well, your sincere friend Philip Therman." Had a long conversation with Mr. Baker on farming, he is one of the shrewdest business men in the county of Sussex; he has been manager of Sharp's tannery for a great many years, many say he has "feathered his own nest," by taking enormous measure when buying bark, giving the poor "habitants" a cord and a quarter for 1½ cords, and marking down 1½ cords in Sharp's books and pocketing the quarter himself, this caused the "habitants" to curse him with every curse imaginable which he listened to with indflerence, measuring the work as if he were an automaton. He also speculated in bark, himself and a few years ago owned as much as 45000 acres, which he has been selling off since he was dismissed from Sharp's service; bought window frames at 75 cents each, and two doors, one at $1.50 the other at $3.00. 5th April, snowed 2 inches during the night; there is more trouble than one would imagine in starting on a bush farm; men bother us for money before the value is done in work, also have fears that they will give up their jobs, also that bad roads may prevent us from furnishing the lumber in time for the buildings; commenced digging our cellar; on getting about 3½ feet deep struck water, surface water from a small swamp in the top of the hill; Tom has given the job of building the foundation of the barn to a stone mason for $15, we to furnish all the materials, he to help us dig the stones. Mallet, Doherty's hired man, had a row with old Doherty; the old man called a French Protestant family, their neighbors, turncoats, Mallet remonstrated and the old man tried to kick him out, but he doused Doherty in a barrel of water, for which he dismissed him; the cause of Doherty's animosity is the fear that his oldest son Bartholemew will marry the daughter, who is a Protestant. Started for lime, Chartier the mason said 3 barricks or 18 bushels would be sufficient. St. Marie is composed of a single street, comprising a large brick. church, post office, cheese factory, a few small groceries and farmers houses, which look well surrounded by fine orchards; the lime is burnt in an oven shaped like a dome with an opening in the top; the roads were bad and the horses got played out and I had to get a farmer with his team to draw the load home. I wrote to Uncle Richard saying we would buy his mare if he would give us time to pay for her; Tom and I asked father if he had any money to spare, he said he could lend us $100 and that it would be just as well as in the bank. Bergeron asked us $60 for a pair of cattle; we offered $40 cash which he accepted, giving us a yoke and chain with them; gave the job of drawing lumber from Guertin's mill to St. John for $1.50 per 1000 ft. Tried the oxen at plowing, they are well trained and go right or left as told; I went to Richford about doors and windows; the falls looked fine with masses of ice being dashed to pieces on the rocks below, they are over 50 ft. high, almost perpendicular and strange to say a horse and cart were carried over them on a huge mass of ice and escaped with only a few bruises. A carpenter asked 40 cents a case to make cases for the windows. Miss McNeill told me jokingly that when our house was finished she was going to marry Tom and keep house for us, I answered her in the same strain; she has pleasing features and is a coquette by nature. J. Blake has finished putting up our house; had to go to Aston for spikes to spike the rafters to the top plates. Delage, sr., the postmaster, would not give me our letters because I was 5 minutes late, he is a very disobliging man and several requisitions have been made to the postmaster general for his removal but to no avail as he is a faithful old conservative. At Aston House a Yankee had one side of the parlor covered with numbered photographs, which he sold at 25 cents each; they are numbered and the men that got the right numbers got prizes ranging from $5 to 10. When the rafters were put on our house Blake put an evergreen bough on the top of the end rafters; all the French people around do so; the "habitants" call it "La Boquet." Louis asked permission to take some tamarac to make fence pins as it is less brittle and stronger than cedar. Mary Dupins and her husband died in the U. S. their 7 children are to be divided between Brodeur, their grandfather and an uncle at East Hastings. Mallet has returned to Doherty's, which shows very little spirit after the treatment he received, but the powerful influence of cupid few men can resist; poor Mallet is captivated by the charms of Doherty's youngest daughter, but to no purpose, Miss D. aspires higher than a farm laborer, at any rate she has often emphatically asserted that she never will marry a heretic, although her two sisters have done so, but they married above their position, which perhaps not even their youngest daughter would not object to, but it is doubtful whether she will ever get the chance as she has not the beauty of her sisters, and the extreme angularity of her features spoils the effect of a clear complexion and fine figure, &c. Maurice D. cleared off with all the sugar he made and only gave father a few lbs.; father wanted us to work it but we could not with all our own work on our hands, the G. boys however took it on halves for the rest of the season. Wrote to Uncle Jerrold, Dear uncle, excuse my not answering your kind letter sooner; all the timber of the barn is squared and framed ready to raise; to-morrow the stone mason will begin on the foundation; most of the barns around here are built on wooden posts as it costs less but is not as cheap in the end as the posts decay. We thought we might as well build a small house as living in part of the barn would be dangerous on account of fire, but as you suggest when we can build a better one we can convert it into a barn; the logs and the rafters of the house are put up; we intend to do the boarding, shingling and laying down of the floor ourselves, and are going to have a cellar

12 ft. deep dug underneath and a stone foundation built, as yet we have not cleared out the stream but when the dry weather comes we will commence to do so; I think the best way to have it cleared will be to get a process verbal for it, that is to get a notary to follow the course of the stream and count all the lots that send water into it and get a legal document passed in the municipal council to oblige all the land holders to work at the stream in proportion to the amount of their land that drains into it; the times are very dull in Canada as you say, farmers will not suffer as much as mechanics or commercial men, in fact agricultural produce sells nearly as high as usual and labor is at half the price that was charged a few years ago, other items end the letter. Read "Uncle Tom's Cabin" a second time, it is one of the most interesting books I ever read. Drew sand and stones to the mason; he asks $30 to build a foundation under the bank 12 ft. high and $15 if we furnish the material; found a snake 2 ft. long; it is a different species from the common kind around here; preserved it in high wines and sent it to cousin Clifford in Montreal, who has a large collection of minerals and curiosities. Our dog Carlo is a great fighter; some of our neighbors consider dog fights great sport; in my opinion men must be very brutal indeed to be pleased with such a cruel pastime. Most of our neighbors spend their evenings in playing cards or worthless conversation; I can well imagine how the civilized and nobler men of future ages will read with pity and contempt how the majority of mankind of this age employed their time; I am sorry to say that Tom and myself have drifted into this bad habit and waste hours of our time in this manner. This spring I have found out the truth of "the borrower is servant to the lender." It is a poor system at best and should be avoided as much as possible by farmers; I have seen a Frenchman lose half a day in going to a neighbors to borrow a scythe; now the cost of a scythe and handle is only $2.25; so that this man who makes a habit of borrowing spends as much time in walking to and fro as would buy 10 scythes. Father has returned with the new boy from Norfolk Distributing Home; I walked to Aston; received a letter from uncle Richard: "My dear boys I received your letter yesterday and herewith enclose you $50; if you want the mare you are per-

fectly welcome to her, as regards the payment you can suit your convenience; since she was in town she went lame on one foot,and the veterinary surgeon told me she took cold in the shoulder from her stall being situated in a current of air between two doors, however you can take her but I trust it will be gone before you come in; I am glad you have bought oxen for they are most useful on a bush farm; Arthur can come in at any time it suits him, as you will want the balance of the money he can have it whenever he likes; we are all well here, aunt unites in love, believe me to remain your affectionate uncle, R. J. Goldsmith." At Vednar's store I changed the $50 note, large bills are useful to him in settling his accounts in Montreal; he wanted to sell me some pine shingles at $2.25 a case, but planed shingles made by hand are better than sawn ones; Tom and I had a difference about Sherman's hay, a private spec of his own; he wanted to sell it to our firm but I considered he asked too high a price; he said I wanted to grind him down as I did everyone else I had transactions with; I told him that as regards making too hard a bargain in this part of the country it was nigh an impossibility as nearly everyone had two sets of prices, laborers as well as storekeepers, and that to protect one's self one had to beat down their prices, My aunt and Walter passed in a cart on their way to Aston; they of a truth do not "live for appearances;" it is all very well not to waste money on a costly carriage as the roads are bad but for respectable people of moderate means a cart for a means of conveyance is carrying Diogenism too far. Lapointe has taken the job of building a foundation to the house for $15; he furnishes everything except lime; this damp sloppy weather is hard on boots and shoes, they have to be greased often to preserve them; I told Andre he would have to give his note for the amount he was owing Tom for hay; he seemed offended but I told him it was customary nowadays in transacting business; met D. Doherty at Laporte's notorial office with Lapointe who has lost his lot of land without receiving scarcely any benefit for it; he agreed to peel 100 cords of bark for Doherty but through misfortune only peeled 80; Doherty who had paid him full in advance threatened to sue him if he did not give him a note for $40, $20 which he received and $20 damages for not fulfilling his contract;

to this Lapointe consented and usury did the rest, leaving him to-day without a home; truly this Doherty nearly rivals a Shylock; bought 25 bushels of oats at 50 cents a bushel. On my way home I went into a brown study over the disadvantages of Tom and I passing the rest of our lives among the vulgar and bad associations with which we are surrounded; it seems to me that man must have good society to live a truly happy and noble life, one cannot hear vulgar and vile conversation without having the finer sensibility of one's nature blunted and destroyed by it. The man who brought us oats from the "French country" can read moderately well in English which surprised us, as most of the French cannot read even in their own language, but their number is decreasing among the rising generation, all through the beneficial result of English influence are being educated; the term French country is applied by English settlers to those parishes where there are no English residents. This man says we are fools to waste our time and money here as we will never be able to sell it for what it costs; I considered I had a good memory for faces but was mortified when he reminded me of our meeting a year ago, however his features are by no means impressive, beautiful and hideous faces are the easiest to remember, those of ordinary appearance last of all. Uncle H. told me we had no right to expect Jonathan to pay us for the wood we sold him; I thought to myself you are a mean grasping old man, so I cancelled the debt; 24th April we find that on account of rocks we have to give up the idea of a cellar deeper than 4 ft. Tom and I ploughed a piece of land on our lots for potatoes. J. Blake had a "bee" to day and raised the barn; received a letter from uncle Richard, "my dear boy I was not surprised at your father getting another boy, avoid all quarrelling and giving offence, in your new house have a room fitted up for him; let him live with you if he likes it, for it will eventually come to that, but you must have command of your own place; if ever he gets to live with you it must be with the understanding that he is not to interfere with you in any way whatever. Russia has declared war with Turkey; flour and pork have gone up and are still going up, your affectionate uncle, Richard." Bought a bushel of seed buckwheat for one dollar; some farmers only sow ¼ of a bushel to an acre of land with stumps in it, as it sends out so many stalks from one seed. Read a book called "the Crusades and the Crusaders," which shows what fools the christians of the middle ages were; went to Guertin's mill through the wood at night, felt somewhat afraid although I really had nothing to be afraid of, as bears are scarce, robbers unknown and ghosts I do not believe in; but all men are born with a certain amount of natural fear; the heroes and the brave are those who conquer and subdue the natural fear and timidity of man. Read in the *Witness*, the Turks have gained a few advantages over the Russians, but the Russians are certain to crush them in the long run; father said he would require the money he lent us as he was running short. 2nd of May Tom harrowed a piece of land for potatoes I "underbrushed;" this is the first thing that has to be done in clearing land, the trees are then cut down, their branches cut and piled and their trunks cut into 12 ft lengths; the brush should be burnt off before piling the logs as the brush would be an encumberance; if the weather is dry and woodlands of value are near, a calm day is preferable, as there is less risk of the fire running; if no wood of value is near a day with a strong breeze is best as the fire spreads better; a small piece of partially decayed wood will burn several hours; on arriving at a brush pile it has only to be held close to the brush and blown gently with one's breath till a flame starts up, but with hardwood brush when the leaves are not on it small chips have to be collected to start it for this reason, it is preferable to cut brushwood before the leaves have fallen from it; after the brush piles have burnt about two hours they have to be thrown together, as even the dryest of brush piles have a fringe of unburnt brush about the edges which should be thrown together before the fire died out; there are different opinions as to whether oxen or horses are most preferable for logging; a strong horse is best on high dry smooth ground, as a horse moves quicker, but in low swampy land or on rocky highland with many roots oxen are preferable; four men are quite sufficient to work with oxen or a horse; a small active boy to chain the logs greatly hastens the work; the pilers have to carry all the small timber on to the log pile, that is not worth while hitching the team to, where they are too far to carry the pilers place them in small.

piles so that the teamster can hitch on to them all at once; the choosing of the spot for the log pile is generally left to the driver on account of his wishing to avoid driving his team in rooty or muddy places, of course at the same time he consults the advantage of his men by choosing an easy place to roll the logs and place their skids, also to place the piles on level land, or still better in hollows to prevent their rolling apart when burning; the driver although he has not as much hard labor as the pilers has by far the most disagreeable job, having often to use his hand in cold damp weather and scrape a hole in the wet earth or mud underneath the log, when it is laying partly imbedded in the earth from having lain there for years and pass the hook underneath the log and hook it on the other side; sometimes roots or rocks prevents him from doing this and he then has to try and hitch his chain to a knot or end of a branch, and if this fails to stir the imbedded log he shouts "lever" and one or two of the pilers have to come and lift the "sog," by which name wet and rotten logs are called; this is generally put on top of the pile as it would not burn if placed at the bottom; to be a good driver one must have inexhaustable good humor, great agility and know all the rules as regard "chaining," and unchaining, giving roll to the chain, lengthening it and shortening it and preventing it from getting over the oxens' backs; when pulling a log from a height; the pile itself to burn well requires to be at least four logs high and put together as closely as possible, in dry weather the piles put together during the day should be set on fire in the evening and then shoved together in the morning; some piles when they are damp require a great amount of chips and small sticks to start them burning, in very dry weather by constantly shoving the piles together they burn up completely, especially hardwood, of which maple burns the best and ranks as the best quality of firewood, but in most cases the remnants of all the piles have to be hauled together in one large pile and burnt; if grain is to be sown two bushels of oats is sufficient to an acre, which is sown on the burnt black surface of the earth and is then "harrowed in;" a strong narrow harrow shaped like a letter V, a narrow harrow being necessary to pass between the numberless stumps, also a man to follow the teamster with a hoe to cover the grain where the harrow cannot get at it, sometimes the harrow has to pass four or five times over rooty ground before the grain is covered; sometimes a harrow will be thrown as much as three ft high when it strikes a root or rock; I have known one man to have his ancle sprained by the harrow striking his leg. I went to Montreal on the 1st of May, went on a fishing excursion with cousin Clifford to Lake St. Louis, but only caught a few small fish as it was too early in the season; brought back the mare with me. Father received the following letter from uncle Richard; "my dear Jonathan, according to instructions I have forwarded you a barrel of flour and Indian meal, a parcel of grass seeds, I could only get one kind of vetch; since the stoppage of the sugar refinery here there is no golden syrup to be had in town, the buckwheat flour they do not keep in the stores here in summer, as they tell me it is very apt to heat and spoil; the prices of provisions are rising rapidly; on account of the war rice is high just now, 6 cents a lb; we had a letter from Richard yesterday he is enjoying himself in London; for want of news I must conclude. Yours very affectionately, R. J. Goldsmith." May 16th, "My dear boys. You need not annoy yourselves about that contract with Blake you can neither sue or be sued so if you have not overpaid him you are all right; the height of the rooms in the house should be at least 10 ft, 12 ft is the ordinary height in Montreal, and is none too high, rest lost." Tom gave me a note for what he owes me, which is now $133; he has decided to keep the mare we bought as a private speculation. During May we planted oats aud potatoes, cleared land and did work on our house. Wrote to uncle Richard: "My dear uncle I have just arrived home, I took a little over a day to drive the 75 miles, the mare is a good traveler and seemed just as fresh at the end of the journey as at the beginning. D. Doherty has been going over our lots and has offered us $50 if we will take back the cut of the hemlock bark; I do not see why he should make such an offer unless the price of bark has fallen in Boston or that he over estimated the amount of bark on the lots. Blake has broke his contract with us and deserted his job but fortunately we have not overpaid him and can easily get the buildings finished for what we owe him. I trust my aunt is better from the effects of the fall and sprained ancle, with love to my aunt and cousins, I remain your affectionate nephew, A. Howard." Went to Merediths; Mr. M. is in New York seeing about some mines; Mrs. M. was very cordial and friendly, she is a model hostess and can equally entertain the rustic farmer or the polished gentleman; enquired if they had any tar left from what they bought to tar the roofs of their barns; said I would buy it to tar our roofs; she told me that Tom Bacon had bought Littleton's house and grounds on speculation and she thought it would be so nice for us to buy it from him and live in the village instead of out in the backwoods, also that her son Nicholas was at an Agricultural College at Guelph, to learn the science of farming that he worked at manual labor at the rate of six hours a day, for which he was paid 50 cents an hour; everything is performed in the most approved manner on the model farm and in the college. The weather was dry enough to burn the brush on the land we were clearing on the 12 May; lived on very plain and substantial food during these months to economize, and find that we are just as healthy as if we had all the delicacies of the season. Saw Andrie's baby, it is the blackest and smallest little Caucasian I ever laid my eyes on. Doherty is making three wagon roads through the lots which is an advantage for us. Logging is very disagreeable work, one gets black as a nigger among the charred timber, for there are multitudes of mosquitoes, sand flies and midges, that keep constantly getting into ones eyes, ears nose and mouth which keeps one constantly rubbing ones face with ones hands. Father tells us the Russians are getting beat by the Turks, but of course it will only be a temporary advantage, the bravest of the brave can hardly resist ten to one. On Sunday went on a fishing and bathing excursion with my cousins; 1 see no harm in taking innocent pleasure and recreation on a Sunday, it is no holier than any other day; to consider it so is only a remnant of superstitious barbarism; a good action may be performed on any day without committing sin, and bad actions should always be avoided on no matter what day; but it has become universally acknowledged that an occasional day of rest is necessary and beneficial to man, and it is more convenient that one certain day should be set apart that all men might rest and take recreation at the same time; it is however simply absurd to try and compel all men to act with what is considered especially saint-like conduct on a Sunday, only to read musty theological works and to observe the day with grave and solemn deportment and conversation; I often felt how supremely ridiculous it appeared to have a mother tell her little child that it was a sin to engage in harmless childish sports on a Sunday or to read any books, excepting those devoted to a description of the golden streets and harps of heaven and other heavenly fiction, which have only been concocted in the brains of some religious novelist, or why do some people consider it a sin for factory people who are shut up all week in a hot smoky dusty city, to go out on Sunday into the country and enjoy the pure air of heaven, admire the beauties of nature, truly this is as pleasing to God as to see them sitting in a crowded church listening to some threadbare arguments and discourses that have been repeated to the christian world for the last eighteen hundred years, or to the discussion of imaginary things which are of no earthly consequence to man's happiness or development. What good I would like to know has all the arguments advanced upon the doctrines of the holy trinity conferred on poor mechanics or any other portion of mankind, and the worst feature of it is that most clergymen devote most of their time to doctrinal teaching, whereas if Sunday-Schools and clergymen taught nature's aud moral laws and scientific truths instead of their doctrinal hash mankind would be the happier and nobler for it. Wrote to Allen Robertson a friend of mine in New Brunswick; "My dear Allen, I have just returned from a fishing excursion on Lake Louis; went from Montreal to Lachine by railway and from Lachine to Beauharnois by boat, after a whole days fishing and trolling we caught only a few small fish; we rowed quite close to the foot of Cedar Rapids and then rowed up the St. Louis river, where we expected to have better success as the water was warmer but without result; on returning we shot the Lacine Rapids, it was not so thrilling as I expected, from the description I saw of it in books. This Spring we have cleared ten acres of land and will sow them with oats and grass seed; land newly cleared is best under grass as it is too rough to keep under cultivation, have also planted eleven bushels of potatoes; have not moved to our lots yet as the buildings are not quite finished. At present we are trying to get a "process verbal" for a stream that runs through our land; if we can get it passed through Aston muncipal council, the stream will be dug 4 ft deep, 7 ft wide and all the brush and logs cleared away on either bank; the distance to be dug is about ten miles and our part of it will cost about $200, but the advantage will be great as it will drain nearly 300 acres of our land; conclude with other news. There has been several thunder storms in May. We fenced in Sherman's clearance as we have the use of it for pasture on condition that we pay the taxes and mend the roads. Father has bought a sewing machine for $20, second hand; he thinks to do all his own sewing on it; a truly disgraceful occupation for a man who passed in one of the best colleges in England as a civil engineer. Read two books entitled "Ferguson's trip across Africa in a balloon," also "The Talisman" by Dr. W. Scott. The Turko-Russian war still progresses; the Turks have still the best of it; France and Germany look threateningly at each other and Austria also threatens Russia. I spent an evening at Carmicheal's; Stephen C. has been married since he went to Montreal and brought his wife out with him; she is very plain and what is still worse vulgar, but is good enough for him; uncle and Clifford came from Montreal and admired the work on our house and barn. Went on a fishing excursion to White river at the end of the range; bought 33 lbs of harrow pins at 8 cents a pound at the blacksmiths; the pins are steel pointed and will not wear out so easily; gave the job of finishing the house and barn to a man for $80, the amount still due Blake, the house to be finished on the 7th and the barn on the 30th of June. I wanted to sell out to Tom for whatever he thought my half was worth, but he would not buy; told him that I would try and enter some military college. A great many people of this range have had the smallpox of which four have died. On Sunday went to the White river with the G. boys and divided ourselves into two crews and ran a race down the river; afterward rowed up nearly to Richford, 5 miles distant, where we lunched on a picturesque island. Since our dear mothers death family prayers have been abandoned; I think, however, that praying now-a-days is overdone, in fact that it is altogether unnecessary; how foolish does it appear for millions of different people, and even people of one nation or parish, praying for directly contrary results; does it not appear far wiser to perform our duty in this world according to the wisdom a Creator has given us and leave the result in his hands. 7th June, sowed the last of our oats; it is doubtful if it will ripen for the land is so rich that it will keep growing longer than oats sown in poorer land, besides it is a week past the right time for sowing it, however it will make good green fodder. Tom sheared father's sheep; this is the right time as the weather is beginning to be very warm and the sheep rub it off; if, however, they are shorn too early they catch cold from the early spring rains. Shingled our house. Tom offered to sell out to me, but I preferred not to buy. Our oxen are what is called breachy, no fence will keep them in, a low fence they jump and a high one they lie down against it and upset it; put an apparatus on their heads covered with sharp points to prevent them. I went to the back end of our 400 acres and considered it was all magnificent land, but a year after was surprised at the change after the fire had ran over it and burnt off all the loose moss and light vegetable earth on the surface, leaving exposed all the roots and stones underneath; however, our lot contains some of the best land in these parts. Our mare is very wild since she has been put in the pasture, and kicks dangerously at one when one tries to catch her. Had a "bee" on our lots and logged about ¾ of an acre, and made 18 log piles, which is very fair as men never work as hard at a "bee" as on other occasions. Had my aunt to bake some bread for us; gave her 60 lbs. of flour and got back 30 lbs. of bread; decided that this does not pay, and in the future if we run short of baker's bread we will make pancakes. On Sunday did not go to church as the mare was lame; read a book called "America before Columbus;" also a book called "My Wife and I." My aunt keeps continually praising Florence Meredith to me; by so doing I do believe she intends to tease me; played checkers with Frenchmen in the afternoon. 19th June, received a letter from uncle Richard: "My dear boys, I have just received yours and will see that the door is sent at once. We are all well and are going to the seaside at Gaspe on the 2nd of July. How is the mare, has she kicked since she ran away with Arthur? Richard has read your letters and says that the door can be got cheaper in Aston. When you are settled in your new house send me a list of the things you need, for I have no doubt that there are many things in our house which we do not use that would add to your comfort. Your aunt and cousins unite in love to you both and to you father. Believe me to remain, dear boys, your affectionate uncle, Richard." We truly ought to be thankful for having such a kind uncle. Took several horses to pasture at $2 a month as our pasture has more grass than our animals can consume. The oats sown on the rich, black soil by the stream, looks better than what was sown on higher ground. Wrote to uncle Richard. "Dear Uncle: We received your letter with the $10 enclosed; we can buy a front door for $3. We have seeded all our new land with hay seed and it has taken well. We will not be able to move to our lots for several days yet, but on doing so will let you know; if we cannot get a stove from father we will purchase one in Montreal as they are cheaper there than here. We have had tarred paper put between the boarding of the stable which will make it very warm. We both thank you for thinking so much about our comfort, also for the postage stamps, Tom unites with me in love to all. Your affectionate nephew, Arthur." We bought 1800 feet of pine lumber for cornice and casings around the doors and windows at $18 a 1000 feet. Spent the evening at Meredith's and was introduced to three young gentlemen from an adjoining village, named Harrison, who were on a visit there. Earthed up our potatoes. Out of respect for the reader's feelings I cannot give verbatim the disgusting conversation and jokes we hear daily and I regret to say that conversation that used to fill us with disgust is now listened to with the utmost indifference. Tom and I had a dispute about the mare; I refused to pay for her keep; sowed our buckwheat on the 29th of June. Herbert C. sat in Willoughby's drawingroom and read a book, never speaking a word to Miss Mabel W. who was there; told him that such ungentlemanly behavior would make the ladies consider him a boor. Went to the church with Mabel; she teaches sunday school; she is not beautiful, but is very accomplished and has graceful manners and is a very kind-hearted, pious young lady, is able to converse in 4 languages, and is a skillful pianist. While in Aston buying locks and keys for our house, I noticed flags flying from the station, the union jack, the stars and stripes, and another flag that is used in all Catholic processions, and the band playing as the incoming train arrived. Sir J. Macdonel was on the train on his way to a conservative picnic. Mr. Mignault read and address from the French Conservatives and Mr. Littleton from the English; he also received a bouquet from the ladies. Sir J. in his speech tickled their fancy by his saying that his opponents called him a priest's man. I often make resolves to devote all my spare moments to self improvement and not be influenced by the bad associations around me, and perhaps the very next evening am enticed by an acquaintance to some dance at an adjoining neighbors, where I hear conversation from young girls of "sweet sixteen" that would, I actually believe, make the ladies of Queen Isabella and Charles the Second's court blush. While chopping a turned up tree into lengths the roots and stump suddenly sprang back into its old place and buried our dog Carlo beneath; it fortunately did not crush him and I quickly dug him out; I have known a man to have been thrown as much as 15 feet and considerably bruised by such an occurence. Paid $7 for 7 doz. small panes of glass, 12th July, moved into our house; father gave us some of the furniture and cooking utensils of the old place and a small cooking stove. Finished earthing up our potatoes for the second time. Aunt Ethel and Sarah came to see us. I said to Tom the first evening in our new house, let us in the future be united in all our plans and transactions, and show to the world that we can succeed; after which I burnt his note to me for $130, but he seemed very cool and indifferent. Father told us that when we had our house finished he would give us some turkish carpets and lace curtains that our dear mother brought from England, which is very kind of him. Uncle and aunt told us that an Orangeman had been murdered by the Roman Catholics of Montreal, whose name was Hackett. Two foolish Protestant ladies wore orange flowers and this color has the same effect on some Catholics as blood has to a mad bull. The followers of this the only "perfect church," vilely insulted and attacked these helpless ladies and Hackett, like a true gentleman, remonstrated and then defended them and in doing so was brutally murdered. "My dear boys, you will perceive that I am still at Gaspe with your aunt and cousins. I suppose that you are very busy with your crops and that you have moved into your new house by this. This is a lonely place and the winters are about one month longer than with you. There is a beautiful bay just outside our windows. We all went in a yacht the day before yesterday; it is very dangerous and I am afraid that none of them will try it again. Clifford, Mabel, Flora and myself went out fishing to the St Johns river, we only caught a dozen trout and some of them were very small It is cool here in the mornings and evenings and very pleasant in the middle of the day. Rain is badly wanted here, they have had only one small shower for weeks. It takes 4 or 5 days to get a letter or paper from Montreal; I miss the papers very much. Richard is taking care of my patients; should you require anything let him know. I expect to return on the 4th of August. With love from all, your affectionate uncle, Richard." Read a book by Capt. Butler, entitled, "The Great Lone Country." Commenced cutting our hay on the 16th of July; some of the inhabitants only cut theirs in the middle or last of August, but the hay by then has lost its nutritious juices and is little better than dried sticks. I dulled my scythe and had to go to a neighbors to sharpen it as we have not yet bought a grinding stone. When I returned, Tom accused me of wasting time and a dispute was the result; he said he would not be under any obligation to me and gave me back a note for the amount he owed me. I worked till dark as we wish to get our hay saved while the weather is fine. It surprises me how we lived at this time, a completely vegetable diet, and in the best of health with much hard work. It certainly requires endurance to mow steadily all day in the sun, with a thermometer at 78 to 89 degrees above zero. Tom commenced digging a well. Andre has commenced to use his new potatoes. In a confab Tom and I had, he said he would like to go to Manitoba or Texas. Old Burke came with a petition to have his son released from Kingston, a great many justices of the peace had signed it, and some priests; we put our names to it. His son half killed a peddler a few years ago. The G's. refused to pay for the pasturage of their horse, because our dog killed a pig of theirs that was running half wild in the woods. Ran the boundary line between Delage's farm and ours; the surveyor was 5 acres out in the distance of one mile when he reached the corner post at the other end of the lot; in returning the line was rectified and the posts changed. Sent by a passing neighbor for a bag of salt, a little put on the hay in the mow prevents it from heating or becoming mildewed, and makes the animals eat it with a better relish; 3 persons are required to draw in hay: one to pack it on the load, one to pitch it up and one to rake after the load. Have been reading history of late. I think we should get a home boy; he would be useful for cooking meals and keeping the house clean. Had to pay the surveyor at the rate of $5 per day and $1 for placing a boundary stone, also hotel expenses $1; the dearest surveyor we ever had; the other one we had only charged us $2½ for our expense. Allowed Andre to put his hay in our barn till he gets one built. While saving father's hay for him, our oxen trespassed on G's. meadow, for which we had to pay $1. Mr. Carmicheal, of Montreal is on a visit with his relations; he is a very vulgar man and is continually talking of having dined with the honorable Mr. so and so. We fenced in a piece of meadow for a pasture by our house to prevent our oxen from trespassing; were offered 1 cent a foot, lineal measure, for the cut of our tamerac timber on our lots, which we did not accept. We cook our meals outside in a stone fireplace to keep the house from being too warm. After mass on Sunday our French neighbors went picking blueberries. We have commenced underbrushing more land; also are drilling and blasting the rock in our well. Some Aston ladies came on a raspberry picking excursion and took tea with us. Father says he has only $20 cash, if so he will have hard work to weather the winter. At present we are making rails for a fence in front of our lots; we make 150 a day, which is fair considering we are novices in rail making. Cut down a cedar somewhat over 90 feet high, the highest I have seen in these parts. Had a dispute with Tom about housework, thought he left too much of it for me to do. Had hard work swamping the rails, sank some times over one foot in the mud. I am thinking of asking my uncle's permission to enter some military college when I go to Montreal in November. A heavy thunder storm has caused the tall, rank oats by the stream to be thrown down, which will make it difficult to cut; next morning the whole of the low lands were flooded as there is only a partial outlet for the stream. Have commenced to use new potatoes occasionally, but it is a waste to use them until full grown. Tom has become quite a sportsman and shot many pigeons in groves of cherry trees. "Dear boys, we have all got home at last from Gaspe. Richard and Charley are not at home and I thought you had better postpone your visit till they come back. I hope to be able to come out and see you very soon. As soon as you get this send me word what money you want, also a list of the things you may require; I am glad you have moved to your new house for several reasons; you will save time and fatigue and be able to keep a lookout on your land. I think it will be necessary to get a cow; the small Canadian cows are good milkers." Extract from reply: "We owe Bedard $27 for blacksmith bill and Mousseau $29 for groceries. We will require $60 this quarter. In the future we will try and buy everything on the cash system as the storekeepers have higher prices for credit." To-morrow we will finish fencing the new pasture we have made; after this is finished we will plaster the crevices between the logs of the house and apply tar to the roofs of the house and barn to preserve the shingles. Carlo discovered an otter under some roots by the stream, but we could not get at it; their skins are worth $10. Gave the job of 1¾ acres of land to Napoleon to log and burn for $8. Received a letter from uncle Richard, sending us $60 and advising us to keep poultry. Tom and I have decided to clear 25 acres of land this year; we will do all the underbrushing and cut all the timber on the ground this fall, and in the winter cut the standing timber. This is a good time to get improvements done as labor is cheap. Sold Meredith fifty cords of stovewood for $1.25 a cord, also twenty cord of wood to Mrs. Guernsy at $2 a cord. Bought ten lengths of stovepipe for 64 cents. Canadian tobbacco

in rolls costs 20 cents a lb. As we will not have as good a crop
of potatoes as we expected (on account of the ravages of the Col-
orodo beetle) we bought some potatoes cheap at 25 cents a
bushel. Clifford came from Montreal. I slept on the hay in the
barn but found it rather chilly; cut with a brush scythe wild
raspberry bushes that was growing upon some of the cleared land.
Moses La. Rivere, brother to Andrie' is coming to live next to
him, he has often arguments with me on purgatory and confession
and advises me to become a Catholic and marry a French girl.
I ridiculed the idea of his paying certain sums of money to his
priest to get his mother-in-law's soul out of purgatory, and tell
him that it is a religious swindle and means of making money.
Louis Brodeur's mother-in-law nearly drowned in a stream; she at-
tempted to cross while driving cows through the woods, she sank
in the mud so much that she could not extricate herself but
fortunately help arrived in time. Wrote to uncle Jerrold giving
him a description of the improvements on the lots. Bought a
cow from Napoleon for $25, a very fine animal, part Durham
and a good milker. We are fattening two pigs. for pork Went
on three days fishing and boating excursion with the G. boys
and Clifford to the Black river, also shot some partridges. Clifford says we ought not to allow Frenchmen working in this
vicinity to stop at our house, but it is hard to refuse them, it
would look disobliging. Bread has fallen to 15 cents for a 6 lb
loaf. Tom and I had another dispute about house work. Tom
went to Aston council but the process verbal did not pass, there
was too much opposition; many of the councillors land that sends
water into the stream voted against it to avoid expense. There
was a review of militia at Richford, one of the raw recruits shot
his captain in the hand. Jonathan G. tells me that Magloire
Vincent had a disgraceful wedding through too much whiskey;
the bridegrooms brother had his clothing torn off him and one
of the bridesmaids had her nose broken; amongst the French
here there is generally only one bridesmaid and a best man, who
are called "Garcon de honeur" and "Fille de honeur." "Salford
England August 20th. My dear Tom and Arthur, I received
both your most welcome letters; I am truly glad to hear that
you are getting along with your farm; you ought to be truly hap-

py boys, out in the fresh country air, healthy and strong, every foot of your property your own forever. I have been trying to buy some land ever so wild; I should not care but cannot get it. I once owned 70 acres but was tempted by an offer of just double what I gave for it and have regretted it ever since. Although you are minors no one can touch your land without the deliberate consent of two old experienced heads; every foot you improve of that land is a safe investment. It almost makes my head ache to see Rupert studying so much over his books the competition is so great now-a-days that brain work is carried to an excess. We leave Salford shortly, remaining at Orford House a few weeks and then go on to Brighton where we will remain a few weeks for the sea air, I went round the Duke of Devonshire's garden and grounds; I saw two immense rocks called rocking rocks so evenly balanced that they could be moved with a touch of the finger; the conservatories were beautiful, containing all sorts of Southern plants and rare trees growing in a glass building larger than a church and heated to rather an unpleasant degree. The Russians and Turks are busy killing, burning and cutting each others throats; Heaven change them and God grant we may never suffer from the horrors of war. Aunt Mary joins in love. Your affectionate uncle, Jerrold Goldsmith." Uncle Richard came to see us and brought us two large jars of preserves from my aunt. Uncle said we would have a fine estate some day. 10th September, this week we expect to finish sowing all our oats. Received a note from uncle Richard saying he had insured our buildings for $300 and our crops at $200 for three years; cost of insurance $5.15. In a letter from uncle Jerrold he says Rupert thinks of entering the Queen's horse guards. Gave Lapointe of Aston a job of ten acres to underbrush at $1.60 an acre. Went to Doherty to give him a notice to pay the balance of his account, had a supper there; their usual fare potatoes, pork, bread, butter, honey and strong tea. Resolved to devote $1 out of every $100 I am worth to some worthy charities. Wrote to uncle Richard; "Dear uncle, Tom unites with me in thanking you for your regard for our interests in having our buildings insured. We have finished plastering the chinks between the logs of our house; Doherty will pay the balance next week; we have given twenty acres to Frenchmen to have underbrushed at $1.60 an acre in low land, and $2 in high lands; where there is more fallen timber to cut it is a great bargain, the usual price is $3; the twenty acres will extend from the Beaver meadows on 35, across the whole front of 34 to Sherman's line. Could you, if convenient, lend us $40 and we will pay you out of the November quarter. We will cut our buckwheat next week;" unimportant items conclude it. Bought a grinding stone for 68 cents. Went to Meredith's, Florence and Maud are at a ladies college in upper Canada, Jessie at a deaf and dumb institution in Montreal; she lost the power of speech and hearing at an early age after a severe fever; and Timothy the second eldest son is at Lennox college, so the house has a deserted appearance with only the mother and younger children. G. boys are making great improvements, most of their meadows could be cut with a machine; they have a small orchard that is wonderfully productive. Gave a Frenchman a job of sawing 80 cords of stove wood with our sawing machine for 35 cents a cord, we to furnish the machine, oil and files and a man to work it. I went to a "bee" at Houde's farm near our place; the family are going to move here this fall; there were twenty-three men which was more than was needed. The Frenchman has given up the job of sawing the wood, says the machine does not saw enough to pay him. "My dear boys, I received your letter yesterday and was glad you were both so well, in fact you are both so busy that you have no time to think of bodily ailments even if you had them. There is no doubt that the clearing of that twenty acres will be a grand improvement when it is finished. I shall take a great pride in your making that a fine farm particularly as I expect your uncle Jerrold will soon come over to see you. It was principally on your account he came out last time. In the letter I enclose $60, $40 from myself as a present and $20 from your uncle Jerrold to pay for a cow which you absolutely need he says, not having heard you bought one. After a year or two you will be able to sell something off your farm when you can keep a boy and have more cattle; that farm of yours when cleared will make a fine stock farm. I hope you will not be obliged to draw cordwood this winter any more at $2 a cord, there is nothing made by it and you really are above such labor. Clifford is going to school again but I think he is getting tired of it. After next year I think he will like to be a farmer, but I fear he has been too much spoiled by town luxuries. I send you a small book of prayers for morning and evening use, as I know that it will give your uncle Jerrold pleasure to know that you apply to the throne of our Heavenly Father for guidance every day, as we require to support the body with daily food so we must enliven our faith and nourish our souls by constant communion with God. I thank you very much for your kind invitation and would like very much to go out and see you for a few days; when you are opening up the stream try and give me a couple of days notice. Of all things plant an orchard; see what a great quantity of fruit your uncle has received from his orchard which I planted myself for him 10 years ago; excuse my writing across my letter, with much love in which your aunt unites, I remain your loving uncle, R. J. Goldsmith." "Dear uncle Richard I received your letter yesterday evening with your generous gift of $40 and thank you for it, I trust by our future conduct and management of these lots we will at least show you that we are trying to be worthy of two such generous and good uncles, who have always taken such a deep interest in our spiritual as well as our temporal welfare; how very good of uncle Jerrold to send us $20 to buy a cow with. We have finished cutting our buckwheat; we will not draw any more wood to Aston but let the purchasers get teamsters to draw it. This winter however we will have plenty to do in chopping the standing timber and making rails. We will follow your advice and make preparations for the planting of an orchard; in a short time we will begin to cut wood with the sawing machine; with love to my aunt and cousins, your affectionate nephew, A. N. Howard." Father's buckwheat has been destroyed by G's cattle; Jonathan tried to take their cattle from father's stable by force and struck father several times, in one spot making his face black and blue; father threatens to sue for damages for assault and battery, if the damage is not paid and a written apology given. W. Carmichael of Montreal acts like a rough, he fired off his revolver in Aston several times. Wrote to uncle Jerrold a long letter. Received a letter from uncle Richard saying that Flora was very busy preparing for her approaching wedding; she is going to be married to a Mr. Butler, a superintendent of a railway. On the 13th Oct. received another letter saying that Flora had returned from her wedding tour and that he expected us in shortly, also that he was sorry to hear of the fresh feud between father and G's. In November received a letter from uncle Jerrold congratulating us on our improvements; supposed that Sarah had returned to her husband for they should think more of each other than all the world, that he was a sober and industrious man, who will eventually make her happy, also asked to be kindly remembered to Mrs. McNeill, who so kindly attended on our dear mother in her last sickness; that we should visit our dear mother's grave often and keep it looking beautiful and attend church regularly. The council decided that the bridge over our stream 12 ft. wide was not a bridge but a culvert, and that we and the land proprietor on the opposite side should keep it in repair. In November Jonathan G. went to a medical college at Chicago; he has earned some money teaching school and his brother out west will also help him; he is a clever fellow having studied enough by himself with the aid of Rev. L. C. Willoughby to matriculate. Mrs. Meredith invited us to spend Christmas with them. Mrs. M. told me they were paying $600 a year for the schooling of Florence in Montreal and that the education of five of their eldest children cost $1800 alone, also showed me a large and interesting collection of curiosities collected by her husband, such as coins, minerals, &c. Uncle Richard wrote saying that he passed through Aston and intended to call and see us but that uncle H. was on the platform and never invited him out, and wanted to know if we had heard of anything that displeased uncle H. Replied, "Dear uncle, yours received with uncle Jerrold's enclosed; we did not hear anything as regards uncle H; he has not been to see us since he was with you last August. We have logged 6 of the 20 acres also plowed some of Richard's old clearance to have ready for wheat next Spring. At present we are chopping down and cutting up the large trees on the 20 acres; when the days are too wet to work outside we thrash oats in the barn. Tom has changed a considerable amount of time with the neighbors by sawing wood for them with the sawing machine, they are to pay us back by helping us to log We hope to have the pleasure of seeing you and Clifford at Christmas, with love to all, your affectionate nephew, Arthur." Mr. Meredith sent father a book of travel; he has written a very interesting book entitled "To the Andes and back." I have commenced a history of the World and intend to devote the spare moments of my life to it, and I never lose an opportunity to collect all the most important events, statistics, manners, habits and customs of all nations from all sources imaginable; histories, newspapers, magazines, etc., and classify them, leaving out all the trivial and unimportant details. On the 25th of Oct. the ground was covered with snow, the first we have had this season. Read for the second time the history of Rome. Had several disputes with father this fall, he thinks we should work on his farm as well as our own, we told him we could not and that he must depend upon his own resources to make his system of farming a success, but that we should never see him in want of anything; told him it was mean of him to try and prejudice our uncles against us, or to tell our friends that we were bad boys because we went fishing or boating on a Sunday or passed our evenings at the firesides of our French neighbors. We have 3 French neighbors now, Andre and Moses Larivere and the Houde family, which consists of father, mother, 4 daughters and 2 sons. Went to Houde's to spend the evening, Andre and his wife were there playing cards; Houde made me take supper with them after which he asked me to join them at cards; told him I could not play, said his daughter Marie would show me how, at which a rather ordinary plain featured brunette came and sat by me she appeared however to be the most intelligent of the daughters and can read and write, of which accomplishment her sisters are deficient. The old lady and Andre quizzed me and said they supposed I should soon get married now that we had a house built; I said I did not think I was possessed of sufficient means, at which Andre laughed and said look at me. I had only a week's provisions ahead; said I thought he had more pluck than ever I would have; under Marie's direction I played with varying success; sometimes when the cards went wrong she would utter rather strong language, such as "Mon Dieu," "Seigneur," etc. Andre lives the best of any French people around here; he nearly always has meat, soup, potatoes, butter, bread, tea, and very often apple and mince pies. 14th December; the water in the basin on the wash-stand was frozen solid this morning; the day is windy and piercingly cold; there are good sleigh roads. Wrote to uncle Jerrold: "My dear uncle, I received your letter, and thank you for the great interest you take in our welfare. I sincerely trust that the improvements on our lots will reach your highest expectations when next you come to Canada, which I trust will be next summer. Uncle H. and family are all well; a reconciliacion has been effected between Sarah and her husband, and she has returned to live with him. Jonathan is studying medicine at Rush medical college, Chicago. In winter Tom and I go to church, we have to take turn about, as some one has to remain at home to keep the fires going and attend to the animals. We planted and replaced this fall some cedars that had died during the summer in the hedge around our dear mother's tomb. We sometimes visit Mrs. McNeill; the kind lady who attended on our dear mother during her illness. I trust Rupert's health will not be injured by the hard study, but the greater the difficulties the greater the victory. There fell about 8 inches of snow a couple of days ago, but it has nearly all thawed away. During the last few years there seems to be less snow during the winter. Mr. Venner, the weather prophet says that during the next half century the Canadian winters will be very mild; also that there is a probability of the rivers remaining open for navigation this winter, but time will prove his correctness. Everything on the farm is progressing favorably. With love to my aunt and Rupert. Your affectionate nephew, A. N. Howard." Changed time with our oxen with our neighbors, one day with the oxen and myself being considered equivalent to three days worth of a man. Invited father to spend Christmas with us, but he spent it at Carmicheal's; cousin Sarah from Davenport, with Philip and Walter spent the day with us; we all then spent the evening at Herberts. London, December 4th. "My dear Tom and Arthur: Your joint letter has just been handed in by the postman, with one from your cousin Mabel. I was so pleased to hear from your uncle Richard of the great improvements you are making on your farm; in a few years more you will begin to be comfortable. Mind you keep out of debt whatever else you do; "the borrower becomes servant to the lender." Let nothing ever tempt you to run into debt, ruin is sure to follow; the man that owes nothing sleeps sound, out of debt and out of danger; better to be a free man on a poor dinner in a ragged coat, than ride in broadcloth with a full stomach and a sore heart; moreover, pay day always comes when there is no money to pay, and if you owe nothing all you have is your own, and he who has debtors has unwelcome visitors; and if you wish to be glad to meet a friend do not borrow money from him. I cannot make out how much land is downright cleared out. Your aunt, Rupert and myself would be delighted to be in the woods and see you all. Have you planted any apple trees? As soon as the woods are cut down in Canada the climate will become much warmer. I felt strong and well in the woods, the air seemed so delightfully pure and fresh, so different from smoky, foggy London air. I should like to get a farm and live in the country, your aunt Margaret could attend to the dairy, and I could see after the men and plow and reap wheat and oats; I should grow potatoes and cabbage, keep fowls and pigs and sell them, and have plenty of sheep and cows; I should have all my own mutton and beef, with butter, eggs and cream. I fear I am getting very old, but I am always hoping to live on a farm, and perhaps it may come to that at last; although like a doctor's bread, he never gets it till he has no teeth to eat it; and if I do not get a farm soon I shall go to it at last with lean sides, creaking joints and a rheumatic old fogy, fit for nothing else but to sit in a chimney corner and grumble at everything. We had a telegram from New York warning us of a terrible storm that would visit us on the 24th of last month, which it did with a vengeance, many ships were lost and houses and trees blown down; our servants were so frightened that they sat up all night. The price of wheat and bread has risen in England. We are all well, thank God. Your aunt sends her love. Give my love to uncle Herbert and his family and to all friends, and believe me your loving uncle, Jerrold Goldsmith." During 1878 I kept my journal very irregular and in March decided to discontinue it. 7th January, '78. When I got up this morning the thermometer in the bedroom was 4 degrees below zero. "My dear uncle Jerrold: We read your letter and thank you for your good advice and will try and follow it. The woodland has so many operations to go through before it becomes cleared land that I am not surprised that our description of the different operations puzzled you; as regards how much land we have cleared since we came on the lots: we have cleared and put under cultivation 13 acres of land and are at present engaged in clearing 20 more; we have not planted any apple trees, but will do so in the spring; a good orchard on a farm greatly increases its value. I hope you will be able to find a good farm as the change would no doubt be beneficial. Cousin Clifford spent New Years with us. The weather here now is very changable, this morning 4 degrees below zero, at noon thawing, and to-night snowing and blowing in a most wintry manner. With love to all. Your affectionate nephew, Arthur." Tom has bought a cutter, or light sleigh, for which he has paid $28. The Russians have captured a Turkish Pasha and 30,000 men. Read a book, entitled, "Jesuitism in Europe and America," which plainly shows their crafty and ambitious policy, that of bringing all the world into submission to the doctrines of Roman Catholicism. We have threshed and stored away in a granary, 40 bushels of oats for seed. Allowed Brodeurs to make rails on halves out of the cedar on the 20 acres we are clearing. Houde has bought some pine trees from us for square timber; some pieces that had decayed knots he plugged up with pegs of wood, but the buyer discovered the fraud and cut him terribly in measuring the sound ones; truly, honesty is the best policy. 29th Feb. Uncle Richard came from Montreal; our house was in a terrible state, as we were having tongued and groved floors put down, and also a flight of stairs; he brought us a set of carpenter's tools from himself, and some very nice furniture and household nic nacs, which our cousin, Angelica Fothergill of Salford, England, had him buy for us; also my aunt, cousin Mabel, and Mrs. Hayton, uncle Richard's sister-in-law sent us many articles and trifles that will greatly beautify and add comfort to our bachelor's hall. We are truly blessed with many loving and staunch friends; uncle returned in the morning. I often long for that time when we shall have sufficient means to live in such refining and elevating society instead of being buried and continuously in the slough of humanity in which we now exist. Houde only paid us $1 a piece for the pine timber, large and small, which was not enough. "Fredricton, N. B. Dear Arthur, I hope you will excuse my not writing before but I did not wish to write till I had renewed the subscription to the "Youth's Companion" I send you. As it is too late to wish you a merry Christmas or a happy New Year, I at least hope you have enjoyed those holidays. I am still attending the university of New Brunswick, which is located here. My youngest brother had an attack of diptheria and after he got better my mother and youngest sister took it. The weather here as everywhere else is unusually mild although we have had enough snow for good sleighing. There has been a great temperance revival here over 1000 people formed the club which they have established, they are doing a great deal of good for Fredricton; my little baby brother is beginning to talk and walk, he is about ten months old. This is all the news; 1 hope you will write soon; ever believe me your sincere friend, Allen I Robertson." Mr. Willoughy held services fortnightly in our school house also had a singing and confirmation class among some of the younger members of the three English families on the range. In a letter from uncle Richard he said "your uncle Jerrold takes an interest in all your movements, and the most minute details about the land are of interest to him." Also read a letter from aunt Margaret: "My dear Tom and Arthur, my last week's mail Angelica sent me a few £ to invest in household articles for your comfort, will you please tell me what articles you require most and I will send them to you; you ought to get a carpenter to help you to finish your house inside, hope you will attend to this and have it nicely finished and consider the importance of making yourselves comfortable; we will be much happier here when we know that you have your house nicely and comfortably furnished, after that your farm work, clearing land &c. Do not forget to write to Angelica, she takes a great interest in you, both for your own and your dear mother's sake; your affectionate aunt, Margaret A. Goldsmith." "My dear aunt I read your letter and thank you for your great kindness in thinking so much about us; how very good of Angelica to have such regard for our comfort, we shall certainly write to her occasionally. You are all so very good to us that it fills us with the most earnest desire to make our attempt at farming a success, knowing how much it would please you all; we will have our house finished inside as you suggest. Everything is progressing favorably on the farm. With love to all I remain, ever your affectionate nephew A. N. Howard." Received a circular from a conservative in Dudley: the conservative party is broken up and there is to be a "general election;" the circular strongly advised the people to sustain the conservative party by voting for it and as good Catholics not to vote for the Liberals or "Rogues," who as a party are denounced by their priests. Received a letter from Angelica; "My dear Tom and Arthur, I was so pleased to receive your letters by last week's mail and to hear of your success, I heard from Mamma, of Clifford's visit to you and how much he enjoyed it; hope he writes to you regularly but I fear hs is rather lazy about it, as he scarcely ever writes to me. Timothy was surprised at the large clearance you are making; he would like to see Canadian woods very much for he has only passed by them in the trains. Will you make any sugar this year? We have been greatly interested in reading Mr. Meredith's book "to the Andes and back," do you often see him or any of the Aston people. You must enjoy the quiet rest in the evenings, and I hope you still delight in the words of God. Our baby is more than two years old and is so lively and talkative. I have no news about your uncle Jerrold, with love from Timothy and myself, your affectionate cousin. Arthur E. Fothergill." I have so much work and so little time to spare that I have decided to discontinue my journal 9th December, '78, I have changed my mind and recommenced my journal; it is eight months and ten days since I left off writing in it; I shall give the chief events that occurred during that period. Mrs. Doherty died; we went to the wake and funeral; the corpse was in a coffin in the parlor, there were about seventy-five people there, several prayers were said for the repose of her soul, I of course kneeled with the rest full of silent disgust at such nonsense; forsooth are the prayers of a few insignificant mortals capable of changing the just and unalterable decrees of a mighty just and merciful God. All of the people except the members of the family feasted, conversed, joked and drank in such a manner, that in outbursts of their merriment I almost believed I was at a wedding; it seemed to me that these people were "Job's comforters and that they came to have a good time generally instead of out of true sympathy with the bereaved family. There were 3 meals during the night. It was truly a strange sight to me; in the parlor the bereaved family sat in silent grief shedding tears occasionally, and around them sat old married women talking in subdued voices about the latest news and gossip. In other rooms, middle aged men and women, with young men and women kept up a continual chatter of conversation, some in subdued voices, whispering love sentences into the ears of their sweethearts. The uproarious outbursts of laughter, together with the coarse jokes that were uttered, made me shudder and think how much of mankind were yet really in a state of barbarism, "even though God had revealed to them alone the only true religion." In a moment these people cease from their coarse conversation and lewd jest and drop on their knees to utter prayers to God. What blasphemy! surely such prayers as these must be an abomination in his sight. After breakfast and prayers the funeral started for Aston; at the edge of the village they were met by about 50 people on foot who joined the procession; when about two acres from the church the priest came out and met the funeral with several singing boys, dressed in white, singing Latin, for which especial honor this fraudulent priesthood charged the snug little sum of $50. Now for a secular undertaker to take people's money for such silly pomp and show is bad enough, but when the chosen priesthood of the meek and lowly Jesus, stoop to such low means of making money, they truly deserve the contempt of all intelligent men. The coffin was now placed close to the altar and several prayers chanted over it in Latin, the priest keeping up such a continual bowing and scraping that I almost thought he was a French dancing master; he also smoked the coffin with burnt rosin and a censor which caused a horrible stench. I cannot see how they think that such incense could be agreeable to the nostrils of their God. The pall bearers then placed the coffin in the grave, which was in the church, and read the services in Latin over her. The privilege of burying her inside the church and the services cost $200, truly this is a money making religion. In March gave the job of logging and burning the timber off the 20 acres ready for the harrow to a Belgian for $5 an acre, we to furnish the oxen; he is well educated but a very strange character and can tell the worst anecdotes I ever heard, some of which however are very witty and laughable. When in Montreal this winter I saw all the sights and had great amusement in tobagoning. In the early spring we set fire to the timber on the 20 acres; it was truly a grand sight to see the flames leaping from one brush pile to another and there was a strong breeze and the whole 20 acres were in a short time in flames, which rose from 10 to 20 feet high and columns of smoke rising hundreds of feet high, but to our sorrow the sight became more magnificent when the fire rushed into the adjoining forest and all the woodlands on our lots became a mass of flame except a portion that was swampy on 35. It was indescribably grand at night to see the flames leaping from one tree top to another and rising very often many feet above them; by morning the fire had ran over 4 miles of woodland on which fortunately there was not much timber of any great value, besides our neighbors and people for miles around had also lit fires which had all blended into one greater one, so that no one could prove whose fire had done the damage. One man in another township lost 12,000 cords of bark, worth $60,000, which made him bankrupt. The Belgian employec as much as 30 men and faithfully completed his contract; they all slept down stairs in our house which might have been taken for a "dead house" at night with all the rows of bodies lying about in every direction; he only paid the men 50 cents a day without board. We unfortunately after sowing 12 acres of land had the seed all burnt, the fire passing a second time over the charred surface which still contained many particles of half decayed wood and leaves; we had to sow it again but it was too late to ripen. After the fire passed over the lots Tom and I decided the best thing to do would be to sell the cut of the timber as the different species of wood worms would destroy it even quicker than natural decay, but our uncles objected. About this time I organized with others an association entitled "Aston Young Men's Association," with the following constitution: Resolved, That this association repudiates all dogmas promulgated by the christian churches that are contrary to human reason and scientific research, and utterly disbelieve that God has specially revealed his will to any particular sect or body of men; that it regards all sects and churches who claim the right to dictate certain doctrines of belief to its followers (on pain of excommunication and damnation for disbelief) enemies of civilization and humanity, and will do all in their power to bring into contempt and destroy said churches and sects, and use its utmost endeavor to persuade all men to disbelieve the fraudulent revelations of all the bogus sects and churches and adopt the most rational view of that question; that God's revelation to man is found in the grand. works of his creation alone and in the wonderful laws by which he governs this earth and its inhabitants; that it accepts many of the precepts and moral laws of the Bible as useful and beneficial for man's guidance in life, but only consider them as the writings of wise men and philosophers, which superstitious and ignorant followers afterwards palmed off on the semi-civilized world as divinely revealed truths; that it will persistently advocate a method of education superior to that now in existence, a grand system of national education that will only teach practical knowledge and the already demonstrated truths of science and history as well as an accurate knowledge of the wonderful laws by which all nature is governed, and try and improve the schools of the world so that they will give the rising generations an education that will enable mankind to attain to the highest possible state of physical and mental perfection, that it will try and demonstate to the world that it is only the good moral laws and precepts of the christian churches that have enabled them to retain their influence so long on the mind of man, and that these same precepts and moral laws are not revealed by any special revelation, but merely by wise and good men making a proper use of the intellectual powers a great Creator gave them, and will try and convince all intelligent men of the folly of attempting to solve mysteries that are too great and out of the range of man's intellect, and the great folly of the christians in shedding so much of the blood of their fellow men and persecuting each other for some absurd difference they had about the divinity of their God, and that it does not concern man's happiness or improvement whether there is one God or one thousand; all that man has got to do is to make a proper use of the great gifts the Creator or unknown power has given him and he will certainly be happy here and in the probable hereafter; that it will try and hasten the day when priest or parson will no longer be required, when every man will be a priest unto himself in the glorious work of elevating himself and his fellow men to the highest possible state of perfection; that each member swears unceasing resistance to the fraudulent and tyrannical spiritual authority that has been usurped by the Popes, Patriarchs, Bishops and Archbishops of every religious organization of the earth, and will always earnestly endeavor to free our fellow men of every creed and color from the thraldom of spiritual slavery; persuade all men "That the world is their country and to do good is their religion." Signed, A. N. Howard, I. G. Goldsmith, C. H. Carmicheal, W. A. Goldsmith. There were meetings for a few months, but the association languished and died for want of members. Uncle Richard and his family passed the summer months at Norfolk and visited us while forest fires were raging, but could not stay long as the atmosphere was full of smoke, which hurt one of his eyes which is weak from over work. There seems to have been quite a mania for the Houde girls amongst the young beaus in these parts, much to the chargin of other belles; as much as 15 young men visit there on visiting nights, which are Sundays, Tuesdays, Thursdays and Saturdays, the remaining evenings are called "the evenings of the jealous," on which no young Canadian goes to see his sweetheart. When a young man enters one of the young girls receives his hat and overcoat and stows them away on a bed in the corner, there being no other convenient place to put them, she then returns to her "cavalier" or first gentleman caller, but if the other is her favorite he comes and sits by her and usurps her all to himself, she generally asks the second one, if a favorite, to conduct her to the waterstand for a drink (which is generally a rough wooden stand with buckets of water on it) and then goes with him to a different part of the room, leaving the poor disconsolate first caller in a state of defeat after this little "coup de etat," to be ridiculed by the other young people for having been made to "eat oats," which is equivalent to the common English term, "cut out." In fact, the two national sports of the French Canadians consist of playing cards and making love. In the dry months I deepened the course of the stream through our clearance and in some places found beaver dams 6 ft. below the bed of the stream with the marks of their teeth plainly visible on the wood. The general elections came off in the spring, the Liberals had only one majority, but their victory was an unsuspected event. We squared the timber for a shed 75 ft. long, between the barn and the house, and put it up with a "bee." One of the men at the "bee" while jumping over the stream sank in the mud on the opposite bank and lost one of his shoes in the mud; while on his knees on the bank with his sleeves tucked up trying to find his shoe, one of his companions gave him a shove which sent him headforemost into the mud, this was greeted by roars of laughter by the rest; when he crawled out of that slough he was the most pitable object imaginable, and the volley of oaths that he sent after the culprit, who ran away, was appalling even to that crowd of rough men, especially those including the name of the virgin, which name seems to be held with greater respect among them than that of God. Some of the more devout remonstrated when he uttered what they considered a terrible oath, which translated literally means "Damn the Host," which certainly from a Catholic point of view is one of the worst oaths. The Orangemen tried to walk in the streets of Montreal and were arrested by Mayor Beaudry, and the Lower Canadian Parliament passed an act making it illegal for Orangemen to have processions; much to the credit of some of the Liberals they voted against the bill, although Catholics. I am not by any means in sympathy with Orangemen, but I think they have as much right to have their processions as the Irish Catholics. The elections for the Dominion Parliament came oft and the Conservatives defeated the Liberals with an overwhelming majority. The main planks in their platforms were protection for the Conservatives, and, free trade for the Liberals. In harvest I always took the lead at mowing, circling a piece and letting the hired men follow me. I have found by experience that if the farmer himself does not know what amount of work ought to be done in a day by a man, that a great many hired men consider it a "soft snap" and impose on him. It requires a great amount of practice to mow in rooty and rocky land without breaking or constantly blunting one's scythe. Had a "bee" for mowing, the best mower around here challenged any man in the crowd to follow him and circled a piece. I went after him, and it was a race all day, but he could not get ahead of me, many atime I regretted doing so and felt as if I would almost faint from exhaustion, and at night every muscle in my arm ached; the straw averaged 5 ft. high, having grown on a dark, rich alluvial soil. In the autumn I commenced digging a drain 10 acres long, 4 ft. deep and 3 ft. wide, which will drain a damp portion of our clearance into the stream. During the summer I went to several "bees." for logging, cutting hay, peeling hemlock bark and building houses, and also instead of spending what little spare time I had in self improvement I wasted it in flirting with French girls and playing cards and other games, for which I often dispise myself for not having firmness of character to shun the worthless society with which we are surrounded. Letters received in '78. "My dear nephews: What pleasure it will give me to drop down some day on your lots and see your fine house and barn and above all a lot of land cleared—good crop bearing land, free from stones and brushwood; what a comfort to you to know that every acre is a freehold forever. Have you got legal power yet for clearing the brook? It surprises me to find it opposed for a moment, being a work so necessary, not only for the redemption of land and the increase of wealth to the country, but also conducive to health. I am quite sure that the body of stagnant water I saw must breed fever and ague, exclusive to the loss to the nation by keeping so much land waste of such great fertility. I find Canada is sending over her sheep and cattle in splendid condition; I hope this trade will increase and that Canada, which I like so much, will flourish. I should like you to buy that cheap land you spoke of, or any that is a good bargain; perhaps if you know of any you will write to me by return of post, but I should not like to buy it unless it was considered very cheap; if you could bid for it at auction and I would send you the money; uncle Herbert got his lot very cheap in that way. Unimportant news. With fond love to you both, your affectionate uncle, Jerrold." 17th Feb. '78. "My dear Tom: I wish to congratulate you on coming of age and at the same time to draw your attention to the fact that it is the most important period of your life, how much your dear mother would be pleased to do the same now if she was alive; but God in his mercy has taken her from scenes and circumstances which are almost breaking my heart as they did hers, but what is her gain now is my sad loss. She is gone to her heavenly home and eternal rest from the sins and sorrows and vexations of this life to enjoy a purer and unalloyed happiness after a checkered life of devotion, and self-denial for the glory of God and the good of her fellow creatures, therefore I should not murmur at the Divine will for her sake, though many of the circumstances connected with it make me feel it more keenly, nor indeed murmur at all on my account, as I should remember that God's will is best in the end, but I do feel also that this is a very solemn time for you, the turning point as it were of your life, that which may stamp your future career not only in this world but the world hereafter, for as we live so we die (generally). Some may be brought to a sense of God's grace and their own nothingness without him in their last days but it is a fearful risk to run. God said "they that seek early shall find me." Now I do not want to impute that you do not love God, but as your father and one having gone over a great part of the ocean of life I must know something of the rocks and shoals which beset man and would therefore like to warn you. In the first place example is said to be stronger than precept and the surroundings here are very far from what tend to make a man a noble man, a gentleman, let alone a christian. It is said "by their fruit ye shall know them," and if you are a child of God you cannot be happy in the midst of evil. A christian may be in the world and may use the things of the world (in a moderate and useful sense, not as the world generally do) but must not be of the world: we are told also to "love not the world or the things of the world," but to set our affections on things above, heavenly things, sound principles which constitute the will of God; to "seek first the kingdom of God and his righteousness and all things necessary will be added unto us:" the kingdom of God is within us: heaven is above, when we submit to the reign of Christ's Holy Spirit, sanctifying all our thoughts and aspirations and bringing our wills into the subjection of the will of God our Father just as he sets us an example "His servants ye are to whom ye yield yourselves servants, to obey sin unto death or God unto righteousness," also "he that knoweth his Father's will and doeth it not shall be beaten with many stripes." God often makes the circumstances of this life produce bad stripes on our consciences when we go against his will till he brings us into discipline, industry is good and commendable, humble patient industry becomes the christian, it may be slow but it is sure and more likely to have God's blessing than impulsive and inordinate ambition, which often overleaps itself and brings its own punishment as many speculators on this continent are finding to their sorrow now, by trying to do more than their circumstances would permit, often defrauding others to accomplish it or making hard bargains with their fellow-men; God's eye is on all our works and his ear is open to the cry of the distressed to-day as much as it ever will be; he may be slow but he will not pass it over, sooner or later he brings it all out; there is nothing which will not be revealed by him in his own good time and punished. The true child of God's place is to desire neither poverty or riches that they may not become "poor, or mean and steal," nor too full and forget their God. A mans life does not consist in that which he has but in that which he is in principles. Dr. Watts says: "could I in stature reach the pole, or grasp creation in my span, I'd still be measured by my soul, the soul's the stature of the man. Too much riches are a curse and a heavy responsibility, for "unto whom much is given much is required," whether in talent of the mind or riches requires great wisdom and grace to use them wisely for good; when life comes near its end we are but stewards over it and unless we make a noble use of it it affords us no real or lasting pleasure; "we bring nothing into this world and we can take nothing out, but riches may produce remorse if badly used and is apt to cause many snares and temptations, if we have not the wisdom to make a right use of it. I have read and know of many instances of young people going to destruction morally, by too great and sudden acquisition of wealth before they knew how to make a good use of tt, and worse, in some instances love of speculation, and intense ambition, in others, all of which is quite contrary to the spirit of christianity. Your land is now all paid for, you have now a nice and easy prospect before you, far better than many of your uncles when they began life, for your land is good arable land for the most part not having so many stones as the home farm. If you act judiciously, in a few years you will begin to realize money, then comes the danger to the young and inexperienced; it is said the love of money increases with the money itself, because it is the means of indulgence in all worldliness; it is also said "to be the root of all evil" in the power it gives and the abuse of it unless the possessor is living under the fear and love of God; the fear of doing wrong and the desire of doing right is not natural to any of us even in a regenerated state, we are prone to go astray without constant reference to the word of God and a careful and serious study of it; to the young it may appear a dry book but it is not so, the more it is read the more it will be found to be the fountain of true life a self interpreting book, the most sublime soul-purifying and comforting book that can be read as a guide in the affairs of life as well as in the life to come. The world has its attractions, companions and lawful duties, which when not ruled by order and system which is Heaven's first law, they tend to distract and divert us from it; I find it so myself and always did through life if not guarded against, but I thank God it is not new to me, I have read much of it in my early days and it has been a great blessing to me and I can truly say it has been a lamp to me in my brightest as well as my darkest hours; its principles and precepts being a check and guide to me in all difficulties and temptations, which naturally beset every one in all positions and circumstances of life; no one can be truly happy without a knowledge of it. You are now about to commence life on your own responsibility, you are as it were a young human fruit tree just transplanted and you will need care till firmly rooted in sound principles; you have had some grafting of good things done for you but you will find there will always be some pruning of unreasonable propensities, to do otherwise you cannot bear good fruit. There is also the parable of the sower and the wheat; I am anxious often when I think of you both (Arthur also) for much good seed has been sown, but what of the fowls of the air (bad company) also the weeds and briars of life (the cares of life) choking it. Oh, my dear boy, I cannot give you the riches of this life but I would warn you with all your getting to get understanding and wisdom, which is more precious than rubies; the wisdom of this world is foolishness with God; the wisdom of the Bible is the sweetner of life; the Bible is the mirror of life where every man can see his own character and above all God's grace to fallen man and the principles by which regenerated man may enjoy something of the Kingdom of Heaven, within us. While in life serving God our reasonable duty is to glorify our Redeemer as branches of the true vine of which he is the head; our fruit should be goodness, truth, mercy, righteousness, brotherly love, and such like: in the Mosaic dispensation Ten Commandments were given for that period, but in the christian dispensation God has given but one commandment "to love one-another," for it includes the whole law of God; love is the fulfilling of the law and does mercy with all righteousness and sees all christians as the children of one father redeemed from the spirit of a sinful world which still offers us the same terms which Satan was permitted to tempt our Saviour with, namely "all those things I give unto thee if thou wilt fall down and worship me" he is still the Prince of power of this world, working in the hearts of all who do not resist and reject him as the Saviour did; even christians still are liable to do wrong and err as others if they from any cause quench the strivings of the Holy Syirit or neglect it, then he takes its place and they are his captives for a time being led astray by some weakness, allurement or propensity; the sincere christian will be sorry and try to avoid the causes that lead to it from a pure love of goodness and a desire to please God, not for the mere sake of appearance or con-

sequence only; the Lords Prayer is a key to that, it is a Bible in
a nutshell, as it were employing great principles, but the one I
allude to is "Lead us not into temptation;" that is the great thing
to know and what to avoid also; we cannot stand temptation
of ourslves; if we know anything to be wrong we should avoid
it and not stop to question it, but reject it at once as Christ did;
his purpose was to be our example as well as our Redeemer;
His sacrifice put away the wrath of God for original sin; His example teaches us how to live as christian followers of him, a
peculiar people redeemed from the spirit of the world, sanctified
unto good works and while using the things of the world not to
abuse them nor let them ensnare us unto the ways of the world;
Christians should be an example to the world and not followers
of it; whatsoever we do should be done unto the glory of God
and for the God of mankind; no Christian can live to himself he
must live to and for God and mankind; we are bought with a
price, the price of Christ's blood and if we reject God's grace and
live according to the will of the flesh and not according to his
Holy Spirit can we wonder if he rejects us hereafter; we are created in the image and likeness of God spiritually with a free will
of our own but are responsible for the use and abuse of it. I regret that you have no better society; the society here reminds
me of Bishop Heber's hymn describing "Ceylon's lovely isle,
where every prospect pleases and only man is vile;" but there is
much to be thankful for, even here if there was only a right
spirit of reciprocity, but this cannot be where the love of God
does not abound, even those who have any little share of it
have something to do to preserve it, therefore temptations and
example of an injurious kind is much against you and the danger to the young of forming injurious and improper habits is
very great if not guarded against; habits are like a chain not
easily broken, therefore you should be careful not to have unnecessary acquaintance with those who do not tend to exalt and
improve you; better have no company than bad company. St.
Paul says let all things be done decently and in order; order is
in business what harmony is in music, it helps the memory some
time and promotes peace and happiness; promptness, punctuality
and conscientiousness are of great consequence also, the first

saves time, loss and accidents, the second respect credit and ease of mind, the third the basis of sound integrity, without which a man is worse than nothing: in work whatever is worth doing is worth doing well and pays the best in the end; exaggeration, prevarication and deceit are only the attributes of crafty and ignorant men, and those who would have a consience void of offence towards God and man cannot do so; the world's spirit is selfishness, the Christians is self-denial; no cross no crown: a Christian has three characters, first the child in the spirit to learn the father's will, second the servant to do it and show it by his conduct, also the soldier to conquer sin in ourselves and others by the guidance of his Holy Spirit and word. I have written this to you to warn you commencing the voyage of life, to lead you more closely to the narrow road that leads to everlasting life that you may not only be happy here but hereafter. I would like to say more to you both but you will find better than my feeble words can say in the New Testament, Psalms and proverbs especially; read often, it is the chart of life and will assuredly make you happy and good; it will bring order, happiness and peace to your house; it is the root and foundation of all true greatness, goodness and happiness; it is my only consolation after the disappointments of life; my sincerest wish is for your spiritual and temporal welfare, but remember that text "what will it profit a man if he gain the whole world and lose his own soul." God bless you both: your affectionate father, J. E. Howard." Montreal Oct 1st 78. "Dear Tom and Arthur, father told me to write and ask either of you to come into town for a few days, I expect you are not very busy as all your crops are in, we have been having heavy rains lately. Edison the great inventor is seriously ill. What do you think of the personel of the new cabinet? The failure of the Glasgow bank has caused a great deal of depression in the business circles of Scotland. Gas stock went down 13 per cent here on account of the electric light, but it has commenced to go up again; if they use the telephone instead of the telegraph it will do away with a great many telegragh operators; how strange it was for your colt to change from a dark brown to a light grey. I must now close as I have to read notes for my lecture, with love from all your affectionate cousin, Clifford H. Goldsmith." October 78 "My dear Tom and Arthur. We expect father back from England in a few days, he says his eyes are much improved he is anxious to return to his practice, the Marquis of Lorne and the Princess Louise will arrive here by the beginning of next month. The great Hanlan and Courtney race was to have been rowed yesterday at La Chine, but the weather was unfavorable so it did not come off, they will not row unless the water is as smooth as glass; the betting is 3 to 1 on Hanlan, which is absurd; there are about 30,000 strangers in town to see the race. I was pleased to see that the country you live in returned a Conservative; it was a glorious victory. Montreal returned 3 Conservative members by large majorities; there was great excitement here at the time. I now attend McGill college; Flora and Mr. Butler have been staying with us for the last few days. Your affectionate cousin, C. H. Goldsmith." "Aug. '78. Horton House, Abbeydale, Salford, England. My dear Arthur: I was so glad to get your letter and hear what you and Tom are doing on your farms, Timothy is always interested too, and likes me to read your letters to him; he is so surprised at the quantity of land you have and to think of your just cleared and sow 21 acres! We had such fine weather for haymaking and had about 15 tons. I suppose you know that Mabel has come over and is paying us a visit now. It is so delightful having her here, and she and little Constance are great friends. On Tuesday she is going on a visit to uncle Jerrold. We had such a nice trip to the lakes at Windermere, Derwentwater; Mabel was with us and took many sketches. We noticed how beautiful all the trees and shrubs were in the lake district." Minor items end it. "Montreal, Nov. 16th. My dear Arthur: When you were in town you spoke to me about selling the timber on your lots. I thought you knew best and consented, but on second consideration think it is the most foolish bargain you could make and that your land would be perfectly worthless; you are aware that wood is getting scarcer every year in your neighborhood, with another railway almost at your door and the great quantity the Grand Trunk consume annually, the wood on your land must become valuable. If the timber rots as you say it will make manure; it is worth more than twice what you propose to sell it for; with regard to buying those 200 acres from Doherty at 60 cents an acre think you had better have nothing to do with it; you and Tom have entered into a joint partnership to settle on and farm lots 34 and 35, as one of the partners I do not think it the correct thing for one of you to enter into any speculation on his own account; remember neither of you are land speculators, it is a question whether you have not too much on your lands already. I know everything I say here is in accordance with your uncle's wishes and as he has left the matter to my judgment I give you my advice in the matter and cannot change unless he instructs me to do so. You do not say one word about the Roman Catholic church tax you would have to pay on the land." In a note at Christmas he sent us a present of $5; in June he wrote from Norfolk where he spent the summer months with his family: "My dear boys I received yours of the 16th, I hear you will have a great deal of trouble with the burning of the 20 acres, in consequence of the rain, we have had very wet weather here: the frost has damaged the vegetables, Mabel will spend the Summer and Autumn in England, R. I. Goldsmith." P. S. Richard still coughs a great deal; I have not decided on a farm here for Clifford as they are exhorbitantly dear. London August 26th 78. "My dear Tom and Arthur. Your letters were delivered this morning and gave me great pleasure: it is always great happiness to me to hear of your clearing the land and improving it: every man that clears an acre of land confers a benefit on mankind; it is so much additional wealth added to the country and while you serve yourselves you add wealth and prosperity to the nation, besides it is your own free hold forever and bye and bye it will be such a pleasure to look at the wealth and estate you have created with your own hands and brains; it requires great cleverness, skill and perseverance to make a fine estate; after the rough work is over you can do the ornamental part, such as planting shrubs and trees, and first of all an orchard and a fruit and vegetable garden, A good fenced in garden is a treasure. How the Canadians out far away get bricks is not within our knowledge, here we require walls for fruit trees, such as peaches, plums and grapes, probably wooden fencing does as well,. When you write to cousin Sarah give her my love and say how glad I am she has a little daughter; give my love to uncle Herbert and his family. I am looking forward to the pleasure of going with your aunt and Rupert to stay for a time in Canada and build a hut, good bye, your affectionate uncle, Jerrold Goldsmith." Received letter from Mr. Hogarth, dated San Mateo, San Mateo Co. California, saying that he had just returned from Arizona where he had the charge of a stud farm for one of California's millionaire's, also a letter from uncle Jerrold asking us to buy for him some cheap land and that he would send us the amount; letter from uncle Timothy Howard to father, Waterford, Ireland, "Dear Jonathan, Your's of the 29th inst. reached me yesterday, Thursday is our only Canadian post day; I enclose a credit letter on Montreal bank for £5 which I hope will help you; the season here promises well and I am glad to hear that your prospects are favorable; the Church family would only be a drag on you, they are most helpless, neither of the boys do anything and the girls weak and delicate; Beaufort was a clerk in a store for a short time at 3*s*. per week which was afterwards raised to 10*s*. and Timothy received £2 as assistant teacher in a school of design, but both are now doing nothing: they are not however dependant on their relations as when our sister Anne died she entrusted her money in my care, the interest of which gives the children £4 10*s* a month; sister Bess last month was 75. I am 72 and continue in my business; I sent you last week English illustrated papers, your affectionate brother, Timothy Howard." June 78. My dear Tom and Arthur. We are at present at Norfolk, Bruntfield Lake. Our cottage is very pretty on the edge of the Lake; I have been twice out fishing with very little success. It rained all last night, whenever it rains I think of your land that you have to clear: this part of the country is very like yours, a good deal of rock and swamp, yet the land is very dear, from $12 to $25 an acre. There is one farm here for which they ask $13.000, which amounts to $40 an acre; the owner must be crazy to ask such a price although he says that the water power on it is the best in Canada. The railway that runs from Sutton will pass through Norfolk. I think Richard's cough is better since we came here; hoping to hear from you soon, I remain your affectionate uncle, R. I. Goldsmith." 6th Dec. '78. Tom and I are cutting cord wood; we have sold to Mr. Meredith. There are about 2 inches of snow on the ground. Frank Dodsley, father's home boy has gone to work for Carmicheals for $15 a year with board and clothes. In the *Witness* I see that the Marquis of Lorne, the new Governor General for Canada, with his wife the Princess have arrived; thay received a grand reception at Halifax and at all the chief towns on their way to Montreal, where they received a magnificent reception; the whole city was illuminated and the depot decorated with evergreens as well as mottoes and arches across the principal streets; they left for Ottawa, the capital, on Monday. The Eastern affairs look unsettled although everything seemed to have been peaceably arranged by the Congress at Berlin Our buckwheat was a heavy yield and we have occasionally buckwheat cakes with maple syrup for a change. Uncle Herbert is better from the effects of a severe fall he received, at one time his life was despaired of. It truly takes very little to extinguish the lamp of life when it begins to flicker in the period of old age. Helped the G. boys to saw wood; it takes 4 men to work a sawing machine, 1 to drive the team, 1 to remove the blocks when sawed and 1 to sit on a bar to keep the log steady while being sawed. Had a Frenchman to kill our pigs, he did not stun it before bleeding it as the English settlers do; said that the animal did not bleed as much when insensible and that the meat was not as white; he wanted to burn the hair oft the pig with straw, the usual way they do it, but we preferred having it moved with scalding water, as burning it off gives the meat a disagreeable flavor. 11th Dec. Rained hard all night. All the snow is gone and the two streams on our lots are flooded. Most of our evenings we spend in playing cards and flirting with French girls. While cutting wood in the damp land of the beaver meadows my boots get frozen so hard that I have to thaw them out before I can pull them off. There has been another fall of snow, just enough to whiten the ground; the evenings now are very long it gets dark at 4 o'clock, from this to 10 gives 6 hours for self-improvement, but somehow after severe physical exertion all day, a sociable evening with our French neighbors seems to have greater attractions to us than useful study. A Frenchman offered us 30 cents a hundred for the cut of our ties, which we refused, as the usual price is $1; paid Mrs. Brodeur 50 cents for a double knitted pair af woolen mits, 30 cents is the usual price. Tom and I cut 4¼ cords of wood in a day of ash which splits very easily. We have finished cutting 50 cords for Meredith; cut a supply of wood for father. John Kirwin has married Norah Doherty, although when quizzed about him she indignantly replied that she would never marry an old bachelor like him. Went to Meredith's; talked in the deaf and dumb alphabet to Jennie; asked Nicholas to come and measure the wood we sold them. Mrs. M. asked me to a party to be held in the village schoolhouse; Florence and Maud were spending the evening at Willoughby's. 22 Dec. It has snowed heavily all night; there are snow drifts 2 ft. deep. Of late I have been thinking of leaving the vulgar and degrading associations with which we are surrounded and of trying to enter some English millitary college. While at Houde's last evening I met the lover of the eldest daughter, he seems to be greatly captivated with her; his arm encircled her waist and her head rested on his shoulder; every minute or so he would whisper loving sentences into her ear; they passed the whole evening thus from 8 till 12, sitting in a corner of the room. For my part I would not like to have to express the sentiments of my heart to the being I loved, before a whole housefull of people, and I think even the most devoted of lovers would find it rather monotonous uttering love sentences 4 hours a night, 4 nights a week for several months duration. The father and mother generally after a game of cards or so with some neighbor who has called, go to sleep; the father on the floor by the stove with his coat under his head, and the mother in her rocking chair. Dec. 24th. Went to Aston and bought the ingredients for our Christmas dinner. Went to Meredith's; played checkers and whist with Florence, Alfred and Jennie. Mr. M. has just arrived from Wyandotte Silver Smelting Works where he is employed; went to a party at the school-house; the fair young ladies of Aston were well represented; presents were distributed to the younger children from the Christmas-tree, after which many of the ladies kindly favored us with singing and music and some of the gentlemen made speeches and related amusing anecdotes; after a pleasant evening the assembly parted after singing "God Save the Queen." Tom and I waited for mid-night mass; the church is a fine stone building; besides the organ there was an excellent brass band, which played some very fine music, but the service and ceremony seemed to me not as good as a poor pantomime, and better suited with all its set forms and mechanical movements for the worship in some Japanese or Siamese temple, than for that of a church in one of the civilized nations of the earth; it lasted nearly two hours and we were nearly frozen, there being no furnace as yet in the church; it was amusing to see the breath of hundreds of people issuing from their mouths as if they wers smoking furiously. It was surprising to me how delicate ladies could stand such cold and there were but very few of them that did not stay the service out. Next day dined at G's; we conversed on school affairs and decided that it would require great unity on the part of the Protestant families to keep the school from falling into the hands of the R. C's., which if it did we would have to pay taxes four times as high as we are now paying. Read "Devereaux," a novel by Lord Lytton, which gives a good portrayal of the crafty Jesuits; went to a dance in the evening at Houde's; spent a pleasant evening during the week at Meredith's, Miss Eliza Grant was there; Mabel Willoughby and Florence played some nice duets; Nicholas promised to come and inspect the rails we had sold him; Nicholas inspected the rails and but very few of them were "culls;" he remained over night and we played dominoes, checkers and cards and related anecdotes till 3 a. m, also discussed the state of society of the present day and what a great influence the "almighty dollar" has in it; Nicholas has rather socialistic views on the equality of all men; I argued that the barriers of the different classes of society would never be brought all to the same level for the very reason that all mankind can never become equal in intellect, education, wealth or merit, but that the day would come when all men of merit and worth would form one distinct class of society regardless of wealth or high sounding titles or names. Lent Nicholas several novels by Sir W. Scott. The English are having a successful campaign in

Afghanistan. Sunday, had a conversation with Tom about the great inconsistencies of the lives of most of the followers of the religions of the present day, who mostly believe that their religion alone is the perfect one even though its followers are in a semi-civilized condition. Now I held that there must be something essentially wrong with all the religions of the earth and their system of training; the rising generations or most of their followers would not be such worthless and miserable specimens of humanity, as it must be acknowledged most of them are. Their apologists however reply that it is not the fault of their religions or their doctrines but that of mankind, who will not follow or live up to them. Now I must say that this is a base and lying excuse, for there have been nations in Europe that have been the subservient and humble slaves of the Catholic priesthood for the last 1000 years, in such countries as Italy and Spain. Now if "God's most holy priesthood" in 1000 years of instruction can produce no better or more civilized people than the Spaniards or Italians, I think all truly liberal men must acknowledge that it is high time for all intelligent men of all classes of society to unite together for the overthrow of such a worthless system and use the intellectual powers a Supreme Being has given them in establishing a new system of training; the rising generations that will produce better men and women physically, mentally and morally than the majority of those which the christian churches have produced; in justice however to all the christian churches I must say that they bring much evil reputation on themselves by not following the injunction of that wonderful book their Bible: "Therefore come ye out from among them and be ye separate saith the Lord;" in fact they have admitted so many nominal christians into their churches that the true christians form but a very small minority, the ungodly and disgraceful lives of these nominal members combined with the leading position they occupy in the churches has a most injurious effect on the lives of the rising christian generations, in fact if they continue to violate this wise injunction of their bible all good men in future years will be ashamed to be members of churches that allow rascals for the sake of a few $1000 to be members of it, although they have risen to ignoble wealth and power by defrauding and oppressing the more helpless portion of humanity; told Tom that if we ever expected to become noble and useful men we must cease drifting into the low manners, habits and customs of the people that surround us and make an effort to acquire a love for the most useful and advanced studies which would elevate us and enable us to become useful members of the best of society, and that the only way for us to avoid a dishonorable use of our spare moments would be to have ever before us useful employment and recreation as well as honorable ambition and high aspirations; Tom said with a smile why my dear fellow to carry out such a course of action during life would cause you to be regarded as a bore and disagreeable fellow by most classes of society of the present day; imagine for instance if in the society of ordinary ladies you refused to converse on the light vapory and useless subjects which they discuss, how soon you would be shunned by them (as "a disagreeable bear") for the society of some one who would listen with profound interest to the trivial incidents that occurred at the last party of Mrs. so and so. While at Aston on the 31st saw the great preparations the Meredith's are making for a great party they are going to have. In consequence of the arrival of cousins Richard and Clifford we have improved our bill of fare as Richard is in very delicate health and would require what we would consider as delicacies; he and Clifford are thinking of becoming farmers; we all dine at G's on Jan 1st, 1879. Nicholas came out for a load of wood next day; in the evening I went to Meredith's to see if they wanted any more wood; Mrs. M. thought they would buy wood closer to their place; they wanted me to stay to the party but said our cousins had just arrived and that I had promised to spend the evening at my uncles. The roads are badly drifted; upset once returning; have agreed to swamp 50 cords of wood for Meredith's for $10; he has bought 2 ft. stovewood to be delivered at his house for 90 cts. a cord; which is very low; Clifford read an agricultural lecture aloud; it advocated econimization of manure and the sowing of clover as a fertilizer, as its leaves derive a greater part of its nourishment from the atmosphere. Of late we have been cutting down and cutting in lengths the standing timber on some land that we are going to clear in the spring, and chiefly spent the evenings in reading many of the useful and choice works our cousins brought with them. For the last three days and nights it has almost snowed unceasingly till it is now 3½ ft. deep. One of Earl Beaconfield's novels appeared to me rather smutty. Devlin asked me to break a "short cut" for him to Aston with our oxen for which he gave me $1.50, but afterwards regretted as I had a very hard ¾ days work with him and 5 other men; were completely tired out when we reached Aston at 8 p.m. the snow was damp and melting which is the best time to have a snow road "broken." The five men walked ahead up to their waists in snow and the oxen followed with a sleigh; slept at Kirwin's, Delvin's brother-in-law, who keeps a store in Aston; had a bad cold for several days after. 13th Jan. drove Richard and Clifford to Montreal; I beat Dubue at checkers; he is the champion checker player in these parts. We hired a man to thresh our oats at $2.50 a day, we to board himself his team and hired man; the first day we threshed 64 bushels; in the evenings played dominoes, checkers and cards; Louis Brodeur talks of going west and says it is impossible to make money here; spent an evening at Houde's, there were six young men, so that three of them were obliged to "eat oats" as the French girls call it; the girls told our fortunes with cards and always foretold that we would marry a girl with hair and eyes of the same color as the pretty fortune teller; they also sang songs mostly of a tragic or sentimental character. Received a letter from Richard asking us to rent Sherman's or some other house close to our lots. "The only excitement at our house is Flora's baby. I cannot say how grateful I am to you both for the kind way you put yourselves out to have us comfortable. There is a hitch in the Soles farm which we intended to buy; some of the cattle having the foot disease and she wont sell the place without them. When I go out your way I intend looking about Melford. I have finished sending out father's accounts and have not much to do now; that specimen of stone found on your land I showed to a mineralogist who pronounces it to be chlorite mixed with iron pyrites and micca; its value is nil." "Dear Arthur yours of the 20th inst. received. As no other house can be had I think Sherman's will be the best as it is the largest; you will please try and make it comfortable; whatever you spend I will pay you when I go out; a few chairs and a table will be all we will need, the rest we will bring from 'Montreal. You might also have the well emptied and some lime put in it if it is not all right; Clifford will go out with the things on Saturday, so a large sleigh will have to meet him; will you go out on Monday? With love to you both I remain your affectionate cousin, Richard I. Goldsmith." W. Charmicheal ran a few days ago with $20,000 and there is great excitement over it. 22nd finished threshing our grain, 154 bushels; had to draw one half of the threshing mill to the next place he was going to thresh at; this is the rule enforced by all those that go threshing about the country; put the straw back again into the barn to prevent its getting wet. Charmicheal's liabilities are over $200,0co, but the assets chiefly in real estate are over $400,000; it was foolish of him to run a-way; his wife and son brought him back from Chicago; he says he was under the influence of intoxicants when he ran away. The train Richard came out on took 7 hours, the usual time is 2½. I drew wood and helped Richard next day to fix up their room in Sherman's house; had many evenings at cards with our cousins; the French games at cards are entirely different to the English. There is much dissension about school affairs, some of the Aston people want us to join our school to theirs as we have only a few scholars, but the people of this school district want to hold out as long as they can. Tom and I had a dispute about house work; Uncle Herbert, Daniel Charmichael and the Reverend L. C. Willoughby, are school trustees. At a meeting they appointed father school teacher at $12 a month; he will only have his two Norfolk home boys to teach; the school is to be kept 6 hours a day. H. Carmichael was the lowest bidder for furnishing the school wood for the small sum of 90 cents a month. Feb. 1st. The weather is neither too cold nor too warm, but a delightful, invigorating atmosphere, although a few days ago the thermometer went as low as 16 degrees below zero; last evening we spent at Houde's, there was a house full of relations and friends, the married people spent the evening at cards and gossip, the young in making love; we had two suppers, the last one at 2 o'clock, consisting of pork, potatoes, bread, green tea, pies and maple syrup. On Sunday dined at Richard's; gave Ethel a book as a New Year's present; sold the G's. 100 bundles of straw, also some to French Canadians; Houde has cheated me out of $2.50 on the contract of rails I made with him, through not having a written agreement; tried to persuade father and uncle H. to agree about what hours he would teach the school; father begins at 10 and ends at 4, uncle wants him to teach from 9 to 3; I succeeded in persuading father to acquiesce. On Sunday went to church and dined at Meredith's; could not wish to spend a pleasanter afternoon and evening with nicer young ladies than Florence and Maud Meredith, in fact, ever since I saw Florence, 12 years ago, she has been my beau ideal of feminine grace and lovliness, and what is better still her accomplishments and intelligence are as great as her physical beauty. Mrs. M. asked me if I was not getting tired of farming in the backwoods; said I was and that I thought of entering the English army next spring, as we expected my uncle to come from England; she said I ought not to enter the army, but buy some farm in a nice location and get married and settle down. Florence showed me 50 valentines that she received; played checkers with Nicholas, also discussed Darwinism. Read in the papers of a British defeat in Africa by the Zulus, 500 British officers and non-commissioned officers and 1000 men were killed, and the colors of the 24th regiment captured; a great dishonor to British arms to be defeated by almost naked savages; the campaign in Afghanistan is not encouraging as the troops suffer from the severity of the climate and want of proper accommodation; Lord B's. government had better make more successful arrangements or his party will be defeated at the general election. Spencer's father, his wife, two sons and two daughters have moved on to the range from Bowansville; he was and old English soldier who married a French woman; the girls are very plain brunettes. The Houde's are to have a dance on Monday as Lent commences next day, after which there will be no flesh eating or dances for forty days. Sunday, 16th February. Tom is 22 years old to-day; it has snowed for the last 5 days; dined at Richard's, conversed on politics, religion, agriculture and commerce; I ridiculed that part of the Episcopal catechism where the godfather has to renounce the devil and all his works for his godch'ld; next day the farmers in our vicinity assembled together to snow-plow the roads with their teams. We did not go into Montreal this quarter on account of my aunt's illness, so uncle sent to us by mail the quarter's allowance At present we are drawing lumber from the mill and finishing the inside of the house; 23rd breakfasted at Richard's; uncle Richard has come from Montreal, they are all going to Lampton to look after a farm for Richard and Clifford; they all took tea with us; conversed on Orangeism and the life of soldiers of the present day; uncle read a chapter of scripture and prayers; next evening went to Preston with Daniel C. and the Houde girls to a dance; the country on this side of Preston is cleared and the wind was piercingly cold; Daniel C. unfortunately upset his sleigh but fortunately none of the girls were hurt; the master of the house came out and gave us a hearty welcome and conducted us to the supper room where we partook of tea and pies and then went to the room where the dancing was going on; some of the dances were new to us but as there was a young man to call them out we made no breaks; I had a headache and no wonder, the room was so hot and full of tobacco smoke; during intervals between the dances songs were sung, some of which were of the plus ultra Byronian style; slept in buffalo robes with many other young men in the dining room. I find that father has sent some of our dear mothers rings, broaches, &c., to his relations; told him not to give away any more as we wished to have them preserved; bought some brussels carpet, lace curtains and hearthrugs from him. Received a letter from Clifford saying that his father had bought a farm containing 200 acres from the Trust and Loan Co., one mile from Hartford and three from Leamington; there is a nice wood on the farm and a good house surrounded by beautifully hilly country; is only 5½ miles from the city of Sherbrooke. "We are all much obliged to you for your kindness to us while at Aston's, I think it improved Richard's health; we will go on the farm on April 2, your affectionate cousin, Clifford." Tom and I have finished the house ready for lathing and plastering. A man offered father 20 lbs. rent for every 100 troughs in his sugar bush and to make 200 troughs besides, which good offer he foolishly refused. 2nd March, lovely hay, the snow is thawing; drew 2000 ft. of spruce clapboards dome which cost $6 a 1000 ft. bought 4000 laths at $1, 25 cents a thousand, and lath nails at five and a half cents a pound. Received a letter from uncle Timothy of Waterford, informing us of the death of aunt Maud, to whom we used to write in our younger days; she was an old maid. Daniel C. and I started for Melford to visit friends there, met a drunken Frenchman, who stopped our horse and struck it on the head, also got a blow in the face in trying to pacify him; when sober he is a really good natured fellow; took a wrong bush road and to our disgust after driving 3 miles it abruptly ended among a tangled mass of fallen hemlock trees; there are so many roads in winter for lumbering purposes that it puzzles a stranger; nearing Melford there is some of the nicest scenery in the Province; maples and evergreens are seen along the roadsides and cosy farm houses surrounded by orchards. On arriving at Wakefield's, the eldest daughter met us at the door with her sisters, Sarah and Winifred; they are very sedate and religiously inclined girls and favored us with sacred music during the evening; Daniel scarcely spoke a word the whole evening, I expect he is bashful; went to the Scotch church the next day, the singing was not as good as in our Episcopal church at Aston; I never saw so many plain and plainly dressed ladies in an English church before; the sermon went to prove that there is a God from the evidences of his works; David shocked Mrs. W. by using some slang expressions, which I saw by the expression of her face, as of course she is too ladylike to take marked notice of it; had a quiet tete a-tete on past events; she told me her husband who died last summer, lost $9000 on a railroad contract, that the railroad was now in bankruptcy, but that eventually they expected to get the money; that night we went to the Methodist church, very fair music and singing and the congregation had a better appearance and were better dressed than that of the Scotch church, but the sermon was uninteresting. A miner at the slate quarry lost $1200 by hiding it in the mattress of a bed, of which his wife did not know and emptied the straw in the rood. Daniel C. had an argument with his sisters about the discipline of the militia, which his sisters criticised; he was greatly annoyed, but the mother, however, stopped the argument; even in the most religiously inclined families brotherly love and harmony does not always exist; Daniel and I have the same ideas on the Chinese question, that all men should be allowed to come to this country as long as they observed the country's laws; next morning took a pleasant drive with the girls in Wakefield's double sleigh; wrote in their autograph albums which seems all the rage with many young ladies of late; In returning home had a terrible time of it; every second step the horse took it sank up to its knees in the snow which is thawing. On my way back heard thunder and saw flashes of lightning, an unusual occurrence at this time of year. Wrote to Uncle Jerrold; went to Meredith's and played chess with Nicholas; Florence told me that Rev. L. E. Willoughby was sold out for debt, but that his wife bought all the things back; it is certainly a disgraceful state of affairs for a minister of Christ: Mrs. M. told me of several of his transactions which were not considered strictly honorable and that some of his parishoners talk of getting another minister in his place. After tea had an evening at cards and music; Florence sang a song very beautifully, entitled, "love me little love me long;" coffee and cake were passed around at 10 o'clock; Nicholas sang some comic songs and Maud played several nice duetts with Florence; returned home at 12. Went next day with uncle to Doherty's to give a notice from Uncle Richard to pay a certain amount he still owed on the bark. Old Doherty is greatly vexed with his eldest son who married a French Protestant although she has now turned Catholic. "March 76. Dear Tom and Arthur. Every day I have been intending to write you ever since my return but only now succeed; at present we are very busy getting ready for the farm as we have to buy everything; everything now is very cheap; I have been offered a new Warrior mower and an Ithaca horse rake for $80, and a second hand mower can be bought for $25; the "Buckeye steel horse rakes new for $20. a sulky plough for $30. We leave for Hartford on the 3rd, taking a car for our freight; there is great excitement in town about the new tariff and of course it does not please everybody, there is one thing sure and that is that it will make everything dearer than at present, bread must go up as they have put 50 cents a barrel on flour; all grain is taxed and coal 50 cents a ton; this will effect wood in some districts; you will see by my Uncle Jerrold's letter that I enclose, thinks of coming out next summer; I suppose the house is very comfortable now with its many rooms; the house on our farm is not finished outside; we are going to have it bricked and a veranda put up; it is very well finished inside; the hardwood woodwork being excellent; if the soil is as good as the buildings the place will do; the barn is immense; you can drive nearly to the top of it, it being against a hill, with love I remain your affectionate cousin, R. I. Goldsmith." "London March 79. My dear Tom and Arthur, I received your nice letters and long account; your money seems a great deal swallowed up in labor such as chopping wood and other work which I suppose you cannot find time to do yourselves; Rupert and your aunt are well and send their love to you; Rupert came up from Oxford yesterday during vacation until the 16th of April next, when he returns. The weather continues dreadful, now rain and hail and the air as thick as pea soup, it is truly disagreeable, I should be glad to buy land but would be unwilling to keep on paying taxes for land that I could neither use or employ, however if you hear of any cheap land for sale let me know, although times may be hard for a while real estate will be sure to treble in value later on; stick to yours and thank God you are not in a pent up stifling smoky city like me, but in a fine free open air, land all your own and plenty of healthy labor to make you strong and sleep sound and live long; may you do so and be happy is the prayer of your loving uncle Jerrold B. Goldsmith." "Dear Tom and Arthur. We have decided that the best place to buy a wagon is in Aston, please enquire the prices for us; we have a hired man and wife for one year; we bought a big Clyde mare for $55 and a good set of double harnes for $24, with love your affectionate cousin, Richard I. Goldsmith." I talked politics with uncle H.; he is a conservative. 21st March, went to St. David; drove as far as Preston then drove up the Black River several miles on the ice, then turned off southeast on a main road or range that was 12 miles long, straight as a crow could fly; the houses were not more than two acres apart, many were very fine buildings of stone; it looked like a long straggling village; Daniel who was with me got off to work; our horses took fright at something and ran away going full gallop for two miles when they collided against a load of hay and broke the neck yoke; how fortunate they struck a load of hay, if it had been of wood they would have been seriously injured; paid 50 cents to mend neck yoke. The lime burner had a kiln not quite finished burning; we fed our horses, bought some bread and maple sugar and waited; on returning upset our load in crossing the Preston River; had to pay a man 25 cents to help us to load it; the lime of St. David is superior to that of St. Marie for fine work; returned home at 2 o'clock. It seems as if Canada's policy of protection does not meet approbation in England. Received a letter from Fritz Hogarth, he has returned to England. Nicholas came for a load of wood invited me to spend the evening at their place; had an evening at cards; Florence is on a visit at Lemington with some friends; spent the night there; the Meredith's live very plain for people of their means, but they show their sense as too much pastry is unhealthy; Nicholas lent me a history of Greece; composed sentimental verse while at M's. Sugar making operations have commenced. Bought scantling from Guertin for $3.50 per 1000 ft; bought a single wagon for Richard, with express box, two seats cushioned, also a double tongue to hitch on a span as well shafts for one horse, all nicely painted and first-class workmanship for $43. Went to Guernsey's; the girls played on the organ, which music I do not care for outside of a church. Went to the Lentel services that are held in the school-house and from there to McDougalls and played checkers; spent next evening at G's. Aunt quizzed me about Maud and Florence Meredith; I do detest the low habit of quizzing, and see nothing to be ashamed of for liking the society of sociable and refined young ladies, which has a beneficial and elevating influence on the rougher nature of men. The ancient Grecians were truly a noble people and would put to shame many Christian nations of the present day by their integrity, courage and patriotism. Mrs. Houde told me, in the gravest manner possible, a story of a young girl that danced the same day she took the Holy Communion, against her mother's wish, and said she would dance even if she had to dance with the devil himself. When the dance commenced a young man entered handsomely dressed and commenced to dance with her, but held her hand so tightly that she screamed; the others tried to free her hand from his grasp but could not, so they sent for a priest, who by applying holy water frightened the Devil away, but in going away he took one side of the house with him, and that during the rest of her life the girl's hand was marked with the finger nails of the devil. I smiled and said, Mrs. Houde do you not think that the persons who related it to you exaggerated? to which she replied, I know they did not, for my mother and several of my uncles were among the spectators, and are good honest people who would not lie about it. I told them that it might have occurred in a similar manner to that of an incident in Spain: "A priest who told a young man that the devil would carry away the body of his father from its grave if he did not pay for masses for the repose of his soul. The young man sat up with a shot-gun and hid himself by his father's grave, and when something appeared resembling the christian idea of the devil he fired and wounded, not the devil, but the same parish priest." April 3rd. It snowed and blew so hard all day that I was obliged to pass the day in reading. Went to Meredith's in the evening, several young ladies were there; had music and singing; the younger children played philopena. After tea we all went for a drive by moonlight in a double sleigh; there was Florence, Maud, Mabel W., two Miss Weldon's, whose father is station agent, and Nicholas and myself. Met Richard Ba on, who was coming to get Florence and Maud to attend the practice of church music, they would not, however, forgo their drive. I treated the party to $2 worth of confectionery and fruit. Stayed over night at Meredith's; Florence remonstrated with Nicholas and myself for playing chess on Sunday. I proposed to Mrs. M. to have a sugar party at their place and that I would furnish the syrup, she was delighted at the idea. I drove Florence to church; the music and singing were very fine but the sermon uninteresting. During the Lental services I attended them regularly. April

HISTORY OF THE FRENCH IN AMERICA.

10th, a lovely day; the sap will run well as it froze last night; borrowed a small sugar kettle and went to Meredith's; Mabel Willoughby, Annie Weldon and two Miss Grants had arrived. Nicholas and I made a fire outside and boiled two gallons of syrup; when sufficiently boiled we poured it in pans full of snow and passed it around; after having a most agreeable time we adjourned to the drawing-room where Mabel W. and Florence favored us with music and singing; to hear the powerful and cultivated voices of Mabel and Florence is a rare treat, and any one that does not enjoy good music is to be pitied. Good music I think has a most elevating influence on the mind of man. After tea we played whist, but when Florence commenced playing a waltz the ladies insisted on our having a waltz and a few quadrilles; one lady had to take the part of gentleman as there was only Richard Bacon, Nicholas and myself; at 10 o'clock cake and cordial was passed around; Mr. Meredith is a staunch temperance man and never allows wine in his house; I drove Mabel home. On Sunday dined at Rev. L. C. Willoughby's; his second wife is a very kind and ladylike woman. I feel disgusted with myself for the many precious spare moments I have wasted of late; even in the superior society of Aston English people one does not derive much advantage as the chief part of their conversation is of a frivolous nature which can never aid a man in becoming useful and great; if I did not know better it would not be so bad, but I love and wish to aid and maintain everything that is good and true, and yet, at the same time, I have not sufficient stability of character to keep me in the path of duty, but I must and will mark out for myself a path in life and adhere to it, and will shun and denounce everything that has not an elevating effect on myself and the rest of mankind. On Sunday the church was decorated for Easter; some of my *Aston acquaintances quiz me about the Miss Meredith's. No ',true gentleman would stoop to such low vulgarity. Read in a book called "Rome as it is." It certainly always ⌊fills me with indignation to read of that church "that declares it cannot err in its spiritual instruction." All men that love civilization, liberty and progress should use their utmost endeavors to overthrow this and all other churches that keep men in the worst form of spiritual slavery. Some of my French friends have often said to me how can you call us slaves when there are so many clever and learned men in our church; I always reply it is possible for a man to have a great intellect and be a profound scholar in most branches of literature and science and at the same time be a regular fool in religion, for the very reason that he has been taught from early infancy that it is a "mortal sin" to begin to think for himself or doubt some of the absurd doctrines that his spiritual dictators force him to believe on pain of "eternal damnation." Received a letter from uncle Richard saying that he would like us to go and see his sons soon on their new farm and also that he had a scheme that he would tell us of. Have clapboarded our house. 18th April, snow is disappearing rapidly; went to a sugaring off at uncle Herberts. Wrote to Mills, the deputy inspector of schools asking his advice on our school affairs. At times I am filled with a desire to be something better than a bush farmer amongst ignorant, superstitious French Canadians, and that there are less opportunities in this place to fit myself for a higher position in life than in other parts of the continent. Drew manure on the meadows. Government surveyors are surveying this part of the country for the purpose of making a new map. Had to pay Houde $2.50 for our share for the work he did in keeping the roads in repair this winter, as we did a good deal of shoveling on them ourselves. Tom and I drew out timber to make a veranda on 3 sides of the house; hired a man to help us for 3 weeks for $8 and board. On Sunday Tom, Daniel C. 3 Houde girls and myself went to a sugar party at Brodeurs; in the evening there was songs and conversation that would even horrify "such a bad man as Col. Ingersol," yet the people belong to the devout and respectable class of the French Canadians and are in good standing in the Catholic church, yet were their conversation to be repeated in any English house the offender would be kicked out; to me it seems that it is the fault of their religion and not that of the people; the church by granting absolution at stated periods makes the people regard sin as almost a necessity and a thing impossible to avoid. It is sickening to me to see people regularly confess and receive absolution and partake of "God's body" while their lives are most base and worthless; many are habitual drunkards and of as low a standard of manhood as one could imagine and still are allowed to remain regular members of the church. Hundreds of frogs are croaking in a neighboring swamp which sounds very dreary. Received a letter from uncle Richard saying that they were very busy buying manure, stock and implements. Commenced logging, which is very hard work. Our hired men seem to expect that I should do as much as them, so I have to work pretty hard to keep them up to the work, in fact take the lead. A man man offered to hire for a year at $175 and board. Engaged Metz Vincent for a month at $10.50. The oxen's necks are swollen from hard work; have to "chop land" till they are better. Had a dispute with one of the hired men; I deducted 30 cents for two mo.nings he came too late, for which he exhausted the French and English language in oaths and bad names. I have given up going to see the Houde girls. 4th May, did not go to church as I felt too fatigued after a hard week's work. The English pros pects in the Zulu war are improved. Hanlan the Canadian champion rower has fine prospects, betting 4 to 1 on him against the English champion; he beat the American champion before going to England. Every evening in the month of May the French go and pray at a cross in the centre of this range; it is called "the month of Mary." The lovers have a great time escorting their sweethearts to the cross to pray. Daniel C. escorted Alphosine Houde; I hardly thought he would degrade himself with such barbaric superstition. On the 5th there was thunder and lightning. I have come to the decision that the greatest hero is that man who can maintain an unceasing conflict during life against error in all its forms; this form of heroism is greater and supremely grander than the reckless courage of the hero that rushes to the cannon's mouth. The musquitoes have arrived a few days ago. Houde's pigs have greatly damaged our meadow by rooting it. It has rained for the last two days. Metz and I were trying to see who could chop the fastest, and in my haste my axe struck a twig and swerved out of its course and descended on my instep making a terrible gash; I made for the house 20 acres distant as fast as I could, jumping over logs and the blood spurted from my boot every step I took; when I arrived at the house I felt rather weak from loss of blood; bandaged the wound tightly and tied a handkerchief very tightly around my ankle and sent for Dr. Bacon; he says I have cut an artery which he tied with some silver wire and then sewed up the wound which is 4 inches long. It was not as painful an operation as I had imagined it would be. It is really too bad to be laid up thus at the busiest season of the year. Read in "Rome as it is;" from what I have read of this church and the effects of its teachings on the French Canadians makes me look on it merely as an improvement on Paganism; the book truly says "Rome's intolerance is only measured by its power." An impartial study of history clearly shows this; but although its power is fast increasing and it is making mighty efforts to retain its hold on the minds of men it will be of no avail, for not 100,000 churches of Rome could arrest the grand march of civilization, for as the ages roll on men will more and more make use of their reasoning powers by which all spiritual serfdom will be abolished, and the nations will cease to hate and persecute each other on account of nonsensical doctrines as in the middle ages; for all men will be in honorable rivalry in trying who can become the best and most noble people physically, mentally and morally by a perfect study of the laws by which a Supreme Creator governs the human race and our planet. I can well imagine how amused the more enlightened men of future ages will be at the absurdity of their semi civilized ancestors, each trying to draw a picture to themselves of their God and the unknown hereafter and then teach their innocent little children that their poor neighbors are damned because their imaginary picture is different to theirs. Have read much of history of late, among others that of Rome, from which it can be seen that lust, gluttony and intemperance destroyed one of the greatest empires of our earth. In some ways a soldier's life has great charms for me, especially I think in a conflict for a just cause, but to an honorable man it must be very distasteful to fight for his country when it has undertaken an aggressive and unjust war. The Afghan and Zulu wars are just over; the obstacles of climate, rugged country and warlike natives are at length in a fair prospect of being overcome by the prowess of British Arms; Beaconsfield and his policy it appears are growing more unpopular with the British people; the Socialists are taking very desperate means to try and gain concessions from some of the European Soverigns. 12th May, it is very warm to-day, the atmosphere is clouded with smoke caused by fires made to clear land. Protestantism has made great progress in Canada since it became a British possession; about 50 years ago Montreal was almost entirely Catholic, to-day about ⅓ of its inhabitants are Protestants, and most of the chief business and enterprise is carried on by them which is a most remarkable example how liberty and education triumph over ignorance and superstition, and so it is with every country in the world whenever Romanism has all to itself and the inhabitants yield unquestioning obedience to its priests; the people are lower in the scale of cultivation than in countries where Protesantism and Infidelity exist; the following countries prove the truth of this; Spain was once one of the greatest nations of the earth but could not hold its power against Protestant England, and as a people are truly much inferior than the English heretics; then Italy, the very center of Catholicism was a few years ago one of the most celebrated countries in the world for brigands, assassinations, vice and beggars as well as for the ignorance of the mass of the population; then again Mexico, Brazil, Chili and Peru are all under the absolute spiritual rule of Romanism, and compare them with the worst of the American States or Provinces, and even the Romanist himself cannot deny the great superiority of the Protestants, although Brazil has ten times more natural advantages than most of the Protestant American States; Romanism can of course boast of some great and noble men, but these men were great and good in spite of the degrading influences of the religion they believed in; poor Gallieo's greatness and goodness cannot be attributed to Romanism (his church) for it persecuted him to death. Pagan Rome and Greece produced some of the greatest, purest and noblest characters of the earth; yet no one would be foolish enough to attribute their nobleness to the diabolical teachings of their priests. It is perfectly plain that the policy of Rome is to keep the masses of the people in ignorance, which policy they have carried out in all those countries where infidel or Protestant influence is not felt and whose inhabitants have not had the courage to rebel against priestly tyranny as in France; see what a country it has become since the revolution; a great part of its inhabitants are infidels, but how much superior are they than the poor, devout, priest-ridden people of Spain. Another feature in the crafty policy of Rome is, that wherever Protestants or infidels have any power and form a large portion of the inhabitants as in Great Britain, the United States and Canada, they establish their own schools and colleges to educate the children spiritually as well as secularly, for fear the Catholics would patronize the national schools or those of Protestants; thus, Catholics where part of the population is Protestant, receive a superior education than in those countries where the population is entirely Catholic and where the priests have everything their own way. I predict that Italy through its being freed from spiritual thraldom, will quickly lose the vice, ignorance and poverty with which it was cursed under the infallible spiritual rule of the Popes, and become a nobler, wealthier, happier and more powerful people. One of the most degrading influences of Romanism is the confessional; can anything be more disgusting than to have a chaste and innocent young lady subjected to the impure questions that every priest is obliged to ask those who confess to them. I could give hundreds of horrible proofs of its degrading influence on the people of the middle ages, and this, too, extracted from works of eminent Catholic authors of good standing who would not have written so had not the condition of the people been in a dreadful state, but I cannot for the sake of decency and virtue. I would suggest to all impartial men to read well a description of the condition of Europe in the middle ages, when Romanism reigned supreme, and compare its degraded state to the more civilized state of the whole Christian and Pagan world since the glorious light of Luther's reformation dispelled the dark clouds of superstition that darkened the earth, and has made the last few hundred years the grandest epoch in our earth's history. I have seen in the Province of Quebec, hundreds of French Canadians, that were considered devout Catholics who regularly received absolution and performed the chief duties of their religion; yet such was the depravity of their lives that some of the meanest infidels have lived nobler and purer lives. What surprises me is the low standard of character generally amongst the Catholics of this Province, who as long as they are not guilty of heinous sins imagine that impure conversation and indecent jests are not wrong, but merely "pour rire," as a young French girl once said to me when I used condemnatory language on an indecent remark a young man had made. I have seen numbers of them who lived ignoble and despicable lives, at the hour of death confess, receive absolution and partake of their "bread god" and in two instances recover contrary to expectation and lived the same sinful and worthless lives they had done before their illness; yet these same men were allowed to remain members of the church and partake of the "holy sacrament," which most Christians believe if taken unworthily "is taken to a man's damnation." Romanism also has been guilty of persecutions that have been so cruel that even "devils" would be ashamed to acknowledge them; and some of these diabolical persecutions have received the approbation of the Popes. Romanist apoligists assert that Protestants have been guilty of persecution, but this does not palliate their atrocities. It should also be remembered that Romanism persecuted men for a contrary belief long before the first dawn of the light of the reformation began to appear on the earth, and therefore as the infallible church set a bad example to the rest of mankind. It should also be remembered that the early Protestants had great provocation. If Queen Elizabeth did persecute the Catholics she was first set the example by her bigoted and cruel predecessor, Queen Mary. It should also be remembered that English Protestantism was weak, and numerous plots were being made for its overthrow and that some of the harsh laws that were made were really justifiable, from the fact"that self preservation is the first law of nature," and Cromwell, if he did persecute the Irish, had great aggravation for doing so. His co-religionists had been atrociously murdered with the expressed approval of the head of the church of the meek and lowly Jesus. But the great difference between the two religions is that the Protestants almost universally are ashamed and lament of the persecutions their ancestors committed, while many of the Romanists glory in some of their persecutions and with lies and quibbles deny others, attributing it to political animosity etc. It is however an acknowledged fact that there still exists at Rome a medal in commemoration of the massacre of St. Bartholomew Now supposing this massacre was done for political motives by Frenchmen, when the infallible popes found out their mistake why did they not destroy the medal instead of preserving it, but even in this enlightened age many of its followers in different parts of the world persecute Bible sellers and Protestant teachers in various ways, but dare not take their lives for fear of arousing the indignation of the Protestant world; but men and priests that would cruelly beat Bible sellers as they have done in Austria and Spain would burn them if they had the power to do so. I was pleased to see however that the American board of Foreign missions have been trying to obtain complete religious liberty for missionaries in Spain and Austria. It is a terrible condition of affairs to have a Protestant traveller fined and imprisoned in Spain in '82 because he could not consientiously take off his hat and kneel in adoration to a God of bread. Any church that would tolerate the Inquisition and not reprimand its members for such diabolical cruelty cannot of a certainty be inspired of God; a church that would allow members in good standing to use thumb screws to tear men limb from limb and burn them at the stake, without a word of condemnation, deserves the hatred and contempt of all civilized men. Yet this church declares that its spiritual teachings have always been infallible—and has the barefaced impudence to say that Luther's was a disastrous revolution. The only way I can account for clever and good men believing in this and other religious frauds is as I have before stated that although they are wise and learned in all branches of literature and science they are childish fools in religion, having never been allowed by their spiritual tyrants to harbor doubts or reason to themselves as to whether this revealed religion is really true or not. I have no ill feeling against the most devout of Romanists, Protestants or Mohammedans; it is only against those religious frauds and imposters who for lust of gold and power try to keep the inhabitants of this earth in a state of spiritual slavery. Amongst Protestant Clergymen however I must say I have met with many noble, generous-hearted men who have devoted their lives to the glorious work of elevating their fellow men by teaching chiefly the beautiful and grand moral laws and precepts of that great moral teacher, Christ. Among the Catholic Priesthood such noble men also exist, but I have never had the pleasure of meeting one for they are much scarcer than among Protestant Clergymen on account of the more rigid ecclesiastical training and tyranny they have to undergo, which in most cases dwarfs and contorts the better sentiments of their nature, for it must be remembered that as the people are under the priests so the priests are under the bishops and so on till all is concentrated under the one man and spiritual despot, the Pope. How humiliating for a priest of intelligence to think I cannot use my reason on religion or in any way use the gifts God has endowed me with but must without questions or doubts teach and preach according to the ideas and wishes of my tyrannical superiors. and even in fact in many of the church superior sects is this intolerant spirit also shown, and the moment a clergyman begins to use his reason on religion and deny the truth of some of the absurd doctrines concocted in the superstitious brains of the barbarians of former ages, he is excommunicated and driven from the sect to which he belongs How very despotic for most of the Christian Churches to form councils, such as the council of Trent etc., consisting of narrow minded ecclesiastics, who set themselves up as the spiritual dictators of the rest of mankind and promulgate doctrines according to their fancy and then take away from their fellowmen the God-given privilege of freedom of thought, and with lying threats of "eternal damnation" on pain of disbelief force the majority of mankind to accept their ideas as inspired of God, in fact in the middle ages the spiritual tyrants were not satisfied with condemning (those who refused to be slaves) to torment in the future world, but must roast to death, all men who had the courage to think and speak for themselves, but as the years rolled on great and noble men by a proper use of the reason God endowed them with saw the unjust wickedness of such despotism and through their efforts and the improved religion of Protestantism, the Christian councils no longer roast men alive; they only condemn them to eternal punishment in a future world for the terrible crime of not submitting to their decrees, which were only the thoughts and ideas of the minds of finite fellowmen; yet the brazen-faced apologists of Romanism have the audacity to declare that their religion is, was, and always will be unchangeable, if so why do they not try and roast their enemies now as formerly, or supposing for instance a party of Catholics were to commit such an atrocity would not the Pope immediately excommunicate them? Of course he would, then if an unchangeable church why did he not excommunicate or at least reprove the villains who committed such atrocities in the middle ages. The reason is plainly this, then the Popes power was almost unquestioned and supreme, to-day it is endangered by Protestantism and civilization, and in this enlightened age were they to encourage or tolerate such barbarity 100,000,000 hearts and hands would be united for his overthrow; yet even in this enlightened age much bitter and cruel persecution still exists, several cases of which I have myself personally witnessed; one case especially, that of a relative of mine, a perfect gentleman and a throughly moral and good man who moved in good society; till that moment he had the moral courage to express his unbelief in some doctrines that appeared to him absurd and improbable, from that moment the circle of society and friends he had moved in thrust him out of it as if he were a viper, and even one of his uncles told him that he did not wish to have any one visit his house who doubted the essential doctrines of Christianity, but such bigoted injustice and cruelty although it may frighten and prevent some men from using the reasoning powers God gave them cannot, and never will, arrest the progre ; of men's enlightenment, for in all ages of the world ve courageous and conscientious men existed who would bravely face the persecutions and contempt of the ecclesiastical world, rather than fall out of the ranks of that noble little band of workers who have ever claimed the right and privilege of men for the pefect use of their reasoning powers on all things spiritual as well as temporal, and have ever resisted those tyrannical Christian councils who usurp to themselves privileges that God has given to all mankind. Fellow-citizens of this great and enlightened age let it not be said in future ages to the eternal dishonor of this age that its best society did refuse to admit men in its midst because they boldly claimed the right of enslaved humanity to think and reason for itself. In my opinion however this little band of workers will, as they increase, form a select society of themselves that will extend the hand of fellowship to every fellow man rich or poor, as long as he has done and is doing his level best to attain to the highest possible state of manhood and will not close its doors on such and for a slight differance of belief or wealth as the Christian society of the present day has done to its eternal dishonor, but will of a certainty refuse to tolerate in its midst all men who advocate the right of any body or class of men to become the spiritual dictators of the rest of mankind. Many Sectarians have often sneeringly remarked to me, what have you "unbelievers" done for humanity, you do not build hospitals or schools, to which I reply, how could we? We do not yet exist in sufficient numbers, besides we do not believe in having schools or hospitals for any special class or body of men, we believe that all men should act not as if they were some distinct race, separated from the rest of mankind, but as if they belonged to one grand brotherhood, created by one God and actuated with a generous rivalry to see which can make the best study of his unchangeable laws and become the most perfect beings of his creation, and therefore we liberally aid all good and charitable institutions organized by Christians but at the same time are doing all in our power to remove their most objectionable features and unite them all in the grand work of healing and educating all diseased and ignorant fellow-men regardless of creed or color. Our aim is not to become some distinct class or sect, but to preserve all the good moral laws and precepts of all religions that hundreds of years of experience has shown to be useful and beneficial to mankind, and which are not the result of any special revelation to man as all religious theologians assert, but merely from a proper use of the glorious God-given gift of man's intellect in the study of the unchangeable laws of nature. For instance, I ask the intelligent reader does he think God would endow men with intellect reason and a discerning spirit and make such revelations or special commands as "thou shalt not kill," and a hundred other laws which the gifts he endowed man with were capable of discerning without any revelation; a proof of this is seen in many of the barbarous and detestable laws of marriage, etc., said to have been specially revealed by God to Moses, which are far inferior to the more beautiful and just laws made at the present day by civilized and humane men. Is it possible that God would reveal laws that are considered barbarous and cruel by the civilized portion of mankind of the present day. I think the reader will agree that they were merely created by some semi-civilized philosopher and palmed off by him on a semi-barbarous people as a special revelation from God. All we wish to do is to purge all religions of the supernatural absurdities with which they are cursed; and to convince Mohammedans that dancing like mad men does not tend to God's glory or the good of mankind; and to the Roman Catholics that the glorious light of science and useful knowledge shining amongst men is more pleasing to a Supreme power than the light of 100,000,000 wax candles; to the Jews that God has never been so brutal as to take pleasure in the blood of lambs and turtle doves, and that the incense of a beautiful and noble life is sweeter to God than all the sweetest incense of the earth combined; and to the Protestants that God takes no pleasure in a man casting himself on the earth in abject humility crying,"vile! vile! unclean am I!" But that all God requires of man is that he should make a proper use of the God-like attributes that he has given him and become the grandest being of all creation with a perfect knowledge of his duties towards himself and the rest of mankind. This class of "free thinkers" should not be confounded with apostate or bad men of all religions who leave the sects to which they belong merely because they cannot live up to some of the good moral laws and precepts that are taught. This, however, I regret to say is generally the case, and all bad men who do not belong to some religion are unjustly classed as freethinkers. It must be acknowledged that this is unjust, for the true infidel or free thinker is one who after he has exercised his judgment or reason on the so called truths of supernatural religion, cannot believe them and of necessity must reject and expose what he conscientiously believes are errors and prejudicial to the interests of humanity; yet I have heard a narrow minded christian remark that he would prefer introducing a Turk into his family than an infidel. The same spirit is exhibited in the education of the children of Christians, their minds are so prejudiced against infidel books that the average Christian lays one down with holy horror on seeing its title, and I actually saw a Roman Catholic Bishop who ordered his spiritual slaves to cease taking a certain newspaper because it published articles criticising the Catholic Church. Truly the Catholics of the Province of Quebec must have very little manhood left to allow their priesthood to dictate to them what newspapers they shall read; surely if human beings, after attaining manhood and womanhood, are responsible beings, they have a right to use their own judgment as to what they read; I must say I have been greatly surprised with the agreeable contrast of the religious freedom and liberty of the members of the Mormon Church, who buy and read what literature they choose; I have even seen in the houses of good Mormons, the *Tribune*, a newspaper that never loses an opportunity of ridiculing and bringing into contempt the doctrins of their religion; were the *Tribune* to publish such bitter articles in the Province of Quebec, I am confident its establishment would be attacked in 24 hours time, for I myself have witnessed a sight I shall never forget, in a French Canadian store, that of a mob who attacked a Bible seller and robbed him of his Bibles, which they burned; I may also draw two other remarkably favorable contrasts for this much persecuted people. The head of their church allowed a Gentile Minister to preach against the Mormon Church in the Tabernacle of the Mormons; this, for liberality, has never been excelled in ecclesiastical history; also that of apostate Mormons, lecturing and denouncing the religion they once professed, without their lives being endangered or even a single threat uttered against them. When I compare their christian toleration and patience with the intolerance and blood thirsty conduct of the Catholics in the Province of Quebec I cannot help thinking how absurd it is for the Catholic Church to have the cheek to come to Utah to try and convert a people who are in every respect superior to themselves. Members of this same infallible church in the Province of Quebec mobbed a hall where Father Chiniguy, a reformed priest, was lecturing against the errors of Romanism, in Aston village, and were it not that a few Protestants including myself stood at the door with loaded revolvers I have not the slightest doubt that Father Chiniguy's name would have been added to the long roll of names of the noble martyrs that have been murdered through the diabolical teachings of Romanism. Also when Father Gavazzi, a reformed Italian priest, lectured in Montreal, a youth 15 years of age died of the wounds he received in a Catholic riot that occurred, he was a brother of the dearest friend I ever had. Under the circumstances I do not think the reader will blame me for entertaining a most profound contempt (not for individual Catholics) but for the religion itself, which is working quietly and energetically with one aim and object in view, that of bringing all mankind under its rule. Imagine what a condition the world would be in with a Pope and his few chosen counsellors as the spiritual dictators of the world. Does not the reader think that with such blasphemous power in their hands and without any power to resist them that they would not hesitate to severely punish all men who ridiculed and rebelled against their decrees. Truly this world would be in a pitiable condition if Protestantism and all the glorious work it has accomplished was blotted out. Catholic apologists often say: "Does not religious liberty exist in most Catholic countries of the present day." But intimate association with good Catholics proves that full and complete religious liberty is not given to any Catholic now in existence; nor in the whole history of their church can it be found that religious liberty was granted to them. It is true, however, that most Catholics can if they wish think as they please at the present day and use their reason on the doctrines of their church, but the reader well knows that if they do so they can no longer remain members of that church, but are expelled as heretics and rebels against the spiritual oligarchical government which that church lying asserts that Christ, the great philanthropist and moral teacher, established on earth. I would also ask some of these Catholic apologists how they account for the remarkable fact that Catholicism and its followers rigorously punished, in the most barbarous manner, all heretics during the middle ages, and that they have only ceased their brutality and cruelty during the past few hundred years since Protestantism and infidelity have become so powerful. I also ask the impartial reader how can he account for the world of the present day being so much more civilized and improved than it was in the middle ages, when Catholicism reigned supreme over what was then considered as the civilized world, and at the same time assert "that Protestants, Heretics and Infidels are wicked and prejudicial to the interests of mankind," when it cannot be denied that they have accomplished most of these improvements and have a greater power and influence than heretics ever had before during our earth's existence. It is quite clear that the oligarchical form of spiritual government of Catholicism is antagonistic and not in harmony with the true spirit of all forms of republican governments, and better suited for the more uncivilized one man form of government of empires and kingdoms, for the reason that Catholicism elevates the church above the state, and all good Catholics are taught that they owe their first allegiance to the Pope, whom they regard as Vicegerent of God. Now supposing that the Government of this enlightened country at any time thought proper to enact a law that was considered by the Pope as prejudicial to the interests of Catholicism, but which the Government thought necessary for the interests of a republican form of government and the production of truly liberal and enlightened citizens. Would not all "good Catholics" disregard the Government's wishes, and at the command of the spiritual king of mankind do all in their power to resist and defeat that law, so that a large portion of the votes of the nation would be given according to the dictation of a foreign power that maintains the interests of Catholicism regardless of all others. Free thinkers and reformers as a class should maintain an unceasing conflict, not only against all religious errors, but against all the forms of error with which this earth is cursed, and prove to the world that nothing is gained by the mere performance of silly rites and ceremonies, and teach to all mankind that grand truth, "that the earth is their country and to do good is their religion." Tom sowed 12 bushels of potatoes to-day. The grass is growing fast and the woodlands getting green. This dry weather we are having is very favorable for burning timber on the land. While I was laying on the veranda with my disabled foot I was struck with the beauty of the scenery around our place. To the south lay the dark-green primeval forest as far as the eye could see, broken here and there by a village with its tin-covered steeple glittering in the sun, also several mountains towering high above the solitude of the forest, till their summits were lost in the clouds. In the east the view extends down a grass-covered hill, side to a babbling, winding brook, across a valley with numerous beautiful, evergreen and stately hardwood trees and up another hillside till the view ends abruptly at the top of a hill in Sherman's clearance with our cattle grazing in it. In the north the view extends 4 miles across an almost unbroken forest; the chief object on the north is the "Beaver Meadows," through which the brook meanders through a stately grove of elms whose shade keeps the carpet of wild grass beneath them of the brightest green. As I watched the water foaming over the numerous rapids it reminded me of the life of man, every part of earth the water rushed over was passed forever, there was no turning back, on it rushes till it reaches the depths of the ocean. And so with man, his life glides swiftly onward, there is no recalling a day, an hour, a minute once passed it is passed for ever; on it rushes until he is hurled into that mighty ocean of an unknown hereafter. In the east the view is obstructed by forest, in the hillside in close proximity to the house. In reading ancient history it appears to me that vice and intemperance were the sources of the distruction of ancient nations. Those of the present day ought to take warning of the danger of allowing vice and intemperance to exist where temperance and virtue ought to reign. It is the duty of mankind of this age to use its utmost endeavors to transmit to the coming age a grander civilization and a nobler race of people than that which our ancestors have transmitted to us. It is truly very sad to see such terrible deterioration as that of such a noble race as the ancient Greeks to their present low condition in the scale of humanity. No man can imagine what exalted and much nobler beings we would now be had all our ancestors from the earliest ages used all the means in their power to develop and improve mankind. The day, however, will yet come when just and wise laws will be made to punish and prevent everything that has a deteriorating influence on the human race and rewards given to all those who materially aid the grand work of developing and educating the human race to the highest possible standard of excellence. 15th May. The piece of oats by the house is coming overground. I put some leaves of the wild cucumber that a French quack doctor gave me on the wound on my foot. Tom drove one of the Houde girls to Aston which is very foolish; I would consider it a disgrace to be seen in public with a vulgar girl like her; a gentleman cannot expect refined laoies to like his company when he associates with such society. The bare and desolate forests of a few days ago are now clothed in green. Tom has hired two Frenchmen of old France; they ridicule the priests, advocate national schools, and have an intense hatred for all forms of monarchial governments and nobility; the socialism of Europe is caused by an oppression of the people driven to desperate remedies to remove their oppression, but of course "two wrongs never make a right." An inventor has discovered a new means of guiding a baloon by paddles. Strange how little progress has been made towards perfecting aerial navigation. Some of the members of the Dominion Parliament are acting in a very ungentlemanly manner by blackmailing each other. Read a book on predestination which had some plausible arguments, but it appears to me a horrible doctrine and contrary to the alleged mercy of God, that he would predestinate millions of souls to eternal punishment; man I believe is a "free agent" and if he lives according to the better sentiments of his nature he will in most cases be happy here and in all probability in the great hereafter; no arguments on earth would convince me that God ever doomed any man to eternal torment without first giving him an opportunity to work out his own salvation. The Frenchmen working for us for 35 cents a day and board are quiet, steady fellows. "Hartford April 15th. Dear Tom and Arthur. You must wonder at my not answering your letters before, but father thought I had written and I thought he had and besides we have had a visit from Angelica; just fancy she came over for only one week's visit. The wagons here cost $80, so we will get one at Aston for $50 I am sorry to put you to so much trouble but hope some day to be able to reciprocate; we have bought $25 worth of manure; have paid $1.50 a cord for wood and drew it ourselves. You will like this place when you see it, I wish we had you near us, when fall comes I want you both to come and visit us, when I will show you a scheme we have on hand, but if either of you could visit us during the Summer we would be delighted to see you; Clifford joins me in love to you both, your affectionate cousin Richard. P. S. Have bought two 2½ Ayrshire cows for $35 each." Read a book on Scottish Patriots, they certainly exhibited the most daring courage and the noblest patriotism to preserve their country's independence. Richard and Clifford have sown a small crop for a farm of 200 acres, only 15 acres in oats potatoes and peas and 12 in meadow, the rest in pasture with about 30 acres in woodland. We can hardly sleep at night from the bite of mosquitoes. Read a book called "ruins of sacred and historic lands;" truly the architecture of the present day is in many cites and countries (of even the civilized portion of the earth) much inferior to that of the Ancients; there are few buildings of modern times that could resist the hand of time 3000 years. Tom has sown 13 bushels of oats. Had a conversation with the G's. about the poor prospects for a young man in this parish; there was a sucessful celebration of the Queen's birthday at Montreal, over 10,000 people viewed the parade of the Militia. Rev. H. Beecher and Marquis and Princess were there. I was right in my conjecture, uncle Richard wants us to sell out and move to Lemingtón to be near our cousins. I take great pleasure in reading Sir. W. Scott's poems they are totally free from those objectionable features of most poets who have generally at least a tinge of the Byronian style; have also been reading Shakespeare's plays a second time. Argued with one of our workman on the advantage of temperance, he says he is "too far gone" and has not the power to resist the desire for strong drink, a truly pitiable condition for a man to be in. 30 May. exceedingly hot for this time of year, thermometer 90 degrees in the shade. England has concluded peace with Afghanistan on favorable terms, gains a tract of rugged mountainous country that will form a natural defense for

India's Frontier. England at present seems to have a very aggressive policy. Sold some seed oats to our neighbors at 40 cents a bushel. Daniel C's mother is so angry with him for going to "spark" French girls that she refuses to cook meals for him, a truly sad state of affairs between mother and son. Are having occasional light showers which will be of great benefit to the crops. At a "logging bee" at Goldsmiths 29 log piles were made they used a horse as well as our oxen. We have had several frosty nights which has frozen all tender foliage. Tom has had serious trouble with Metz Vincent about money he advanced him on work; have read many standard novels of late by Chas. Reade; W. Thackeray and George Elliot. Arphosine Houde is deeply in love with Daniel C. they went yesterday on a pleasure excursion to Sutton. Henry Milton arrived with a letter of introduction from Mr. Sherman, I gave him all the information he required, he has bought the cut of the bark on Mr. Sherman's lot. Sunday 15th June, to-day is called "Fete de Dien," the Canadians have great processions to their churches in honor of their bread God to which they have the audacity to want Protestants to take oft their hats if they encounter the procession, I had my hat on one occasion knocked partially off my head and when it passes all the people drop on their knees on the dusty road. The weather is cloudy and only 60 degrees above zero. Gave Tom Mallet a ditch to dig at $2.00 an acre 3 feet deep, I myself am also finishing the long ditch I commenced through the clearance. Read the lives of "Nelson and Collingwood," two of England's greatest naval heroes. Herbert Charmicheal has returned from St. Louis, where he could find no employment, and looks quite pale after the privations he endured. 20th of June although a cloudy day the thermometer stands at 80 in the shade. Our oats look splendid; the hay crop promises the best we have had for years; the French Prince Imperial has been killed in Zululand, a pity seeing he was a goodhearted, gallant young man; but of course my sympathies are with the French Republic, I admire their policy and how they have restored prosperity to the country; his mother fainted when she heard the news and no wonder, the only child she had on whom all her hopes were centered. I pity poor Mrs. C.

she has a careworn appearance and although she has a violent temper and is a very vulgar woman, this does not justify the disrespectful conduct of her son Daniel, who has commenced to drink and smoke since he associates with Houdes. Oh how things have changed since my dear mother's death; the young people of this place have all deteriorated since they have lost the elevating influence she used to exercise on them. I am sorry to say Tom has also commenced to take a social glass; have tried to persuade them to give up the habit; showed how it ruined hundreds of thousands every year and that few men knew how strong the habit becomes, till it is too late; thousands of talented men have thought they could drink in moderation and be safe, and through it ruined themselves and their families; even the pernicious effect it has on others ought to make a good man avoid it for the same reason that one of the greatest Christian teachers gives, "if eating meat cause my brother to offend I will eat no meat." Went to Mrs. C's. she appeared very jovial from which I imagine she has been before the throne of Bacchus. Have given the job of plastering the inside of our house for $12, we to furnish materials and a man to attend on the plasterer; Tom Mallet offered his services for $12 a month and board, but he is so impudent that we dislike to hire him. But persons wishing to get on in the world should not be influenced by their feelings, all must be sacrificed excepting one's honor and health to climb the difficult road to wealth. I often feel what a pity Tom and I are not surrounded by better society, after having spent an evening at Houde's or some other neighbor the shallow pleasure derived while there is more than counterbalanced by pain and regret afterwards for having wasted my time amongst them; have read Tennyson's poems of late. While at G's they said the land on this range was too rocky for successful farming; the Carmicheal's have not paid their school taxes on account of some quibble of the condition of school affairs; told him that any one who for some trifling quibble would refuse to pay his taxes and try to put our school into the hands of the R. C's. did not deserve the name of Protestant, and was a fool in the bargain, as the taxes of the Roman Catholics are much higher than ours. I am mixing the first "coat of plaster put hair in it to prevent it from falling; have also commenced clearing out the stream on our lots, a very unpleasant job, we are up to our knees in mud and water. Some French "bark peelers are staying at our house I write this while listening to their jabber, songs, jests, grinding of axes and the frizzling of their pork, that is being fried for their supper. Read of a machine invented in England that turns out woolen goods, cottons and silk with only a few men to work it while the old machine employed 30 men. The Zulus' are still holding out, their King Cetawago has shown a considerable amount of tact as general. Tom Murphy saw a bear, we chased it in the raspberry bushes with a revolver and gun but could not hit it. Tom's mother is a half breed Indian and he has inherited many Indian characteristics; he walks like one and is terribly revengeful. I commenced cutting hay in the Beaver meadows. It has commenced to rain in torrents; hope we will have fair weather to save our hay. The Vincent family were all taken up for being drunk and fighting in the streets, four of the brothers and the father got released by paying a fine of $45; Metz who works for us escaped but was caught in the wood by two bailiffs. I have at last persuaded the C's. to pay their taxes. The roads are in a bad condition, especially the "big swamp" a mile long is covered with peat to the depth of 18 ft.; some places the road trembles when the wagons pass over it. Have hired the three Houde girls to rake hay at 50 cents a day; they can perform nearly as much work as a man; it is a very heavy crop this year. I mowed three acres of father's hay in one day, worked from daylight to dark; the hay was not a heavy growth and the land entirely free from stumps and stones I felt completely tired out at the end of the day. Sir Garnet Woolsley is in command of the British forces in Zulu land in place of Lord Chelmsford, who is the poorest Peer in Great Britain with the small income of $4000 a year. Letilier, the Lieutenant Governor of the Province of Quebec has been dismissed much to the disadvantage of the Liberal party with whom e was in sympathy. Red cherries are ripe, they flourish in every clearance and grow in great profusion by the road-sides throughout this part of the country, but they have more kernel than fruit. I have been appointed secretary to the English school. Have given out the cutting of some of our hay at 50 cents an acre. Have had a great deal of work to do on our roads; in a letter dated 14th July, Richard asks us to try and hire a boy out our way for him says "our hay is nearly all in, only 26 loads double ones. People say farmers are always great grumblers but I trust we will not acquire the bad habit; our oats are well headed out. Mr. Milton called in to have Tom write a letter in French to his sweetheart a French girl at St. Augustin. In making hay it should not be allowed to get wet, especially after it is partially dried, nor should it be drred too much, one day of good sunshine is sufficient for an average crop but when a very heavy growth a day and a half is required and it has to be spread over the ground's surface. Gave one of Milton's bark peelers a job of clearing out five acres of the stream, merely the timber that had fallen in and the brush on the banks at $1 an acre. The Miss Carmichaels have arrived from Montreal, being expelled from a ladies college in Upper Canada, and are the wildest girls I ever saw, the youngest s very good looking a "dare devil sort of a girl who swears like a trooper; the other one is just as bad only that she is more of a hypocrite; I thought what a pity these girls were not properly educated, it certainly seems disgraceful for a man worth half a million to let his children run wild; they were sent to school of course but that was all, the rest of the time they spent as they liked on the streets; their mother being deaf and an "easy going" sort of woman, did not care for them and the father was too much occupied in business, the consequence is the boys are the wildest vagabonds in the city and there is no prospect of the girls ever becoming ladies, although they are educated in most of the accomplishments a lady should have. Had a school meeting, I gave the trustees the amount of the value of the dissentient property in the parish, which amounts to $25,800; they struck a rate of ¼ of a cent on the dollar and decided to keep school at Meredith's house. Tom Murphy discovered a nest of bees on Sherman's lot; we went with lanterns at midnight and cut the tree down and "smoked out the bees" and brought back two pailfuls of honey. 12th September cut our buckwheat and housed it; engaged Tom Murphy for three months at $10 a month and board. Have commenced cutting saw logs for a new barn we are having built; the putting up of the frame and the squaring of the timber we have given to a French Canadian for $40. The C. girls are thoroughly enjoying themselves in attending French dances and spending evenings at French houses. 16 September. Have commenced cutting our oats; gave Metz Vincent the job of drawing sufficient stone for a stone stable 6 ft high which we have decided to build on the hillside underneath the barn. In the Autumn the game of "bluff with cards" for apples amongst the French is very prevalent. Had a "bee" to raise our new barn which is 40 x·50 ft.; Tom would insist on having whiskey for the men as they always have it at other "bees. Several of the men stole the whiskey out of a cupboard and got beastly drunk; the French however are a good natured people and there were no serious fights; had the crowd been Irishmen I expect they would have been breaking each others heads. John Murphy went in search of his son Tom (who had went to sleep off the effects of the liquor in a mow of hay); by taking a pitch fork and probing the hay; we however obliged him to desist from this rather dangerous method of searching for his son. Have hired two stone masons to help us to build the stone stable under the barn. In several nights of the past fortnight there has been a mild frost. There has been a revolt at Cabul, Afghanistan, and the members of the English Embassy have been murdered, it is however only a faction; the Ameer still sides with the English. Received a letter from Richard saying he "expected us to go and see them after our crops were in. We had only one acre of potatoes and tried to keep off the beetles by picking, but our efforts looked ridiculous so we had to put on London Purple which destroyed them all and stopped our neighbors cattle from trespassing." The Senate of Quebec have refused to give their sanction to the "bill of supply" for the Lower House in hope to make the Liberal party resign, but that party nobly holds out. Nearly all the elections that have taken place; for ·members, since the last general election shows that the people have confidence in the party. We have commenced to clear land behind the Beaver meadows. Went with Tom Murphy to Valcour in a south east direction east of East Hastings; drove 40 miles and saw some interesting coun-, try with many orchards. Mr. C. came from Montreal, although a very clever man he is very vulgar, for instance, in speaking to me of his stepmother he said "her photo could be sold to frighten away rats;" the whole family are vulgar in the extreme; the boys talk about dog fights, cock fights, boxing matches, rows in taverns etc., the girls of their flirtations and their numerous admirers, the father of "my walking down the street with the honorable Mr. so and so and of dining with M. P's. and other notable persons." Russian Territory is steadily approaching India, much to the alarm of Russia-phohists. The Chinese have recovered their Province from Russia. The Liberals of Quebec have only now a majority of three but still hold out. Uncle Richard sent us the following letter to him from uncle Jerrold. "My dear Richard. I was glad to hear from you as I have been anxious about your son Richard's health; the farm is a good idea as it will be a healthy and useful amusement; I am obliged to put off my visit to Canada till next summer when I expect, please God, to visit you; this is almost certain as I find my old illness returning and my former trip nearly cured me; tell Howard's I hope to see great improvements on their farm. Agriculture, and in fact everything is as dull as ditch water here, but most wonderful of all my old practice has fallen down to almost nothing; for 40 years it has been a little California to me and why it should so suddenly collapse I cannot imagine, probably the new energetic practitioners are shelving as veterans on the retired list; as far as I myself am personally concerned it matters little as my bread is baked and dinner cooked, yet I am so sorry to see so many better men than myself at the end of their career losing their practice and with nothing laid by for their old age; trade is depressed all over the world except in France, the country of all others whose ruin was predicted; here in England it is awful, we have been badly used; every nation has taken our money and in return, even our Colonies actually prohibit our trade—although we admit all goods at merely a nominal rate, or altogether free; happy, thrice happy are you in Canada farming homesteads, out of turmoil and the sight of misery; 1 trust you will keep an account of the profits on your farm to give me an idea of the profit and loss; you will probably for the next two years spend a great deal of money before you get any returns, the English laborers I fear are gone into habits of lazy demorilization, idleness, cheating and lying are their chief characteristics, and the servant "gals" are upstart, impudent, reckless hussies, running about from place to place careless of the future, never thinking of saving their own or their employers money; they live flighty, flirting extravagant lives and end their days in a workhouse, a sourse of annoyance all their lives and at last an expense to the overtaxed middle classes. The floods, overflows of rivers, countries under water, and storms have at last ceased; great fears are entertained of a bad harvest and a general scarcity; I should think that breeding of stock on your farm would be better than raising corn; the weather is fine but close and dull. You may bye and bye hear of a war declared between Russia and England. I shall be glad to get a letter from Tom and Arthur although I owe them one; love to your family and friends in Montreal and the Howards; believe me always your affectionate brother, J. B. Goldsmith." In a letter to us he says "if you have as much rain as we have it must prevent you from clearing out the stream; that will be a rare piece of fertile land yet. I hope you will be able to use the stream bye and bye for irrigating the adjoining lands; water is a most valuable fertilizer over here and a little stream with a dam to send it over the adjoining fields renders the property of double value; that stream of yours looks to me like a tough job to clear out, plenty of work late and early, but perseverance will do anything. I hope you have no dealings with the stores and that you do not run credit for a single farthing; the stores and credit have been the ruin of thousands; better to live on a dry crust with hard work than to eat fish and meat and be at the mercy of a storekeeper; some of them have no more conscience than a butcher's dog and no more feeling than a cobbler's tapstone. I am sorry that I cannot go to Canada this year as Rupert cannot be spared from his studies at Oxford. It was a good idea to build another barn nothing better than plenty of room, except it be plenty of stock and corn; I expect to see you, please God, get rich and prosperous farmers with good clear fertile land and plenty of everything. Rupert had a friend of his from Oxford here who is just saying what lucky fellows you are, not living in this smoky city where the air looks like dirty pea soup, and they would like to go out there and plough and dig and cut wood on their own freeholds; his friend, Roberts, a young man from Australia is longing to get back to his Australian fields; he hates London but must remain at Oxford University three years until he takes his degree; he says he would not live here if he was made King of England. The Whigs Radicals, Conservatives and Irish home rulers are the four political parties now agitating this country." The Elms, Hartford Sept. 30th. "Dear Tom and Arthur. Yours of the—received. I am glad to hear that you have all yonr crops in, we can't say the same as our corn now is only being cut; we had such miserable weather that our oats and buckwheat have only been in a few days; we have commenced at our potatoes and then we have mangolds and turnips which will take us three weeks to finish; of course fall ploughing goes on at the same time and we have commenced putting up a barbed wire fence. To-morrow I am going to Montreal will return in about a week; could you come and see us when I come back, by the 10th. "Dear Tom and Arthur; Richard left yesterday and did not have time to finish his letter so he deputed me to do so; we will be at Lemington Station to meet you when you come. The country here is looking lovely, it is wonderful weather for Oct. 80 degrees in the shade; excuse this horrid scrawl, your affectionate cousin, Clifford." Had a discussion with J Murphy on Irish affairs; proved to him from history that the first conquest of Ireland, by Henry II received the sanction of the infallible Pope, Adrian; also argued on religion, I told him that it was plainly evident to unprejudiced and impartial minds that there was no perfect system of religion on this earth, nor even a perfect system of education and that the degraded condition of the majority of Catholics and other Christians was a plain proof of this; he argued that the Apostolic Roman Catholic Church was the only true and perfect church and that its doctrines were exactly the same now as in the time of the Apostles; I told him that some of the chief doctrines were perhaps the same, but that in its discipline and the spirit that actuated the policy of the church were entirely different, that it forbids its priests to marry, which is only a command of the rulers of the church, for that Christ himself restored Pope Peter's wife to him and never commanded any of his teachers or preachers to abstain from marriage; and that Christ commanded his teachers and Apostles to preach the Gospel to all men without money and without price, but the Catholic priests in this province would sell a poor man's homestead for the dues he owed his church, which was in direct contradiction to the commands of Christ; and that in Italy the priesthood of the Catholic Church had burdened the people with the expense of building gorgeous and stately cathedrals, costing millions of dollars, while the people were in a pitiable state of poverty and ignorance, that of course this had nothing to do with the doctrines of Catholicism, but at the same time their unchristlike conduct and acting in direct contradiction to the beautiful spirit and principles that pervade the true gospel of Christ ought to cause them to be regarded, not as the ministers of Christ, but as selfish and fraudulent priests; also that the more enlightened religion of Protestantism with a praiseworthy liberality allow men to a certain extent the use of their own judgment in applying the great truths of Christ's teaching to themselves as a guide through life, but that the rulers of Catholicism with a truly dogmatic tyranny lay down the law to every member of their church which they accept in humble childish faith as from God himself; also ridiculed their diabolical belief that all men who absolutely refuse to believe their supernatural nonsense "will suffer everlasting torment." Murphy said that he thought this quite right that a man should be punished for refusing to believe the truth. Read in the *Animal World*, a British newspaper published by the society of the prevention of cruelty to animals. Uncle Herbert and Aunt Margaret told me that a young man could never meet with much success by living here. Have read the "History of France" of late. Tom has just returned from "The Elms," Richard and Clifford's farm. I have named our place Elmbrook. David Grant, master of the Orangemen, has sued Mayor Beaudry of Montreal for illegal imprisonment, but lost his suit which was for $10,000. The Afghan revolt is not quelled yet; several regiments have left England to reinforce the troops. The Zulu war is over and the great savage Cetawayo is a prisoner. There has been a murder in Montreal, one woman killed another. The dead lock still continues between the Liberals and Legis.- lative Council, which has a faint resemblance to the English House of Lords, they refuse to sanction the Bill of Supplies; it is likely that Joly, the Liberal Primier, will appeal to the people and be successful. The Russians are progressing very slowly with their campaign at Merva and have suffered a defeat from the Turcomonds. The Russian and British Empire are fast approaching each other, it is quite possible that there will yet be a deadly struggle between the Lion and the Bear. Am suffering from toothache, smoking somewhat eases it; have commenced to build tramways into the threshing floor of the new barn; while clearing land behind the Beaver Meadows I glanced around me and saw land stretching away acres upon acres in every direction, of a dark, rich, alluvial soil over six feet deep which only requires perseverance and hard work to clear and drain it and make it some of the best land in Canada. I felt that we should give our farm a longer trial before we thought of leaving it; the ground is very damp, at every footstep the water oozes out of the ground. Grant's steam planing mill was burnt at Aston last week. Aston has a bad reputation amongst insurance companies; at one time some refused to insure buildings in it. Tom and I discussed the objections and advantages of going to live near our cousins at Hartford. The objections are that land is very dear and those farms that can be had cheap are exhausted and worn out; labor is also very dear and we would have to adopt a more expensive mode of living as the farmers around there keep up a considerable amount of style; the advantages would be improved society and none of the drudgery that is on a bush farm. Trade and commerce in Canada have begun to revive; the Conservatives say this is to be attributed to their policy of protection, the Liberals, that it is to be attributed to good crops and the economy that all classes exercised after the hard times; perhaps there is some truth in both their claims. The Liberals have suffered a defeat in the German Parliament; the elections in Belgium have decided in favor of national education. Edgeworth, of Richford came and looked over the timber on our lots; I sold him all the ash timber on 400 acres and 20 cedar trees for $50; bought cloth for a tweed suit for $4.90, lining and buttons $1.90, tailor for making it $5; bought a pair of rubbers 60 cents. On going over our accounts found that we will be $25 short this quarter, but I think my uncles will say nothing as we are making great improvements; wrote this in the cars on my way to Lemington Oct. 30. This is a "mixed" train travels very slowly; left Aston at 12 o'clock; the country on each side of the track between Aston and Davenport six miles is unsettled, neither is it settled between it and Dudley, excepting a few farm houses; the primeval forest has been cut away and there is a second growth of poplar, birch and maple. The country is flat with a few knolls here and there; nearing Dudley the land improves; Dudley is an English village, with three churches one Roman Catholic; it is not as centrally situated as Aston and has not half as much trade; Livingston the next stopping place consisted of a few houses surrounded by a dense growth of Tamarac, spruce and balsam, the land is level and swampy; the conductor informed me as we were traveling at the rate of 25 miles an hour; passed over a small river and through some railroad cuttings from 50 to 85 ft. deep; the country commences to be more hilly and heavily wooded with clearances here and there. We are now approaching Melford and Rawlings and are passing through fine undulating country and pleasing scenery with fine farm houses, orchards and glistening streams; the river St. David divides Milford from Rawlings; there is an English college here called St David's college; it has many fine residences of brick covered with slate; its trade is no longer carried on in the same manner as in villages but everything is sold separately; has dry goods stores, groceries, hardware stores and confectionaries; has a bank and three churches one Roman Catholic; the river is about three acres wide; changed cars here for Lemington; since I left Aston a little snow has fallen; there are three women close to me who I imagine must be walking advertisements of some manufacturer of perfume; it shows very poor taste to use it to such an extent; the railway track runs parallel with the river St. David; there are fine groups of cattle and sheep grazing in well fenced fields; in some of the flocks there are at least 50 to 75 sheep; the country looks charming with its hills here and there covered with evergreen groves; the river is getting smaller as we go towards its source, the current is very swift and has many pretty islands in it. On approaching Waterloo the country is very picturesque; the river is covered with foam; there is splendid water power here; to my discomfort a Frenchwoman came and sat in the same seat with a brawling baby in her arms. The bed of the river has huge rocks in it and looks very fine with foam and water dashing against them; the country is getting wilder the clearances smaller and it is snowing considerably; the country again commences to be more cleared and numerous little streams join the river. At Benton there is a huge saw mill and immense piles of lumber; the banks of the river after leaving Benton are covered with a second growth; it was dark when we arrived at Sherman, disembarked at Lemington; got shaved and bought a pair of cloth gloves for 50 cents, it was 3 miles from Lemington to Hartford, I rode with a farmer as far as Hartford, walked from there to the Elms ½ a mile. Fred Steele a cousin of Richard's was spending the evening at the Elms, he is studying for the ministry at Lemington College. Had a warm discussion with Fred on ritualism in the Church of England; went to church next day at Marsdon, which consists of a grist mill, store, a few houses and a small Episcopal chapel also a post office; the congregation was small and well dressed and of better appearance than is usual with rustic congregations; the clergyman preached a nice evangelical sermon, but Richard says he is high church at heart but is afraid of displeasing the congregation; strolled over the farm after dinner, most of the soil is light and sandy and about ⅔ of the farm is lying waste, but by fertilizers and a proper rotation of crops, Richard and Clifford expect to make it a beautiful and fertile farm. Read some of the standard authors till a very late hour in my room. Went for a drive with Richard next day, many of the farms around here exhibit a want of thrift; many fields covered with moss and have not been cultivated during the last 10 years, but on towards Carlton the farms were better cultivated, in fact Carlton is considered one of the finest farming districts in Quebec. I am reading as much as possible; all the new books I find in the library. Have helped Clifford to cut some driftwood on the Salmon river also brushwood along the river's bank. Had a discussion with Richard on the system of promotion in the English Army. I said no Duke ought to be allowed, as the Duke of Cambridge, to be commander-in-chief of the British Army, unless he deserved it by merit. Helped them to pull out their mangolds and turnips also to thresh their grain with a mill which threshes 100 bushels a day; they have 80 bushels of mangolds and turnips. Went for a drive with Richard, saw some fine fruit farms also passed a picturesque spot, a schoolhouse surrounded by forest with a fine waterfall close to it; there are very few rocks in this part of the country. Richard and Clifford take 21 English and American newspapers and magazines; if I had means I would take all the leading newspapers and magazines of the world and purchase all historical and scientific works and write the best history of the earth ever written. It seems sad to me that some of the many men of wealth and leisure do not devote their lives to the classification of literature and scientific research; sometimes my heart is moved by ambition and I think can I not rise to a higher and more useful position in the world; I have often serious thoughts of entering the English Army but I know my uncles would be terribly indignant. On 17th left Richard's they invited me to come next summer and that we should all go on a fishing excursion to Lake Megantic; at the station were a band of college boys playing lively airs in honor of a friend of theirs who was going to England to enter the English Army. On reaching Rawlings went to Melford to see the Wakefields; there was a small party and dancing in the evening to which a few friends were invited. Daniel W. is at a military college at Quebec. Went out riding with Winfred W. next day and although I consider myself a fair horseman this young lady almost frightened me the way she made her horse gallop across the country, over ditches and everything else that came in our way, and up a precipitous rocky range of hills to a slate quarry and visited some of her friends who very kindly insisted on our taking lunch before leaving. The manager told me that it would take $80 worth of slate to cover a barn 40 x 50 ft. Miss W. is a very agreeable companion, having good conversational powers and n ne of the disagreeable affectation that some city ladies have. While at Sherman I was greatly struck with the remarkably fine water power, it has one of the finest in the province; it's main street has magnificent stores that would do credit to a city of 50,000 population let alone 10,000; is a manufacturing town and one of the most progressive in Canada. I am greatly surprised at the great superiority of all the English towns compared to the French. Rawlings is one of the prettiest and neatest towns in the province, and has an almost wholly English population. While at Montreal I received the quarter's money and read a book entitled the "British Legion in the Spanish war;" both Uncle Richard and Jerrold served as surgeons in it. Mr. Hayton uncle's brother-in-law, consul for three of the South American Republics and Denmark; in Montreal related one evening some of his adventures in the Danish war while the gentleman were having their wine, but after adjourning to the drawing room the conversation among the ladies was not so interesting or useful, being composed chiefly of those "little nothings" which almost universally pervades the conversation of the best society; I trust however, for the interests of humanity that the good society of future years will not allow "society gossip" to form the chief material of their conversation. The eldest Miss Wakefield only gets $14 a month for teaching 30 scholars; what a shame to pay a teacher (who in a great measure forms the characters of the rising generation) less than a man who digs ditches. The Liberal party has been overthrown, some of it's members turned their political coats and deserted their party like craven cowards; I am exceedingly sorry as I am confident the majority of the Liberal party had the true interests of the country at heart and not so many public leaches as the Conservatives. On my return home skidded logs on an average 80 logs a day with two men the oxen and myself, but the ground is very rough and unfavorable; pork is very cheap $9.72 for 100 lbs. Tom and I talked about our future plans; I advocated a progressive policy to put up every stitch of canvass before the breeze of enterprise which would either waft us into the harbor of success and wealth or into that of bankruptcy. About this time (as hundreds of other young men have done) I wrote many love sonnets which I will, however, not inflict upon the reader. Mrs. Grant and her two agreeable daughters offered to make whatever pastry we might need for Christmas. Received a letter from G. Barclay saying that Minnesota was a grand country and that we ought to sell out and go there; we take Harper's Weekly one of the best illustrated papers in the U. S.; Ethel received a sewing machine from her father, cost $45. As we had no work of our own I went to work at Roussin's shanty for cutting and skidding logs; scrambled a mile over logs and through brushwood till we reached it at dawn, but found that they had men enough. Have at last received Uncle Richard's approbation for the sale of the cut of the timber on our lots for $500; Roussin would not give any more on account of most of the timber being destroyed by fire on the 400 acres. While spending an evening at Meredith's Mrs. Meredith told me that two beautiful young ladies were coming to visit them at Christmas and said I must come and spend a few days at their house, which with thanks I accepted. Received a letter from Fritz Hogarth, he is again in his native land, Germany, but thinks of returning to America, as the prospects cannot be very good there. "London—My dear Tom and Arthur. Your dear uncle wishes me to say how pleasant it was to receive your last letters and we are all very glad to hear that your farming has been so successful; may God bless and prosper you in all the undertakings in the approaching New Year is our prayer, dear Tom and Arthur, your affectionate aunt, Margaret Goldsmith." In a letter from Uncle J. he says, "Now I look upon you two lads doing a great service to the country, you are redeeming from the wilderness a great property and by your efforts adding forever to the wealth of the nation besides making a most honorable provision for yourselves; every stroke of work will tell to your honor and profit; talk of soldiers, heroes and great generals, why the man that adds one acre of land towards the everlasting support of the people, deserves more honor than 100 soldiers; he kills no fellow creatures makes no widows or orphans, but adds to the wealth and happiness of the land he lives in; although officers are a necessity and deserve some honor in their place. We have more frost with snow. Your letters were only received this morning, the postmaster says that it takes from 12 to 14 days for a letter to reach it's destination in Canada; your farm ought soon to begin to pay, but sooner or later it is sure to do so, provided you work for yourselves, but if you depend on paid labor you must expect to be always in difficulties, the man that depends on the labor of others is in danger of debt and live a most unsatisfactory life; labor strengthens the body and contents the mind as well as fills a man's purse; this rule holds good in everything especially farming; if you are once set down as men that cannot work yourselves, every one will impose upon you. Uncle Richard has made me very unhappy by telling me that your Cousin Richard is in consumption; it will relieve my mind to hear about him. We, like you, fear that Russia is so aggressive and treacherous that we will have to thrash her which she deserves for she is a cruel and diabolical power; we also expect a fresh dissolution of Parliament and a fresh election; Russia hopes that the Whigs who are it's friends will come into power and allow it to continue it's encroachments towards India. The son of the Czar and the war party at his back will find themselves mistaken, for any party that favored Russian aggression could not remain in power in England. Your aunt is playing at the piano and singing that beautiful hymn "I will arise and go to my Father." We have a piano also in the dining room, your aunt is so fond of music and we have so many visitors. To-morrow is the Lord Mayor's day; we all send our love to you and pray God to keep and guard you in the ways of truth, love, peace and happiness, your most affectionate uncle, J. B. Goldsmith." "Elmbrook Dec. 30th. Dear uncle. Many thanks for the illustrated papers you sent us. I write to you on a subject which I trust will not displease you, that is to ask your consent to give up farming and enter some military college; I have always had a wish to enter the army, but when our dear mother was alive I could not think of leaving her alone so that when Uncle Richard proposed to sell us lots 34x35 I decided that it was the best I could do, as we would be near our dear mother; after her death however I could not give up farming until we had paid Uncle Richard for the lots, but now that he is just paid I feel free to express to you my desire to enter an English military college. You may no doubt think it strange that I should wish to abandon farming after having said so much in praise of it to you in my letters; I have nothing however to complain of our success since we settled on the lots, as they are worth over $2000 and we are almost out of debt, but when I compare the society of ladies and gentleman with that of the people around here I am disgusted and think what is the use of living in this world without a perfect education, without which the greatest happiness of man is lost, namely the true enjoyment of associating in the best of society; I know there are a good many disadvantages in the army, the worst of which is that a person might be maimed and have to live the rest of his life in a miserable and almost helpless condition; I also know that the army is no place for one who is not willing to sacrifice everything for his own and his country's interests, except his honor, but I will willingly undergo any amount of hardship and hard study to raise myself to a useful and honorable position of independence; there is a military college at Quebec where those that enter have nearly all their expences paid by the government, and also another at Kingston, Ontario, where the cost is only nominal, I would however prefer to pass at some English military college; if pleasing to you I would give Tom my half of the land as he intends to continue farming; I trust you will have the kindness to grant my request and I assure you I shall do all in my power to pass a successful examination. We spent Christmas at Uncle Herberts; the snow roads are in good condition but the weather is exceedingly cold as much as 40 degrees below zero; wishing you all many happy returns of the season, with love to my aunt Rupert and yourself, I remain your affectionate nephew, Arthur N. Harvey." Wrote also to Uncle Richard on the same subject. Mr. and Mrs. Meredith request the pleasure of Mr. Thomas and Arthur Howard's company on Monday evening the 29th at ½ past 7 o'clock. Staney Brae, Dec. 26th 1876. Went to the party with Tom; had a most enjoyable time; there were about 80 people present; after dancing till 12 supper was then served, consisting of two sorts of soup, three sorts of meat, fowls, fish, pastry and every sort of cake imaginable, oysters, numerous sorts of fruit and nuts for dessert, in fact everything that could be desired except wines and other liquor, as Mr. Meredith is a strict teetotaler; had the sitting room and the drawing room to dance in; some of the aged ladies and gentleman played whist and conversed together. On New Year's day made calls on all my Aston friends with Mrs. Willoughby, as Rev. L. C's. horse is sick; then called on Meredith's and spent a delightful afternoon, skating on some good ice close to the house, also tobogganing and snowshoeing; towards evening had music and singing; Mabel Willoughby and Miss Bacon of Toronto, who is a charming young lady without any false pride or reserve are visiting at Meredith's; after dinner a party of us drove to an amateur theatrical at Preston. Went to a church social next day held in the school-house, all the English families contributed the necessary amount of cake, fruit refreshments etc- A few days after went to a select party at Meredith's. Have had an unceasing round of festivities for the last three weeks in Aston and on our range amongst the French. While at Uncle Herbert's a few days ago they said much in disparagement of this part of the country; I said bush farming is all very well in its way for men that are capable of no higher occupation than that of a hewer of wood and a drawer of water, but those who have higher aspirations should devote their lives to higher pursuits, and supposing we do spend our lives here and become wealthy what advantage would it be to us, for we could not mix in good society as our manners would be too coarse, for we cannot constantly come in contact and associate with vulgar people without deterioration in their manners and character; the first thing a man should acquire is a good education; a man may lose everything else by unforseen circumstances but can never be deprived of a good education; the chief cause of ignorance and vulgarity among farmers as a class is because it is possible for him to make a living without education or being a gentleman; in most other professions man must of necessity have a good education and be a gentleman to succeed; I said to the Goldsmith boys we can trace back our noble ancestors to the time of the Crusaders, yet think how low our branches of these families have fallen until we are to-day little better than common laborers and with our ordinary education and vulgar associations can never expect to rise from this despicable condition unless we make a determined effort to do so; we should awake to the sad reality that we have just arrived at the threshold of manhood and have scarcely accomplished anything. While spending an evening at Meredith's I was introduced to a Mr. Vansanford and his daughter he owns a large farm at Lexington, which is a fine farming country; Miss V. has very interesting features, but is very delicate and as "pale as a ghost." Went the same evening with a large party of Aston ladies and gentlemen to a ball at Preston; next day joined a party of young ladies and gentlemen at skating, on Aston river; in the afternoon played checkers with one of Aston's champions, but lost three games out of five; was surprised at the tasty manner in which he had furnished his house, with articles which are very rarely seen in the houses of the lower class; forgot to mention that a few evenings before Christmas I, with a party of young gentleman brought a load of evergreens to the parsonage where we, aided by a bevy of fair young ladies to make wreaths etc. to decorate the church; at a concert in the Town Hall, comic songs, humerous readings, duetts and songs by ladies were sung; Mr. Bramult was the greatest gentleman favorite; a Miss Kate Watts read a poem by Longfellow, entitled "Hiawatha," which was a decided failure; Florence Meredith sang several songs and received thunders of applause, being acknowledged as the general favorite. G's. sent us a present of some pork, having killed two pigs that weighed over 700 lbs. This is a custom among the French people to send a piece of whatever animal they kill to their nearest neighbors. In speaking of the best soldiers of Europe I argued that French soldiers were too excitable, too easily elated and depressed to be considered as the best. I gave the job of making shingles to Louis Brodeur, and to do the boarding and shingling of the new barn for $40, which is very cheap; we furnish the "cut" of the cedar and of course the boards and nails at that price. The campaign in Zululand is over at last; terrible railway catastrophe in Scotland; largest bridge in the world gave way, precipitating the train into the river 90 ft. beneath; 300 lives lost. 15th Jan. 1880, lovely weather, not enough snow to make good roads in the woods, where it requires more snow than on the level main roads; aunt and uncle quizzed me about Florence and Maud, told them that if 100 people were foolish enough to quiz me it would not prevent me from enjoying their charming and good society, or that of any other amiable young ladies I was acquainted with. Changed time with G's. to help them to cut wood with their sawing machine; most of the English young men here have by constant association with the French deteriorated so much as to frequently use vulgar and coarse language; there is one feature however I respect in the English in these parts, is that they respect the presense of ladies and women and never utter coarse language in their presence, which is more than I can say for the French. At present Tom and I are drawing lumber to the sawmill for our barn; while spending an evening at Andre La Rivere.s, he and his brother-in law and some other men used such outrageously indecent and and filthy language in the presence of his wife that even I, accustomed as I am to hearing such language amongst them, was horrified; I would not have thought that even the lowest specimens of humanity could utter or tolerate such language, yet this woman seemed greatly amused and laughed heartily at it, yet they are the most devout family of Catholics on this range (12 miles long) as the reader must acknowledge when I tell him that in two years they have not missed one Sunday at church or failed in making their confessions and receiving absolution, and observe all the holidays and feasts in a most rigid manner, in fact they are considered by all their neighbors as the most devout and pious couple that live on this range. Oh Roman Catholicism! with your teachings and discipline, cannot make nobler men and women than what I have seen of your followers in Quebec or read of them in Poland, Austria and Spain, the boasted infallibility of your teachings must of necessity be a mere collection of fraudulent lies and the religion of the majority of your followers the mere performances of rites and ceremonies, in place of a beautiful and noble life which is far more pleasing to God than all your hastily muttered prayers and prolonged feasts. Have papered our house. "Montreal. My dear Arthur. Nothing could have given me greater surprise than the receipt of your letter, in fact I think of nothing else, and I hope you will pardon me when I tell you that I laughed heartily when I first read your sentiments on military glory, I am sure that your

Uncle Jerrold or any one that knows any thing of military life will tell you that it is all a lie and in reality one of the meanest professions that was ever studied, that man who can practice the greatest amount of chicanery and deception, makes the best general, and any honest man in the army to-day will tell you that promotion goes by favor to-day as it always did. King William, that preceded the queen, asked an old lieutenant why he was so bald, because he replied "so many junior members of the profession are stepping over my head." A young man in the army or navy to-day without influence or a great deal of money stands a poor chance of promotion. If a man's country is in need of assistance during an invasion or otherwise there are times he may be called upon to serve, but that has never been the case during your lifetime or mine; during the present time there are thousands of young men that have served in the army that are walking about unfit for other occupations; were I to go to-day to the young officers in the different branches of the service, I could get 10,000 from the rank of captain to ensign that would be delighted to change positions with you, I could get the same number of young men in Montreal, and many of them with good salaries that would be only too glad to jump at the chance you want to kick from under your feet. Supposing that it were possible to have a commission placed in your hand to-morrow I would not advise you to accept; why did Mr. Bentley leave the service; he was in the Royal Engineers, proving that he was a man of brilliant abilities; it was because his father became bankrupt and he could not live on his small allowance; why did your cousin Fred Sanford leave? because his private income was not sufficient; besides at the end of the four years it would take you to pass, you would be too old, as to the Canadian service, a man would be foolish indeed to trust himself to their tender mercies. In your letter you ask a straightforward question will I consent? I say *no*, neither as an officer or as a private, for the simple reason that you would soon get sick of it, and it would be exposing you to many unnecessary temptations that you are now free from; in your present position your regular income and your prospects are excellent; if you are tired of the locality I would not be opposed to your moving, but do not throw away your advantages and the fruit of your hard work. Should you and Tom think of leaving I would advise you to divide your land into four lots of 100 acres each, build a cottage and plant an orchard on each, and I will have no difficulty in selling them for you, but this I would not do if I were in your place without your Uncle Jerrold's consent, for he has both your interests at heart and loves you with a father's love, had it not have been for him you and I might have been in different circumstances to-day, you are now following one of the most noble and honorable of all professions, one that the late Prince Albert was proud to cultivate; three of a gentleman's sons in Montreal are giving up their situations in banks and going on farms without prospects as good as you have; so far as society is concerned I think you are tolerably well off; there are some very nice pople in Aston, Willoughby's and Meredith's; as far as the matter of education, it is in your own hands, you can in your spare moments perfect yourselves in all the higher branches of education, as for your manners they are more gentlemanly and graceful than those of many young men who mix in the best society in Montreal; the true Christian is always a gentleman and that of the purest type, he has dignity and self-respect without pomposity or frivolity; he has natural ease which always gives natural grace; as to your future prospects socially, I think they are very good; then you can get your farm improved and a new house built, I can introduce you to good society where you can choose a nice wife with a little money, that will be always useful on a large estate like yours; the lact is Tom and you have been working too hard and living too economical and you have got downhearted, but you must shake off this fit of the blues and take a brighter view of things, and in due time with God's aid and blessing all will be well. Your Aunt Mabel and Flora unite in love; I forgot to say that Flora's husband has been ordered to Michigan by the railway authorities, and although his salary as manager there will be greatly increased we shall feel lonely at their departure. Your loving uncle, R. J. Goldsmith." Richard Bacon who is studying for the ministry says, I ought to study for law. Daniel C. has gone to live in Montreal; he has taken a photo of his dear Alphosine with him and kissed her before a crowd of amused spectators on the railway platform before leaving, telling her to remain "tonjours fidele." Received a terribly indignant letter from Uncle Jerrold which has been mislaid; the next one was as follows. "My dear nephews. I have been sorry for feeling angry with Arthur, although my feelings of anger arose from my love for you; for through my long life of experience I have always found that the man who cries for the moon is the most intolerable; he is always a nuisance to himself and his friends; I mean such a one as always thinks of doing impossibilities and never sticks to one thing. It is generally caused by vanity and an idle roving disposition; fellows who can do nothing always tries to do everything and nothing cures them. And finding dear Arthur before he has perfected his education writing to the public papers I feared he was wasting his strength by trying to jump to the top of the house instead of beginning at the foot of the stairs. thousands of such men are about here every day in rags and starvation. To be truly great is to do the work before you; to be good is to love God and your neighbors and be contented. To be safe it to have an unwavering faith in Christ. Mistaken ambition and misapplied energy has been the ruin of half the world; so I beseech you my dear boys to beware of crying for the moon like senseless children, and if you should take it into your heads to do anything great or glorious try the first steps of the ladder or you will be sure to fall never to rise again, which God forbid. The ground here is covered with snow and we suffer a great deal more from cold in England than you do because we are not provided against it; our stoves and fireplaces are all small; Rupert is on a visit at Wissenden Hill, Trowbridge Wells, Kent. I shall be glad to get letters from you about your farms and all the news, your Aunt Margaret likes to have me read them to her; and I like them too for they are good clever letters and most interesting to us; your aunt unites with me in kindest love to all; and always believe me your sincere friend and loving uncle, Jerrold Goldsmith." Notwithstanding these good kind letters I cannot, and will not give up my project, not at least until I have positive proof that it is utterly unfeasible, so I have written at greater length to both my uncles, and to the colleges at Quebec—West Point and Kingston. Jan.

14th. "My dear Arthur. Doherty called and paid the balance, which leaves a bill due by you on your lots of $130. I was amused at your ideas of the requisites to get on in the army, if you suppose that the best men are promoted or that promotion goes by merit you never made a greater mistake in your life; why is the Duke of Cambridge the commander- in chief of the British army, Lord Chelmsford sent to South Africa, or even why did the Iron Duke get command of the army in Portugal, because the Marquis of Wellsley was his brother and had a seat in the House of Peers. There are very few persons by force of character get on in England, France or the United States; nor you cannot name a single man that has got on in modern times in the United States or France that has not been educated at West Point or the Ecole Polytechnic. During Napoleon's time it was different, yet even he had a first class military education, was trained "to arms" from his earliest boyhood, and in his first career was backed up by Madame De Stael and some of the first women of the Empire; it is true he had the genius to take advantage of the situations; he took the tide at the flood and led on to fortune. How many millions have perished under him whose history is unknown, who probably may have been more worthy in every respect. Lord Chelmsford acknowledging his incompetentency in the Zulu war has, or is about to have, a command given him over the heads of other men, but in your case it is entirely out of the question, you would be too old as I have said before, at the expiration of the four years study; I think, 18 is the age, and for the whole of Canada the British Government only gives four appointments each year; one for the engineers, one for the cavalry and one for infantry; this according to merit out of 300 or 400 applicants. We are all well here; I hope to see you in February; I am glad you have made the house so comfortable; I trust you have raised sufficient wheat and vegetables for yourselves; your aunt has a splendid receipt for curing meat. I suppose you heard of the death of the wife of your uncle Dr.. Goldsmith in Ireland. With love to Tom believe me to remain your affectionate uncle, R. I. Goldsmith." Carmicheal's have allowed lumbermen to live in the English school house but have told them they cannot stay there unless they pay a sufficient sum to have it insured in case it was burnt through carelessness. Father, one evening I was going to Aston, quizzed me about Florence, which I told him was a very ungentlemanly and a low, mean habit, that for my part I did not care, but that idle rumor might reach her ears and cause her pain, for ladies are more sensitive than gentlemen; also that no true gentleman should use language that might possibly hurt a lady's feelings; that it was right that young gentleman should take pleasure in the society of young ladies apart from any motive of love, for that gentle and graceful manners refine and add grace to the harsher and rougher manners of young men. Alas! why promise, strive and hope, and still go on from bad to worse; unhappy is the wretched man that cannot guide himself aright, but slowly drifts on rocks and strands; truly his is a wrecked and ignoble life. Skidded logs for J. Murphy with our oxen; he has taken a large contract from the proprietor of a steam saw mill at Richford. Tom is drawing ties by the 100 and I am chopping cordwood; went to several church socials where the refreshments consist of cake and coffee; the ladies chiefly favor the company with singing and music, the gentlemen by humorous readings and recitations. Have lately got a boy from Norfolk Distributing Home. Sold Guertin some Elm trees at 40 cents a tree. Herbert C. is in love with Margaret Guernsey; told me he prefers her to Cousin Ethel for the latter is too "stuck up;" perhaps the reason he thinks so is because she will not tolerate his vulgarity. Houde's eldest son has been married. Daniel C. was "garcon de honeur" with Alphosine as "fille de honeur;" at the festivities in the evening one of the women guests was so overcome with intoxicants that she had to be carried out of the room where the dancing was going on; in justice however I must say that such cases are not numerous among the French I have associated with; a French club has been started, it has a very fine building with reading room, billiard room and private rooms for meetings, some of its not active members are English, but I think it shows very little spirit on their part to submit the list of books they intend to purchase, to the parish priest for his approval before buying them, yet of course they are not so much to blame; for a literary society started in an adjoining village met its death through not submitting to the dictation of the priest, for they bought some works of an infidel tendency and were ordered to remove them from their library which much to their credit they refused to do, the priest however was not to be defeated and in the parish church next Sunday advised all young men that were good Catholics to have nothing more to do with an association that kept in their library books that ridiculed the doctrines of their "holy church" the consequence was, the ranks of the association was daily thinned by deserters, but of course the poor fellows cannot be blamed so much, for any young man who should boldly stand up in defiance of the "Holy priesthood" would suddenly be brought to his knees in penitent humiliation; by first refusing to him the "Holy Sacrament" for any man incurring this penalty is looked upon as worse than the vilest criminal, and is immediately shunned with holy horror by all his countrymen, the reader must acknowledge that the average man has not the moral courage to sacrifice on the altar of truth, the fellowship and respect of all his nearest and dearest friends, and place himself in the cruel position of being in the condition of an exile in his native land; there were however a few noble spirits in the association who preferred liberty to anything else, but I am sorry to say they might almost as well have tried to kick against an iron wall as against the priesthood;. for they had to suffer that quiet form of persecution that is almost equivalent to that of former ages. I was myself personally acquainted with one of them, a very moral and intelligent young man who kept the best store in the village; but from that day that he was man enough to claim for himself the God-given privilege of liberty, his custom gradually dwindled away and the young lady to whom he was engaged turned him from her father's house; he was truly an exile in his own country, and shunned and despised by the friends and playmates of his childhood; with a burning contempt and hate for such a religion he came to the United States, a land of liberty and progress, even though freethinkers and heretics are so numurous in it. 13th of Feb. If this snow continues it will put an end to sleighing. On Sunday the two Miss Guernsey's visited us; their style of conversation was something like this—I like them style of cups

I aint going to; you dont say! well I declare; dear me; did you ever? this tea is awful strong; oh my! well well! and their laugh was like the report of a Woolich infant; of course I like to hear ladies laugh when it is like the music of a silver bell; but harsh discordant giggling laughter is disagreeable even in the most beautiful of women. Have read Rokeby, one of Sir W. Scotts poems which Florence advised me to read, it is her favorite. Three Irish Canadian feminine friends visited us from Richford, the wife of a tavern keeper and her two daughters, so highly perfumed that it pervaded the whole atmosphere of the parlor, after they had been within it for a few moments; but one cannot approach within 10 ft of the mother without smelling an abominable odor of gin, the poor woman is a hard drinker, but is nevertheless endowed with one of the warmest Irish hearts I ever met, I merely mention this to show that no man who truly loves the honor of his family or the interests of humanity, should engage in this traffic of selling slow poison to his fellowmen; it also reminds me of a striking imaginary comparison my father made of it, that "all spirituous liquor was the blood of the devil." Received numerous valentines, some very flattering and nice, and some very disagreeaple ones. I often spend an evening with Mr. Mc Dougall at Checkers, was introduced to his daughter who is on a visit there; and had "an evening at cards." She is a very affable and agreeable young lady; father has been advising me not to try and enter the army, but to study for law. We have some trouble in driving one of our young horses with an older one; have to equalize their strength by shortening the whipple tree on the oldest horses side. Uncle Herbert asked me in a contemptuous sort of a way what young ladies I would go to see now that the Miss Meredith's had gone to college; I felt like telling him it was none of his business, but this would never do, for grey hairs must and ought to be respected even if they do grow on the heads of clowns and donkeys. The Socialists have made an unsuccessful attempt to blow up the Czar of Russia. Have borrowed books from father on chemistry, practical geodesy, trigonometrical surveying, geometry, mensuration, and other books pertaining to the profession of civil engineer, am also taking lessons in French and of late have made it a practice to read only French newspapers which is a means of perfecting my knowledge of their language; had a conversation with father on the cruel harshness of the christian society of the present day in keeping true and good men and women out of its select circles because of a slight difference in their social standing, that I hoped to see the day when the leading spirits of the best of society will say to all good men and women our circle is open to all gentlemen and ladies who have cultivated manners and are good men and women, and we will not exclude you even though you cannot afford diamonds and costly silk; how many noble and elegant ladies are driven to despair and ruin through being shunned by their former christian friends, after the unavoidable bankruptcy of their husbands or fathers; is it not the place of their wealthy lady friends to come to them and say, we insist upon your still moving and associating in our circle of friends, even if you come in the plainest and coarsest of apparel, for although we admire and appreciate beautiful and costly apparel our greatest admiration, love and respect is reserved for the grand and God-like attributes with which the characters of every good man and woman are endowed, and would it not be the duty of these ladies the victims of some unavoidable calamity to have the moral courage to wear only that style of apparel suited to their reduced means and also to associate with as much ease and grace among their richer friends as formerly; and the duty of all gentleman to be as gracious to the poor lady as to the richer one, to show all men that they have greater admiration for true worth of character than for costly diamonds or silks or satins. It is an outrage to the better sentiments of mankind and contrary to the beautiful maxims and precepts of Christ; for the christian society of the present day tolerate in its midst vulgar and unprincipled men and women who have risen to ignoble wealth through defrauding their fellow men, and yet at the same time refuse admittance to the honorable men and women of the poorer classes, but I must not omit mentioning one of their most cruel and unjust rules, that of "visiting the sins of the father" on his innocent offspring, for instance, the children of gamblers; swindlers, drunkards etc. are not tolerated in the society of the children of the better classes, good society has no plac   or them, they must either have no society at all or mix with the vilest of the vile, this is a cruel injustice, for in many instances the innocent wife and children of such villians love and admire what is good and true, and the children would become noble and useful members of society if the christian society of the present day were not so intolerant and cruelly select; why should the host and hostess of that christian mansion that is to be the scene of a delightful party to-night, in sending out their invitations, pass over the names of the wife and children of a notorious drunkard and gambler, who live but ½ a block away and who is nobly doing her utmost to educate her children to become useful and honorable members of society; would it not be far more God-like to receive them occasionally with a hearty welcome to their stately christian homes, and show the poor children of that gambler the beautiful fruits of industry and virtue, and would it not be more Christ like for them to say to their children, whenever you meet the children of that gambler, our neighbor, be just as polite and gracious to them as if they were the children of the greatest gentleman in this city; they are trying to be good and true men and women, and it is your duty with your greater advantages to do all in your power to help them you must exert to the utmost all your influence to make them become refined ladies and gentlemen by gently reproving and teaching them the usages of the best society, and make it your duty to give them your perfections without acquiring any of their imperfections; would not mankind generally be much nobler and happier from such a course of instruction than from that which most Christians give their children of the present day, viz: "My dear children you must not speak to the children of that low, depraved gambler." Thus the followers of the meek and lowly Jesus build up an almost insurmountable wall between what is good and true and what is wicked and depraved and because poor innocent little children are born on the wrong side of that wall, they (instead of doing all in their power to aid the poor little innocents to cross over it) by their inhuman indifference and pride keep millions of their fellow creatures on the wrong side. Truly their christianity must be with the majority of them almost a dead letter when "Christ's head of the church" would bless cruel Philip of Spain and persecute noble Gallieo; or when the enlightened Protestants would bow humbly to such as the Duchess of Hamilton and pass without notice the virtuous and good women of an humbler position in life; or Christ's so called priesthood bless such a woman as the degraded Isabella of Spain and burn to death such a glorious woman as Joan of Arc. Father, however, only partially agreed with me; said that some unfortunate beings were judged too harshly by society, who does not always take into consideration that many children are led astray by evil associations as well as inheriting very often the failings of their parents. 1st March; the snow is nearly all gone. While at Merediths, Mrs. M's. mother came into the room to get the *Orange Sentinel*, an Orangeman publication, published in Ontario; she spoke to me as follows. "Oh, how har you, Mishter Howard. Shure its a long time since I saw you. What splindid weather this is." I saw plainly that Nicholas was on thorns, and he cut her conversation short by asking her to have the kindness to leave us alone as we were about to play a game of chess. There are few families in the world that have not a skeleton in the closet. Nicholas since he has been to college is not so choice in his language and must have met some wild young fellows there; he is, however, I am glad to say, a model of politeness before his mother and sisters; in my opinion he is too much petted by his mother. Read "Handy Andy," one of the most laughable books I ever read. 5th March; inquired the price of steers 1 year old, for Richard's farm; they ranged from $8 to $12. 8th of March; was very warm and close the first part of the night, froze towards morning and commenced to snow this forenoon. The inhabitants have commenced to tap their sugar bushes. Received an answer from the Secretary of War of the U. S. saying that there would be no vacancies for foreign appointments till 1882, so that destroys all prospects of my entering West Point. I had written to that college and received a prospectus. If I am too old to enter the Canadian or English colleges, I shall have to abandon the idea. Father has had only 6 bushel of wheat from 3 sown; this sort of farming does not pay. The following conversation occurred between Tom and a Frenchman in the dining-room while I am writing this, so I record some of the Frenchman's remarks: "This is cold weather for boots like mine. I just called in to light my pipe. My feet are nearly frozen, the d—d shoemaker made my boots too tight; I should have moccasins. I do not like Canadian tobacco. I am glad I am finished swamping rails, for it is d—d mean work; I came near getting my horses' legs broke amongst the roots and rocks; some of the rails I had to draw on my back as far as ¾ of an acre. You'll have more timber than you need for your barn from 390 logs. I have sold my rails to Frechette for $4.50 a hundred, he ships them to the old parishes where he gets a big price, he also ships squared timber for the frames of barns and houses. While at Houdes the other evening, Alphosine accidently tread on her brother's toe and he made a most disgustingly vile remark. Extract from a letter to Uncle Jerrold: "A man requires the society of gentlemen and lady friends to be a perfect gentleman, education alone is not sufficient; even supposing I had a perfect education, I could not pass my life among the vulgar people that surround us without contracting some of their vulgar habits aud ungramatical language. Every day of our lives we hear vile and degrading language and the most gross breaches of the usages of the best society of the present day. Now if I was a man with a will of iron, muscles of steel and the heart of a diamond, I might not be influenced by such associations, but no ordinary man situated as we are could pass his life among such associations without undergoing a terrible deterioration. Recived a letter from Uncle Jerrold, in which he said I was jackenapes and that some of my ideas were diabolical. According to newspapers the Nihilists of Russia aim at the overthrow of religion as well as that of the Emperor. Received an answer from my letter to Woolich. "Horse Guards War Office. Sir: I am directed by the Field Marshal, Commander-in chief, to acknowledge the receipt of your letter of the 21st ultimo, addressed to the Governor of the Royal Military Academy, and acquaint you in reply that a British Canadian is eligible for admission to the British Army. The regulations for admission to the Royal Military College and the

Royal Military Academy are enclosed and will give you all the imformation you require. I am to add that the pay of a 2nd Lieut. in the infantry is 5 s. 3 d. per day. I am, sir, your obedient servant, J. N. A. Dillion." General Regulations for the Government of the Royal Military Academy at Woolich: The Royal Military Academy is maintained for the purpose of affording a preparatory education to candidates for the Royal Artillery and Royal Engineers. This education will be chiefly technical and will in no obligatory subject be carried beyond the point useful to both corps alike. Regulations for admission, &c.: Admission to the Royal Military Academy as cadets will be granted to the successful candidates at an open competitive examination. The examinations will be conducted by the Civil Service Commissioners, and will be held twice a year, namely, in Dec. and July. Notice will be given from time to time of the day and place of examinations and for the vacancies to be competed for at each examination. The limits of age will be from 16 to 18; the candidates being required to be within these limits on the first day of Jan. next, following the winter examination; and on the 1st of July for the summer examination. The candidates for admission to the Dec. or July examination must send to the military secretary, and later than the 15th of Oct. or 15th of May respectively an application, to be accompanied by the following papers: (*a.*) An extract from the register of his birth, or in default, a declaration made by one of his parents or guardians before a magistrate, giving his exact age; (*b.*) A certificate of good moral character, signed by one of his tutors, or the heads of the schools and colleges where he has been, and at which he received his education from his 12th year to the date of application, or some other satisfactory proof of his good moral character. The number of trials will not exceed three. All candidates will be inspected by the Medical board, and no candidate will be allowed to proceed to examination by the commissioners unless certified by the board to be free from bodily defects ailments, and in all respects as to height and physical qualities, fit for Her Majesty's service. Cases of exceptional shortness will be refered to the War Office for special consideration. Candidates will be required to satisfy the commissioners in the following subjects: (1st.) Mathematics, viz: (*a*) Arithmatic and the use of common logarithms; (*b.*) Algebra, including equations, progressions, permutations, and combinations and the binomial therein; (*c.*) Geometry up to the standard of the 6th book of Euclid; (*d.*) Plane Trigonometry including the solution of triangles; 2nd. French, German or some other modern language the examination being limited to translaation from the language and gramatical questions; 3rd. Writing English correctly in a good legible hand from dictation and English composition; 4th. The elements of Geometrical drawing, including the construction of plane scales and the use of simple mathematical instruments; 5th. Geography; a thorough knowledge of each of the four branches of Mathematics will be required. The commissioners may, however, if they think fit, dispense with this preliminary examination except as regards Mathematics. English composition and Geometrical drawing in case of my candidate who has satisfied them on a previous occasion. No marks will be allowed for the above preliminary examination excepting for Mathemetics (2,000); for English composition, (500) and for Geometrical drawing, (300). The future examination will be proceeded with immediately on conclusion of the preliminary examination. Candidates who fail in their preliminary examination will be informed of their failure as soon as possible and they will be released from further attendance. The subjects of the further examination and the maximum number of marks obtainable for each subject will be as follows: 1st. Mathametics, viz: Further questions and problems on the subjects of the qualifying examination and the elements of the following subjects: Theory of Equations, Analytical Geometry, Conic Sections, Solid Geometry, Differential and Integral Calculus, Statics and Dynamics. N. B. In all subjects great importance will be attached to accuracy in numerial results; 2d. English and English literature, limited to specified authors and English history limited to fixed periods being notified before hand (2,000) numbers required in Mathematics, (2,000) in English; 3rd. Classics, viz: Latin or French, a candidate will not be allowed to take up both, (2,000) marks in each of these; 4th. French, the examination to be partly colloquial, (2,000); 5th. German, the examination to be partly colloquial, (2,000); 6th. Italian, Russian, Spanish or Hindoostan, either of these at option, the examination to be partly colloquial; 7th. Experamental science, viz: (*a.*) Chemistry and heat or (*b.*) Electricity and magnetism, (2,000) marks in these as well as the optional languages; 8th. General and Physical Geography and Geology, (2,000); 9th. Drawing free hand. A certain number will be deducted from the marks gained by the candidate in the preliminary examination in Mathematics, English composition and Geometrical drawing. The resulting total will determine the candidate's place in the competitive list. The successful candidates being those who stand first on the list up to the number of vacancies competed for. Optional subjects in Mathematics. Detailed syllabus. Further questions and problems on the subjects of the qualifying examination. Theory of equations, first principals witn easy exercises. Analytical Geometry; problems on straight line and circle Conic Sections; Elementray properties with easy problems, both on Analytical and Geometrical methods; Differential Calculus, Differentiation of functions of one independent variable; Taylor's and McLenrin's theorens, applications; Maxima and Minima of Functions of one independent variable; method of Infintesmals, first principles with easy applications; tangents and normals to curves; involutes and envolutes; Integral calculus; Elementray integrations; intregation considered as summation; rectification and quadrature of plane curves Statics; equilibrium of forced and comples in one plane; friction, center of gravity; mechanical powers; problems on Elementary Statics; the Graphical or Geometrical method of treating such problems should be studied as well as the Analytical to applications of the differental calculeus will be required; Dynamics, Elementray principals projecticals; motion of a heavy particle on a smooth curve; centrifugal force; simple pendulum, problems and exercises. No applications of the differential calculus will be required. Terms of payment for cadets at the Royal Military Academy are regulated by the following articles of Her Majesty's warrant of Dec, 1870. for the pay and promotion of the army. The payment on behalf of a cadet is as follows: for the son of an officer in the army or navy, who has died in the service, and whose family is left in pecuniary distress subject to the approval of our Secretary of State, £20, and so on in proportion up to £80; for the son of an admiral, or of a general officer who is colonel of a regiment, or in receipt of Indian Colonel's allowances, £ 80 a yr; the son of a private, £125; the pay of a cadet is 3s per day, it is assured to cover the expenses of regimental clothing, messing, washing and other contingencies; all other necessary expenses of this nature as well as weekly pocket money, postage of letters, bootmakers and tailor's bills for repairs etc.; which cannot be covered by his pay, shall be chargable to his parents or guardian in addition to the regulated contribution, a sum of £25, to cover expenses of uniform, books etc., and bring with him all the articles of clothing of which he shall receive notice, and which afterwards must be kept up at his expense. He shall also be required to pay the regulated contribution in advance for each half year he remains under instruction, and a deposit of £5 for contingent expenses. The Field Marshall, Commanding in chief will be the president of the Academy. The Academy will be under the control of a governor appointed by and responsible to the Secretary of State for war through the Field Marshall, Commanding-in-chief. The organization will be on a military basis; cadets will form one company mnder a Captain assisted by 4 Lieut. charged with the disciplineant of studies and the drill, one of whom will be Adjutant and Quarter master. The professors and instructors may either be military men or civilians; they will have limited power of punishment, within and without the halls, at the discretion of the Governor, to whom they will report all punishments they may inflict. The Chaplain will be specially appointed by the Secretary of State and will give instructions in classics. No professor will be allowed to give private instruction to a cadet at any time to prepare candidates for admission into the Academy; the Governor will have absolute power of rustication and removal, and also of sentencing a cadet for misconduct, to lose places in the list of successful candidates for commissions; when expulsion is necessary the case will be referred to the Secretary of State through the Field Marshall Commanding-in-chief; the name of such cadet will be made known to the First Lord of the Admiralty, and to the Secretary of State for India, to prevent his being admitted into other branches of Her Majesty's service course of instruction will be 2½ yrs.; if any student fails to come up to the required standard of 2 examinations or be found unable to qualify in his studies for a commission within 3 yrs., to be counted from the commencement of the first term he joins, or to acquire a sufficient proficiency in military exercises he will be removed; no extension of the period of three yrs. will be granted from any cause except illness; the following subjects will form the course of obligatory studies; first mathematics, including a thorough knowledge of plain trigonmetry, practical mechanics with the application of machinery; 2nd fortification field and permanent, such a course as is suitable to cadets, qualifying for the artillery and the requisite amt. of geometrical drawing; 3rd, artillery, such a course as is suitable for cadets qualifying for engineers; 4th military drawings with field stretchings and reconnoissance; 5th military history and geography; 6th French or German at the students choice; 7th chemistry and physics; 8th drills and exercise; in addition to this, students will be allowed to take up certain voluntary subjects; no obligatory subject shall gain cadet ranks unless he obtain a minimum of 1 half marks in it; no cadet will be insured a commission unless he qualify by obtaining at least 1 half marks in obligatory course in mathematics, mechanics, fortifications and artillery, and 1 half of the total aggregate of the marks alloted to all the obligatory subjects; no voluntary subjects shall gain a cadet any marks unless he obtain a minimum of at least ½ of the marks, assigned to that portion of it in which he is examined; the marks gained in the voluntary subjects will be added to those obtained in the obligatory subjects, to make a second total according to the which cadets shall be finally placed. The Academy has 19 Professors; the Governor has £1500 a yr. inclusive of all allowances except quarters, in addition to his unattached pay as general officer, Sec. Treasurer £400 Capt. of Co. 12s. and regimental pay, also forage for one horse, quarters, fuel and light, and 2 soldier servants; Lieut's 4s. Highest pay of Professors, £550 lowest £350; a cadet is removed from the Academy for moral or physical unfitness. Copy of a letter sent to Uncle Richard. Feb. 3rd., "My dear uncle, I recd. your letter yesterday and was sorry to hear of Uncle Timothy's wife's death, also that Richard's cough is worse, was pleased to hear that we may expect a visit from you shortly, please send postal card a few days before and either Tom or I will meet you at the depot; you name the Duke of Cambridge as a proof that promotion in the English army is by influence and not by merit, and certainly it is a very strong proof, as he never gained the position he now holds by rendering any service to his country, but only through influence, but then we should remember his position is only nominal for he has never seen active service, and were a great war to break out and threaten England and her colonies, he would not have the ability or experience to guide the movements of the army, and some other general better suited would be chosen; some time ago when there was danger of war between England and Russia, it was not the Duke who was to have command of the forces, but Sir W. Napier, and supposing there had been a war and any victories had been gained, it would not have been the Duke but Napier that would have had the honor of them; England in time of war must of necessity only regard true merit in preferance to any influence; Nelson, one of England's greatest heroes had to struggle for a long time without the aid of influence, but his courage and ability triumphed over all; the Duke of Wellington may have gained some advantages through the influence of Lord Welsley, but if he had not possessed ability and merit, the appointment would have only been a disgrace instead of an honor to his name, therefore, influence without merit is far inferior to merit without influence; if a man through ambition cultivates whatever abilities he has he will quickly find friends who will lend him their influence, but as you say, the first thing a young man should do is to educate himself; as the age in the U. S. is from 17 to 22, I am certain I can by a little hard study, fit myself to pass the primary examination, and if you and Uncle John will have the kindness to consent I shall go immediately to the U. S.; become a citizen and by a little skillful manoevoring get appointed by one of the members of Congress in some of the States; I know well that no man can succeed who has not a fixed purpose in life, but would make this mine and would spare no effort to make it a success; I hope you will pardon my alluding to the subject again after your 2 refusals, but I still hope you may yet consent, when you see how dear the object is to us; I have received prospectuses from Kingston, West Point and Woolwich military colleges; at West Point the age is from 17 to 22, which puts it within my reach; the cadet receives $540 a year, commencing when he enters the college and which is ample to pay all expenses; hoping soon to hear from you, I remain your affectionate nephew, A. N. Howard." When I wrote to the President of the United States I forwarded him the following letters, but I have already mentioned of the answer I received. I was informed that there would not be any vacancies for foreign appointments before '82 and that placed all hopes in that direction out of the question. Head Quarters; Newburg, 23rd June 1883. Sir; I was yesterday favored with your letter of the 12th of February, and this day I transmitted the papers which accompanied it to the President of Congress with a letter of which the enclosed is a copy. Your early attachment to the cause of this country and your exertions in relieving the distresses of our fellow citizens as were so unfortunate as to be prisoners in Ireland, claim the regard of every American and will always entitle you to my particular esteem. I shall always be happy in rendering you every service in my power. Being with great truth, sir, your very obedient servant, George Washington." Mr. Reuben Howard. Headquarters, Newburg, 23rd June, 1783. Sir: I do myself the honor to transmit to your Excellency, a copy of a letter I have received from Mr. Reuben Howard of Cork, Ireland, and sundry papers which accompanied it. The early part this gentleman appears to have taken in the cause of this country, and his exertions in relieving the distresses of such of our fellow-citizens whom chance of war threw into the hands of the enemy, entitle him to the esteem of every American, and will doubtless have due weight in recommending him to the notice of Congress. I have the honor to be &c. G. Washington. His Excellency, the President of Congress. By the United States Congress, assembled July 18, 1783. On report of a committee to whom was referred a letter of the 23d of June, from the Commander-in-chief, enclosing the copy of a letter from Mr. Reuben Howard, merchant, in Cork in the Kingdom of Ireland, and other papers. Resolved, That the Commander-in-chief be requested to transmit the thanks of Congress to Mr. Reuben Howard, and express the just sense Congress entertain of the services he has rendered during the late war to American prisoners. Chas. Thomson, Secretary. Sir: I am honored with the care of transmitting to you the enclosed Resolution of Congress, expressing the sense that August Body entertain of your goodnesss to American prisoners. Impressed as I am with sentiments of gratitude to you for this expression of your benevolence, I feel a very particular gratification in conveying to you the thanks of the Soverign Power of the United States of America, on an occasion which, while it does honor to humanity, stamps a mark of particular distinction on you. Wishing you the enjoyment of health with every attendant blessing, I beg to be persuaded that I am, with every particular respect and regard, sir, your most obedient servant, G. Washington. Mount Vernon, August. 1784. Sir: Capt. Stickney has presented me with your favor of the 25th of May, together with the mess beef and ox tongues, for which you will please accept my best thanks. I don't grow tobacco, nor am I possessed of a lb. at this time, otherwise I would have the pleasure of consigning a few hhds. to your address, under full persuasion that no person would do me greater justice in the sale of them. Wheat and flour of last year's produce is either exported or consumed, that of the present year is not yet in market. What prices they will bear is not for me to say. But though I do not move in the mercantile line, except in wheat, (which I manufacture into flour,) I should, nevertheless, thank you for any information respecting the price of these articles. With very great esteem and respect, I am, sir, your most obedient servant, G. Washington. General Washington subsequently presented Reuben Howard with a gold ring in which was set a minature portrait of himself which is still preserved in the family. These letters were printed for private circulation only amongst the members of the different branches of the family. G. N. Howard, (grandson of said Rueben Howard) merchant and vice-consul for Prussia, Sweden, Norway, Portugal, Brazil and Mecklenburg Schwerin at Cork. Have been reading the Histories of Germany and Spain of late. Mrs. M. has asked me to spend a few days at their house at Easter. Father has received a letter from Jim Parker, the first settler in these parts, he has discovered a mine in Colorado, and has had a village that has sprung up around it named after him. Some iron ore has been discovered near Aston and is being drawn to McLean's foundry at Durham. Went to Davenport to see cousin Sarah; went with her busband to the neat little church in the village; it is free for the use of all Protestant denominations, which shows how the divisions between the Protestant churches are being removed and that the differences between them is only nominal. It seems that these divisions amongst them has been a source of strength and aided their remarkable growth and the glorious work they have accomplished. In this the first era of their existence they have accomplished double the amount of growth and good than the early Christian church did; let the reader study impartially both periods and he cannot be otherwise than of the same opinion. Was surprised to see Mrs. Cross, who was one of the first settlers on our range, teaching Sunday school; in former days she had a tongue like a two-edged sword, but I suppose advancing years has induced her to put it to better use than "back-biting her neighbors." Called at Devlin's and was surprised to see a picture of "God, the Father." What terrible blasphemy! According to their own scripture, Moses could not look upon the glory of God; if so, how could any human artist paint the features of Him; and does not their own scriptures say, "Thou shalt not make any graven image, or the likeness of anything in heaven above or the earth beneath; or bow down to them or worship them." Yet I have seen hundred of these deluded people kneel down with the most disgusting servility before the image of some saints who were only weak and finite men like themselves. While speaking with Meredith's hired man he told me that Nicholas hardly ever does any work, but gets it all done by hired help and is most of his time reading or smoking in his room or under the shade of some trees. If he continues thus he can never become a prosperous farmer. "The Elms,. Dear Tom and Arthur: Your letters received. We have bought 5 steers this spring for $15 each; they are small for their age having been brought up on straw, but all who have seen them think they are a great bargain, as we can get at least double for them next fall; we have 6 steers, 2 heifers, 4 cows, 3 pigs, 10 sheep, 2 colts and 2 horses, which is very little stock for a farm of this size; it is enough, however, until we have enriched the soil, after which we will have 3 lots of steers, 30 always maturing 3 years and ready to sell. There is little money to be made in this Province by raising grain, it pays better to fatten cattle for the British market. In your letter you still appear anxious to buckle on armor. I fail, however, to understand your patriotism, as you are as willing to enter West Point as an English one, where you would have to swear allegiance and fight against England if called upon to do so. I think the idea of your getting into West Point is an impossiblity, for each state can only nominate 1 or 2 names. When I was in New York the number of applicants was over 2000 for that state, and it was by competitive examination held by the members of Congress. I think the President only appoints ambassador's sons and merely for the educational facilities of the institution and occassionally some relative, when there is a tremendous rumpus in the papers. You say at Kingston military college the expense is nominal, that is right, only as far as instruction goes. Our friend Mr. R's son is going to leave on account of the expense, but is a miserable place at any rate and not worth entering; if I were in perfect health to-morrow I could not get into the army if I wished to, being too old as you are also for the Canadian and English military colleges, and I hardly think you could get an American member of Congress to appoint you (a stranger) when he has to deny 100 of his countrymen every yr. A friend of mine, D. D. Turner, a graduate of Cambridge would have paid any amount of money to get into the English army and although only a few years older than the appointed age he could not succeed, besides it is a miserable life at best, I have personally known several officers who left to go to college to study for a profession, and I entirely disagree with you about poor uneducated people, there is no where that a real gentleman shows more to advantage than among the lower classes, "honor and shame from no condition rise," act well your part there all the honor lies." As for study, all our great scholars have been self-taught; you can study anywhere and if you have a taste it will always be a pleasure; I think Clifford and I can hold a much more easy and independant position as farmers than military men; in a great many cities the principal people will not call on the military or invite them to their houses, on account of their being too dissipated; your cousin Mr. Fothergill tells me that this is the case at Salford, England; if you and Tom make up your mind that you would like to try legitimate farming in a cleared country I would write to Uncle Jerrold if you should wish it; I have a nice farm in view for you of 200 acres, 80 cleared and rolled, with a fine rich soil that can be purchassed for less than $2000; the great thing in buying is to see that the fences are good and that the stables, pastures and meadows are in good order, for if they are not you will lose 2 or 3 yrs. in trying like us to get them in order again; Clifford and I were much interested in your 2 pieces of poetry entitled "the Scottish Knight," and the "Irish settler;" I am now interested in reading a "history of our own times" by Justin McCarthy, he is a Liberal and writes very impartially, giving praise to Beaconsfield as well as to Gladstone; at present our men are drawing rails and manure, The U. S. army is so small (24000) that I fail to see how they give employment to all the graduates every yr.; in time of peace vacancies are not plentiful; the yr. before last the officers of the U. S. navy were not paid, as the Congress had not voted money for that purpose; with love to you and Tom, your affectionate cousin R. I. Goldsmith." Tom and I have been making rails, also draw logs for Guertin's mill and made "sap troughs" at the rate of 50 a day in ash timber trees of medium size, cut in 2½ ft: lengths, split in 2 halves and "hollowed out" with an axe and adze. "The Elms, Feb. Dear Arthur, The Kingston Military College leads to nothing, after cadets have finished their study, 3 or 4 if up to the mark, and those the best out of the whole college get employment in the English army; kind to Canada, we pay for their education, then England takes the best away if good enough for her;) the Canadians will not stand this much longer. England will have to educate her own soldiers, (volunteers are enough for us.) A. and B. batteries in Canada very seldom have a vacancy, so with an average of 30 scholars each yr. at Kingston, the chance of being one of the best 4 is very poor; the col'ege at Quebec is only for training volunteer officers for Canada I believe; even if you were young enough to enter, the life would disgust you, in time of peace (a time we all hope for) an officers duties is a little fatigue drill dancing and drinking, the latter you have to pay for whether you drink it or not. There are religious men in the army but they are few and far between, and are generally considered out of place, as it puts them in a false position. If England makes an unjust war against another nation you cannot even raise your vo:ce against it in protest, and every man you kill is a question between yourself and your maker, although you gain some medals and applause at the time, you will finally learn that the applause of society is too often the applause of the devil; by judicious reading and avoiding bad society, and being just in all your dealings, you will always find yourself respected by that society most worth cultivating, and you will eventually secure to yourself an honorable position in this Canada of ours, which is yet in its infancy, and which if we could only realize it, our individual conduct will either make it a good or a bad country. To enter a ball room with brassy assurance to be smiled on by a a people both artificial in manner and appearance, and to mix in society made up of wealth, dishonestly acquired in most cases, is ambition that would soon wear out: there is a society however not numerous, but select, which consists of true men and women who judge each other by what they are, they believe that a gentleman is a man educated in his own language, leads an honest life and above all things is sensitive with regard, for the feelings of others, all this I believe you have Arthur, but what I would suggest is, that you move to a cleared farm where less work would bring a greater return, and where you would have a more congenial social atmosphere; with your large income you could keep a housekeeper and live in comfort, while the proceeds of your farm would enable you to make an annual bank deposit; I believe where you are you are wasting your time and money, and the Frenchmen should you become intimate with them will ultimately drag you down to their level: you must excuse my going so much into the sermon business, but had I no regard for you I would not do it; we have bought a Suffolk sow for $17, also a Durham 9 yr. old cow for $26 also 10 tons of hay at $4 a ton, to draw it ourselves. Hope you will decide to come and farm near us, your affectionate cousin R. I. Goldsmith." It is perfectly absurd for Cousin Richard to speak of military men in this way, for as the world is not civilized enough to abolish war military men will rank as they always have in the world's history, as one of the best and highest classes of society, brave and gallant men possessing that grace of manner and stately demeanor that wins for them so much admiration and respect in the best society in the world. And I confidently assert that more true and perfect men can be found in the army than in any other class of people in the world, and that not 1 lady in 20 would prefer the society of your ignorant and boorish farmers to that of men in the army, therefore I maintain that this preference shown for the society of military men by the most refined and perfect ladies all over the world is a certain proof that military men are as a class the most perfect gentleman, to this of course there are exceptions, there being in the army as well as all other professions a certain class of men who bring dishonor on their fellow-officers who despise their low ungentlemanly conduct, and would not tolererate them in their midst if it were possible to remove them from it; there is however a rigid Puritanical class of society, whose homes are too solemn and its inmates too grave and devout to tolerate the bright sunshine of the witty and charming conversation of these perfect gentleman, but that class of society may rest assured that even if they did invite them these military gentleman would no more think of going to spend an evening in their Puritanical drawing-rooms than they would of spending it in the cell of a dark and gloomy prison. Extract from letter from Uncle Richard dated April 1st. "Tom and you have done a great deal of valuable work on your lots which will tend much to your ease and comfort hereafter. I feel like a bird out at Richard's farm. Liberty is a sweet thing, especially to those who have been enslaved to many of the foolish usages of civilized society. I am glad to hear that poor Parker has fallen into luck, poor fellow has suffered much from the tribulation an vicissitudes of life, but I always considered him a clever, shrewd man. My son Richard, while out west for his health, gave a very doleful account of that country, and said he had no doubt the time would come when the tide of emigratiom would turn back east; said he saw more idle people seeking bread in California than in any other part of the world. In Lower Canada now the rush seems to be for Manitoba, and were it not for bad water and scarcity of timber it would not be such a bad place. There are several in Montreal that have returned in disgust. Few can tell better than yourselves of the trials and hardships in a new country. Most of your hardships are now over and in another year or two your farm will begin to pay. Excuse my saying that in your composition you have one bad habit that of dropping your articles and consonants; this custom is only adopted by illiterate Americans; you say, "at saw mill;" "for new barn;" otherwise your composition is excellent; of course I know there are few men whose composition is perfect, but I know you will receive these remarks in the spirit of love in which they are given." Have piled our timber at Roussin's saw mill. Walter Bacon has written a novel and published it; the Bacon family are all very clever, and with only their widowed mother's aid have educated themselves. Since I last wrote in this journal I have gone to concerts, balls, private parties, church socials and private theatrical entertainments and played a "checker tournament" with all the best English checker players of Aston, and came out at the lists as champion of the English players, a truly empty honor for a man to waste many precious hours in acquiring. Oh, inconsistent man that I am! Have heard oaths and vile conversation amongst the French, and in the best society of some of Aston's English ladies have seen so called christian ladies that one day sang praises to God in his church and spent the next in standing and speaking evil of their neighbors. In justice, however, I must say I have met with some beautiful exceptions, but regret to say they are very few. At the English schoolhouse I saw a panoramic view of the "Holy Land," which was very instructive. Spent a most enjoyable evening at Merediths; 10 or 12 intimate friends were there from Preston, Richford and Aston; passed the evening in listening to singing and music, playing whist, and a few waltzes; after a choice supper at 11 o'clock we dispersed; I returning on foot 7 miles over a road ankle deep in mud greatly regretting that I had not accepted the invitation to stay all night. I went next day with a Frenchman to attend to the boiling of the syrup; had a sugar party in the English schoolhouse, at which a most unfortunate quarrel occurred between two young gentlemen (so called.) Mr. C. was sitting on a barrel and Mr. N. asked him to get off as he wanted to get some articles out of it; Mr. C. did not immediately comply and Mr. N. shoved the barrel and knocked it over, at which Mr. C, who is very quick tempered, of Irish descent, made a hard snow ball and let fly, almost stunning Mr. N. and giving him a black eye; fortunately no ladies were present and the affair was hushed; they are both aspirants for the fair hand of Miss Mabel Willoughby, which in a measure may account for it. 8th April; beautiful, mild weather; have commenced drawing out manure on the meadows. It astonishes me how Frenchwomen swear and imagine there is no harm in it; such expressions as "My God," "Saviour of God," Holy Ghost," Holy Virgin," Good God," Jesus Christ," &c., are all hourly and common-place terms with them. I must say to the credit of English and Protestant women, that I have never met a respectable women among them that would be guilty of such language. Have read Tennyson's poems, but prefer those of Sir W. Scott and Lord Byron. This afternoon snow fell 2½ inches deep. There was a delightful little party held in the English schoolhouse at Aston this week. Had a dispute with Tom about his horses; he says that I must not take them to go to the village without asking his consent; told him that I had to pay half the expense of feeding them and that it was only just that I should be allowed the use of them once or twice a week. The Liberals have defeated the Conservatives in England by a large majority. Herbert C. had a sugar party, but it was a decided failure, even though he had printed and distributed cards of invitation, as but few representatives of the fair sex were at it; Nicholas M. and Adam Grant who came to it, stayed over night at our house and played cards, dominoes and sang comic songs and related some anecdotes that would have been more appropriate in Charles the Second's reign. Tom and I have commenced cutting timber on land we are going to clear; we have given Freddy Burke 20 acres to clear at $5 an acre; it is where Roussin's lumbermen have removed most of the timber. Bought 2 calves at the village for 50cts. each; Jimmy Burke has been released and is more depraved than when he entered the penitentiary, and uses most horrible language in general conversation. I have persuaded Mrs. Meredith to teach school, that is, her own children in her own house, for the sake of not letting the school fall into the hands of R. C's. Have joined the French club, which is named St. Andre. Have been deepening the course of the stream lately; which is cold work, up to one's knees in water and mud. The Meredith's went one evening this week to attend a "May Queen" celebration; Florence and Maud are coming back in June and will, I suppose, be full fledged, graceful and charming young ladies. Freddy Burke has broke his contract; Meredith's have bought a farm adjoining theirs, 185 acres with small house, barn and stable on it for $1600; it is very cheap being only one mile from Aston village; 3 years ago the old Frenchman that owned it offered it to me if I would pay him $200 a year for life, which I refused and he died a year after. Walter Goldsmith dined with me at Merediths and is extremely bashful with young ladies. Croquet is all the rage in Aston now; country villages are always behind the time in everything, especially French Canadian ones, lawn tennis has been in vogue in other places long ago. While out on a boating excursion some of the English young men decided to take a bath as it was 6 miles up the river and far away from civilization; the Frenchmen had each a small piece of dark cloth attached with a string around their necks with the name of the Virgin sewn on it; I was informed the little piece of cloth came from the robes of the bishop of this diocese and cost 50cts. each, and that any Catholic found dead without this badge of Catholicism the body would not be buried in consecrated ground; I expect this only holds good for the ignorant French in this Province, for I hardly think that intelligent Catholics in the U. S. or England would pay 50cts for a little bit of the worn out robe of a bishop; they, however assured me that all Catholics wore this badge in all parts of the world. The water was not very cold considering it was the 10th of May. Have made a pleasure boat to keep on Aston river; have christened it "Grace Darling." Metz Vincent has married; I pity the poor creature whoever she is. We have been very busy of late clearing land, drawing lumber for the new barn, fencing, ditching, and repairing our main road. Had a dispute with Vincent's; they took the contract of clearing 3 acres of land, commenced work at 9 in the morning and quit at 4 in the evening and still expected to make big wages, but discovered their mistake as they only earned at the rate of 35cts. a day, and were so enraged they threatened to thrash me within an inch of my life. Have of late been trying to organize a volunteer corps. Received the following letter: "St. Jean. Sir, your letter of the 31st of May has been received and I have noted its contents which I have transmitted to the brigade major of the military district No. 6, to be forwarded to Ottawa for the consideration of the minister of militia. I have the honor to remain your obedient servant, Lieut. Col. Doherty, Of late Tom has had morning and evening prayers regularly; our hired boy Jerrold is very useful about the house; have contributed $5 annually to the Norfolk Sheltering Home for Orphans; Nicholas and I often attend the St. Andre club and play billiards, cards, checkers, &c., and read the newspapers which are chiefly in French. Rev. L. C. Willoughby does not denounce error enough in his sermons; his sermons would I think be very suitable for angels to listen to but are not practical enough for frail and mortal man After the services a child was christened; this has always seemed to me a ridiculous ceremony; the idea of a babbling infant being received into the church of Christ and 4 adults taking vows on themselves that this child will renounce the devil and all his works when perhaps it will live to be a housebreaker or a murderer, and what seems still more absurd is that I have seen many godfathers and godmothers both in the Church of England and the Catholic Church make this impossible promise when they themselves had not renounced the works of the devil. I have actually seen at the Catholic Church in this parish an inveterate drunkard and wife beater allowed by the parish priest to stand up as godfather for a poor innocent little infant; I thought at the time the poor little thing would be better without any godfather at all than to have such a brute as this. Mr. Milton is staying with us a few days till he has sold a small quantity of bark that still remains on Sherman's lot. On the 24th May there was a pic nic at Preston in honor of the Queen's birthday. Commenced to sow potatoes in the new land but found it so rocky and rooty that I decided to give out the job to Louis Brodeur; he is to sow 12 bushels of potatoes and give us 40 this fall. Uncle Richard has been out to see us. "18th June, Dear Uncle, I hope Flora has perfectly recovered from the shock her nervous system received from the fire; how very brave her husband was to rescue her from the burning house; how fortunate her furs and jewelry were insured. We have been very busy clearing land since you left us; have sown it all except a small piece we have reserved for turnips. Our crops consist of 16 bush. of oats, 2 acres of buckwheat, several acres under oats and 1½ under potatoes. The Colorado beetle has not yet made its appearance; our crop of hay promises to be one of the finest we have had for many yrs; in many places it is 2½ ft. high; I expect both barns will be full as the old barn is half full from last year. Have also done much work at clearing out the stream; the black alluvial soil we dig out of its bed will form good top dressing for the highland meadows. We are raising 9 calves on milk and Indian meal. Our "home boy" is very useful, keeps the house tidy and cooks the meals; we will have to feed, clothe and give him schooling for the first 3 years and after that pay him wages. Last week I heard of a great bargain of land, 1500 acres well covered with timber for $1 per acre, is situated in the Co. of Suffolk and within 4 m. of a rly; some of the land is low and has good pine timber on it, but the greater part of it is high land covered with sugar bushes; one of the lots is within one mile of Richford; public roads pass by all the lots; I think it is a great bargain and that even the timber on it will be worth in less than 5 yrs the price that is now asked for it; the annual tax on this property is rather high now on account of the rly tax but altogether does not exceed $30 a yr; the titles are all without a flaw;

what I propose is that Tom and I buy this land; he will sell it payable in 5 annual installments of $314, which includes interest; this we can easily meet with the returns from our farm and income. Now that I cannot enter the army I want Tom and myself to be something more than market gardeners, to possess one of the finest estates in this part of the country. I hardly think you will object to our taking advantage of this great bargain which will be a good and safe investment for all our spare capital during the next 5 yrs. It seems to me that good land well watered and timbered at $1 per acre is the best investment a man could make; however we leave it to your decision. Tom unites with me in love to you all, your affec. nephew, A. N. Howard." Mr. M. sold his lot situated 2 m. from Aston for $800; during the copper mine mania he refused $10,000 for it which he must now greatly regret. The flies are very troublesome to the animal world and men at this time of yr. While working at father's by an almost perpendicular rock, 30 ft. high, it reminded me of my younger days when us boys divided in parties under the Union Jack, with stars and stripes, with wooden swords; used to take great pleasure in attacking a minature wooden fortress in its summit and burning it. Played croquet at Guernsey's with Mary G., went to Meredith's, listened to music and singing, Maud showed me some sketches she took while in Ontario. After tea had outdoor games with Nicholas and a cousin of his from Scotland; Maud and Florence are delightfully unaffected and were the apparently pleased spectators of our athletic sports; had an interesting 2 hours conversation with Maud, Mabel, Florence and Nicholas on the veranda in the cool evening air of early summer. At church next day the 2 Bacon's officiated, one of them has been ordained a clergyman. Daniel C. has bought what is known as Dupries farm from the B. A. Land Co; 100 acres for $450, 8 yrs to pay for it without interest; it has a fine sugar bush some hemlock bark and is heavily covered with timber. I hoed fathers potatoes for him. I have resigned the secretaryship of the dissentient school and been elected trustee. Went to a "bee" at Carmichael's, the dinner and supper were very poor, lewd jokes and oaths were numerous throughout the day. Received a letter for our boy from his widowed mother in

Liverpool. We commenced cutting our hay on the 10th July; Tom is still thinking of leaving this place and going out west; offered to rent me his half if I would clear 10 acres a year on it, I refused. Had an argument with J. Murphy about Gallieo, he tried to persuade me that he was cannonized as a saint by the church, told him that instead of being made a saint he was persecuted by the bishops of the church and imprisoned for having the moral courage to assert a scientific truth that "the world revolved around the sun instead of the sun around the earth. 10th July, dear uncle, we received your letter last Saturday and apologize for not answering it sooner, the reason was we were busy all week cutting and saving our hay which will keep us busy for at least 2 months as we will have to cut father's hay for him, of which he has about 6 acres and 38 acres of our own. I regret you have decided against our buying the land but of course as you say any business that is stretched too much is likely to break. We have had very dry weather lately, there has been no rain for several weeks. My uncle Herbert has not yet returned from his visit to his son the Dr. in Iowa. A great many farmers around here have great difficulty in getting laborers for haying on account of so many being employed at bark peeling, unimportant items close it. Daniel C. and I have in contemplation another visit to Wakefield's, he became hopelessly in love with the eldest daughter several yrs ago, but of course she rightly considers herself far above him, is fairly educated and has $2000 in her own name but is very plain and freckled, red hair and protruding teeth; I trust it is not the $2000 he is in love with, for my part altho I like money exceedingly for the great advantages it can purchase I am confident I never could be mean enough to try and persuade an ugly young lady that I loved her for the sake of a paltry $2000. I can understand genius and talent making a man love an ugly lady, but in my opinion riches, never! Nicholas and his cousin Morton from Scotland often come to see us. While looking over a photograph album with Florence and Maud one evening, Maud made some indirect remark about Richard Bacon's photograph at which Florence blushed deeply, which filled my mind with the most painful of thoughts, but never mind "faint heart never won a fair lady," so I must strive on manfully through life, battling unceasingly against its many difficulties and temptations, and live to be worthy of her even if I do not win her, true love has an elevating and enobling influence on mankind, but man should not allow even it to gain an overmastering influence upon him, for in so doing it often ruins weak men's lives, for instance, those men and women who say "because the dearest object of our affections did not recriprocate them we have lost all ambition in life," are truly to say the least, weak and puny specimens of manhood and womanhood. The beetles have appeared on the potatoes, Louis B. has applied Paris Green to them. Mortin, Nicholas' cousin is "very green" while at our place Nicholas persuaded him to try the experiment of sleeping in a tree saying that trappers and huntersoften did so and enjoyed it, he belongs I should say to the middle class of the Scotch people, and is thoroughly honest and a good hearted fellow. At Carmicheal's "mowing bee" I took the lead of 20 men and none of them could keep up with me, and am now acknowledged as ths best mower in these parts. Mr. Bacon, telegraph operator of the St. Norbert Rly. is engaged to Miss Grant; if some lovers only knew how absurd they appear in the eyes of the world they would not act as if they were the only happy individuals in existance. Sold Mr. Grant 2000 bundels of hay for $120; spent the evening there, played cards and talked nonsense with the 2 Miss G's, who are terribly affected and would make good disciples of the aesthetic Oscar Wild, laughed at poor jokes, heard pretty lips use bad grammar, sipped wine, nibbled cake and passed a moderately pleasant evening. 9th Aug.; the oats in the back clearance are nothing extra, and the potatoes almost a failure, so we did well not to sow them ourselves; Tom is now glad he took my advice. Went to a picnic of St. Andre's club on Pine Island, situated in the river that runs from Richford to Preston; there never was a gayer party of young men, as we ascended the river next day with our well filled lunch baskets singing French and English songs; on reaching the island for the first time in my life I partook of a small piece of "frog's leg" which a party of those who went out fishing had cooked in butter, it was perfectly delicious, and tender as a chicken, and I shall always defend Frenchmen hereafter when I hear them ridiculed for eating frog's legs, the flowing bowl was also passed around with many a boisterous shout, and most liquors from champagne down to whiskey, and beer were largely partaken of, I however with a few others did not imbibe, which was very fortunate as many of the gayer spirits were so intoxicated that in going down the river we had all we could do to keep them from getting drowned; have hired Mrs. Vincent to do the washing and mending of the clothes for Tom, myself and our hired boy, for 35cts. a week; while at La Rivere's conversed with him and his brother-in-law on religion and morality; so disgustingly low were their ideas on these subjects that I look on them as but a few degrees better than the brute beast, for when men's intellectual faculties are crushed and enslaved to this extent they lose all their worth and beauty, and reduce man from being one of the noblest of God's creatures to that of being one of the most servile and debased; told G's of a concert going to be held at Davenport, they talked of going 2nd class, I said a young man should not travel 2nd class, a millionaire might afford to do so but not a young man who has yet to make a position and friends in the world, and I thought it unwise of a man to pass many hours in a vulgar atmosphere for the sake of a few shillings; went on a visit to Hartford; there has been typhus fever at Lemington college through bad drainage; I find that one of the Bacon's a student there "cribbed" and was nearly turned out of college for it but the examiners took pity on him as it would nearly ruin his prospects in life, besides they are short in their supply of candidates for the ministry; drove to Johnsville, some fine farms and pretty scenery, deep ravines with groves of woodland not very far apart. Clifford and I went to Carlton which is a magnificent farming district, has some of the finest rural scenery in the province; every valley has its stream or river, and most of the roads are arched over by stately avenues of trees; the whole country is a network of well tilled fields interlaced with groves of primeval woodland which resembles many parks as the ground underneath is free of brushwood and covered with grass on which large herds of cattle graze; Carlton has an excellent young ladies' college. Mr. Christie's farm buildings look like a small village with its many roofs and tall chimneys, for cooking roots for cattle; his workman's cottages, barns, graneries, stables and his own house and that of his sons, are all well surrounded with a stately grove of trees; no sand is seen here as at Hartford, and the few rocks that were here have by thrifty industry been built into walls, so evenly that they are an ornament the country; Christie is the richest and best farmer in Canada, yet strange to say he has a very poor education, not even a good elementary education; has made most of his money in the shoe business and is now one of Canada's Senators. 1st Sept.; went on a pleasure excursion to Norfolk; the excursion is in aid of an R. C. church that is being built there. On leaving Aston the land on either side is sandy; most of the primeval forest has been cut away and a second growth taken its place. Where St. Herbert rly. crosses our "range" the land becomes more rocky with a rocky ledge 100 ft. high, and the soil also improves this I have noticed is generally the case, that wherever rocks are the land is scarcely ever poor or sandy, pass Leurier's brickyard and over the stream that runs through our land, also over Guertin's river a branch of the Richford river; the country now becomes more cleared and level but looks bare with no primitive forest in sight, before reaching Richford pass through several deep cuttings with board fences 12 ft. high to prevent the snow from drfting in; are now in sight of Richford, a pretty view, the r'wy runs along the river's bank which is about 100 ft. above the river; Richford is a pretty village in a valley with a steep range of hills on either side; after leaving Richford the country becomes exceedingly rocky; passed a few small whitewashed houses in a clearance, forest right up to the track on one side and a small strip of clearance on the other; the train travels quickly considering the many curves in the road; this road is well fenced in with board and wire fencing; small clearances on the left; the land is still considerably rocky; cleared land on both sides for a short distance; forest again on both sides, no swamps as yet seen, all high land and hardwood timber, pass through some deep cuttings in rock so high that we cannat see the top of it from the car window; some fine fields of grain and the houses of new settlers; a fine grove of maples and much cordwood along the line; have reached cleared country again with some ledges of rock in it; arrive at South Richford, a small stopping place with a few wooden houses and a considerable quantity of bark and ties; country is getting more level and of better appearance; a great many board fences to keep the snow from the track; primeval forest on either side, but clearances can be seen on rising ground in the distance; on both sides a splendid growth of forest clearences, again newly cleared with stumps and stones in it; a range of hills in the distance, forest and clearance alternately; pass 2 small stopping places; there are a number of Frenchmen yelling in the car next this one; they have imbibed somewhat too freely; a clearance growing up in second growth; country getting more and more cleared, cross a stream, country beginning to look more attractive, numerous streams, land low and marshy and covered with brushwood, clearances again with rocky land; the smoke from the engine is very unpleasant as all the windows are open; arrive at Warrington, a very straggling town; pass what some Eastern yankees call a "bone orchard;" the country we have passed through is far from picturesque or offers brilliant prospects to intending settlers; have entered wild wilderness again, trees of stunted growth, scorched by fire, clearances newly made, stopped at a small station, forest again on either side. The country now suddenly changes, and the scenery becomes interesting; Norfolk village is surrounded by 14 hills; passed by Bruntfield Lake, one of the most beautiful in the Province of Quebec; its surface is dotted with dozens of islands; Norfolk is a scattered village; hired a boat with some of my French friends for 75 cts., rowed to one of the islands where there was a fine sandy bottom with water only 4 to 5 ft. deep for acres in extent, where we bathed; there was a boat race in the afternoon; I rowed about the lake by myself, amongst its beautiful little islands for 2½ hrs. without stopping; 300 people dined in a beautiful grove, many dined at the hotel, a remarkably good one for such a small village; after that there was a bazaar where christian ladies sold things for double what they were worth, and never as a matter of course would give you back small change if any was coming to you, I have also noticed that with these religious undertakings they generally chose the brightet and most good look-

ing ladies to induce foolish young men to be more lavish with
their money on that account; they also threw tickets for watches
and then the fortunate one who threw the hightest number with
dice received it; I must say this seems to be a low way of making
money to build a house for God; they were also several
speeches made, one speaker reproved the French for coming to
the U. S.; towards the close a most beautiful young lady went
through all the crowd soliciting subscriptions for the church; it
was amusing to see how many young men by their manner gave
her to understand that they gave the money for her sake. Read
"History of our own times" by J. McCarthy, England may well
be proud of her orators, statesmen and heroes. 8th Sept., smoke
of brush fires so dense that we cannot see 5 ft ahead of them.
Houde's wells have dried up, he draws water from our streams.
The French Canadians are a very productive race; the clergy
encourage them to "increase and multiply" as it all adds to the
power of their church; in conversation at G's I discovered that
in our range, 12 miles long, with several hundred people on it
there is not a single Frenchman that cannot say he has never
been drunk; the government ought to legislate against this growing
evil. The English have routed the Afghan Insurgents; Gen.
Roberts is a clever general; Baroness Burdett Coutts is determined
to marry her secretary, Mr, Bartlett an American, against
the advice of the Queen and her friends; she is an old maid over
60 yrs., and worth several millions. Spent an evening at Meridith's;
from the top of their house (which commands a very extensive
view of the entire surrounding country) we saw the light
of bush fires in all directions, which illuminated the distant horizon
somewhat as sheet lightening does. Spoke with Mr. M. on
politics, he is a staunch conservative but agrees with me that no
Englishman should vote otherwise than the Liberal ticket in this
province, for in reality the Liberals are the Conservative party
and the so called conservatives, ultermontanes, or in other words
that party supported by the influence of the priests. Mrs. Harrison
was on a visit there; Mr. M. sang a German song with
Florence, after which Florence sang one in Italian; without doubt
she has a cultivated, sweet and powerful voice; Mrs. H. sang,
her voice has something strained about it, still I imagine she had

a fine voice in her younger days. Two train of thoughts occupied my mind that night before going to sleep, the first was, to sacrifice everything to mount the ladder of fame, to make that my aim and let nothing else divert me from it, the 2nd was, to pass through life in a peaceful quiet manner, or to use a prayer book term "be satisfied with that state into which it has pleased God to call me." Had an hrs. conversation with Mrs. H. next morning, she is a kind hearted lady, and exceedingly well read; it did not require long acquaintance to engage in friendly conversation in America, as is generally the way with ladies in England; she was an agreeable exception to that class of ladies who can converse on nothing else than the senseless gossip of society. On reaching the church was informed that bush fires were burning near our place; came home at full speed on horseback; 2 miles of country was literally covered with flames; at times I thought I would be suffocated, but got through at last and found the fire raging on both sides of the road quite close to our house; Tom with other men were on the roofs of the buildings with buckets of water wetting the roofs, and others were hauling water with teams, I started with a party with axes hoes and spades, and dug trenches in the earth to stop the advancing flames; the ground is so dry that the decayed vegetable matter on the surface is almost impossible to extinguish; Kirwin came from Aston with men to help us, he was very drunk but had just enough sense to be in great fear that the bark on his lots could be burnt; fortunately it rained towards morning which enabled us to take a rest; Clifford C. has gone to the exhibition at Montreal, the first time he has travelled in a rly, since he was an infant 20 yrs. ago; I also know of a young lady in Aston who has never seen a steamboat; went to the exhibition in Montreal, hotel prices are very high; bought a tweed suit at"the Boston one price clothing store" for $8.50, the dearest suit I ever bought for it only lasted 2 weeks wear; entrance fee to the exhibition is 25 cents; for a description of it I give a letter I wrote to Uncle Jerrold on my return. "Dear uncle. I have to apologise for not answering your kind letter sooner but I waited till Tom returned from Montreal, we both went to an exhibition held there during Sept. which was a success considering that there was one held at Toronto at the same time; I enclose in this letter a plan of the grounds; no. 1 is the road leading to Montreal; 2, the road to Mt. Royal; 3, road in front of exhibition grounds leading to St. Lawrance Main St; 4, restaurants, side shows and gambling dens; 5, cabstand, 6, board sidewalk in front of exhibition; 7 and 8 a fence 12 ft. high in the front of the grounds with 2 gates for foot passengers entering, and 2 for exit; 9, building with post-office, telegraph office and rooms for exhibition committees and secretaries; 10, an enclosure containing a captive baloon which made ascensions nearly every day; 11, refreshment tent; 12, a seat; 13, the right side of exhibition grounds with a shed running the whole length for cattle, some of which were thoroughbreds, also 2 wagon roads for entering the exhibits; 14, a ring for the inspection of cattle; 15, a watering place; 16, an open enclosure in which were cultivators, harrows, mowing machines, rakes, threshers, patent churns, in fact nearly all the modern appliances of agriculture; there was also an apparatus for making sugar by evaporation by steam in pans instead of over a fire in kettles as formerly; 17, a shed with a central passage through it which contained nothing but pigs of all sizes and breeds, some of which had a hideous appearance, so fat that their eyes could hardly be seen, but everything was perfectly neat and clean; 18, a restaurant at which a very fair meal of bread, meat and vegetables with coffee or tea could be had for 25cts.; 19, an exhibition of tombstones; 20, the building containing mechanical and manufacturing departments; 21, refreshment tents; 22, a restaurant, 50cts. a meal; 23, back part of exhibition, a wagon entrance in it and a shed running parallel with it, containing cattle and Shetland ponies; 24, railway platform; 25, Manitoba car containing its agricultural exhibits; 26, left side of exhibition with a shed similar to that on right side, containing mostly heavy draught horses with a few exhibits of thoroughbreds and racers; 27, a building filled with sleighs, carts, carriages, wagons, gigs, and almost every style of vehicle imaginable, also saddles and row boats, some finely built ones of cedar costing as low as $32; 28, the crystal palace, a curiosity in itself, having been built in 8 days, the 1st story had a large assortment of furs and fur clothing of every description, a large collection of pianos and organs with lady and gentlemen performers; soaps, confectionery, drugs and chemicals, all arranged with great taste; immense glass show cases with every make of biscuit imaginable, dry goods of all sorts, hardware, bells, saws and 100 other different hardware articles, also an altar and images of the R. C. church of such miserable workmanship that I believe were the great Grecian sculptors still living they would die of disgust. On the 2nd floor was an art department containing thousands of beautiful pictures and paintings, a department for sculpture, also photography, stationery, minerals, fancy work, stuffed animals, small machines such as sewing and knitting machines, &c., musical, brass and stringed instruments, also a department containing every style of ladies' and gentlemen's dresses, also hundreds of smaller exhibits too numerous to mention; but I need not give you a minute description for you have seen exhibitions in Great Britain that would make 3 of this; sufficient to say that it was a success and a credit to a colony of 4,000,000 inhabitants, but it is almost certain that ere another century passes the exhibits of Canada will equal if not surpass those of any European nation; 29, a fountain; 30, tents of newspaper reporters; 31, ice water; 32, first class restaurant; 33, Manitoba hall, in which I was surprised at the size of products that had been harvested 4 weeks before maturity. It seems strange to me that thousands of French Canadians emigrate annually to the U. S. when we have millions of acres of fertile land in our own country; the majority of the clergy also strongly condemn their leaving this country, but it is the high wages that tempt them across the border, also all their children can get employment in factories as young as 7 years. 34, ring for the inspection of horses; 35, a restaurant. The day the Governor General arrived there were 75,000 people in the grounds; minor news closes the letter. I regret now having come in so early as all the exhibits have not yet arrived. The flags of most nations are flying and liquor of all sorts flowing, and what with the hum of machinery, the banging of hammers, the neighing of horses and noise made by other animals, with the buz of human voices, renders it almost a second babel; a brass band plays constantly in the grand pavilion. Visited the

Witness printing establishment, it employs 120 hands; saw a monster Hoe printing press which turns out newspapers almost faster than they can be counted; paid 10cts. admission to the art association and saw thousands of beautiful paintings, water colors, etc. Have seen some good plays at the Academy of Music, the best theatre in Montreal. Went through the McGill college grounds, they are very beautiful, with green grass, shady walks, vine covered bowers and arches, summer houses, fountains, flower beds, etc., the college buildings are of stone and look very imposing on the side of the mountain. There are four different classes of seats in the Academy of Music, orchestra boxes on either side and overlooking the stage, $5 each; dress circle seats immediately in front of the stage, $1; general admission, 50cts., and "up amongst the gods," or in the "nigger heaven" as it is called in the U.S., 25cts.; for my part I prefer the general admission ticket, that is of course when not accompanied by a lady, as the seats are just the right distance from the stage to see the actors at an advantage and the seats are just as comfortably cushioned; the orchestra boxes are richly furnished, soft carpets, luxurious sofas and chairs and costly curtains that can be opened or closed at pleasure, and in them sat some of Montreal's richest citizens with their dignified and beautiful wives and daughters; up amongst the "gods" were chiefly college students, policemen, cabmen and laborers, and I am glad to say no women; there were no cushions here and saw dust was on the floors; all the seats in the theatre are like a semi-circular stairs, similar to those in a Roman amphitheater. After returning home I decided to return with Tom and a party of Aston friends to the exhibition; write this on board the cars "en route" for Montreal; between Aston and Preston the country is flat with very few clearances and much of the forest has been cut away and damaged by fire; crossed the Preston river on a bridge about 80 ft. above it; the country has a bare, barren appearance and has numerous small whitewashed houses. Preston has a small Episcopal church, a large R. C. one, and Morrison's large extract factory with a few saw mills forms the chief support of the village; flat uninteresting country covered with occasional clumps of poplar groves. Many passengers have to stand for want of seats; large tracts of land growing up in poplars; most dreary looking country between Preston and St. Leonard; are now passing through a district burnt black as cinder; after passing St. Leonard the country is more cleared and there are some fine, good-sized fields; fine farming country, but too flat to be picturesque; this part of the country once formed some of the best agricultural land in the Province, but the French have destroyed its productive powers by taking crop after crop, year after year without rotation of crops or manure, and the country which might have been made very beautiful looks about as uninteresting as one could imagine, with the monotonous similarity of its little whitewashed houses, large plain looking churches and its numerous whitewashed crosses with a jauntily painted cock on the top of it, how this bird can advance interests of christanity I cannot imagine unless it be to remind these devout christians of the base treachery their first infallible Pope, Peter, was guilty of to his Lord and Master; I have often heard lecturers and orators eloquently describe R. C. Churches as "Poems in Stone;" this, however, cannot be applied to the majority of R. C. Churches in Canada, especially in the country districts where the most of the churches resemble large stone or wooden barns with a steeple on one end of them and I can well imagine how much it would try the christian patience of the many saints of the past years if they could but see the horrible caricatures that the R. C. Churches exhibit of them in the country villages of Quebec. The greatest part of this country is cleared but the farmers show a want of taste by cutting away all the trees and not leaving or planting any on their farms which would greatly add to the beauty of the country; clearances grow less and second growth of poplar takes their place. The country from Aston to St. Jean is very level. Mr. Morrison, the best citizen Preston had, died yesterday; he was a true christian and a good man. Have reached cleared level country; no taste shown; the farms have been divided year after year till many of them are actually one acre wide and a mile long; the country has the appearance of being covered with numberless roads running parellel with each other. St. Jean is a very old town and has several convents and seminaries where the pliable minds of the rising generation are moulded and fashioned according to the will and pleasure of the tyrannical rulers of Roman Catholicism; the country about the town is somewhat more interesting as there is greater variety among the houses. The clearances now stretch away for miles on either side almost as far as the eye can reach; the cars shake so much that it is almost impossible to write pass several small stations that are surrounded by a few small whitewashed houses, a store and church. The country now begins to assume a finer aspect with groves, green fields, herds of cattle and flocks of sheep; passed a dried up river; it is the dryest season we have had for many years; now come in sight of Bethel mountain, which rises abruptly from the surrounding country and look very fine covered with trees which grow almost to its summit which is enshrouded in a beautiful mist of many colors and the sun shines brightly down upon it; pass through a small tract of second growth forest; cleared country again, its English settlers have left many beautiful pine and elm groves; arrived at St. Lawrent where Mr. Waldon has moved to as station agent from Aston, much to our regret as he was one of the most energetic church wardens of the English church, it is however a promotion for him. This is a very pretty village of tastely built stone and brick houses surrounded by a beautiful undulating country thro which the broad and placid current of the Bethel river flows, which forms a pleasing scene with the numerous little pleasure boats and steamers plying up and down its surface. The country between Montreal and Bethel river is flat with some nice groves here and there; cleared land can now be seen as far as the eye can reach with small herds of cattle grazing upon it in many places. The quality and smoothness of the surface of the country from St. Jean to Montreal ought to make it one of the best farming districts in the province; passed a small village, many farmers have stacks of fodder outside, many houses have chimnies built the whole height of the house at one end of it, a few of the houses are thatched; another small village; nearly all French villages are named after some Saint; passed the Victoria bridge, the largest tunnel bridge in the world, and entered Montreal the commercial metropolis of Canada; passed thro a manufacturing portion of the town and reached

Bonaventure depot, a very unsightly depot for a city of 150,000. Our party of Aston young men decided to economize and went to a cheap lodging house where for a large room with 6 beds in it we paid $5 for 3 nights. We were all pleased with Lotta's acting but were disappointed with the play entitled 40 days around the world. We take our meals at a 15 cent restaurant, meat, vegetables, coffee, bread and butter, all neatly served and of good quality for 15 cents. I cannot see how they make it pay even tho they are well patronized as many as 50 dining at the same time. Saw the torpedo experiments in the harbor which blew an old ship over 100 ft. high out of the water. The price for tin type photos in Montreal is 12½ cts. Had a glorious view of the surrounding country and Montreal from the observatory on Mount Royal through some powerful opera glasses; saw the illuminations on Dominion square, which were of all sorts of fanciful and fantastic devices, hundreds of rockets and fire baloons ascended in the air, some of the latter so high as to almost look like stars. Tom has gone to Charlesburg on a visit to Mr. and Mrs. Bentley. On my return I found that Timothy Somerset, father's hired boy whom we had left in charge of our place had deserted it and returned to father's; I thought it very inconsiderate of father to allow him to do so. I replaced some decayed planks in the stable floor and made a gate for the entrance leading to our house, also made picket and rail fence in front of our farm; we are having very bad weather; in the evenings read Rollin's Ancient History. Louis Brodeur came to dig the potatoes, but found them such a poor crop that he asked me to release him from his contract, which I of course did, as the crop is worthless through no negligence of his; we will dig the best of them ourselves and leave the rest in the ground; Dined at G's. on Sunday; they live better than they used to; have pastry, different sorts of meat, etc., more frequently. If abstaining from meat is rewarded in another world, Tom and I will have a great many marks to our credit as we have scarcely tasted it all summer, our diet consisting almost altogether of bread and milk; no, I take back that remark, we will derive no credit for it, for we do not believe that a Great Creator takes any pleasure in seeing his children abstain from a moderate use of good and wholesome food. I played croquet with Ethel; she seemed to have less of that grave sedateness that usually characterizes her manners. Had a lengthy discussion with father on the condition of ancient people and those of the present day; I said that the ancient Greeks and Romans although Pagans, were in many respects; nobler and more civilized nations than among the nations who are guided and instructed by the infallible R. C. church of the present day. Received a letter from Jonathan Goldsmith, who 4 yrs. ago worked on his father's farm; he is now a doctor in Benton, Iowa, has bought out his brother's practice, who has moved to Galena. Have hired father to teach the English school for 2 months for $20, and Miss Guertin a French Protestant to teach in another part of the school district for 4 months at $12 a month, and Florence Meredith to teach for 2 months at their house for 20; this division was necessary on account of the dissentient scholars being so scattered. Have bought lot 19, next Uncle Herbert for $800, payable in 4 yrs., have named it "Oak Hill;" trappers in early times gave it that name on account of a majestic grove of oaks that grow on a hill that commands a very magnificent view of the surrounding country; about 80 acres of this 200 acre lot are cleared and contain a fine orchard of 80 trees, and a very nice house and barn; it is one of the most beautifully situated farms in this part of the country, the clearance having in it numerous fine groves of butternut, cherry and maple; 50 acres are covered with a large sugar bush of maples, averaging 50 to 90 ft. high, and the pastures abound with springs of clear ice cold water; the back of the lot is covered with valuable hardwood and softwood woodland; the distant view from the summit of the hill is exceedingly picturesque and beautiful; to the south-west is Richford, with its glittering steeple and sparkling river; in the distance are the summits of Mounts Bethel, Royal, St. Peter and other mountains; to the west lies Aston village, and several smaller ones; to the south-east are seen the towns of Melford and Rawlings and the hilly country which surrounds them, on which herds of cattle can be seen with the aid of an opera glass, between the hill and them, lies a valley in primeval forest with clearances interspersed in it; to the north-east the view extends over primeval forest to the villages of Dudley and Davenport with the cleared land in their vicinity; the chief draw back is that year after year crops have been taken from this once fertile soil till nature refused any longer to repay a thriftless farmer's toil, but it has lain idle for a few years and has recuperated some of its former fertility. Mr. St. George, the agent for it, reserved the right to the original owners of half the profits from any mineral that might be discovered on it, also the right of first mortgage till the place was paid for; the deed of sale cost $5, which I had to pay. Rev. L. C. W. complimented me on my enterprise and said he hoped to see me a wealthy farmer yet; showed him a letter to the Montreal paper that I had written condemning the system of Catholic education in the Province, and found that his sentiments coincided with my own. Met Miss Kate Watts, who told me that she had been introduced to Tom at Mr. Bartley's. I was mnch disgusted last week in reading a Protestant newspaper, *The Christian Weekly*; which says of a picture of Christ by Gustave Dore: "the face, the crown of thorns, the bleeding brow, satisfied the ideal even better than that of Guido's Christ, which is so universally admitted to be the nearest approach to it." What nonsense, to say that it is the nearest approach to it when it is well known that no reliable picture of Christ descended to this age, nor is it at all likely that humble and great philanthropist ever went to the expense of having a portrait of himself painted, and I know that a Protestant editor is too much a man of intelligence to believe as the French Catholics here do, that "when the Virgin wiped his face with a handkerchief the portrait of his face was miraculously left upon it;" and what also appears more absurd to me is, that although I have seen hundreds of Christ's pictures, the great majority of them have but little resemblance to each other. Went to the Guy family entertainment in Aston Town Hall; the scenery and acting was very good; there was a skillful violinist who with his violin imitated a cock crowing, a door on rusty hinges, and 2 pigs trying to pass under a gate; there were also athletic performers who exhibited extraordinary strength and agility. At present we are chopping cordwood for Roussin on our own lots, on land we intend to clear, at 75cts. a cord. Louis Brodeur's wife has a mournful expression on her face of late, as her husband is becoming an inveterate drunkard; truly from the beggar to the king, all men have their sorrows and difficulties to contend with; what strange beings men are, some have boundless ambition, but not a proportionate amount of talents, and like baloons of weak material, their ambition drives them so high that they burst and fall down in ruin; others have great talents, but have no energy or ambition to make use of them, and others appear to be totally indifferent through ignorance and the influence of evil associations to all that is beautiful and good. In a letter from Clifford he says; "I and Richard were at the exhibition and stopped at our uncle's Dr. Steeles house; all our crops were very good except the potatoes, those were too dry for roots; our fall ploughing is nearly finished; have sold our sheep, they destroy and unfit pasture for cattle; there has been fine weather for some time past, but it has now turned wet; our new barn and stable are nearly finished." Houde's have moved to "the White river," a tract of land situated in the center of the triangle formed by Aston, Preston and Richford; in one day they moved away; a French Canadian can almost leave his place of residence as quick as an Arab can; thus we have only Andre La Rivere as neighbors now; Moise La Rivere having moved away some time ago, losing all the improvements he made on his farm, their wives used always to be quarrelling. Gave G's cedar timber to make shingles from, for the new barn they have built; they have no cedar on their lot which is nearly all high land and under hardwood. Our old homestead has lost the neat appearance it used to have when our dear mother was alive, though it was in the backwoods, everything indicated taste and refinement during her life, and best of all, her loving, gentle spirit had an elevating influence on us all, the whole community has deteriorated since her death. Read a letter for Joe Vincent's wife from her sister-in-law—"My dear sister i rite you a few lines to no if you are in good helth as this leaves me at present. Sari an is getting on well he sends his love to you also metz sends his best complents to you all. Marie and osine send their best love to marie. I sends my love to you all; tell Joe, Metz says they must have a good spree together next time he comes here."

Miss Guertin gave up teaching the school, because some of the parents said she had no diploma; this however is unnecssary for a school that does not receive aid from the government, and I am confident her education was suffient to teach the scholars, some of whom are not out of the 2nd reader. Received a registered letter from Uncle Herbert notifying me to prepare material for a fence between his lots and mine; Uncle Richard thinks I have acted unwise in buying Oak Hill; told him that now I had decided to become a farmer I had determined to make it a success, also, that activity and enterprise were necessary in life, and that if we did not keep our energy and income fully employed we would be in danger of taking life too easy and spending our surplus money in unnecessary luxuries, whereas if we had obligations to meet, it would increase our thrift and energy; while at Meredith's one evening, talked on politics with Mr. M., and later in the evening on the exhibition church concerts and bazars to be held at Durham with Mrs. M.; Florence and Maud had an oyster supper before leaving. "My dear Tom and Arthur, I have understood from several friends here that hay is going to be very dear this winter, they are buying it here and shipping it to England, I write these few lines to put you on your guard, for buyers are going around buying the contents of barns; I have no news, Flora and baby are still with us; when I last heard from Uncle Jerrold they were all well; I have had letters from Richard and Clifford, they are both in good spirits, I think from Richard's letters that he is somewhat better, this damp weather is trying for weak lungs; the ground here is slightly covered with snow, with much love to you both, your affec. uncle, Richard I Goldsmith." Had a long discussion with Uncle H. and Auut M. on the many inconsistancies of many of the christian churches; two of their pigs died almost immediately after they were fed this evening, both exhibited the symptoms of poisoning, it is thought that some Paris green must have fallen accidentally into their food. Ethel, Phillip, Walter, Clifford C. and myself played cards, later on in the evening tried to organize a class for study for the purpose of perfecting our education; brought to their notice that nearly all the great men and women that the earth produced were educated, and in many instances self-educated, that we never could expect to make a success of life if we did not posess a thorough education, without which we could not associate with those people from whose society both pleasure and benefit is derived, who, instead of dragging a man down lower, as some society does, elevates and enobles him, developing all those good qualities that are necessary, to form a noble manhood and womanhood, that our first great difficulty would be, to exercise that amount of self-denial and discipline it required to enable us to say, I will devote every moment of my life to what I consider as useful and good, and will always be my earnest endeavor to avoid in thought, word or action, everything that my better sentiments tell me are useless, no matter how pleasing or harmless they may appear to be, if we once made this resolve and firmly adhered to it we would soon acquire a love for everything that is useful and beautiful, and studies and conversation, that we may now regard as uninteresting and tedious, would soon be considered by us as recreation and pleasure; that none of us could expect to become anything great or good without unceasing industry, and a perfect economization and proper use of every minute and moment of our existence on this earth, that there is enough precious time wasted on this earth to make every desert a garden of fruitfulness, and to banish all poverty, ignorance and misery, from the face of the earth; that it is our duty as rational beings to use all the means within our power to elevate ourselves aud our fellow-men to that glorious Godlike position that God ordained that every man should occupy on this earth, and which all men and women would occupy now if they made a proper use of the glorious gifts God has endowed them with; that we cannot justly offer such excuses as "have no time, or do not posess the proper opportunities as others;" this is not the real cause, in 9 cases out of 10 the real cause is, want of true ambition, energy and perseverance, how will these excuses defend young people who indulge in silly games and conversation when it would take 20 such lifetimes as theirs to acquire all the useful and elevating knowledge that now exists on this earth; that young men cannot expect to be much better than boors or clowns when they gaze vacantly into the fire in the evenings after their day's work, or waste their time in senseless chat, losing the splendid opportunities that the long Canadian winter evenings afford; the cost of the best educational works are so low that it places them in reach of all classes of society; that it is a disgrace to the present age, the manner in which even the members of the best society waste their time while their education is only superficial. We failed however to organize a class. Extract from lettrer to Clifford: "I offer as an excuse for my not writing sooner, our distance from the post; bad roads and extra work caused by the approach of winter, you can easily understand that to miss Saturday's mail causes a week's delay as we only go once a week to the village." 1st Nov. rose at 6, sharpened our axes; Vincent's called for our washing at Mr. V's request, gave him a French bible; cut a cord of wood each during the day. 2nd Nov; commenced working at a shanty for making saw logs that has been made on Houde's lot by Mr. J. Y. Morrisson, nephew of the Morrisson who died this fall, he owns a saw-mill at Preston, Mr. Baldwin, son-in-law of Mr. M. deceased, is manager of the mill and lumbering operations; he came to this country a poor lad and rose by degrees, married Mr. M's daughter, and is now a wealthy man. I get 75cts. a day and board; our usual bill of fare is pea soup, potatoes, green tea, bread and syrup; the men for cutting the logs are put in "gangs" of 3 in number, one to cut the butts and tops of the trees, and measure and mark the logs in 12 ft. lengths, the 2 others saw them. The walls inside of the shanty are filled up with berths above each other, with a little straw underneath, and our overcoats over us, form our complete sleeping outfit; when I say that 60 men sleep in a shanty 20 by 30 ft. with a fierce fire burning all night, the reader can imagine how close and warm it is. I have at the request of the son of the boss joined his gang at skidding logs; I find I am quite a favorite with all the men as I join them in their jokes, games and anecdotes. It is quite a sight to see the men kneeling at their morning and evening prayers with their eyes wide open; beads in hand, taking cognizance of everything that occurs around them, and even while on their knees will occasionally make some remark in the secular conversation and immediately after rising from their knees commence using indecent language and oaths, yet these men are not considered as reprobates by the holy church but are respectable members in good standing to my own personal knowledge; in evening conversation some of the men began speaking of Protestantism and said that Protestants "were the servants of the Devil." Eat our dinner in the woods when we are far away from the shanty; I was surprised how much frozen pork and bread I could eat at noon; hard work and exposure to cold requires solid and substantial food. 3th Nov. raining hard, we all asked the boss for a task to have our day count; he gave each team and 4 men 50 logs to skid; the boss also gives out small contracts for cutting logs at $5 per 100; the boss has decided that 2 men is sufficient to roll the logs on to the rollways; because I dulled my axe and took an hour to sharpen it the boss wanted to deduct ¼ of a day, so I left and commenced plowing at Oak Hill; had an argument with Murphy at Langevin's, his neighbor, who is a liberal in politics; the argument came to a close at 12 by Langevin saying that a freemason could be a good Catholic, at which Murphy put his fingers in his ears saying that's enough! that's enough! Made a plowing bee and plowed several acres on Oak Hill. Told Florence that we could only keep the school open 2 months as the funds of the school had been much diminished on account of several dissentient rate payers having sold their land to R. C's; said it was immaterial to her. Mrs. M. asked me to a party on Dec. 1; have been plowing on Oak Hill with our oxen of late, but snow prevents further work. Mrs. Mortemain who has charge of Norfolk Distributing Home came to see Jerrold; she visits all the Home boys to see that they are well treated. Went to Meredith's, played whist with Florence, Mrs. M. and Maud, Florence also favored us with music and singing. Tom has sold the two colts to Mr. Baldwin, one nearly a yr and the other 5 months for $60. 20th Nov. heavy snow storm; read history; Persians, Egyptians and Carthagenians are far inferior to the ancient Greeks in civilization and virtue. Extract from a letter to Clifford on war: all lovers of virtue, liberty and progress should use their influence towards encouraging the civilized nations of the earth to abolish war and adopt the more humane and civilized method of arbitration. If even 3 of the most civilized nations declared that war must cease their influence and power would be sufficient to prevent all civilized nations from going to war and eventually induce all civilized nations to disband their armies and have only a police force to preserve the peace among the lawless portion of its citizens; this would save the civilized world millions of money annually as well as put to nobler use the energies and talents of millions of men; the great difficulty to suppress war is to get a few of the most powerful and civilized nations to make an earnest effort for that purpose, this done the object is more than half accomplished, yet it should not be difficult to suppress war among the christian nations, for it is in direct contradiction to their religion as well as to the better sentiments of humanity. It is a great inconsistency to allow nations to murder thousands of men wholesale and not to allow individuals to do it in retail, who are punished with death for what in many instances may justly be termed retail war, even though they had great provocation; yet nations are allowed to waste millions of money and murder millions of men for the most trifling of causes. The cost of actual war is not the greatest but that of keeping large standing armies, some nations keeping ½ a million men in a state of idleness which heavily taxes the remaining citizens to suppoat them, also the loss war always causes when it passes through a land, cities are burnt, the harvests are spoiled and the nations wealth wasted by war's turmoil. There have been enough proofs however of its cruelty and destructiveness in the history of the world to leave only one argument for it that is "that it is a cruel necessity that cannot be done away with," a senseless argument at best, as there has never been a real effort made to accomplish it, therefore until a great many attempts are made and are failures, then and then only will the "cruel necessity" argument have an appearance of truth in it. If the nations can have international postal regulations and laws for the pursuit of criminals from one country into another; why cannot civilized nations abolish war as slavery and many other cruelties have been abolished. It simply needs one united earnest effort of a few of the most civilized nations to remove from the civilized world this error and disgrace of the age we live in. The certainty of the great increase of happiness and prosperity of nations thro the blessings of peace should make all civilized nations unite and decide on some means of preventing the devastation and ruin caused by war in the civilized countries at least. While at Meredith's Florence gave me a letter to give to Maud at Rev. L. C. W's, but as I had several other engagements I forgot to do so, on arriving home enclosed it with the following note and had it posted by a neighbor. "Dear Miss Meredith, I apologize for my great negligence of yesterday evening in not giving to your sister the note you gave me; a mistake like this in commercial transactions might be overlooked but with a lady it is inexcusable; trusting however that you will accept this expression of my regret for my great forgetfulness I remain yours sincerely, A. N. Howard." I have again entered Morrison's shanty. Nicholas came out to see us, was surprised to see me working at the shanty; had a discussion with the clerk of the shanty who is a bigoted Catholic, one of those I saw that burned the bibles of a bible seller in Delage's store; it was on the temporal authority of the Pope; I argued that even a devout Catholic could not with justice advocate temporal power for the Pope; the clerk said Ferdinand of Spain gave the Pope a certain amount of Territory and what right had the Italians to take it from him, I replied Ferdinand could not give what did not belong to him, kings, emperors and princes only rule "by the consent of the people" and have no power to transfer their authority to another unless it receives the sanction of the people, but allow for arguments sake the Italian people consented to this transfer it only gave the Pope power to rule as long as his government pleased the people or at least the majority of them, the moment the majority thought his temporal rule injurious to the country they had a perfect right to take away his temporal authority; in barbarous ages it might have been different when people were fools enough to believe kings reigned by divine right but in this enlightened age monarchs can only reign by the consent of the people. The Italians under the Popes were in a pitiable state of ignorance, superstition and vice and crime flourished throughout the land as is generally the case where liberty and liberal education have almost ceased to exist (Clerk) whose fault was this; it was the Pope's; all the schools excepting a few of the higher institutions of learning taught chiefly to the mass of the population how to repeat their catechism and prayers in the same manner as they now do in this province; even when Englishmen wanted to light Rome by gas the Pope would not permit it; is it to be wonderad that the people rebelled when they saw nearly all other nations ahead of them in prosperity and happiness, (Clerk) but it was not the Pope who prevented the progress of education, he has always encouraged it. How then is it that the inhabitants of protestant and infidel countries are more enlightened; prosperous and educated than those under catholicism, even the most partial Catholic has to acknowledge this, for the condition of the European and American protestant and catholic nations of the present day clearly make it "a self evident truth," but we need not leave Canada to see how much superior the republican form of spiritual government of protestantism is to the one man ecclesiastical government of Rome; compare protestant Ontario with Catholic Quebec and even you cannot deny that the protestants are better educated and more prosperous in Ontario than the French catholics of Quebec, (Clerk) are not the jesuits the best educated men in the world; not the best but one of the best educated class of men as are also the priests of your church, but this has nothing to do with the masses of the people and if catholics are well educated in Gt. Britain, Germany, France, the United States and a few other countries they are indebted to modern civilization and protestantism for it and not to their own church, but I have diverged from the subject of our discussion, which is did the Italians have a right to rebel against the temporal authority of the Pope. I claim that as the Pope did not govern them according to the wishes of the majority of the Italians the people had a perfect right to deprive him of his authority and establish another sovereign of their own choice; since they have done this Italy has begun to improve, schools are being established on a more liberal basis and the nation is rising rapidly in power and importance in Europe and will be no longer a bye word among nations as a people worthy of contempt for having fallen from being the greatest nation of the earth to one of the weakest and most contemptible. In the middle of Dec. I worked for Murphy with our oxen at skidding logs. Herbert C. seems to be in love with Margaret Guernsey; I am sure I do not admire his taste; in the first place the girl does not care for him besides she is an invalid subject to fits and is a plain uneducated girl. Went to a party at Meredith's on Nicholas's birthday, several Aston and Preston people were there, had an enjoyable evening; dancing, music and conversation; J. Murphy was staying at Brodeur's, but quarreled with Mrs. B. because he said she was ignorant in arithmetic— Eve's proud spirit rose within her. With haughty step she crossed the room; with anger in her hazel eyes, she on old John pronounced his doom. As I do not know how to count, you from my house can now depart, and live with those that better count; thus through your fault old friends must part. Worked a few weeks for Murphy; had a most disagreeable time skidding logs in frosty weather on low, swampy land for $2 a day for our oxen and myself, and have had since then a very bad cold. Murphy is greatly pleased with a speech of Mr. Bright of the English Parliament, he said: I am sure Ireland will get home rule and that the Queen will favor it. Could not convince him that the Queen had nothing whatever to do with it. Received circulars from G. Ghaffe of N. Y., about phonography, offering to sell a book for $2.10, or to give a primary course of instruction by mail for $10 or a 3 months course for $25; sent two beautiful Christmas cards to Florence and Maud, cost $5, also some nice ones to the Miss Grant's and Mabel W. G. boys say they do not care whether Richard or Clifford come on a visit here or not, because they never invite them to their place; they should remember that people must have passable manners at least to be invited into good society. Wrote to uncle Jerrold a long letter defending my purchase of Lot 29. People are very unwise to buy goods on credit, have discovered that there is $20 difference between our account at Delage's store and his one; storekeepers generally charge higher for each article when sold on credit which quickly mounts up. The English Liberals do not believe that England's interests require "the sick man" to be doctored to keep him alive. The Quebec government is going to give grants of phosphates to agricultural societies instead of money, which is a good idea. The Conservatives throughout Canada are jubilant over the success of their policy of protection, also the success of their premier sir J. Macdonald, in forming a company of mil-

lionaires in England and the U. S. for the construction of the
Canadian Pacific railway; it is to build the rly in 10 yrs and receives certain grants of land, portions of the road already constructed by the government and a bonus of money. Went with
a party of the shanty men into the French country to St. Leonard,
they bought several bottles of whiskey "pour nous rechauffer,"
or in English to keep us warm; reached the house of the boss
at 12 at night, his mother got up and gave us for supper bread,
milk and pork, a rather disagreeable mixture; slept with his son
Joseph on a buffalo robe on the floor. This is a strange country;
to-day I was in coarse overall clothes working with common laborers, to-night taking a drive through the country with our handsome sleigh, fine horses, silver mounted harness, a $60 fur overcoat
and a $200 gold watch, and I am now sleeping like a tramp on the
floor with a coat under my head for a pillow; such is life with its
ups and downs pleasures and vexations, happy is that man that can
accommodate himself to its many changes; this is a nice farm with
comfortable barn, stables and house all whitewashed as usual, but
very neat and clean; the farm is all cleared except a sugar bush; this
part of the country is all cleared except a small strip of woodland here and there reserved for fuel. St. Leonard is comprised
of only a church, a few houses and a store, all whitewashed,
church, houses, fences, well, poles etc.; went to mass with the
family; the priest, a clever and eloquent man, preached a very
argumentative sermon in defense of Romanism, almost thought
he had preached it specially for me; after mass the sons of the
boss attired themselves in the gayest of apparel and asked me if
'*vien tu avec nous pour avoir egard a les fille*," or in English,
'will you come with us and pay attention to the girls;" Of
course as they had five nice looking sisters I could not commit
such a breach of ettiquette as to leave them, although it would
have been more agreeable to me to have driven with the boys
10 or 12 miles, and seen some more of the country; one of
the sisters however rewarded me with her company the whole
of the afternoon and evening, even though 12 or 13 young beaus
came from the surrounding country, I am afraid however that
she thought I was dull and uninteresting, for although I tried
my "level best" to make my conversation as interesting as pos-

sible, it is utterly beyond my conversational powers to confine my conversation for 6 long hours to endearing sentences and sentimental flattery, the reader can well imagine the predicament I was in, sitting there by that girl with 3 or 4 young men doing their utmost to make me "eat oats" or in other words, have her leave me and go and converse with one of them; and what added to the awkwardness of the situation, general conversation is not considered polite, each beau must confine his attention and conversation to "his own girl." If it had not been for the experience and knowledge of French customs and manners that I acquired from the Houde Girls, I believe I should have been driven to despair, and have left the house with some excuse and an apology. Spent Christmas day partly at father's and Uncle Herbert's; I begin to think that Uncle Herbert's love for us is not very great; he wrote to uncle in England saying that we had sold rails to Meredith's at ½ price, which had not one word of truth in it, for we cleared $20 profit on the rails we sold them; paid Guertin what we were owing him, he is the most obliging and kind-hearted Frenchman I ever met, and in justice I must also say, one of the most devout Catholics. Uncle Richard's supposition that hay would be dear is incorrect, as it only sells for $5 per 100 bushels of 15 lbs. Visited Mr. Dolliver, an honest, genial old farmer, the family consisting of brothers, sons, nephews and uncles, forms a compact and neat little settlement of 20 families, all of the same name, who support a neat little Episcopal church of their own. I pay the village barber 50cts. a month for hair cutting and shaving; I often feel that if I could only act according to the better sentiments of my nature, how much better and truly happier I should be. Jan. 18th '81. "My dear Tom and Arthur; immediately after receiving your letters I had your buildings insured for $1000, cost $10 for 3 yrs. Our new barn at the "Elms" when finished will have a stabling capacity for 80 head of cattle; the building cost an unusual price as there was not enough water in the rivers, and for what little spruce and hemlock lumber the millmen had, they charged $10 per 1000 ft.; the day is not far distant when spruce or hemlock will be worth $20 per 1000 ft. at your place; must now close this note; love from your aunt and cousins to you both; your affec. uncle; R.

S. Goldsmith." The Elms, "My dear Arthur, we have bought 5 tons hay at $7 a ton, and hardwood stovewood at $2 a cord; the best quality of horse hay is $1 a ton higher; lately there has been a great many auctions around here, but the things are sold at full value, as the friends of the seller buy them in when enough is not bid for them; I was sorry to hear that you had bought Oak Hill, as you will be likely to have trouble with the G's; we have had our stables whitewashed inside, as it makes it lighter and destroys vermin; we have had the barn-yard fenced to have a place for the cattle to sun themselves in, without going astray; with love from Richard and myself, I am your ever loving cousin, C. H. Goldsmith." Montreal, 6th Nov; "my dear Tom and Arthur, in reply to yours of the 30th I herewith enclose you $42, and have given you credit for the $6 you sent me for insurance, and the $24 on the account you owe me, which is now only $34, I should have asked one of you into town this quarter, but Flora, her nurse and baby, with the houseful of other guests are with us and there are no spare bedrooms at present, but I shall expect both of you in on a visit at Christmas; I was sorry to hear that you had bought lot 29, you are crowding a heavy burden on your shoulders, I expressed my opinion fully and freely on a former occasion, on the subject of buying more land; lot 29 was the most objectionable lot you could have bought, for the simple reason, that a week after you take possession, your Uncle Herbert and family will quarrel with you; take my advice, throw this burden off your shoulders as quickly as you can; had you got it for nothing it would have been an injury to you; you have more land in your lots than you will ever require; your affec. uncle, R. I. Goldsmith." If I am to be eternally dictated to in this way, even though it is by kind and loving uncles; I shall be obliged to go out into the world alone; I can use my own judgment and be dependant on no one. London. "My dear Arthur; I received your letter in the *Weekly Star* on the system of education in Quebec; do not be angry with me when I tell you that you never can be a successful writer; I thought you had passed that infant age when every young donkey fancies himself a poet or an author, or destined to do great things, the moon fit generally lasts up to the age of 14, but seldom does the dominion of donkeydom bother a man at your time of life; millions of letters have been written on the same subject, but a more common place, childish, drivelling letter I never saw, if I were not your friend it would be much wiser on my part to say nothing against your letter, for it is human nature to have bitter feelings against anyone that upsets the hobby of another, but I have done my duty and told you the naked truth, however disagreeable; I hope the land you have bought will not with your other farm be too much for you both, although a great bargain; however as you have bought it, stick to it, and let the world see that you have not made a foolish transaction, which I trust and hope you never will so far as poor human vanity can go, still I must say I have every confidence in your manly good sense, perseverence and steadiness, and I believe the many prayers of your dear mother's loving heart, will and have been heard, and that you will be good and happy; with much love to you both, your loving uncle, Jerrold B. Goldsmith." He does, I must say play havoc with my essay on education, but I shall yet show him that I will, and shall be a successful writer, I am glad at all events that he is favorably disposed to my purchase of Oak Hill, if I can only bring Uncle Richard to reason about it, I will work early and late to make it the finest estate in these parts. In a letter from Uncle Jerrold to Uncle Richard he says, "if I could get a large tract of land bye and bye I would purchase it. It is very unfortunate of me, not to have invested my money in gas shares, during the scare or panic on the discovery of the electric light, they have risen 33 per ct. since then; possibly electricity might some day supersede gas; but I do not see why electricity may not be applied to gas in its present form, and so increase its illuminating power; I suppose the Howard boys' father does not interfere with them now; in a letter to Tom and I he says, "we have had potatoes exhibited here (larger than your body) from Southern America, but there are drawbacks in these countries; the atmosphere is overcharged with electricity, human life is much shorter, the human passions are violent, and life is every way unsafe; on my fields I should prefer the small and more numerous vegetables which are more life- nourishing and wholesome than the big and less abundant ones of a more enervating climate; God has given to every part of the world, blessings in different forms, in Canada you have long cold winters, but a clear invigorating air which produces vigorous nerves, and strong limbs with a clear complexion; I would rather live in that Canada of yours than to be a dried up, cynical profane Yankee with his shrivelled belly, yellow skin and nose-trumpet slang, too often giving to the world, utterances offensive and immoral; you write sensibly and truly on the condition of Ireland. On what part of the map can you find "no man's land?" Ans.: in Ireland with the Irish." What's mine is my own, but what's yours is everybody's else; what confusion there is in Ireland, first landlord's, then farmers, then tillers, and last of all a class of thieves and cut-throats. Waterford, Nov., 1880. "Dear Arthur; your long and interesting letter arrived, and was not less welcome for being very unexpected, Tom and you seem to have had a hard struggle at first on your land, but you appear to have succeeded well, I should like to go and see you, but I never expect to have that pleasure as I have not been in good health for the last few yrs.; I was very sorry to hear of the death of your mother, I had reason to know what a terrible loss it must have been to you, it is no wonder that you who had no opportunity of studying Irish affairs should think some of the demands made by the Irish people to be unjust, even many people who have lived all their lives in Ireland have not been able to agree about the Irish land question, let alone Home Rule, with regard to the land, it seems to me that the Irish farmers have from generation to generation done nearly all that has been done towards reclaiming the land from a state of bog and forest to its present state, and have built most of the barns, houses and fences on it; the present sevants, representing both themselves and their ancestors have a large claim to a great part, perhaps nearly half of the present value of the land, yet they have almost no legal claim, and this is what causes the bitterness of feeling between landlords and their sevants, feeling that in many cases they have been legally robbed of their life's labor by unprincipled landlords raising their rent; I agree with you that there is not much use trying to fix rents by laws; what I desire to see is, the same thing that was done in Prussia 70 yrs. ago with most satisfactory results; the

Prussian Government took up the estates of the large landlords giving the owners bonds for the full value of their land and allowed the servants to buy the farms, paying the price to the government in yearly instalments, so that now Prussia is a country of contented pleasant proprietors, and Gt. Britain and Ireland are almost th. only European countries in which almost all the farmers do not posess their land; France is another country that has been greatly benefited by the conversion of sevant farmers into proprietors of the land they cultivate. Elmbrooke 15th November '80. Dear uncle; yours recd. last Saturday, with quarterly allowance enclosed; some time after Christmas; either Tom or myself will be able to accept your kind invitation. I regret that the purchase of Oak Hill is against your wishes, and I suppose I shall have to dispose of it if you so decide; we have rented one of the sugar bushes on it for 50 lbs. of sugar, and the man has "to rig the bush himself;" there has been small snowfalls last week, but they have disappeared as quickly as they came; extracted from the guide book of Montreal in a condensed form for the information of the reader, "Montreal derives its name from Mount Royal, the name given to a mountain in its vicinity, by Jaqu Cartier, (on his visit to the town of Hochelaga, situated at the base of the mountain) in 1535; it is situated on an island formed by the confluence of the Ottawa and St. Lawrence rivers; in 1628 it only consisted of 3 or 4 log houses; in 1642 Maisoneuve and his 40 associates planted the colony of Ville Marie de Montreal, to them belongs the honor of being the founders of this city of palaces; it was surrounded by hostile savages for 120 yrs. and struggled through the vicssitudes of floods, earthquake and war until 1747, when it was described as a city containing several churches; colleges, and houses of stone and wood neatly built, and surrounded by a high wall and ditch. In 1760 it, with the rest of French Territory fell into the hands of the English; the first newspaper established in Montreal was an English paper, named "the Gazette" in 1778. Its contemporary, "the Herald was first published in 1811; in 1801 two acts of parliament authorized the formation of a company to supply the city with water, and another act granted the petitions of the citizens to remove the fortifications; the first steamer that navigated the St. Lawrence was built by an Englishman, J Molson, in 1809,which was 2 yrs. after Fulton's successful efforts at steam navigation; Canada's first bank was the bank of Montreal, established by English-Canadians in 1817, with a capital of only a few hundred thousand, and it has increased to $12,000,000 in 1880; Montreal's streets were lighted for the first time in 1819; 2 years later the lachine canal was commenced; in 1850 a provincial exhibition was held; in '56 the grand trunk railway was opened for travel; in '60 the Prince of Wales opened formally Victoria bridge, one of the wonders of the world, being 9,000,000 ft. long; in 1760 its population numbered 3,000, in 1880, 150,000; the value of its imports in 1833 were valued at $5,160,000, in 1853, $16,000,000, and in 1873, $54,287,000; its imports in 1833 were $3,475,000, in 1873, $40,460,000; in 1833 it had 133 sea going vessels, in 1873, 720; it is noted for its excellent quays, which are built of limestone and forms a continuous display of masonry, unequalled on this continent; there are at present 5 lines of steamers plying between Montreal and Great Britain; Montreal was not incorporated until 1832; the largest theatre only seats 1200 people; its largest church 12,000, and is 255 ft. long and has 2 towers 220 ft. high, its bell weighs 29,400 lbs.; Christ's church is 187x70 ft. and its spire 224 ft.; some of the railways are G. T. R. R'y of Canada; South Eastern; Quebec, Montreal and Ottawa; Boston & Montreal Air line; Deleware and Hudson Canal R'y. Some of its markets cost over ¼ of a million dollars; the mills and water power in its vicinity give employment to over 10,000 persons; it has 3 telegraph companys; its street cars pass at intervals of 8 minutes. Letters that I rec'd in 1880 that I forgot to enter in their right places: "Grange, Waterford, Dec. '80. Dear Arthur, I send you and Tom the history of Ireland, by A. M. Sullivan, M. P.; I recommend you to skip the early part of Irish history and begin about 1000 A. D. Mr. S. as you will perceive is a Catholic, but I think he is very fair minded. Notice his remarks about Henry II, and the Roman invaders of Ireland, who got beyond his control and quarreled amongst themselves. Sullivan thinks Henry would have ruled Ireland well if he had time to attend to it. I see collections are being made for the Parnell defence fund in Canada.

A few days ago I attended a meeting where he spoke, 10,000 people were present, your cousin, truly, E. Howard." March, 1880; extract from letter from uncle Jerrold: "Since I heard of Arthur's mad army freak I thought it right to make enquiries and find that an officers pay is only 5s and 3d. for the first 3 years, and that he has to pay 5s. a day for his mess, and that no man can remain in a regiment under £200 a year. Army life is unhealthy shabby, monotonous, mean and subservient drudgery; in a table published, out of the whole British army only 3 have risen from the ranks to colonel; the pay of a colonel here is little more than what a good mechanic can earn. Arthur is not fitted for the army; the polished humbug and flattery of their artificial manners would not suit him; neither would the change of climate, damp beds, poor diet and close air suit his body; he would pine for his farm and freedom and forest and die." Extract from a letter from Uncle Richard: "Would you please try and get some contractor out your way to take a contract of building a barn on the Elms for us; the lowest bidder arouud here was $650. I expect to go out and see you shortly, Arthur can drive back to town with me; when I see you we shall have a long chat about farming prospects." Extract from letter from uncle Jerrold: "And the bright day will come soon when emperors and kings will cease to set men to cut each others throats and call it heroism. How is your uncle Herbert's daughter? Does she know how to make butter, cheese, and how to manage a dairy? Does she know how to manage a garden, how to make and mend clothes, cook food properly and keep accounts? If she does not know everyone of these things I shall not leave her a penny in my will." April, 1880. Dear Arthur: Yours in pencil received; Mr. Murphy who addressed it reduces me in the social scale, he calls me Mr. Goldsmith, putting aside my right to M. D. Mr. is only used to address servants or very humble individuals, we are all esquires now a days. In the U. S. they have a good plan of putting the name alone without any appendages. I do not care how I am addressed, but some people are very sensitive on this head. I trust you will be able to hire young Murphy for us as we like him very well, he is a good, steady fellow. Our neighbor, McLaren, will not have his line surveyed, will not take a notice and will not allow the surveyor to run the line; this will put us to the trouble of getting an order from the court. There is a good deal of trouble in this world." From uncle Jerrold: "If you have anything to do with your father in business transactions, you are forever ruined, both in comfort and prosperity; he is one of these unfortunate and unlucky men that drags everyone down that has anything to do with him; so surely as you let him get his little finger in your affairs he will worry you to death. I have no personal enmity against this unsettled and unmanageable man, but I should regret to see you involved in the discomfort and hardships your mother suffered Never of course see him in want of the comforts of life, but if you enter into any agreement or have any dealings with him whatever, I shall only say good bye to all, and you may say good bye all happiness and prosperity. If he makes any proposals to you, just listen to him, but make no decided answer but let him go on until he starts something fresh, and so on." Horton House, Salford, England, Feb. 1880. "Dear Arthur: It was such a pleasure to hear from you, for though I am constantly hearing of you and Tom from them all at home, still it is a greater satisfaction to get a letter from yourself sometimes. How improved your farm must be; Mama says she wishes it was near the Elms so that they might see more of you. You must be surprised to see Richard and Clifford hard at work on their farms after seeing them play at farming with you, I suppose that none of you are busy yet, but our land is being prepared already though it is only the 10th of Feb.; we are having quite mild, spring like weather; our baby is such a pretty little creature and Constance is delighted to have a sister; she will be baptized, Angelica Theodora; would not your dear mother have liked the names; I feel our children have had a great loss in her removal, for she would have prayed for them. I always think of you, especially in that prayer in the morning service, "And make thy chosen people joyful." I trust you and Tom are filled with joy at Christ's love for you. We are going to a drawing-room meeting to hear an account of the American church in Asia Minor. It is interesting to hear about christians in all parts of the world.

Timothy is very fond of travels and has made such a correct map of the latest explorations in Asia. Hoping to hear soon from you, and with Timothy's love and mine, I remain your affectionate cousin, Angelica E. Fothergill." Letter from a former neighbor, Ned Blake, to father: Chohdoes Falls, N. Y. Mr. Howard, my dear friend i sit down to rite you there few lines hoping to find you in good health as it leaves me at present, we are all well and the children is all well and we got two of them working in the factory and last pay day my oldest boy got $8; we got here all well and like the place well enough so far and I have been working for the farmers ever since. I came here and I got $1 a day, and write to me as soon as you get this letter and let me know how the folks is, and let me the news all about the plase i levt, and let me know how Dinnis Doherty getting along and let me know all the particulars about the farm I and please rite as soon as you can and rite a longer one and let me know all about the country and give my best respects to all who inquire for me and no more at present from your friend Mr. E. Blake. Don't forget to write soon now." "June 1880, Dear Tom and Arthur, you should have asked my consent before buying that land; I again strongly advise you to have nothing to do with it; never go into debt if possible, debt is the ruin of this country and the people in it, it drives thousands annually out of house and home, you are not land speculators, you have 400 acres of land which is ample, more than enough, devote all your energies to the improvement of that land, make it a good farm in every sense of the word; every cent you can spare for the next 10 years invest it on your land. That farm, if you continue as you have been doing, will make a fine estate for you in future years, that will be the pride of your eyes and the joy of your heart. You must bear in mind that farming is the most useful and honorable of all professions; there are scarcely any real farmers in this country, the majority are too ignorant and too conceited to be taught. After your place is improved you can sell it and move to another locality. But heretofore it has been all drudgery, now you are only on the threshold of farming and you will take more pleasure and interest in it every year; your land is better and stronger than anything around the Elms."

Elmbroke, Dec. 1880. "Dear Edmund: I have to apologize for not answering sooner your letter of the 12th inst. Was sorry to hear that your health is worse of late, but hope it will improve and that you will soon come and see us, as I believe the change of air would do you good. Aston, though not a fine or rich country, has at least, pure air and good water, the two greatest essentials for the health of man. Many thanks for the papers and pamphlets you so kindly sent us; I agree with you that landlordism is injurious to the prosperity of a country as is also the law of entail which is in a great measure the cause of large estates; there cannot be a single doubt that 10,000 acres can be better cultivated by a large number of small farmers who possessed their land than under the management of a single landlord; Belgium, France and other countries are clear proofs of this. The law of entail is the chief cause of the formation of two extreme classes of society, one extremely rich and the other extremely poor; this state of affairs should be discouraged by civilized governments, for the great wealth of the rich encourages them in unnecessary extravagance and the poverty of the poor keeps them in ignorance and misery, therefore it is the duty of all governments to make laws that give equal opportunities to all classes of its citizens, the English government is in many ways to blame for the poverty and discontent of many of its subjects in Gt. Britain as well as Ireland and especially for the trouble they have brought upon themselves in governing Ireland unwisely; they have in many ways been unjust to the Irish people, and no people can be expected to bear injustice without resistance and rebellion; the interests of the empire demand that better laws should be made in favor of the agricultural classes of the whole united kingdom, which would enable all classes of its subjects to possess the land they cultivated, for even tho the resources of the nation are great and many agriculture, and it alone is the backbone of its strength as well as that of all other nations. but at the same time all the world can clearly see that England will never dismember her grand empire or lose control of a single foot of her territory as long as she has power to keep it together; with the distant colonies she must of necessity give them Home Rule on account of the distance from the seat of government; with Ireland however it is entirely different, for centuries it has formed a part of the nation and to give it its independence would be to create a menance and source of danger in close proximity to the seat of government of the empire; all that Ireland can ever expect is to have the same privileges as all the other subjects of the united kingdom and an equal amount of representation in the British Parliament in proportion to their population as compared with the rest of the population of the united kingdom, and none of the nations of the earth can dare to remonstrate with England for doing so, for there is not a nation of the earth who has not acquired a portion of its territory by unjust conquest, and if all unjustly acquired territory had to be returned to the original owners it would throw the whole world into a terrible state of confusion, even this great and glorious United States would have to be dismembered and give back the brightest jewel in their possession New York to the Dutch, from whom it was unjustly taken by the use of main force by the English. I was surprised to see in an article in the *Nation* you sent me headed the burglaries iu France, as regards the expulsion of the jesuits why should that newspaper be indignant at this course of action of the French republic when even the infallible popes have in past yrs expelled the jesuits from Rome. If such men as Mr. Sullivan and the editor the *Nation* adorn their religion with falsehood's pride and praise their country beyond the limits of truth and moderation what might we expect from such men if their party once had absolute power; a glance at the earth's history on similar occasions gives us the correct answer; it is not such men as these or the language that they use will free the ish people; if the English are really so "tyrannical, cruel and unjust;" let the whole nation rebel for if their cause is just they surely ought to have a larger battle field than a cabbage garden. If their cause is just and they are as a people noble and courageous they must and will succeed, but if they hold vile doctrines of intolerance and think more of country heads than educating themselves, and take unfair advantages to shoot landlords from behind hedges, and praise the iniquitous doings of their church in former days, and declare that whoever willfully refuses to bow his neck to the slavery of their chuch, is lost; what better can they expect when they defend and praise the tyrannical Pope, who even blessed Phillip and encouraged him to try and take away from the spiritual revolutionists of England the liberty they had gained, and are guilty of as many inconsistancies if not more than those whom they style their oppressors; robbers that are robbed cannot be pitied; assassins that are assassinated deserve the same; tyrants ruled by tyrants deserve their fate,for if these tyrants ruled the other tyrants Ireland still would be in a sad state. No people can ever rise to an honorable position among the civilized nations of the earth, until they are a better educated people than thousands of the Irish are to day; their clergy ought to take this matter in hand, and have them taught a little practical and useful knowledge as well as the doctrines of their religion, which would prevent the humiliating disgrace of this intelligent and noble people, of seeing their countrymen becoming the political dupes of such political intriguers as John Kelly of New York, which brings upon this class of their countrymen the contempt of all respectable Americans. For some Irish agitators I have great respect, but for such men as Mr. S. and the editor of the *Nation* I have profound contempt, for these men have three parts of bigotry to one of patriotism, and seem to be perfectly incapable of speaking on national affairs without being influenced by religious fanaticism, and led by it to the greatest exaggeration. Mr. S. in the 18th chapter of his history says, "Wexford! Glorious Wexford! Now showed that one of Ireland's 32 counties could successfully engage more than one quarter of England's army; well and bravely Wexford fought that fight; it was the wild rush to arms, of a tortured Peasantry unprepared, unorganized, unarmed." This statement condemns either Mr. S. or the Irish people to deserve the contempt of all truly honest and brave men; if the first, as a falsifier of his country's history; if the second, as a miserable people, full of internal dissensions unable to organize any united action against those that they consider as their country's oppressors, for if Mr. Sullivan's statements are true that "the unorganized Peasantry of one country could resist more than one quarter the army of Gt. Britain," England could not resist the united action of Ireland's 32 counties. I was also much amused at another portion in the same chapter where he says, "the Pope had been utterly misinformed and kept in the dark by Henry the 2nd." Now it appears to me that if a Pope can be deceived and fall into error in simple temporal affairs, that he cannot be infallible in spiritual things, which are so much more difficult and impossible for the finite mind of, even a Pope, to comprehend, also in the same chapter he says, "they are full of the most powerful invocations of the saints, and in all other particulars are exactly such prayers, and express such doctrines as are taught in the unchanged and unchangeable Catholic church." This false and absurd statement can only be received as truth by men who have been taught from earliest infancy that such is really the case, but never by men who carefully study both sides of a question and impartially use their judgment on it; a clever Catholic of ours defends Mr. S. in the following slippery manner by saying that, "Mr. S. only spoke in referance to the great dogmas of religion, and had no reference to the discipline of the church." If so he should have said, "as are taught in the Catholic church, whose dogmas are unchangable," but even supposing that this was his meaning, it still contains the same amount of falsehoods, for the dogma of "the immaculate conception of the virgin" did not exist in the church but has only been promulgated quite recently. The Canadian Pacific Rly. is in course of construction and will be completed by 1891; the Co. has recd. a bonus of $25,000,000 and 25,000,000 acres of land, many think the government has acted unwisely in granting such a large monoply to the Co. who are to own and work the road forever, and have power to run several lines to any part of the dominion; it has also the power to prevent the building of rival lines for several yrs.; there are advantages and disadvantages on both sides, but if the Co. acts at all justly it will be of great benefit to the country, as the great North-West will be opened up much sooner than if the government had to construct it; this, with the Panama Canal are the two great works now in progress in America. Business is briskening up, especially the lumber trade in this part of the country, there being as much as 5 shanties for making logs in the vicinity of our lots, but the snow is not yet deep enough for lumbering purposes; wishing you all many happy returns of the season, I remain, your affec. cousin, A. N. Howard." Extract from letter from Uncle Jerrold. "It appears to me that a great many Canadians emigrate to the United States; I see by the census that more emigrate from Canada to the U. S. than from England to Canada, but many of these are merely emigrants from England to the U. S., who pass through Canada; as far as I could see when I was in the United States there seemed to be more misery and poor creatures in New York City out of work than in London; I meet persons (who have come back) every day who give a bad account of the U. S.; the weather here is good and the harvest and crops a good average wheat and hay are good, both in England and Ireland, but I regret to say the potatoe disease has appeared in Ireland, and they expect a scarcity; this people are unfortunate because the lower class of people are an idle, thriftless, quarrelsome superstitious and dirty people, who are difficult to deal with, roving from one place to another and never set their minds on what is before them, but dreaming and planning something far oft and out of their reach: they will not pick up half-pence under their noses but look farther off for gold, and get nothing at last. The nasty humbug beggars are accusing every one in England of their misfortunes, all of their own making; the Yankees seem the only people that can manage to keep them in any decent order; out West they shoot down all men who are quarrelsome, yet the Irish are a curse even to the United States; still with all their bad habits I hold that the Irish are fast improving under English rule, through the country being over populated it is a hard struggle for life. Sir. W. Raleigh introduced a curse when he brought into Ireland the potatoe; it is an uncertain and perishable product, and cannot be used like corn in trade and barter. How sad it is that your cousin Richard is in such delicate health, I am afraid his passing as an M. D. in Montreal, New York and London was too much for him, but I trust his visit to Mexico will do him good. E, Howard sent me a pamphlet on the treatment of tried prisoners in Ireland; "during cold winter nights prisoners have had to lie down on the bare prison floors with only a rug that weighed four pounds as a covering." Dr. McDonnell says, "I found prisoners with cold extremities, shrunken features and chattering teeth." If such is the case the prison officials are cruel and unprincipled men. Hamburg, Germany, Nov. 1880. "Dear Friends: It is a long time since we heard from each other. Since I last wrote to you I have been married and am living here; I have started an export business and am doing well. How is it that neither of you have taken steps in the matrimonial line? I tell you a man does not know what life is till he is married, especially if he has a good and loving wife; I assure you nothing on earth would induce me to change back to my former life again. How are you getting along now? Drop me a note and let me know about your doings and your prospects. With pleasure I think back to the time that I lived at your old homestead, when your good mother was alive. I was then a boy and alone in the world; I shall always feel grateful for the kindness I received at your house; let us keep up a correspondence and always remain good friends. You have followed me through my meandering across the Continent of America, through England, Norway and Sweden, and back again to my native land; so I trust you do not want to drop me now. I am always glad to hear from you and your doings and you have my best wishes for your future prosperity; remember me kindly to all friends. Trusting to hear from you soon and that this will find you in good health, I remain, your sincere friend, Fritz Hogarth." We have beautiful singing in St. Mark's church at Aston, of the lady voices those of Mabel and Florence are the most cultivated and powerful. Have spent several pleasant evenings at Meredith's playing parlor croquet with Mabel, Florence and Maud, they are all charming young ladies; Maud has all the life and spirit of a school girl. Kirwin's lawyer, Limard, sent me a lawyer's letter informing me that Kirwin was about to enter an action against me for defamation of character for $500; the same afternoon I met the lawyer on the street, he said with a bland smile, Mr. Howard, do you not think you had better come to my office and try to make a compromise with Mr. Kirwin I replied, I have nothing to compromise with Mr. Kirwin. All I said in his store was: Mr. Kirwin you are fortunate in having such faithful clerks, if you can always have such good ones you will make your fortune some day yet. Our hired man had drawn some wood there and the clerks marked the amounts of each in a pass book as the man arrived, and when the settling day came, Kirwin wanted to pay for two loads less than the amount the clerk had marked down. But I must say, Mr. Limard, that I am exceeding sorry that times are so hard with you that you are reduced to take such a case as this in hand. He replied that I might have to be sorry for myself when I had the costs to pay. The affair, however, ended there and I firmly believe, to use a common term, that it was a "put up job." 29th Dec. Tom left with Metz Vincent for Chinton, 40 miles from here, where there are some rich English farmers, one especially, who ships several tons of maple sugar of his own make to the Eastern U. S. States annually; a few poor French Canadians live there who are mostly day laborers. Clifford C. has been drunk and fired off a revolver about a dozen times as he drove madly along the range; this is the first time an English resident has degraded himself so low; he has a bruised face and two black eyes through a fight he had with his drnnken French companions. New Years Day, 1881. Spent the day at G's and fathers; went to a church social in the evening at Mr. Hume's the station agent; we had the usual church social refreshments, sandwiches, cake and coffee; Florence sang some very amusing Scotch songs; the evening passed in pleasant conversation and music and closed with "God save the Queen," and "Auld Lang Syne." I never leave the beautiful and elevating society of Florence without having my heart filled with good and noble aspirations; may a Higher Power bless and preserve her from all the greater trials and sorrows of life, and enable me to be worthy of, at least, her friendship by using aright whatever talents I may possess for the benefit of myself and fellowmen. Tom returned next day from Chinton; he gives a horrible description of the manners and conversation of the French families he visited there; even though he is my brother and I have never had any reason to doubt his varacity, I could not believe that fathers and mothers would tolerate such conversation in their families were it not that I have seen the same in a lesser degree in this part of the country, Letter from uncle Jerrold in Feb. 1880, that I omitted to place in the journal of that year. "My Dear Arthur: If you could by any possibility become an officer

after many years of humiliation, your position would not be so
independent as that you hold to day. I must say I am greatly
disgusted at the wicked sentiments and diabolical trash in your
letter, where you talk the old rot and base cant of fools about
the glory of killing your fellow-creatures. There is no glory in
your yearning to fight for your country, at least at the present
moment in a time of peace; if the interests of your country required it in time of war it would be altogether different; I am
sorry to say there are too many young fools like you in this
country; take my advice, remain on your farm where you will
be more useful as a producer than as an exterminator in the
army. Let every cobbler stick to his own last. The man that
wearies of the work before him always thinks he can do something better; it is a sure sign he is fit for nothing. I have been
in the army myself and I shall never forget how I have been
humbled for want of money and also by the petty tyranny and
annoyances of those over me, even though I was well introduced
and a classical scholar. How I longed for some honest calling
to be rid of the swearing, ribald and senseless men about me.
If you want to be a hero obey God's commandments and pro
duce smiling fields; if you have the material of a hero in you
conquer the woodlands and wilderness you possess; there are
enough brutes of the hero stamp already—too many ready for
bloodshed and battle without another donkey to stain his hoofs;
much better to draw a cart and more pleasing to God and useful
to humanity than braying out ridiculous bombasts of war and
destruction. Alas! Poor Mr. H. was always hatching some
addled egg of this sort, some petty project out of the usual track
of sober business, and so he was always an unsuccessful,
troublesome, unhappy man, ever failing, always grumbling,
always dependent, and at last a burden on his wife, who had to
support him out of her income. Whatever you do I hope God
will keep and protect you, your loving uncle, J. B. Goldsmith.
What a happy position you both have now, honorable, peaceful
and innocent, and how useful to your country; every acre you
redeem is wealth and power added to the nation. If you are
called on to fight for your country I am sure you will do it, but
heaven forbid that you should ever long for a soldier's life as a

proffession or means of self glorification." Read a life of Napoleon, by a Catholic; it gave him great abuse and in a most absurd manner tried to show that his treatment of the Pope was rewarded by God with his downfall. Went to Melford with Philip and visited our friends there; in its immediate vicinity the country is beautifully hilly; in crossing the range of hills we had a superb view of the village of Melford and the town of Rawlings in the valley beneath, with the stately and placid river of St. David flowing between them. Went to the quarry, several miles distance, up hill all the way; they were the steepest hills I ever drove up. The process of quarrying and splitting the slates was interesting to see; there were cranes worked by an engine to hoist the slate out of the quarry which is over 200 ft. deep and 300 wide; I ascended on a load of slate out of the quarry, the wire cable was only 1 inch thick and vibrated unpleasantly as the basket swung over the yawning chasm, I felt how foolishly rash I had been when informed that 2 men had been killed and one disabled 3 weeks ago by the breaking of the cable; went to the cemetery and saw some fine monuments but thought at the time that the grandest monument of all is to deserve the gratitude and respect of future generations. Pine has been sold by some of our neighbors at 5 cts. a cubic foot or 25 cts. a standard for the cut (standing in the woods); I am getting more disgusted with the French girls around here; for vulgarity, lack of modesty and frivolty, I have never seen their equal; they may be refined and educated French women in the country districts of Canada, but as yet I have never seen one nor have I seen a French Canadian in the country villages and rural districts who would not use obscene language in the presence of his wife and sisters; some English and Americans are also addicted to this bad habit but I have always noticed that they showed their respect for the gentler sex by abstaining from it in their presence, not so with the French Canadians, fathers, brothers and lovers all freely indulge in obscene conversation and jokes without the slightest restraint in the presence of their mothers, sisters, sweethearts and wives. At a social at Meredith's I was greatly ashamed of the awkard manner of the G. boys, who did not know what to do with their hands and feet or take a proper part in the general conversation; all young men should be able to walk about, sit or stand in a drawing room with a perfect easy and unconscious grace and be able to converse and maintain an interesting conversation with ladies, old as well as young; of course there are hundreds of other accomplishments a young man should study and acquire but until he acquires these two he can never truly enjoy the society of ladies and gentlemen. Mr. Meredith has commenced a course of very interesting historical readings at the socials on early Canadian history. Extract from a letter wrote to Edmund in Oct. 1880. "It is actually 6 yrs since I last wrote to you, since then we lost our dear mother, the greatest loss a young man can have, a loss which nobody but himself can estimate, he never knows her real value till she is taken from him, and thus I feel if I ever become a good and useful member of society it will, next to a higher power, be all due to the beautiful example and wise instruction I received from my dear departed mother. If mothers only knew how much the civilization of future generations depended on their example and teaching they would soon fully appreciate the glorious duties they have to perform in the work of elevating and perfecting the human race by moulding, fashioning and encouraging the pliable and delicate minds of the rising generations to love and admire everything that long human experience has proved to mankind as useful and good, and to abhor everything that long experience has shown to be prejudicial to the interests of humanity; how much better and practical this would be than to teach the innocent creatures a lot of ridiculous prayers to saints and catechism composed of a number of imaginary doctrines; everlasting honor is due to all the christian churches for whatever good they have accomplished by teaching their good and beautiful moral laws and precepts, yet at the same time all intelligent men who study the present civilization of the human race come to the positive conclusion that christianity has only accomplished an atom (as it were) in the glorious work of perfecting the human species, and that the age is fast approaching when the most civilized portion of mankind will only teach their children the practical truths of this life and give to them such a perfect system of education that it will develop the physical and mental condition of the human species to the highest possible state of perfection. I can easily imagine how these noble women and men of future ages will look back with pity and contempt on the histories of most of the religious dupes of the present day and especially on the history of the devout catholics of this province who mumble long and useless prayers, waste precious time in keeping too many holy days and listen to the same monotonous latin service every Sunday and to long sermons on the worthless and imaginary doctrines of their church and actually are told to abstain from wholesome meat on Fridays and in Lent, but are allowed to drink poisonous whiskey and chew filthy tobacco, and their poor little children are in thousands of cases only taught to repeat long prayers and a useless catechism. Truly we can never expect our race to become noble beings through the teachings of churches that tolerate such a state of affairs. Some devout catholics have told me that there may be errors of discipline in their church, but that the dogmas (which are of more consequence) are perfect. Now I would like to know which is of the most importance to mankind, the practical self-evident truths of life, or the imaginary truths of the bogus dogmas that most religions have promulgated. I think that eventually all intelligent and unbiassed men will acknowledge that the essays written on hygiene have done more good for mankind than all the imaginary spiritul dogmas promulgated by the thousands of religions that have existed and do exist on this earth. I see by your letter that you are very patriotic, this is much to your credit as it is one of the noblest sentiments that ever actuated a man's heart; Ireland is certainly in a deplorable condition and in need of legislative measures to redress the grievances of the people, but I must also say that many of the demands of Irish politicians are simply absurd namely "that as the Irish people owned all Ireland once all the English should be dispossessed of what they have owned hundred of yrs; the government will however, in my opinion, eventually make laws in England as well as in Ireland unfavorable to the preservation of large estates; no government should allow to exist the law of entail, this of itself is the chief cause of all the large estates in Gt. Britain; it seems to me that strong drink, superstition and ignorance are greater enemies to Ireland than the English people; some Irish patriots ought to encourage education for without a liberal education they will never be able to gain complete liberty or preserve it when acquired. I was greatly interested in the book you sent me; all this author's works are favorites with young people, he is in fact the boys novel writer. I shall never forget how much I enjoyed reading "midshipman easy," small details close the letter; while at Meredith's pursuaded Mr. M. to let Florence teach the school as she will only have to teach her brothers and sisters and that it was the only means we had of keeping our school from falling into the hands of the R. C's. While conversing with Florence and Maud they told me that Mabel W. is teaching Aston school and that she only received $15 a month; said it was greatly to her credit also that this was an age in which most people considered it a disgrace to be mere consumers and give nothing in return in which they agreed reminding me of their father's maxim "from the kitchen to the piano." Extract from letter to Uncle Jerrold, "Does it not appear foolish to make young men study Latin and Greek before they are thoroughly instructed in their native language, and other studies of more consequence, especially when thousands of these young men that study these dead languages have no use for them in life; if there are fine, eloquent expressions in Latin or Greek let them be preserved with the languages for those that have the time and think it worth their time to study them, but not to oblige those who have other aims and views, and who wish to make the most of a short existance on our globe, but the opinions of individuals will not be of much avail, it is only when a large proportion of society adopt different opinions on this subject, then, and then only will this error in modern education cease; in the mean time young men have to submit to the laws of society which are absolute. The improvments on our farms are progressing, this yr. we have sold 2000 bushels of hay, and by February we will be clear of all debt, clear of all debt did I say, oh, no, we still have a debt, a debt we can never pay, 'tis to you dear uncle, a debt of gratitude, for you have always acted a father's part towards us, without asking any return, or imposing a single condition on us, therefore, dear uncle I trust that we may both be spared for many yrs., you to enjoy life and see the benefit caused by your bounteous hand and generous heart, and Tom and I to prove our gratitude by our earnest endeavors to become honorable and useful members of society, and when the dark periods of life appear, for this life is not all sunshine, for all men from the beggar to the king have their faults, difficulties and aspirations, true thoughts will help to sustain us with a dear good uncle and loving mother. In a letter from Clifford he says "can neither of you pay me a visit for a couple of weeks, it seems a long time since I saw either of you, we shall have a good time together." Extract from a letter from Uncle Richard, dated 18th Jan. '81. "Your Uncle Jerrold has censured me for "allowing Arthur to buy that lot" I told him I knew nothing about it, that the deed had been signed before I knew anything about it; he also asked for information, if it was true that Arthur sold rails to Meredith for half price." I told him that it was not so, some spiteful person must have written falsely to him about it; I regretted to hear that Arthur worked out by the day with your oxen; there should be no necessity for hiring yourselves out to any one, in doing so you lower yourselves very much. I do not agree with your Uncle Jerrold "that Arthur should keep the land" *I say get rid of it as quickly as possible*, if you keep it you will have trouble with your Uncle Herbert, besides you have sufficient land for your labor and capital. Richard is staying in town and goes out driving every day." On the 19 Jan. attended the birthday party of Florence and had a most enjoyable time; also attended a general missionary meeting at which 7 clergymen of different Protestant denominations spoke; while at a Church Social at Mr. Wheeler's, Dr. Bacon, Nicholas and myself conversed by ourselves about the Arlington scandal, he is secretary, and treasurer for the muncipality, and has been guilty of conduct that has brought shame on his wife and children; a dressmaker of this village has sued him and brought his name before the courts; his wife is nearly broken-hearted; they belonged to a very small but select circle of the best French society in the parish, and he also holds a lucrative position as inspector of schools; strange to say that every secretary of Aston muncipality, 4 in number, have absconded during the last 25 yrs., and that one has fallen into a worse disgrace. Montreal, 2nd. Feb. "Dear Tom and Arthur; we shall be happy to see either of you at your earliest convenience, we had a letter from Clifford, who would like very much to have one of you go and see him; I should like one of you to visit Clifford; we have plenty of room in our house now as we have no visitors; poor Richard is very low, it gives him hard work to get up stairs." Five days later he writes, "I enclose you your quarterly allowance, was glad Tom went to see poor Clifford, poor fellow, he must have been lonely out on the farm alone; Richard is very weak, his strength is decreasing. We have had a great deal of trouble heating our house this winter, sometimes too hot, sometimes too cold, also much annoyance with our servants." Extract from letter from Clifford; Feb. 17th. "Tom and I were to the poultry show at Sherman; there was the best selection of poultry I have ever seen; Tom will return on Tuesday; you will of course be charmed to hear that I accompany him; the weather has been very pleasant." Horton House, Abbeydale, Salford England. "My dear Arthur, I enjoyed your last long letter, and wonder I have not answered it sooner; I write now especially to wish you and Tom a happy New Year; I was surprised at your not being quite satisfied with your farm life, for certainly the want of congenial society is a serious drawback, but still it will be possible for you to remove, and I suppose your land is increasing every yr. in value; your cousin Rupert also wished to enter the army, but he is too old; he has been staying with us lately, after taking his degree at Oxford; he is going to become a barrister; I was pleased to see how strong and muscular he looked, all the students at Oxford take plenty of exercise. The governor of the university made the students make a road down to the river; he said they were taking a great deal of useless exercise, and that they ought to turn their energy to some account. We have had some bitterly cold weather, but are enjoying a thaw now; it came just in time to prevent a water famine in London, for it was feared the main pipe would soon freeze, which it did at Plymouth, causing a great deal of inconvenience. How do you like Rev. L.W,s. 2nd wife? I suppose his little daughter is quite grown up now; do you ever go to hear Cannon Baldwin preach when you go to Montreal? I remember my dearest Aunt Sarah used often to attend his services and Bible readings, and liked his evangelical preaching so much; it is well to be stirred up and kept in remembrance of spiritual things by some earnest fellow Christian. I wish you could see your sweet little cousins, Constance and Dora, they are sweet, fine childran; Timothy joins me in love to you both, and I remain, your affec. cousin, Angelica E. Fothergill." I sent a valentine to Florence. While attending the service at St. Mark's Church it seemed to me very inconsistent of its members to all reply when the minister read "Thou shalt love thy neighbor as thyself," "Lord have mercy upon us and incline our hearts to keep thy law." Many of them have been saying this for the last 15 yrs. and yet they have never made the slightest effort to be of any benefit to the large masses of ignorant and superstitious people about them; and what is worse, by their indifferent, lukewarm, half-hearted religion, bring dishonor on the church to which they belong. Extract from an essay I read at a church social: "I feel confident that you are all interested in the great advance education has made, and is making every day towards that period in our earth's history, when those who are in ignorance still remain, will have no one but themselves to blame. No eloquence can convince the world of the benefit of liberal education better than the world's progress in wealth, inventions and commerce since the reformation; since which period a better and more liberal system of education has been adopted. The world's remarkable progress in civilization since Luther's reformation can only be attributed to two causes, namely, greater liberty and a more thorough education. Though a great and glorious work has been accomplished by them, it is but a fractional part of what they have yet to aomplete; the. tyranny, ignorance and superstition are still ascendant on our earth, casting a gloom over some of its purest portions, they will soon be dispelled and vanish, as the light that dawned at the reformations spread throughout the earth. This heaven-sent reform has changed the whole course of Christian history—a history that at first was the grandest of the earth, but afterwards became as cruel and degraded as that of the Pagans, and in many instances more so; oh! so-called Christianity, how many pages of your history, stained and darkened with blood, cruelty and superstition, will you have to account for in that last and terrible day, whose horrors you strive to make your followers fear; yet by your doings and example one might imagine there was not a God of justice, to punish your many crimes. Any impartial person can read with interest, pity and admiration, of the wars and courage of ancient Greece and Rome, for they, in their religion had a God of war; but cannot read without horror and contempt the history of the Popes and Monarchs of the middle ages and those of the present day, who believe in a gospel of peace, and at the same time allow millions of their fellow-men to be murdered; and in the middle ages committed atrocities worthy of "imps" and "devils." We cannot expect the world to become civilized at once by the influence of the purer religion of Protestantism. Education and liberty, though their work is slow, it is certain and sure. The greatest religious ecclastical despotisms will either be buried or destroyed by them; even in this desert of vulgarity and ignorance their light has begun to dawn. A desert of vulgarity and ignorance! You may reply, how can this be? Are we not the subjects of one of the most civilized countries in the world? Are not our neighbors the believers in a church that declares it cannot err in its doctrines? Do we not live in an age that claims a great advance beyond the savage age that's past? How then can you prove that we live in a desert of vulgarity and ignorance? Very easily my friends, very easily. Have you ever taken a tour throughout this province, and seen this people in a semi-barborous state, with their intellects darkened by the power of superstition and ignorance? have you ever gone to one of their school examinations? where you would see a sight that would astonish you; where you would see school examiners listening to the teacher examining her scholars; in the gravest manner possible, and in most cases give a satisfactory report of their progress; yet these men could no more read or write than they could decipher the hieroglyphics on an ancient Egyptian tomb. To the Cure of course it was a matter of indifference; he is satisfied as long as the scholars can repeat their prayers, at a speed that defies the most skillful phonographer to report them; he does not even take the trouble to have the prayers pronounced properly, but allows the scholars to disguise their language with a squeaking twang, somewhat like that of a heathen Chinee. If you have noticed this system of education in our benighted province, you will also no doubt, have noticed its effect on the inhabitants, and cannot have failed to have noticed the manner in which they patronize art, and that in most cases the productions of their artists are nothing better than horrid daubs. Perhaps on entering the house of a well-to-do farmer your curiosity was aroused at seeing a picture of an ordinary looking man sitting on the clouds, and made a disrespectful remark about it, thinking that it was merely a representation of "old father time," when to your astonishment the lady remarks: "oh no! that's a picture of God," I can well imagine your reply: "what! the great Jehova! The Almighty Creator of our universe! it cannot be; pardon me madam, but you must be mistaken. To which she replies: "well sir, perhaps it is not exactly like him, but I don't see any harm in it, it makes us think the oftener of him." On leaving that house a total change takes place in your mind; you begin to feel contempt and disgust for the so-called "perfect church," and if you have travelled amongst the ruins of ancient Greece and Rome, or seen some of their noble looking Gods, you would no doubt exclaim: "those noble Pagans of ancient days were able to make finer and nobler looking Gods than the Christian Pagans of the present day;" as our neighbors are chiefly composed os this class, it will cause no surprise here this evening when I say that I cannot count a single individual of education among them, until I became acquainted with your interesting community, which appears to me as an oasis, when compared with the surroundings; here are at least a people that can speak their native language correctly without using those expessions that would arouse the indignation of Lindley Murray at seeing the beauty of language disfigured, that he in its purity had ever sought to preserve; here youth, manhood and old age, meet together for their mutual edification and pleasure; here a few united families established their church under the greatest difficulties; a church that has always upheld the glorious principles of liberty and education, a church that where ere its steeples are seen civilization and prosperity reign; when the influence of our church is more extended, and more communities like this established, then will education's civilizing influence have power to do its noble work. Ladies and gentlemen, as lovers of liberty and progress, we have a great and glorious work to do, in advancing the interests of humanity in the land in which we live, if we, as Protestants with all our greater advantages of superior education, and greater spiritual liberty, are not guided by our better sentiments, we can never expect our fellow-countrymen to adopt our more rational and civilized religion, we should not be satisfied with having hired missionaries to enlighten the world, but every one of us that loves truth and humanity, should by our noble and useful lives be missionaries in the grand work of liberating all the spiritual slaves on this earth, by extending to them the hand of fellowship, and inviting them to come forth out of their servile and debasing spiritual serfdom, under the despotism of a fraudlent priesthood, and live in the glorious liberty and be guided by the noble spirit that every man posesses in an undeveloped state, let us not be deceived as our Catholic neighbors are, by thinking that our religion is perfect, and that its truths are alone sufficient to convert all men, and eventually enable it to become all powerful on this earth, for nothing is more absurd and impossible; if Protestantism does not continue the grand work it has commenced, but advocates merely a milder form of spiritual serfdom than that of Catholicism, and attaches more importance to vague and uncertain, supposed to be revealed truths, than to the practical and self-evident truths of life, it, like all other religions, will be scornfully rejected and overthrown, by the more civilized men of future ages. The superior religion of Christianity triumphed over Judaism, and the more rational religion of Protestantism has made a more wonderful progress than that of Catholicism during the short period it has existed, but if its grand army comes to a halt in the march of freedom and human liberty, hundreds of thousand's of humanity's patritots will step out of the ranks and continue marching onward and upward until they become the freeest and grandest creatures of God's creation; let us be in the advance guard of this glorious united army (that is to be) and become protestants in the truest sense of the word, protesting not only against the errors of catholicism but against everything we consider erroneous. In a great measure the enlightenment of the French in this province depends on the example of the English Canadians, therefore we should strive our utmost by useful and noble lives to win their admiration and respect, which would do more good than the employment of hundreds of missionaries. The government of the country cannot be expected to accomplish much for the advancement of the people or to adopt a compulsory national system of education for the very reason that the majority of the members of parliament are the slaves of the clergy and subservient to their will, from this it might appear that there was little hope of bettering the people's condition but on reading history we find that there are two ways by which ecclessiastical tyranny is generally overthrown, firstly by rebellion against the unprincipled priesthood whose chief aim is to keep the people in a state of spiritual subjection, or secondly thro the priesthood being obliged to encourage among their followers a more liberal education through the pressure brought to bear on them by the liberal influence of protestantism and infidelity. In the revolution in France in 1789 we have a remarkable instance of the desperation and cruelty to which an ecclesiastically and politically oppressed people can be driven by the tyranny of their spiritual and temporal rulers; tho the deeds of the revolutionists were bloody and cruel no impartial person can deny the fact that altogether it has been a blessing rather than a curse to France; it was as a terrific thunder storm, frightful at the time but an absolute necessity to clear away the enormous clouds of ignorance and superstition that hid in darkness the whole of France; since then France has become a grander and happier nation and ranks to day (notwithstanding its infidelity) as the most civilized of all the catholic countries of the earth; in Italy also the grand desire in the hearts of the people for liberty upset the infallible tyrant from his temporal throne, since then that unfortunate nation has begun to recover some of its former greatness; all those who have studied this question acknowledge that such revolutions as the above would in all probability have occurred in Canada had it not been taken from France by England, to use a vulgar but very forcible expression the clergy under English rule "could not get enough rope to hang themselves," as they did in Italy and France, for it was quite natural for them in adopting a policy for the church to retain the sympathy and affection of the people as much as possible by a wise and judicious policy and besides they knew under a heretic government they could not tyranize over the people as under devout Catholic governments which are very often the servile servants of the church; in such countries they can of course assume a more domineering policy; it was also quite natural when a heretic power had conquered the country, for the people themselves to be filled with thoughts of how they might preserve "their religion, their language and their institutions," instead of joining their fellow-countrymen across the ocean in the cry of "Liberty, Fraternity and Equality." Thus through our conquest of the country almost all hopes were cut off of the people ever freeing themselves from priestly rule by rebellion, for as I have already said its conquest by heretics created a bond of sympathy between the priesthood and the people. Thus the chief hope of the improvement and enlightenment of the French Canadians depends on English influence and example, which, alas! many Englishmen, unworthy of that honorable name, have not given to the Canadian people, but by their despicable lives have brought shame and dishonor on their religion and nationality, and many Frenchmen are, through their inconsistencies, kept from professing Protestantism which is now the purest form of christanity. In fact the followers of Protestantism can never expect to do away with priestly tyranny, superstition and ignorance until the majority of them make the grand resolution to become individually the friends of humanity by becoming the most noble men and women on the face of the earth. There is, however, already a visible improvement throughout the province; the priests are obliged to encourage a more liberal system of education, fearing that their children would attend our schools and colleges. That day is fast approaching when the education of our French Canadian countrymen will consist of something more than counting beasts and saying prayers. They have already several fine schools and colleges and will ere long be able to compete with us in the race for knowledge as their mother country does with ours across the ocean's wave. Some expressions I have used in connection with the religion of our

Canadian friends may seem rather impolite and appear to them as an insult, but I do not mean it thus and would not intentionally hurt their feelings, and I am certain if they try and show us the errors of our religion we will not be offended, but will be grateful to them for showing us whatever errors it may contain, for we all acknowledge that it is far from being perfect. We should all remember that this is not an age in which errors can be hid, whether they be spiritual or temporal they are certain to be found out by the light of civilization and judged accordingly by mankind. We should not be offended at what another says against us, if it be true the remark ought to do us more good than harm, if not true our conduct and lives ought to be sufficient to prove it false, in which case our accuser should rather have our pity than our hatred. Thus I would have our Canadian friends act. Let them study their own history and ours impartially and consider the low condition of the great portion of their people, and if they can prove that my statements are false, in that case I deserve their just contempt; if not let them do away with those doctrines and customs that dishonor both their religion and nationality, and join their Saxon brothers in the grand work of liberating mankind from the most objectional features of the thousands of religious sects that exist at the present day. Ladies and gentlemen, should not we try and accomplish our fractional part in this grand work, by earnestly striving to put to a nobler use all our spare time than we now make of it, and unite with our French friends in forming a literary association with a public library containing all the best magazines and newspapers as well as most of the best books on the most useful subjects of the day. A library that our village would be proud of, which would preserve many of its young men from the low degrading influence of bar-rooms, and many of its young ladies from wasting many hours in reading sickly, sensational novels. Will not ours be the deepest of ingratitude if we do not take advantage of the glorious opportunities that our age affords us—an age of cheap literature, clever authors, eloquent orators and excellent newspapers, that are capable of imparting knowledge and pleasure at the same time; yet if we do not avail ourselves of these, and pass through life in a careless, sluggish way, in senseless conversation and silly games, without a single aspiration to become nobler men and women than our ancestors, will we not deserve the everlasting contempt of future generations." It was well received by those present and did not seem to give offense to three French Catholics who were there; several days after this I canvassed and had 23 gentlemen and 19 ladies subscribe their names to the following document: "We, the undersigned, hereby agree to pay an entrance fee of $1 and a monthly fee of 25cts. to form a literary association in this village, the entrance fee to be paid at a public meeting to be held on the 20th of March, 1881, at the English schoolhouse, at which the laws and by-laws for it will be made." Of the names 8 were French gentlemen and 4 French ladies. Have been working for Houde of late at $5.50 per week and board myself. He and Mr. Frechette are making squared timber for building purposes and fence rails to sell in the cleared country about St. Jean; have also let out contracts for squared timber at 1½cts. per ft. lineal measure. While at Houde's Mr. Houde made a remark to his wife at which all his family, sons and daughters laughed. It was of the vilest description, language that it would be imposssble for me to give the reader an idea of; I would not have thought that Houde would utter such language in the presence of his wife and daughters, as he is considered a very respectable and devout catholic by the majority of Canadians in these parts. Saw the announcement of Richards death in the newspaper; I need hardly say how sorry we were for he ever was a kind, dear and good cousin to us. Tom and I wrote uncle Richard as follows: "Dear uncle, I cannot tell how surprised and grieved I was to hear of the death of Richard; none bnt those who knew him intimately can know how great your loss has been. Though death has removed him from the busy scenes of life, and time may shroud his name with oblivion, the memory of his name will always live in the hearts of his friends, who could not do otherwise than love and respect him. Trusting that you will all receive consolation from that unfailing source from which it may be obtained. I remain, ever your affc c. nephew, A. N. Howard." "Dear Arthur, I received your kind letters of condolence on the death of your dear cousin, although I have been expecting the blow for the last 3½ yrs., yet when it came we felt the shock severely; dear Richard's end was peace, he died in the Lord, with the sure and certain hope of the resurrection from the dead, through the redemption of our blessed Saviour; may God bless you both is the constant prayer of your afflicted uncle, R. I. Goldsmith." Waterford, 5th March. "Dear Tom, I had a long letter from your father a couple of weeks since; he commenced in March 1880, and finished in March 1881, in the last part of his letter he informs me that he received a letter from Ethel Churchill, suggesting her brother Beaufort going out to help him, and learn farming, and that he would write to him and was pleased with the idea. I, however do not approve of the movement, but am powerless in the case; Beaufort has been out of employment for the last 12 months, business got damped by the land league and Home Rulers, but there is not much work in him anyway, and I doubt much if he is likely to do any good, or make himself useful to your father, but as you may not have heard of the matter, I thought it well to apprize you, as it seems from Ethel Church's note, that he offers to give Beaufort half his cattle and land, and teach him farming; there was some correspondence carried on previously, but I did not expect it would amount to anything, now however it seems settled and I cannot prevent it; when his mother, your aunt, Anne Churchill, was alive, she asked me to take charge of what property she had, and I have had it in charge ever since, and have been endeavoring to make the children do something for themselves, but they do not seem to have any life in them, and are living on the interest of the money their mother received at the death of her husband, who was, as I suppose you have heard, a marine surveyor for the British government at Canton, China. We are having just now a run of very keen Easterly winds which are very trying, almost worse than frost and snow; Edmund says he will write to you shortly; I suppose you heard of the terrible death of your uncle Capt. Richard Howard; fell between his ship and the pier in one of the East Indian Ports, and was crushed to death; his wife is now stopping in London with a married sister, who is not very strong. We were surprised to hear from your father that Arthur had been trying to enter the army, I should not have thought an energetic young man like him would like a profession with so much idle duty as the army has now—and I hope may remain so; in the trial and manufacture of arms there is interesting and valuable progress going on to encourage interest in an intelligent mind; war is brutal in all that belongs to it. I am writing for this post and must conclude; yours affectionately, Timothy S. Howard." On the 20th March I had the school-house in Aston prepared for the meeting of the literary association that was to be; only five that had subscribed their names arrived, and immediately commenced to run down the project, offering as many objections as they could, and Mr. Wheeler, our school trustee said they would charge $25 a yr. rent for the hall over the school-house; I used all the persuasion I could, but could not get them to organize, although there arrived sufficient to do so; there is great scandal about St. George and his wife, who are always quarrelling and making peace again, this time St. George has engaged a lawyer and his wife has returned home to her mother. "The Elms, March 20th. Dear Tom and Arthur; I must apoligise for not having written to you sooner. As you suppose, I got a great shock when I arrived in town and was met by Aunt Prim who told me that poor Richard had died that morning, although I knew that he was very ill but I had no idea he was as bad as that, it must have been a great relief to him, he suffered so much and so long; we miss him very much; it seems as if there was a blank that can never be filled; what a cold morning it was when I left your place, 17 deg. below zero; we have been having very good weather for sugaring here lately, the roads are almost bare in many places; wagons are used between here and Sherman; there is very little frost in the ground; while in Montreal 1 of your horses was drowned in drawing logs on the ice down the river. what a disgraceful thing, the assassination of the Czar of Russia; it was doing evil with the idea that good might come of it. The Land League appears to be subsiding, the Coercion bill seems to have frightened them into more moderate language. I got a great bargain the other day, 3 tons of straw for $5; straw is $6 a ton at Sherman; could not Arthur pay me a visit in the beginning of April; must now close as it is bed time; yonr affec, cousin, Clifford H. Goldsmith."

Wooden troughs are used in the old system of making sugar, and the trees are tapped by making a small sloping cut in the tree with an axe, and placing a "spout" underneath it; the boiling is done in iron kettles over an open wood fire; when the sap begins to ascend in the maples, which is generally in the middle but often in the first part of March, the trees are tapped; the wooden troughs are easily got at, as they are always stood up by the tree the Autumn before; after the trees are all tapped, the sugar maker cleans out all rust out of his kettles by polishing them with a brick, and clears away the snow from the fire place which has two forked posts on either side, with a pole across, from which the kettles are hung; Pine, Balsam, Ash, Brasswood and beech, are the usual woods used for troughs; a good workman can make 50, but the average is 30 per day; the camp is generally built in the center of the sugar bush, there is also a revolving post with an arm fastened to it, on which the sugaring off kettle is hung, so that immediately when the sugar is finished it can be swung off the fire; large, heavy logs are placed on the outside edge of the fire, and 4 ft. of cordwood burnt between them; "tapping" with an axe, kills the trees quicker, than with an auger, the cut also being exposed to the sun dries up quicker; the camp must always be built close to water, in some cases it is a mere shelter of boards, in others, a small log building; a disadvantage of troughs is, that much sap is wasted by them upsetting when the snow melts, also in emptying it into the buckets, when gathering it, 3 troughs are placed to a large tree, 2 to an average one, and 1 to a small one; the means of holding the sap at the camp, is generally a long trough, and sometimes in hogsheads; a piece of coarse canvass is generally used, to strain the sap, and a piece of flannel to strain the syrup; the sap is generally gathered by hand, but often with a horse and sleigh fastened on it; a piece of fat meat is hung over the boiling syrup to prevent it from boiling over; eggs are often used to purify the syrup, by raising a scum on its surface, which is skimmed off, the boiling syrup is tested by blowing it through a small hole in a wooden "pallet;" "not quite done yet, but soon will be, he mutters," after a few minutes he tries it again, and a white silken bubble floats upon the air. The boys now get tins of snow and prepare to make "wax," as it is called here by the English; they pour some syrup on the snow but it does not crystalize, after a few trials it partially crystalizes, and makes "wax," the sugar maker judges when it is sufficiently boiled by testing the brittleness of the wax, and when finished is swung off the fire and gently stirred till it is partly crystalized and is then put in moulds. Old Brodeur has suffered great agony for several days past from inflammation of the bowels, yet his family sent first for the priest and for the dotcor several hours after. On the doctors arrival he indignantly said, had I been sent for a few hours sooner I could have saved his life. The poor old fellow looks ghastly, the cold sweat of death is on his brow, his hands are clasped in agony, his features pale and shrunken, without doubt death has him in its grasp; he is unconscious and raving and strange to say he raves in English, on account I suppose of his having an English nurse. His wife who has been on a visit in the U. S. arrived in the morning just as he died; the son started off immediately for the essentials for the funeral. Many a pleasant hour have I passed with the poor old fellow in listening to his early experiences in the backwoods; he was a jolly, honest and liberal old man, remarkably so considering the superstition and ignorance he was surrounded with all his life. That night I went to his wake; there were about forty people praying when I entered; I knelt with the rest; La Berge lead the prayers at such a breakneck pace that even the most skilful linguist could not tell whether they were the prayers of Frenchmen or the Hottentots of Africa. La Berge went asleep by the stove when the prayers were over; Joe Vincent applied a heated poker to his bare feet, the effect was startling, La Berge sprang to his feet with a volley of oaths in French and English; he used the most terrible French oaths from "twist God" to "d—d virgin." The first appeared to me more ridiculous than terrible as it merely meant the twisting of a piece of blessed bread, but to an R. C. who believes it to be truly the body of God, it is certainly an awful oath. The females constantly indulged in such choice expressions as "My God, Savior of God, Holy Spirit, Holy Virgin, etc.," in fact the general conversation was but a few degrees better than that which might be expected of savages. The next time they prayed, La Berge, the blasphemous wretch had the audacity to ask for mercy on the dead man's soul, when his own had most need of it. The only appearance that a dead man was in the house was that white sheets hung from the ceiling around the bed and one over the corpse with a gigantic cross upon it. Suppressed laughter and course language were indulged in all evening. The corpse was put in the coffin at 3 o'clock; they were going to put it on the bare shavings in the coffin till one of the Carmicheals suggested that a white sheet be thrown over them. Mrs. B. came and took a feather pillow from under his head and replaced it with a straw one; this was very practical, but I think it showed a want of feeling. Next evening as the funeral passed the country people took off their hats. I was greatly disgusted at the short work the priests made of the ceremony over the remains of this worthy old man as compared with the pomp and ceremony of Mrs. D's funeral; but of course this religion is a lucrative trade and must be carried on on a strictly business-basis. I did not care about his being deprived of pomp and ceremony, but what filled my soul with indignation was the thought that this so-called priest of God will mutter no long prayers for the repose of this man's soul, but chanted masses and repeated long prayers for Mrs. D's soul because her family could pay $200 for them. Does the reader think that a just God will allow these $200 prayers to cause him to make a distinction between those two souls; I think not and cannot believe that any intelligent being (except blind with fanaticism) believes that a man's condition in future life can be benefitted by the prayers of a fellow finite man and still much less by prayers that are purchased by filthy lucre. And yet it was only a short time ago that I read in an Eastern newspaper that the catholics were working in the greatest harmony with the other christian sects in the good work of trying to convert the "Mormons," whose religion in my estimation is in most ways infinitely superior to catholicism and more in accordance with the scriptures, and whose people are in education, thrift, industry, honesty and temperance vastly the superiors of all the catholic nations of the earth wherever that dogmatic church receives unqestioning obedience from its children. I cannot help thinking how absurd and inconsistent it is for some of the leading men in this great republic to entertain such a bitter hatred and foolish fear of the Mormon church, and at the same time maintain neutrality and in many cases exhibit friendship towards Catholicism, which with its barbaric ceremonies and awful power is a far more dangerous enemy than Mormonism ever could be to civilization. Is it wisdom or justice for such a paper as the Salt Lake *Tribune* to make such a clamor about the danger of Mormonism and totally ignore the frightful increase of Romanism which is far more despotic in giving religious liberty to its followers than is the Mormon church. The gentlemen of the *Tribune* well know that no man can think for himself on religion in the Catholic church; the doctrines have all been cut and dried by its dogmatic councils, and have to be swallowed without questions by its followers on pain of being expelled as heretics. Surely if the *Tribune* wishes to defend the true interests of humanity it ought to attack the abuses that exist in other churches as well as those which it claims exist in the Territory of Utah. If the Mormon church has a hierarchal form of government of apostles, patriarchs, bishops, elders, teachers and deacons, it should be remembered that they are manly enough to earn their own living and preach the gospel according to scripture, "without money and without price;" nor do they wear gaudy robes, nor have the people to kneel before them as they pass through the streets as is the case in some countries of Europe and which I have myself witnessed in Quebec. In fact the Mormon church might well be called a spiritual republic, as all men possessing ability have the opportunity of being elected to some office in the church, and I have noted with great pleasure the treatment the poorer classes of the people receive when they call on the heads of the church, there is none of that false sanctmonious dignity that is affected by the catholic bishops I have seen; nor is their any of that cringing reverent awe in the faces of their visitors that I have seen in the miserable, priest ridden slaves of Quebec while they stood in the presence of their bishop. But I do not want the fair minded reader to misunderstand me as will the reader of a narrow mind, who will at once come to the conclusion that these favorable comparisons are drawn merely as a matter of policy, but I merely do it in justice and out of admiration for this conrageous people who have thrown down the gauntlet to the whole world in defense of their convictions, and I feel confident that a people who have suffered and accomplished as much as they have are capable of exerting a great and powerful influence in this earth therefore I would like to see this people happy, united and animated with a worthy ambition and stern determination to prove to the world the falsity of the slanders that have been heaped upon them by sects and individuals who are in many ways inferior to them and more addicted to ridiculous and worthless pomp and ceremonies than the Saints, which appears to me attach more importance to the practical truths of life than many of the other religious sects; in fact what I read of this people before coming here I imagined I would find one of the most superstitious and degraded class of people of all the christian churches, and to my most agreeable astonishment I found a people vastly the superior of the great majority of the catholic nations of the earth; this superiority appears to me of still greater credit to the priesthood of this church when I consider that a great many of the Saints are composed from the poorer inhabitants of Europe, and when I have entered the neat and comfortable homes of these emigrants from all parts of the world and heard from their own lips how prosperous and happy they were, and attended their mutal improvement associations and saw young ladies ahd gentlemen address the audience extemporaneously on scientific and literary subjects I thought to myself how appropriately the words of that great teacher Christ could be applied to some of the bigoted sects and individuals that are trying to convert them: "Thou hypocrite first cast out the beam that is in thine own eye and then thou shalt see clearly to remove the mote from thy brothers." I trust however when I bring before the public the history of Utah and Mormonism I am now engaged on to clearly show from an impartial gentile point of view how many pages of this people's history deserves the respect and admiration of the world." On our way back from the funeral met the funeral of a man that died of delirium tremens; have commenced drawing manure to Oak Hill with our oxen, Tom is drawing rails for Houde with his team. The Nilhists of Russia threw glass bombs at the Czar and nearly blew off both his legs, they were amputated but he died, 20 persons were killed and wounded. Hanlan the Canadian oarsman is champion of the world; at times I feel disgusted with myself for having remained so long in the contaminating society of this place, however as there is no possibility of my entering the army I will now devote my life in trying to make farming a success, that is if our kind uncles do not interfere too much with the management of our farms, if they do I shall abandon farming and study for some profession. 24th March took a trip to Quebec, after I changed cars at Rawlings I took notes of the scenery, country hilly, spruce and balsam; second growth, not a picturesqe landscape by any means, many of the clearances are newly cleared, some rocky ledges appear through the hills, woodland on the right clearances on the left, no primeval forest in sight all second growth, forest and clearances intermixed, all the clearances have stumps in them, some neat clapboard houses, forest on both sides, railway passes through a valley, very uninteresting country, second growth with strips of clearances here and there, the houses are chiefly frame and are better than the log houses of far back settlements, a very high range of hills on the left, a narrow strip of clearance on both sides, pass the first brick house, large railway cuttings, clearances and woodlands interspersed, a beaver meadow and small stream, brushwood on both sides, clearances with a few dilapidated houses and nice looking farms, second growth again, a few clearances with average looking farms and a distant view on the left of a long low range of hills, farm houses, deep railway cutting, land newly cleared, some house in them painted a flaring red, second growth and clearances interspersed, ravine and hills with little rills, edges of ground on either side obstruct the view, country newly cleared, it would make fine farming country if properly developed; arrived at Waterford 72 m. from Pt. Levi; saw mill, bark, ties and cordwood near it, some fine views of hills in the distance, underbrush, country much wilder, a few clearances, country hilly, medium looking farm houses, a small stream, light sandy soil, hardly any stones; red seems the favorite color with farmers in these parts; tumbling down looking farm houses, a thick growth of balsam trees about 30 ft. high, view of hills in the distance, there are a great many cuttings on this line, a few clearances, view obstructed on either side by rising ground, miserable looking clearances and brushwood intermixed, view of church steeple in the far distance, miserable clearances, dilapidated houses, brushwood,cleared summit of a hill in the far distance with houses on it; a drunken man has raised a row in the car, the air is full of tobacco smoke, the floor thickly covered with tobacco spits and half intoxicated lumbermen are yelling what I expect they imagine "are the sweetest songs imaginable," yet poor but respectable farmers wives have to sit for hours in such an atmosphere as this dreary uninteresting country; it is amusing to hear the loud and animated conversation carried on by the people, lumbermen relating their experiences last season during their lumbering operations on some of the large rivers in the province, old farmers with their short clay pipes, home spun clothes and dog skin caps discussing profoundly the latest politics and a few well to do commercial Frenchmen with that air of dignity that shows how much superior they consider themselves to farmers and laborers; numerous fine farms on the right, desolate wild country on the left, country now more level covered with tamarac and poplar second growth, clearances and brushwood alternately in the distance, a ridge of hills with houses on it, scrubby brushwood, a small sugar bush with a farm house, second growth, dreary swampy country covered with tamarac and poplar; arrive at St. Andre, has a bark factory, a small river runs through the village, has some very nice houses and a few city-like houses, ridge of hills on the right running parallel with the rly, clearances here and there on its summit, brushwood on both sides, a stream with a saw mill on it, ridge of hills again in sight on the right, can see an immense distance on the left over a vast unbroken forest, a cross at a corner where several roads meet; a Frenchmen tells me that these crosses (which exist all over the country) "are for the people to assemble at and say a few prayers when the weather is so bad as to prevent them from going to church;" surely God would be just as pleased to have them say their prayers at home as to wade over muddy roads to say them before a piece of whitewashed timber in the form of a cross; pass a village with stacks of hemlock bark, rly ties, cordwood, rails, &c.; a prettily situated village in view in the distance, some sugar bushes; I have never before gazed towards the horizon and seen such an extensive and unbroken tract of forest, houses on the summit of the ridge to the right, some pretty little houses but generally too close together as about St Jean; the boy that sells candy, fruit, stationary and newspapers must have a good opinion of the capacity of the passengers purses, he passes around so often; brushwood obstructs the view, rocky land in a half cleared condition, over the ridge of rising ground on the right, brushwood and clearances interspersed; arrived at a small village 49 m. from Pt. Levi, has a church and a tannery, is a small loose straggling village with much bark and cordwood about it; the same continuous range of hills are still visible on the right; the country is newly settled here, pass a small saw mill; second growth of ash and balsam with farms here and there; another small village with acres upon acres covered with stacks of hemlock bark, the largest part of this village is I hear ¼ of a mile away, another village consisting of a few houses; hotel, store, postoffice and depot, another small collection of houses, stunted evergreens, small clearances second growth, a stopping place, a few houses, forest trees are somewhat larger, range of hills on the right level and swampy on the left; a Frenchman has just remarked that great numbers of that people were going to the United States; pass through a very extensive bog covered with peat, stunted spruce and balsam, very level and uninteresting country; a small village; the range of hills on the right deserve the name of mountains; pass thro a large swamp covered with stunted balsams, spruce and tamarac, cleared land, a mountain on the left, high rocks, towering at least 100 ft. and in some places several hundred ft. above the rly on either side; arrive at Pt. Levi, which consists of a long row of straggling houses at the foot of an immense rocky cliff that overhangs it; the harbor of Quebec is 2 miles across, its greatest depth is 28 fathoms; tho the water is fresh the tide rises from 17 to 24 ft. the harbor is large enough to contain the whole British navy; in 1844 the county of Quebec contained 45,000 pop. the city and suburbs 43,000. 28,000 being Canadians of French origin, 8,000 British of which 7,000 were Irish, 1,500 natives of England and the rest Scotch; 36,000 of the city's pop. belong to the church of Rome; crossed the harbor in a handsome ferry steamer; went to a cheap boarding house, paid 25 cts a meal and 25 cts for bed; there is only one theatre which is French; asked for the nearest stationers and found it ¾ of a mile off also that all the stores were closed altho it was only 8 o'clock; read in the *Mercury*, a very small English newspaper, published in Quebec; next day had only fried cod and bread and tea as it was "un journee maigre" or in other words a day of fasting; took a walk on Dufferin terrace, which is a beautiful promenade in summer, it is on the side of a steep hill along the edge of which an ornamental fence runs; there is also an elevator to carry people up and down from the upper to the lower town; a few years ago a man slipped on the edge of the cliff and rolled over, he could not regain his legs and rolled to the bottom and was killed; passed a garden in which were the monuments of Wolfe and Montcalm, the brave English and French generals that fell in that battle that gave to England the possession of "the Gibralter of America;" there were several cannon on the terrace pointing over the lower town on to the river; on mounting a long dizzy flight of stairs reached the citadel from which a glorious panorama of the country lay before my eyes, the interior of the citadel is at least 20 ft. below the surface of the hill on which it is built and is encased with thick walls of cut stone; a circuituous road goes around inside of the citadel, passed the soldiers quarters and arrived at a covered gateway and asked a sentry if strangers are allowed to visit the citadel, he called out the sergeant who invited me in while he finished his breakfast of herrings, bread and coffee after which he ordered one of the soldiers to show me about the citadel, saw a great many cannon and howitzers and large piles of shells, and some cannister shot, as well as a cannon captured from the Americans, and the spot where Montgomery fell; also guns captured from the French and Russians; the officers, instead of each having a separate house, all occupy apartments in a very fine, large building; some of the married ones have houses in the city; the stables are built of stone, and contain some very fine horses; saw the entrance to the underground tunnel that leads to a round tower in the direction of the plains of Abraham, and the powder magazines; started for the falls of Montmorenci, 8 miles distance down the North side of the St.

Lawerance; paid the cabman $2, drove across the St. Charles River, was surprised at seeing so many dogs used for drawing small carts; somewhat over 100 yrs. ago, ladies in Quebec used to drive in sleighs drawn by dogs; Charlevoix says "that horses were first introduced in 1665;" drove along the road called "Le Chemin de Beaufort." The farms are very narrow but have nice houses, all of them have chimnies and open fire places; there are numerous stone houses, and those of wood have in many instances the Italian style of roof, many of the houses deserve the name of country gentleman's mansions, surrounded as they are by trees, gravel walks, &. In some places there was 6 ft. deep of snow, and we drove over the highest fences, in other places it was quite bare; passed Beaufort Lunatic Asylum, which has a capacity for 400, is a very imposing building of cut stone, surrounded by beautiful grounds, river St. Lawerance in sight; the meadow land slopes gently towards the river's edge; passed a large stone church at Beaufort village, also one of the smallest churches in the world, only 12 ft. square; reach the park-like grounds that surround the falls, in which there is a hotel, where strangers register their names, and pay 25cts.; citizens of Quebec are admitted free; the prevailing trees in the grounds above the falls, are Spruce, and Arbor-Vitæ, also Aspens, Alders and mountain Ash; a ravine runs from the St. Lawerance river in the shape of the letter V, the sides of the ravine are almost perpendicular, about 300 ft. high, and covered with evergreen shrubs; the river falls perpendicularly, nearly 250 ft. high at one pitch; the St. Lawerance only falls 160 ft. at Niagara; the waters below the falls were white with foam. Returned home on the 26th; there are 17 rly. stations between Rawlings and Point Levi. Extract from a letter from E. Howard. "We are much less disturbed in Ireland than you may perhaps think; the outrages have been much exaggerated for political purposes; no one, out of Ireland can form an idea of how things are here; it was very cold for Ireland last January, ice 6½ inches thick." From Uncle Richard, "A patient of mine has bought land from Mr. Baker of Richford; could you without inconvenience let me know what the quality of the land is; I had a very kind loving letter of sympathy from your Uncle Jerrrold a few days ago; I paid him £2000, that I had borrowed from him; I suggested to him to have £1000 here, but he said I could do so if I gave him 8 per ct, for it; as that was impossible, I sent it over to him; I could get a promise of 12 or even 15 for it, with the greatest prospect of losing interest and principal; Montreal bank at par is paying 10 per ct., but the stock is selling at 186, which makes it scarcely 4½ per ct.; as things stand here, all securities are very shaky, and the man that can invest his money or his own labor in his own property is lucky. I have been attending the hospital since the 1st of Jan., my time expires on the 1st of June. I, and your aunt are going to the U. S. to see Flora and the addition to their family; I should like Arthur to visit Clifford before your busy time commences; I have a notion of selling the Elms if I can get a purchaser, and try and get him a better farm if possible, near Montreal; as you may imagine, we are very lonely here now; with love to you both, in which your aunt unites dear Tom and Arthur, your loving uncle, R. I. Goldsmith." For a belief in God, revelations we do not need; the universe and all that in it exists, are the revelations we receive. Had an argument with father, that a people had a perfect right to rebel against a monarch, and even destroy him, if he infringed on the liberties of the people. "Grange, Waterford, March '81. Dear Arthur, I should have answered your long letter sooner, but have had an unusual amount of correspondence of late; even now I fear I am unable to answer your letter at any great length; I agree with some things you say, as to the undesirability of long estate, and on some other points, such as the horrible loss caused by war, but I suppose we must continue to diff.r about many things in Ireland; the Irish Catholics have never been allowed to govern themselves like other countries, and have not the self restraint and moderation in expressing themselves, that comes from experience in self government; it is quite likely that Ireland would make many mistakes if she set about managing her own affairs all at once, just as a man who puts on skates for the first time; but the experience gained in floundering about is useful, and in due time I expect we would do fairly well; at present, Irish affairs are entirely managed by Gt. Britain, and we have no chance to learn how to manage them, in fact Irish questions in parliament, are generally settled in a way contrary to the expressed wishes of a majority of the people; if any Canadian province were treated in the same way, I am confident that in a few years its people would be as disloyal as the Irish; the Boers in Transvaal are good Protestants, but that does not prevent them from fighting for their liberties, rather than allow themselves to be annexed and ruled by the British grvernment, and nearly all the civilized world admires them for their indep ndant spirit. Last January we had some of the coldest weather that has been known in Ireland for 60 yrs., there was ice 6 inches thick over a ford near here, and snow lay on the ground for a week, the roads being in a good condition for sleighing; quantities of ice float down the river, which is over a furlong wide, at Waterford bridge it has not been frozen over since 1814, and ice is not even floating on it more than once in 10 yrs.; there is a factory in town for making ice, to be used in bacon curing in summer, but quite lately a cargo of several hundred tons of ice was discharged at the quay from a Norwegian vessel. You would be surprised at all the earth (three ft. thick at the base) and stone fences (called ditches) dividing the fields in this country; they waste much room but where a man does not own his farm, he cares less about economizing the land; in England the feudal system of Sevant farming does less harm than in Ireland, because the British manufacturers and commerce, give employment to those who cannot find work on the land, but Irish manufacturers and commerce were almost destroyed by British laws in the last century, and have never since recovered, besides Ireland is naturally poorer in mineral wealth than Great Britain, so that in Ireland nearly every farmer's son or laborer's son has to find work on the land or emigrate, which state of affairs has caused an unnatural demand for farms and tempted Irish lanolords to constantly raise their rent. When bad seasons have come landlords have in many cases heartlessly turned out those peasants who could not pay their rent, and 30 years ago this resulted in many thousands of men, women and children dying in the ditches or in emigrant ships, yet the Irish people had raised more food than was sufficient to support themselves in those terrible famine years, but the corn and cattle which they raised were nearly all shipped off to England to pay rents, while the people were left to starve, and their houses pulled down to prevent them from going back to live in them. If Ireland had been a self-governing country, no such laws would have been permitted to exist as those by which Irish landlords confiscated all improvements made by their tenents and raised their rents to starvation point; but then as as now, Ireland was governed by the Imperial Parliament, which has always been ignorant of the wants of the Irish people and has always governed Ireland in support of the interests of the landlords. Until the ballot act was passed, 10 or 12 years ago, the Irish people had not even the means of voting for members of Parliament of their own choice without a prospect of being evicted by their landlords. Now things are changed for the better in some respects. We have for the first time a pretty compact body of men in Parliament really representing the wishes of the Irish people and determined to win from an unwilling government some substantial reform of the land laws, which Gt. Britain has forced on us against our wishes. The Irish people are also determined not to go on paying high rents to which the landlords have no moral claim. What Parnell and the Land Leaguers demand is that the Irish tenant farmers should have a legal right to buy the landlords' interest in the land they cultivate; so as to put an end to this miserable Irish land question in the same way that the same question was settled in Prussia 70 years ago. As regards Mr. S, he being a religious man, is like many other religious people, both Catholic and Protestant, a little superstitious in some doctrines, but I think he is freer from bigotry and intolerance than most Protestants. I myself am about as far from being a Catholic as any one I know, but I would prefer to entrust my religious and political liberty to such men as Mr. S, than half the Protestants I have met, so far as my knowledge and observation goes, and I have lived 30 years among them. Irish Catholics as a body have no desire to persecute Protestants, which is remarkable, considering the amount of persecution they have received at the hands of the Protestants. Catholic worship was forbidden under heavy penalties, and Catholic priests were hunted down like wolves in Ireland in the last century, but the Irish Catholics when in power under James

II did not attempt to persecute the Protestants for their religion. It is also remarkable that the first community to establish complete religious liberty was the Catholic colony in Maryland, under Lord Baltimore, in 1670. Their example was followed by the Catholic governor of New York and the Quakers under Penn some years after, while Massachusets bitterly persecuted Quakers and other sects. In Eastern Canada in past times the Catholics, although in a majority, showed no desire to persecute the Protestants. We are all prejudiced more or less, and therefore in his case we must make allowances for his prejudice. Open rebellion for Ireland is not a wise course of action, the odds against her is too great; agitation both in and out of Parliament and passive resistance to unjust laws as is now carried on by the Irish people are much better weapons for a weak nation against a strong military and naval power like Great Britain. The Irish have, I am sorry to say, often been divided in times past, but at present and for many years about five-sixths of the people have been united in their demand for self government such as is possessed by the Canadian Provinces. Ireland would I think be more loyal to the Imperial Parliament if allowed to manage her own affairs of which most of the members of the Imperial Parliament know so little. I fear that mutual jealousies among nations will for a long time prevent any such arrangement for the temporary or permanent abolition of war as that which you have so carefully sketched. Your affectionate cousin, E. Howard." While playing checkers with Dr. Bacon, Dr. Oliver entered; he and Dr. B. are warm friends; Dr. B. nursed him when he was half dead from delirium tremens and preserved his life when his wife and prosperity friends deserted him. Poor Dr. O. is a talented man and once had a very extensive practice, but through drink and opium is a miserable wreck. The Guy Family entertainment has again visited Aston; the most amusing part to me was Mr. Guy, Sr. who imitated every laugh (so naturally) from infancy to tremulous old age that he took the house by storm; those of warm hearts and temperaments enjoyed a hearty laugh, and even the most phlegmatic of the ladies and gentlemen condescended to allow the risible muscles of their faces to slightly move. While at Grant's Miss E. Grant wanted me to subscribe for a newspaper at $1.30 a year and that I would get 2 chromos worth $1 with the paper; told her I could not see how the publishers could carry on such a business without bankruptcy. Spent a pleasant evening at Meredith's; Mrs. M. is suffering from a bad cold she caught while dancing at the Town Hall. Mrs. Murphy tells me that Kirwin is a brutal and drunken husband to Nora Doherty. Spoke with Mr. M. who was underbrushing near the ouse; Cold weather this afternoon, Mr. Murphy. "Thin indade youre right thare, its the quare conthrarey weather we have been having of late. How's youre father and brother?" "Quite well, thank you." "And you uncle's people, how are they?" "All quite well, thank you; I suppose you intend to clear this piece of land this year?" "Yes, this spring if I can manage it. Did you hear anything of Ireland in the papers of late?" "Yes I received several Irish papers a few days ago; the coersive measure passed and seems to have frightened most of the Land Leagures into more moderate language. The Government has bought 100,000 acres of land from some of the landlords and are going to sell it to Irish peasants; this is a proper move in the right direction, but what is 100,000 acres amongst a few million people." "Yes, youre right there, and shure its a disgrace how some of the land league members have deserted their leader." "Well, I see nothing surprising in it. Mr. Parnell might have known that the most devout Irishmen think more of their religion than of their country, and that it would give them offense to see him associate and receive such a good reception from the red republicans, who are looked upon by all good Catholics as most ungodly and wicked men. Parnell has also through this cause lost the sympathy of many of the clergy." "Well, yes, I suppose he should not have gone near those French who hate and would overthrow all religion if they could; still I think that the chief cause of the desertions was the bribery and the British gold. Arlington the municipal secretary called to take the census. The French are very gay of late, have dances several nights in succession, danced up to 12 o'clock and then stopped as Lent commenced; one young man less devout than the rest proposed that they should dance a few hours more which all the young women refused to do and appeared horrified, yet these same women and girls laugh heartily at songs that are 50 degrees below decency. It seems so absurd that people should surfeit themselves with food and amusements for the several days preceding Lent and then deprive themselves of many of the God-given comforts for 40 days. Extract from a letter to Edmund: "The Irish can never expect England to give them their entire independence on account of its close proximity to England; let us hope however that the Irish will ere long succeed in getting justice; how much better for Great Britain and her colonies if her statesmen could be brought to see that their policy is unwise on account of its being in two opposite extremes, in Ireland too oppressive and in Canada too indifferent, causing the majority of the Irish to be always in a state of discontent and the Canadians to look on England's hold on the country as merely nominal; this can be clearly seen by reading some of the leading newspapers in both countries; in Ireland columns full of bitter reproaches against the government and in Canada articles on annexation to the U. S. or of appointing a Canadian governor, also suppositions as to whether Canada will be annexed to the U. S. or become a nation of herself; one would think "John Bull" would have acquired wisdom by the war of 1775 but he seems to have forgotten it and to-day is in a fair way of losing one of the most valuable of his possessions through foolish indifference this time instead of unjust taxes and stupid obstinate rulers as in 1775; just think of one of the leading English newspapers said some time ago that "England did not care if Canada was to become an independent nation or be annexed to the U. S." I cannot agree with you on the question of protection. I am of the opinion that it is of immense benefit to young countries with their resources in a yet undeveloped state, especially where there are other countries (in close proximity) with their industries already established and capable of retarding the undeveloped industries of their neighbor by flooding their markets with cheap goods. There are, I think, 3 periods in the existence of some nations as regards protection, firstly when a country has only a few inhabitants, then of course nearly all manufactured goods have to be imported from other countries, there not being a sufficient number of consumers to

make the "home market" large enough to make home industries
worth while, the 2d period is when the country becomes more
thickly inhabited and a greater revenue is required to make railroads, deepen rivers, and harbors and make, canals, &c. How is
this revenue to be raised? this is the question that has given birth
to protection; the protectionist says $5 to 6,000,000 are required
to perform these many public works which are absolutely necessary for the development of the country; our policy is to raise a
great part of the amount by imposing a duty on all imported
goods that can be manufactured with profit at home instead of
raising the whole amount by direct taxation, from which the nation only derives the benefit of the amount of work done on the
public works, whereas by raising part of the amount by an increased tariff we give an impetus to home industries by infusing
enterprise and confidence into capitalists who at once build factories and are enabled with the tariff's aid to compete with foreign
industries that are more firmly established and who manufacture
in such large quantities that even for a cent a lb. or yd. clear profit.
they can afford to export their goods to foreign markets and hold
those markets for many yrs against the feeble competition of the
undeveloped home industries under the theoretical advantages of
"free trade;" the tariff is not at first so high as to be prohibitory
but is only gradually increased each yr as the productive power
of each industry is capable of supplying the home market; this
policy is strictly adhered to till every profitable industry produces
or manufactures sufficient to supply the country's wants; this is
not accomplished for many yrs as the inhabitants, or at least a
portion of them grow wealthier; they indulge in costlier jewelry,
furniture, dress and in fact everything they use and possess, on
all these the protectionist imposes a duty, that is on all that can
be manufactured with profit in the country and by so doing hastens
the development of the industries of the country and at the same
time derives a revenue sufficiently large to construct all the necessary public works; the moment of course that the home industries wholly supply the home market the government's revenue
from the tariff is nil and the nation enters upon the 3d period of
her existence; her statesmen have now to satisfy themselves whether her manufacturers can compete successfully without the tar-

iff's aid with the industries of the adjoining countries; if her neighbors are less wealthy and powerful she of necessity will have to continue protecting her industries until she can persuade her neighbors to adopt free trade; if however her neighbors are about her equal in development and wealth free trade is the most advantageous policy for all parties, but with nations situated as the United States was 40 yrs ago and as Canada is to-day free trade meant that their inland prosperity should be sacrificed for the trivial advantage of getting a greater amount of return cargoes for their commercial navy by buying manufactured goods in foreign countries instead of having them manufactured in their own towns and cities. Now in the name of reason and common sense which is of most importance to Canada and the U. S. their inland prosperity or the prosperity of their commercial navy; surely the prosperity of about 5,000,000 sq m. of inland territory is of more importance than that of the inhabitants of about 10,000 miles of sea coast with a few seaports and a few thousand seamen; ships and seaports would not have developed the U. S. as protection has done or induced the surplus population of Europe to emigrate to it in preference to other countries, or caused the annual emigration of thousands of F Canadians to its thriving manufacturing centers from Canada to its New England States, which are inferior to Canada in soil and not much superior in climate. It was the great stagnation in Canada's labor market that caused them to do so for naturally as a class they have a great aversion to emigration on account of their devotion to their language, religion and institutions. During the last few years however our government has adopted a national policy viz protection, which has had the beneficial effect of starting manufactories and opening old ones that had been closed during Mackenzie's suicidal policy of allowing American goods to enter Canada at 18 per ct. ad valorem while the Americans charged us 35, but his stubborn persistance in this policy gave him and his party an overwhelming overthrow in the last general elections by the conservatives who had adopted protection as one of the planks in their political platform; since then thousands of Canadians are employed in Canadian factories instead of being obliged to emigrate to the U. S. with England I acknowledge it was totally different, when she first began to advocate free trade, there was no other nation then in existence that could compete with her industries, she had then, as now the greatest fleet in the world, that could land her exports in colonial and foreign ports cheaper than the goods could be manufactured by the undeveloped industries of those countries; it was therefore to her advantage to persuade all her less powerful neighbors to adopt free trade; the keen and sagacious Yankees however were about the first to perceive that England, by carrying out this policy would be able to keep most of her surplus population at home, in her manufacturing towns, and retard the development of U. S. industries by crowding her markets with cheap goods, they also saw that protection was the only means of preventing this unfavorable state of affairs, and adopted it with the present grand result. The best policy for the U, S to-day would be, to maintain a tariff equal to that which all other nations levied against her goods, but as a matter of course adopt free trade if possible, with such countries as Japan, China, the South American Republics and Brazil etc., and sell as much goods as possible to them before they devolope their own industries, but the moment they begin to tax American goods, to retaliate by taxing theirs. When all the civilized nations have through the beneficial means of protection, caused each nation to be self sustaining by manufacturing all that is possible in each of their own countries, the tariffs can then be removed as useless, but kept in readiness in case the industries of the country commenced to languish or be crushed by those of other countries, for all men who have studied the question must acknowlege that it is wiser, juster and more advantageous that each nation should manufacture everything for itself that can be profitably produced in the country. Why should England manufacture all the cutlery of the world, and possess the sole advantage of that industry? why should the U. S. not manufacture her own when she has all the necessary materials at home; if England alone possessed the only coal and iron mines in the world, then it would be more natural for her to do all the manufacturing for iron manufactures. Of course in all natural and artificial products there are some articles that a nation cannot produce or manufacture with profit, such articles as a matter of course the nations should not tax each other, for it would be very foolish indeed for them to tax these imports, making them unnecessarily dearer for the nation's inhabitants when no earthly good could be gained by it, as from natural causes the nation would never be able to manufacture or produce these articles with profit. There is also another feature to be noticed, that is in cases where one of the products of a nation is in danger of becoming exhausted, for instance, if the United States or Canada became alarmed at the rapidity which their forests were being cut down, their government would have a perfect right to impose a prohibitory tariff on all the lumber exported to European countries, and even pass a law allowing no one of its citizens to cut down a tree without planting a young one in its place, but of course in such articles as cattle or wheat, no restrictive laws are necessary, as these countries have an almost unlimited supply. In my opinion, in future yrs. protection will almost universally be adopted by weaker nations, as a safeguard to protect their manufacturers and mechanics from the unequal competition they have to maintain against those of wealthier and more powerful nations; when I say universally I do not include any of those petty states or nations, that can never expect to have sufficient population to make all home industries profitable or practical, as a matter of course when the majority of nations have adopted protection, it will no longer be an increaser of revenue, but its most valuable and important use, it will always retain that of being a preserver of the balance of manufactures and commerce between all the nations of the earth, and as such, its value and efficacy will each yr. become more generally known, till the great majority of statesmen and politicians will have to acknowledge that protection as a preserver of the balance of trade is as necessary at the present day, as were the wars of the allied powers of Europe with Napoleon the Great to preserve the balance of power in Europe. From an address of the Irish Home League I extract the following: "in 1782 Grattan and the volunteers won for Ireland glorious freedom, and laid it down as an incontrovertable truth, that no body of men on this earth has the right to make laws for this kingdom, but the king, Lords, and commons of Ireland; but in 1800 Pitt and Castlereagh, by bribes and bayonets destroyed the glorious fabric of Irish liberty; in 1881 50,000 armed men are in Ireland, 35,000 soldiers and 15,000 military police; public meetings have been prohibited and dispersed; since 1841 Ireland has lost 3,000,000 inhabitants by emigration and famine, till now we have only 167 inhabitants to each square mile, while Belgium a smaller and less fertile country has 459; the population of male voters in Gt. Britain is 2 to 5 of the male population; in Ireland only 1 to 5; in England and Scotland the police are the servants of the local representatives, in Ireland they are under the command of a central executive." Extract from a letter from E. Howard. "The disadvantages of the law of entail can be seen by the rapid manner in which property accumulates in one family, it is in fact nothing but a remnant of the feudal times, it is simply impossible that a tenant farmer can take as much interest in improving and benefiting the farm he rents as the farmer who owns his farm, this I think is part of the cause of the thousands of hovels that disfigure the farms of Ireland. Only two ways exists for England to preserve Ireland as a part of the empire, first by severe laws and a large military force, to keep the oppressed people down by physical force, but by this means there would always be the danger of an enraged Peasantry determined on revenge; rising with one accord and filling the land with blood and murder, or if the military succeeded in keeping the Peasants in subjection, the Peasants would have to adopt the second alternative, that of wholesale emigration from their native land, which has a ruinous effect on Great Britain's strength and prosperity, for every thousand subjects that leaves Great Britain's shores decreases the nation's greatness and increases the strength of America, hastening the development of the grand and wonderful resources of a country that will, in all probability, take England's place as the greatest power of the earth ere another half century has elapsed. The British government, however, is slowly adopting the second and best way of preserving Ireland and uniting it in sympathy and nationality with England, that is to govern it with the sternest justice and give all classes of people (by wise laws) the opportunity of becoming patriotic and prosperous citizens. When this is done it should bring to speedy justice and punishment all those who by contempt and intrigue are enemies to the laws of our great Empire. Some of the ultra landlord party in Ireland appear to think that they have been treated rather severely; they should remember, however that dangerous diseases require desperate remedies. Let us hope, however, that when the Irish begin to feel the benefits of the wise and lenient laws that are being made for them that they will not be unreasonable or unjust, but become industrious and patriotic citizens. If they do not and think they can force England to give up what she has possessed hundreds of years and acquired no more unjustly than half the territories now possessed by the christian nations of the world, they will discover their mistake as the years roll on and that the sons of England would not permit even Gladstone to give away what our ancestors fought and died for and for which England would face the whole of Europe to morrow if they dared to interfere or dictate to us. The British government should, however, encourage the reclamation of every foot of waste land and awake to the reality that it can never be as great a country with a few hundred millionaires and millions of beggars as it can with less extravagantly rich land holders and a more fair distribution of land among all classes of its people. Great Britain is capable of sustaining several million more population than it at present contains; therefore the English government should adopt every means in its power to make the country sustain as great a population as possible, for one happy and contented subject in Great Britain close to the seat of power is worth five subjects in the colonies. Yet at the same time it should not show an apparent indifference to the colonies, but take in hand the management of all the foreign policies of the colonies, allowing them to send a certain amount of representatives to London, a city by no means unworthy to be the capital of the greatest empire that has ever existed. Doing away with the volunteer system in the colonies and replacing them with regular British troops who would not sympathize with the colonists in event of rebellion, and have colonial troops distributed in Great Britain, the heart of the empire, and Australian and Canadian troops in India where there would be no danger of their sympathizing with the Hindoos.

And Hindoos and Mohammdans would make good soldiers for
Ireland and Great Britain, as they would be less likely to sympathize with the people in event of riot or rebellion. It cannot
be that British statesmen have not noticed the dangerous spirit
of independence exhibited by Canadian politicians of late years,
which is caused by England's unwise colonial policy—a policy
that directly encourages the colonies to become full fledged
nations instead of forming one grand united empire with the
mother country. It is quite time that English statesmen should
awake to the reality that the loss of Canada, India and Australia
would be the death blow to the earnest hope of every patriotic
Englishman, that is that the British empire should continue to
be the grandest power upon this earth for centuries yet to come,
which she cannot be in event of the loss of her colonies and even
less than that. England by herself in future years could only
exist as one of the second rate powers of the earth. When her
stupid king lost the United States she lost one of the brightest
gems of her empire's crown. A country of $3\frac{1}{2}$ million square
miles in extent, with a climate unsurpassed for the production of
every kind of grain, fruit and vegetable required to gratify the
wants of the most luxurious and fastidious; a country with thousands upon thousands of navigable rivers; a country now containing 50,000,000 intelligent, industrious and energetic inhabitants who are perfectly acquainted with its wonderful natural
resources, and are yearly adopting the best and wisest means for
their development. Under these circumstances and knowing the
effect that the example and success of the U. S. will have upon
India, Austrilia and Canada, should not the English government
use the greatest wisdom in its colonial policy, seeing that the
separation of this great empire by the vast oceans will be always
a source of weakness, and that nothing but a mutual spirit of
patriotism between the colonies and the mother country, and the
wisest of legislation can keep united the grandest and mightiest
empire that ever existed." I went to Leamington on a visit to
Clifford; next day went to church at Marsdon; had a conversation with Mr. C., he is a member of the Episcopal synod; said
he had brought before that body a motion to have the posting
of secular notices on their churches prohibited, as he thought it

was sacrilegious; also said that a steeple to their little chapel would be an improvement. Clifford supposed they would put it on the end facing the road, which Mr. C. said would not be orthodox. Read in some of J. Carlyle's works, one of the greatest writers of the present day; a history he wrote of Frederic the Great is used as a text book in the schools of Germany. Visited some sugar bushes with Clifford; many of them resemble parks and have comfortable sugar shanties, with the lately invented appliance called "evaporating pans." The sap is let into the pan from tanks by turning a tap, the pan is divided into compartments and placed on brickwork, one end considerably higher than the other, the sap enters the highest and comes out in syrup; have visited several picturesque ravines heavily wooded averaging about 150 below the surrounding country with foaming streams in them, have also went out boating and duck shooting. Clifford and I tried to make a geneological tree but got somewhat confused in arranging the different Aryan, Semetic and Inrainan branches of the human race. Uncle Richard came from Montreal, visited a neighbor of Clifford's with him who is sick; he has been 60 yrs on his farm which altho once good land is utterly exhausted; Clifford has rented 30 acres of meadow for $45, which I consider too much considering its quality; made a collection of specimens of forest wood for uncle, he left in the evening; Clifford and I have boxed considerably of late with boxing gloves. Rev. Morely Punchon the great Methodist preacher is dead; have been reading some of Edgar Poe's poems of late, a pity that such a great genius should have not met with better success; one entitled the Raven is very beautiful; had an argument with Clifford saying how science now clashed with sacred history and that from the the formation of the different stratas of the earth it was clearly proved by scientific men that the world was never created in 6 days, he said he had heard religious apologists affirm that 6 days meant 6 periods of time and not 6 days, told him that I considered that a mere eqivocation for the commandment given to Moses clearly said "for in 6 days God made heaven and earth the sea and all that is therein and rested on the 7th day, therefore thou nor thy servant shall do no manner of work, &c;" now if 6 days meant long periods of time how could man abstain thousands of years from work when he rarely lives to be 80; read a book by Prof. Dawson entitled "the origin of man," it is in harmony with sacred history, he is one of the most learned men in America. There is a great temperance movement amongst the Catholic clergy of this diocese and I am sure it was greatly needed. Extract from letter from Clifford dated April 1st. "The river here is clear of ice, the grass is quite green already." Extract from letter from Edmund: "The commercial and manufacturing prosperity of Ulster are partly the result of its linen trade which was not interfered with by the British government while the woolen and other manufactures in the south of Ireland were intentionally destroyed by hostile legislation; the rate of fire insurance in Belfast has for several years been very high owing I believe to the habit which some Belfast business men have of burning their buildings when business is bad; Ulster men are clever and energetic at business and rather inclined to boast of their success but I do not care for or esteem them in other respects, altho I have met some agreeable exceptions to what I consider the general standard of Ulster character; I do not see that strong drink can be any part of the cause why Ireland is behind Gt. Britain commercially seeing that of the 2 countries I believe Gt. Britain to be the most drunken, altho both are bad enough and I think you will find that from Brazil to Mexico the catholic countries are more temperate than either Canada or the U. S. although commercially less prosperous; last summer I spent several pleasant weeks in London and saw and heard many of England's famous men in the Houses of Parliament; the English have concluded peace with the Boers. Rules I have adopted for daily observance: to rise every morning punctually at 5 o'clock, take a bath and observe scrupulous care in my toilet which increases man's health and longevity, devote ½ an hour's quiet thought in planning out how much useful work and good actions I can accomplish during the day, to never allow trivial incidents to prevent me from performing the daily duties of my life, that I think the ½ hour spent thus is more pleasing to a Supreme Power than in mumbling monotonous silly prayers to God, the Saints and the Virgin, as the majority of the nominal christians do which must be an abomination to the Supreme Being when he knows that the majority of these men and women make no determined effort to make a proper use of the gifts he gave them; in all my conversation and actions to avoid as much as possible everything from which no actual benefit can be derived, to perform everything I undertake in as good and short time as possible, to keep ever before me the thought that every minute I waste and every useless word or thought I indulge in is a sin to a Higher Power, humanity and myself, never to hastily utter a sentiment or perform an action that I am in doubt of its worth until I have submitted it to the rigid examination of my reasoning powers and to cast it away if it meets the disapprobation of my reason and better sentiments, to earnestly encourage in myself and all men an ardent love and devotion for every time that our reason tells us is beautiful, good and beneficial to mankind, and to cultivate in myself and others an intense hatred and abhorence for everything that our reason clearly shows us is detrimental to the interests of humanity and to do all in my power to remove from our earth whatever is prejudicial to the interests of the human race; to always, on all occasions and in all places, denounce in as forcible and polite language as possible whatever I consider as wicked and foolish, that I will never cast myself down with a base sense of defeat and shame in my heart or cry out that I am a lost and helpless creature, for my reason clearly shows me that every man is endowed with noble attributes and gifts in an undeveloped state, that if he only makes a proper use of these he will and can become a noble and god-like being, that I shall never lose an opportunity to hasten that day when every man will be absolutely, spiritually and politically free, when popes, bishops and christian councils will no longer dictate to mankind what they are to believe, a day when all men will be taught that a noble and self reliant people making a proper use of God's gifts is more pleasing to him than the degraded condition of the majority of the present race who are a cringing, servile, superstitious, helpless, ignorant class of slaves under the usurped tyranical power of hundreds of fraudulent hierarchal governments, to always keep before me the thought that no man has ever been truly learned and that all men that live can learn from day to day on this side of the grave; (manuscript missing). During the latter part of March cut firewood for our own use, made rails and drew manure to lot 19 from Houdes place; in the evening studied grammar, rhetoric, Latin and French; from a discussion I had with father it is absolutely necessary for Gt. Britain's prosperity and greatness to have a contented, prosperous and patriotic Peasantry; the English people will ere long see the necessity of developing to their utmost the agricultural resources of the British isles, and that agriculture is of even greater importance than commerce or man ufactures, as the latter has always a certain amount of uncertainty about them, especially since the new policy of protection has come into existence, which in my opinion has and will, seriously affect England's export trade; in future yrs. when all is colonies and most of its foreign customers have developed their manufacturing industries by protection, there also cannot be a doubt that when the U. S have finished developing their industries, that it will become a successful competitor with England in the markets of the world, the greater natural resources of the U. S. will then more than counteract the advantages Gt. Britain derives from her more central position, and the better development of many of her industries to that of the U. S., besides it is almost certain that most of the nations of the earth will adopt protection when they see the beneficial effect it has had and does have, on those nations that adopt it, for this reason England should not place too much trust in manufactures as a means of retaining her surplus population at home; she may for some yrs. more do most of the manufacturing for India and Africa, but even these countries will in a few yrs. awake to the advantages derived from manufacturing for themselves, therefore under these circumstances it is the height of madness in the English Government to tolerate landlordism, under which system Gt. Britain can never support as large a population as under the freehold system; it ought to do away with all laws restricting the sale of large estates and their subdivision amongst all the children in equal shares, also that every man that owned a large estate should allow none of it to be kept in useless preserves for shooting game, and should keep his large estate in just as useful a state of productiveness as that of the small farmer, or in event of his not doing so, to be obliged to sell the greater part of it, in fact a law should be passed in a country so thickly populated as Gt. Britain that would allow no man to own over 100 acres; the government should also reward with large premiums all farmers who keep their farms in the highest state of cultivation, and fine all those whose land is in an imperfect state of cultivation; it should also do all in its power to increase the subdivision of land, by increasing the facilities for its transfer, and not have the transfer of a few acres of land cost £50 as it now does in Gt. Britain; manufactures have however done a great deal for England's greatness, it has employed several million of her surplus population, and is the chief cause of her maritime greatness by giving her commercial navy employment; when modern manufactures were in their in fancy England with her central position, enterprising civilized inhabitants and wealth, was able to take the lead in manufactures, and supply its colonies and foreign nations for many yrs. with its manufactured goods, and by these advantages and start it has become the greatest commercial nation of the earth. As to the present strikes in the large manufacturing centers of Gt. Britain, they have been only caused by a temporary commercial depression that has visited nearly every civilized country on the face of the earth, which has been brought on by want of thrift and extravngance, but to all appearance the commercial crisis is quickly passing away, and again the light of the furnace and the sound of the hammer will be heard throughout the land; of course it is plain to all who take an interest in the subject that England will have to find new markets for her goods as the yrs. roll on, as most of the European nations and Englands colonies have begun to manufacture for themselves, but for many yrs. to come England will rank as one of the greatest manufacturing powers; the superior quality of her goods will enable her to sell considerable quantities for many yrs. to those nations whose industries are only partially developed, besides this as the millions of inhabitants of Asia become civilized they will buy largely of European manufacturers and for many yrs. be profitable customers until they commence to protect their own industries. While spending an evening at Meredith's Nicholas inadvertently made use of a very vulgar expression in the presence of his mother and sisters, who censured him severely for it, he of course apologized and appeared greatly ashamed; this comes from being only a gentleman in society and not one at heart, alas how many families there are whose manners are only for society, and not for every day life, a gentleman who is not as courteous to his mother and sisters, and even to the poorest of his lady acquaintances as he is to a duchess or princess, deserves rather the name of a despicable hypocrite than that of a gentleman. Several of the oldest French settlers have died on our range this Winter and Spring; gave Joe Vincent and Jim Spencer the "job" of making several acres of fence on Oak Hill, $1.50 for making new picket and rail fence for an acre and $1.10 for rebuilding an old picket and rail fence, all the material of course was drawn on the ground for them; while unloading some shingles that I sold to Meredith's I discovered that Herbert Carmichael had written a lot of trash on one of the shingles about Florence and myself; I wrote underneath: H. C. should keep his witticisms for servant girls and bar maids who would no doubt appreciate them. I have decided if Uncle Jerrold and Richard will not force me to sell Oak Hill, to become the best farmer in these parts and go to an Agricultural College a few months every winter and study agricultnre from a theoretical as well as practical point of view, but if they continue to dictate to us about the best way of farming, which they know less about than myself, having never had any practical experience, I shall give them back all they have given me and whatever I may have earned myself and start out into the world on my own resources; aunt and uncle are becoming very devout, and have family prayers every Sunday; I have noticed that even the most wordly people turn their thoughts to religion as old age advances upon them. Oh inconsistent religions! When will you so educate your followers that all their lives will be so beautiful, noble and exalted, that they will not be filled with doubts and fears at the approach of death, but with calm unfaltering courage leave this battle field of life, like heroes and not like cowards, but what better can we expect when these fraudulent churches teach their dupes that to eat a little piece of bread and confess with humility our sins to a fellow man, is as necessary and even more so than a noble life, for these priests teach "that a man who lives a noble and exalted life is damned if he refuses with scorn their prayers and aid," and yet believe that God created all intelligent men as responsible beings, who have to render no one an account but himself, and that no prayers or intercessions bought with gold can better his condition, in the great and mysterious hereafter. Old Doherty, who is 72 years old, has married again to a widow 32 years old with four children, much to the indignation of his two sons, Bat and Dennis, who fear they will lose the property he possesses. Bat tells me he sold $800 worth of produce off his farm of 75 acres last year, of which $200 was derived from honey. As uncle Jerrold now as well as uncle Richard insists on my selling Oak Hill I have consented, but will give up farming and study for some profession. Part of a conversation with father: The cause of the low position that most farmers occupy in society is the want of a higher system of education amongst them. This defect is chiefly caused by careless indifference, and partly by the occupation itself, which men can follow with even moderate success without even a common school education. But education is necessary for the profession of agriculture, and even if it were not, farmers should educate themselves to become gentlemen if nothing else. Beaufort Churchill has arrived and is thinking of buying Littleton's place from Roussin for $2,000; and for cash he would sell it for several hundred less. It is a valuable property, on the edge of the village, 60 acres in extent, 10 of which are in woodland; a brickyard on it; a beautiful large house on it, with mansard roof, galleries, verandas, and surrounded with a grove of stately trees with delightfully shady avenues, and grounds tastefully laid out in gravel walks and flowerbeds. 17th of May. I will have to make what I can out of Oak Hill this summer. I am now living on it while I plant the spring crop. On the 20, Tom, our hired boy and myself planted 20 bushels of potatoes. Joe Vincent and Jim Spencer made 22 acres of fence besides what I made myself; I objected to part of the fence they had made in the woods where the poles were too far apart which would allow calves to get through, and in other places where they had merely made a "slash fence" of brush instead of poles, the former only lasts one year as the weight of the snow crushes it down in winter. I had difficulty in training a young horse to plow with one of the old ones, but after three days I succeeded and can plow without a driver. The Elms, May 10th. P. S. I have sown several acres in grass seed which is very difficult to sow in windy weather. We have had only two showers this spring and are very much in want of rain; father and mother have returned from Port Huron; Flora has had a little son; in about a fortnight D. V. I shall have all my pressing work done; we had a most welcome rain last night, like Epp's cocoa, grateful and comforting; this part of the country is looking green and pretty now; the postscript of this letter is like a school girls, almost as long as the letter. C. H. Goldsmith." While driving home I was surprised to see how much the Aston end of our range is deserted; only one French family in 6 miles of country filled with small deserted clearances; those that left were merely half lumberers and laborers; later on I have no doubt a better class of settlers will settle on this land, but not until the splendid fertile lands of the great Northwest are settled. Took a ride across the country last Sunday to see some French friends; in returning a magnificently grand thunderstorm overtook me; I was nearly thrown from the horse through a flash of lightning in front of us on the road which caused the horse to suddenly rear on its hunches; It is quite natural, however, that a dumb beast should be afraid, but I think in man such fear is absurd. I was much amused at the way the French young ladies shrieked, "My God, how terrible!" whenever there was a crash of thunder. Next day four French women came 3 miles with some cows that I had agreed to pasture for their husbands on ot 29; their conversation was so disgustingly low that even I, unsensitive being that I am, was filled with astonishment and contempt when I considered that they are regarded "as respectable women and devout members of an infallible church; had a conversation with Israel Dufresne, his opinions are very barbarous as regards his duties towards his children, upon my word if a brute beast could speak it would describe its duties towards its offspring a somewhat the same manner. He said "I feed and clothe my children and have them taught their catechism and prayers, surely no one can call me a bad father;" truly this is a strange age, civilization, liberty, virtue and education are advancing side by side with barbarity, immorality, tyranny, superstition and ignorance; went to a private party at Aston in company with Nicholas, Florence, Maud, Mabel W. Miss A. and Mr. M. and Mr. C. (who are trying amateur farming on Christie's farm) in a double carriage; while we young gentlemen were taking off our overcoats in the gentlemen's dressing room Nicholas made a remark about a lady acquaintance worthy of one of the gayest and most unprincipled courtiers of either Charles II. or Queen Isabella's court; heaven knows I am bad enough but I have never said nor ever will say anything against a lady that I would be ashamed to repeat in her presence; whenever I associate with true ladies they exercise an elevating influence on me and I would no more think of uttering anything improper against them or in their presence than if they were so many angels; after much dancing and a most enjoyable time generally and a sumptuous supper we returned home at 2 in the morning. Extract from a letter to my cousin Ethel Churchill: "You will no doubt be surprised to receive a letter from me as I suppose you have forgotten by this time our early correspondence in childhood; I now write at your brothers request with the hope of persuading you to come and live with him in Canada, he arrived here on the 29th and since then I have been showing him different farms about the country, one of which he prefers to the rest on account of its being situated on the edge of Aston village which has over 2,000 inhabitants and is a centrally situated and rising town well connected by rly with most of the leading towns and cities in the province and has one of the finest markets in this part of the country, it has also a small select circle of society which as a rule is not met with in rural towns, I mention this as with ladies this is generally the first consideration; (gave an elaborate description of Lyttleton's farm) from what your brother tells me it appears that he would like to become a farmer for those that really like it it is one of the finest and most independent professions a man can follow; in following most of the other professions and trades a man is dependant on the public for his living whereas with a farmer it is exactly opposite; kings, statesmen, doctors, lawyers are all dependant on the farmer for their sustenance, banks may fail, stocks become worthless, goods decrease in value, house burn and ships sink but a good farm can never be lost except through the fault of its owner; it has often been a surprise to me that farmers as a class are so much inferior to other professions or even tradesmen and mechanics intellectually, but I am glad to say the farmers of this country are at last beginning to see the necessity of a thorough enducation, without which no man can attain to that position that every man with true ambition should amongst his fellowmen of the present age. We saw the owner of the farm who asks £600 for the place, a very low price, but a rather large sum for your brother to pay, cash down. Your brother thought that you and your sister would be kind enough to lend him $2,000 and reserve to yourselves the right of first mortgage on the place. In doing this you would incur no risk, and at the same time have a beautiful home to live in without paying the enormous rent you are now paying in Ireland, and you would be able to live at about one-half the amount it now costs you and get 6 per cent. interest on this safe investment of your money. In event of any failure on your brother's part the right of first mortgage would secure to you your money, but I think that this is scarcely possible as my brother and I commenced under less favorable circumstances and have succeeded in a most satisfactory manner. Land in Canada is certain to rise in a few years, when emigration from Eastern Canada to the great Northwest ceases, which at the present time causes a great many eastern farms to be thrown upon the market. From a letter to uncle Richard: "Mr. St. George, from whom I purchased Oak Hill, has written to me saying that if I desire he will give me 8 years to pay for the place instead of 4. I had written to him saying that I did not wish to dispose of the valuable hardwood timber on the place at the exceedingly low price it now commands; also that a longer term of payment would enable me to adopt a better system of cultivation and feed the produce on the farm instead of selling it which is certain in the course of time to impoverish the best of land. I merely state this to show you that I did not make a foolish bargain in purchasing this valuable and beautiful estate and that it was easily within my power to pay for it; however, as you and uncle Jerrold have commanded me to sell it in many of your letters, I submit and will say no more on the subject. I send you an account of my expenditures on the place: First instalment on the land, $100; to notary for making deed, $5; for provisions for a plowing bee, $1.50; for snow plowing main road during the winter, $1.50; for manure, $8 for 35 double loads; wire for fence, $1.25; 16 bushels of seed potatoes, $7.50; 24 acres of fence, $21; 29 bushels of oats, $10.50. Fortunately the late frosts did not damage any of our crops as they were not over ground; the orchard is heavily loaded with apples, but the plums were destroyed by the frost." From a letter to Clifford: "On Oak Hill I have sown 22 bushels of oats, 15 of potatoes, and am at present preparing 3 acres for buckwheat; the rest of the farm is in meadow and pasture. When will the Jews, Christians, Mohammedans and Pagans stop their senseless wrangling about imaginary doctrines and revelations and devote more of their time to the more practical and glorious work of elevating the human race and beautifying this earth. Mr. Meredith has contributed $18 towards painting the inside of the church afresh and I have collected $14 towards it. Beaufort C. is stopping with us at present; he seems a half dead and half alive sort of a fellow, with no energy or ambition; a lukewarm individual of a somewhat religious turn of mind; showed him all the sights of Aston; descended No. 5 shaft at the copper mines, 300 feet deep; the mine is only partially worked, the four other shafts are full of water." Extract from a letter to uncle Jerrold, 5th of June. "We received last week the quarterly allowance that you so generously send us; we did not go to Montreal this time as we were too busy at work on our farm planting the spring crops. This spring has been very unfavorable for clearing land on account of the wet weather in May; the rain, however, has been of benefit to the hay crop, which to all appearance will be very heavy. The fertility of the lowlands on Elmbrooke is astonishing, year after year they produce heavy crops of hay without manure. Most of our clearance in Elmbrooke is under hay which is one of the most profitable crops around here; in fact we are obliged to hay the land the first year it is cleared and keep it under hay and pasture until the stumps have sufficiently decayed to have them removed, this generally takes 6 or 8 years. Although the clearance on Oak Hill is some of the highest land in this part of the country and has not been manured for many years the crops are in excellent condition. We have taken a great many animals to pasture as it is one of the best and cheapest means of enriching an impoverished soil. Have visited Clifford since dear Richard's death; he, poor fellow, appears very lonesome as Richard was his inseparable companion for the last few years after his health began to fail.." Montreal, 17th June. "Dear Arthur, your uncle Jerrold still insists on your selling Oak Hill, in this I think he shows his foresight and profound judgment. The crops will have to pay you for whatever you have spent on the place, you have no further interest in the lot so cease bothering about it." While at G's my aunt quizzed me about Florence and Maud; I grew indignant and told her I did not see anything ridiculous in my preferring the company of refined and amiable young ladies to that of vulgar, ignorant country girls. Andre La Rivere had a bee; 15 men were at it; in the evening played cards, sang songs, etc.; there was not enough of the fair sex present to have a dance. A few rules I have added to those already mentioned: "Never put off till to-morrow what I can do to-day;" "To be affable and courteous to all men and try to be agreeable and good company to all classes of people; Devote from 7 to 10 each evening to literature; Never to spend $2 where $1 is sufficient; To cultivate the habit in reading of skipping whatever is uninstructive and useless by which I shall be able to accomplish 5 times as much good reading; To avoid all ostentatious display in dress or otherwise which is a sure sign of a weak and vulgar mind; To always keep alive within me an earnest and honorable ambition to accomplish all I can for myself and the age I live in." June 15th; part of a letter to Uncle Richard: "We are at present sowing buckwheat; the weather has been very warm of late, without any rain, which if it continues will seriously damage the hay and grain crops on high lands," Extract from a letter from Clifford: "Very few people believe that war can be abolished; it is just as impossible to abolish the war of nations as that of individuals, it is impossible for us to change human nature. When a nation's government or king becomes enraged against another whom they think they can beat, then they will have war and no treaties can prevent them. You can no more stop war than you can stop murder. In ancient times their weapons were so clumsy that comparatively few were killed, but now they kill many in a short time. I think we shall have war until the time of the millenium. The only way to prevent war that I can think of is for some one to invent a weapon so deadly that one man armed with it would be equal for a million similiary armed. This would put a stop to it as it would be sure death to all parties engaged." In answer to the above: "I cannot agree with you that it is as easy to abolish the war of nations as that of individuals. For a government that governs with wisdom and justice can easily prevent insurrections and rebellions amongst the people it rules but could not prevent the individual crime of murder or entirely suppress it; I think it is absurd for you to imagine that it would be as difficult to persuade the Christian governments of the world to abolish war, as to persuade all men to cease from murder, for in the first case we have only a few thousand intelligent men to convince, who as a rule strive to make laws for their country's good; whereas in the latter case millions of ignorant and wicked men would have to be reformed; I still maintain that if 4 nations like England, France, Germany and the United States, formed a treaty between each other to settle all further disputes by arbitration, and do away with the awful expense of their armies, that no power on earth could dare attack them even though they did not have a single soldier; the millenium arguments are simply ridiculous, the idea! Civilized men forsooth, must continue murdering each other for the sake of fulfilling some ancient prophecy, this is as bad as the scriptural defense of slavery, "a servant of servants shall he (the Negro) be." I feel confident that long before that long expected Christian period arrives, the more civilized portions of our earth will have abolished this cruel relic of barbarism. Uncle Tom of Waterford writes. "Beaufort's father's family are all extremely delicate, and Beaufort himself is too weak to stand hard work, besides nearly all his money would be taken up in purchasing the place, and Beaufort could never direct even the hired men; it appears to me ridiculous that he should own a farm let alone manage one; if Beaufort was a man likely to put his shoulder to work and stick to it, I should be glad to see him settle down near you " From Uncle Jerrold; "at least half of the property in Gt. Britain is "held in trust," and a man who violates this trust is liable to penal servitude; I have bought Oak Hill from you and will hold it in trust for you; your Uncle Peter's family have very little more allowed them than you, and they have not only saved money but have most nobly, like fine hardworking independent souls, written to say that they only require for the present £3 a month; in another case where I have been making an allowance to one of my family he has with the manly spirit of the Goldsmith family, which has ever distinguished our name as hard workers and self-reliant, with perhaps one exception, sent me back the whole of the yrs. allowance, and 3 pairs of bracelets, of diamonds, pearls and emeralds, with 2 emerald rings for your Aunt Mary, in acknowledgment for her kindness to him while in London; I do not say this by way of hinting at any return; my only and greatest reward will be to see that what I do now for those I love will be of use, and place the dear ones, my own good relations and the children of my darling sister in a free and independent position; you can redeem Oak Hill later on if you wish, by paying me 6 per ct. interest on what I pay Mr. St. George." This is one of the many letters that Uncle Jerrold has written to me saying that I could keep the place, but Uncle Richard is determined that I shall not keep it, because I did not ask his consent, and he thinks he knows best, although I have given him practical proofs that it is one of the cheapest and most beautiful farms in this part of the country, in fact parts of both their letters to us of late have been extremely hurtful to my feelings; he and Uncle Richard well know that Tom and I have worked like slaves and even deprived ourselves of the common neccessaries of life, to make our efforts at bush farming a success, and yet they sometimes write to us as if we were idle and extravagant, for my part I will not stand it much longer. Extract from a letter from Uncle Jerrold: "I protest against Arthur's acting contrary to your Uncle Richard's wishes in keeping that lot, and have written to your uncle to the same affect, once more for all I repeat to you again and for the last time, as I hope it may not be neccessary again, you must be solely guided by what your Uncle Richard says in all your transactions, you may remember in my letters to my dearest sister, your good mother, I wished to let her see that the annuity of £100 a yr. was right, as I knew she always felt a reluctance to incur obligations to any one, but in her last letter to me she annulled and repudiated this by saying, she only accepted my gifts as a token of my brotherly affection, and added, that so far as her whole life went, that it was she who was indebted to me, at the same time it is but fair to tell you, that in event of my death I had provided absolutely for the payments, although as the case stands I have not executed any deed or stamped document, so that as matters stand at present my income to you is not compulsory, and depends on your acting with that care and prudence for which I have hitherto esteemed you, God forbid that anything should arise to prevent me from performing towards you what I consider as my sacred duty and promise, and which it would pain my heart to discontinue, and which please God I shall never do; do not take this in anger, or as a threat, it is only intended in kindness and love; you will be glad I know that your cousin has passed his examination at Oxford; we have had all day and all night the most violent thunder storm I have ever seen in England, the great downfall of rain has done good to the land; I hope you will soon be able to make a little money out of your land; it looks odd to us in England where we pay heavy rents and awful taxes and yet save money; told Uncle Richard that the fact of so many farms being to let is greatly exaggerated, as he would find very soon if he came here to buy or rent one; for the land Arthur has bought I shall pay for, deducting 6 per ct. interest from your annuity, and so save any expense." "July 10th. Dear uncle; I received your letter a few weeks ago, but waited till Uncle Richard came out and arranged about the lot. I have to thank you for your generous offer to pay for Oak Hill and give me time to pay for it at six per cent. which offer I would have accepted had not uncle Richard positively forbid me to have nothing more to do with the lot after th s fall after I have taken the crops off of it and he has repaid to me the $100 I paid to Mr. St. George on account. The potatoes are in fine condition and the Colorago beetles are kept from doing damage by applying Paris green and London purple to the leaves with a watering pot; the hay crop I am sorry to say is much inferior to last yr. about ⅓ less; as regards running into debt you say truly that it is the source of ruin to thousands, that is to those who become debtors thro reckless extravagance; with us however it was entirely different, I went into debt for Oak Hill it is true, but it was one of the cheapest bargains I have seen for many yrs. in this part of the country; I did it with the best of intentions to have an estate that I would be proud of when you came to see us; I had decided to throw my whole energies into farming and make it a success; such a debt as the one I incurred I am proud of and if no farmer were allowed to incur such debts as these few of them could rise above the position of market gardeners and laborers. It is true we have 400 acres besides Oak Hill but it would cost us more to clear 100 acres of it than the whole 200 acres of lot 29 with 100 acres cleared on it free from stumps; I cannot tell you how my uncle's persistent refusal to allow me to keep this beautiful farm has dampened my hopes and hurt my feelings but I have had to submit altho I could have paid for the farm easily from its own resources alone in the 8 yrs I had to pay it." "Elmbrooke June 22, dear uncle Richard, I of course will have to submit to your decision about Oak Hill but at the same time I would respectfully remind you that what you call unwise land and property speculation has been the very means by which you have amassed the greatest part of your present fortune; I will as you say devote a little more time to mental culture without which not even the man most perfectly endowed with physical gifts can ever expect to rise much higher than a common laborer; the progress of the man now-a-days that depends on physical labor alone for the accumulation of wealth as compared with the man that uses his brains is as the progress of the carrier pigeons of former days compared with the electric telegraph of the present day; a man at best working every day for 50 yrs could only accumulate by rigid economy and high pay about $15,000, which is but a trifle as compared with the vast fortunes amassed in a few yrs by men who use their brains as well as their hands; with but few exceptions most men to meet with more than ordinary success in life must have a good education, it is the most necessary of all things before a young man devotes all his energies to any other particular object. Uncle Jerrold speaks about our having so much hired labor but you well know that I and Tom with one boy cannot save 70 acres of hay alone. In earthing up our potatoes we used the cultivator you gave Uncle Herbert and found that it was a great economizer of labor, we have also put floors in the mows of the new barn. 4th July, since last I wrote in these pages I have been in one continued round of business, pleasure and hard manual labor; I have taken 3 horses and 11 cows to pasture and had some lively electioneering to keep our school from falling into the hands of the R. C's; have struck a rate of 2½ mills on the dissentient property and decided to keep the school open 4 months in some central place in the parish; have been many times at Meredith's during the spring and early summer, they have had a great many visitors as much as 14 staying at their house at one time. Received an introduction to Mr. B. brother to Miss Brown of Toronto of happy memory, whom I shall never forget, what with evenings at cards, rides and drives thro the country, picnics, croquet, lawn tennis, and conversaziones, we all had a most delightful time. Mr. M. had a severe accident, nearly broke his arm and received many bruises by falling thro the floor of a chemical works at Montreal, he is a chemist as well as a mineralogist and has been making several experiments lately. President Garfield has nearly lost his life by the hand of Charles Guiteau, either a lunatic or villain, has shot him in the groin, the ball has not yet been extracted; a new invention is to be tested by which the doctors expect to be able to locate the exact position of the ball without probing the wound. Wrote to Mr. Blair, secretary of McGill College, to send me a prospectus of the College, as I have decided to go to college; study for some profession and give up farming, in which I say to a person who has capital and respectable neighbors farming is an independent and honorable profession but this is not the case with those who have no capital and are obliged to live amongst a vulgar community. "Montreal, my dear Mr. Howard; we were all indeed deeply grieved when your mother was called to be with Jesus and I well understand how truly you miss both her affection and wise counsel, but you have one to go to all the day long who is more than a mother to those who really trust and seek his counsel, and I trust you will look to him before you take any step in the purpose you now speak of, as regards the information you require I may say that the course of a student desiring to enter law is to attend the chambers of an advocate and for which he is indentured for 4 years, one yr allowed him, if during his course he takes the degree of B. L. A. which takes 3 yrs. to attend lectures and examination in every session in March, the student attends these lectures during the 3 yrs of his indentureship; I send you a calendar which explains examination; the fees for lectures are the two first $5 and $20. A lawyer might take you into his office for your services though in some you pay to be indentured, of course you have to board yourself; you ought to consult your uncle Goldsmith who would I am sure do all he can for you; it is astonishing the number of well educated young men who take to farming, prefering the independence of the life to the busy and trying life of professions; that is a good aphorism "man wants but little here below nor wants that little long;" the blessed return of the Lord Jesus for his believing people may be this yr., and then dear friend we shall with your precious mother pass an eternity of happiness with him "who washed us in his own blood and made us kings and priests unto God, and his Father" &c.; Rev. 1 chapt. 5 and 6 verses; we are just at the end of the journey, our lamps are burning with oil, (the spirit,) and we shall enter in when he calls. Your affectionate friend, W. C. Blair, Sec." Have also read Tom Moore's poems, his longest is Lalla Rookh, which brings Eastern scenes to perfection before the eyes; have been reading Byron, there seems to me a tinge of sadness about many of his poems. "20th July. Dear Tom and Arthur, the only way I can account for your Uncle Jerrold's letter, saying that you could keep Oak Hill, is that it was written 2 days after he wrote to you, all you have to do in the matter is to write to him, stating that the property has been bought for him in my name, he ought to understand my sentiments by this time for I have written several times to him saying, that if you kept the property it would ruin you, and put you on the road in 5 yrs.; you have plenty of land, one acre of your land on lots 34 and

35 is worth the whole of the 200 acres at Oak Hill; it is also too near your Uncle Herbert, and there has been too much quarrelling already; when you bought that land you were what Mr. Gladstone calls "land hungry;" it would have made you what Western people call, "land poor;" should your Uncle Jerrold desire to keep the lot, I shall have the deed made in his name." ".Montreal, July 30th. Dear Tom and Arthur, I have just recd, a letter from your Uncle Jerrold, he has again changed his mind and says he intends to keep the lot for a few yrs.; I find from sad experience that it is easier to buy property than to dispose of it, the Elms farm costs me £72 a month, besides keeping up the house, then there is my city and sea-side residence to keep up; I have had several advantageous offers for Oak Hill, and have again written to your uncle trying to persuade him to sell it; for you to keep it would only make slaves of yourselves; all I have said on this subject has beeen prompted for your sole benefit; I may have been mistaken but time will tell." The Princess Louise and Prince Leopold her brother, have left Canada for England; there is some scandal between Mr. Chaplean, Prime minister of Quebec, and another M. P., which is not very creditable to Canadian Statesmen; Mr. C. thinks his work ought to be sufficient to pay for his board, but father does not; received several Land league circulars from E. Howard, the Irish Peasantry have certainly grievances to complain of, but many of them have been redressed by Gladstone's government; by the census of 1880, Canada has 4,350,933 population; in 71—3,670,000; Bradford, our county has 21,199, in '71—19,177; a very slow increase in 10 yrs.; there is considerable excitement about an infidel M. P., Mr. Bradlaugh, who refused to take an oath on account of conscientious scruples; a suit was brought against him for sitting in the house without taking an oath, and he was fined, although he afterwards consented to take the oath; it was decided by the House that as he had once refused to take it he should not be allowed to take it, 20 policemen prevented him from entering the House, Lord Selbourne and many other eminent lawyers are of the opinion that the House exceeded its lawful bounds of power in refusing to allow Bradlaugh to sit in the House after he had been honorably elected to the Parliament

by the people. I had an argument with father, and said that all men irrespective of their religions, or belief should be allowed to have a voice in their country's government as long as they kept the secular laws, and were worthy citizens. An Insurance agent wanted me to insure my life, I said if I was a married man I might consider it my duty to do so, but as I had no one dependant upon me I did not care to pay $60 a yr., even though the money would be refunded to me in 20 prs.; although hundreds of speeches have been made on Protection, thousands of clever men in both the Conservative and Liberal party, hold directly opposite views on a subject that is of so vital importance to the manufacturing and commercial prosperity of their country; the adoption of that policy however, has had a most beneficial effect on the country. 30th July; have hired a man at $26 a month and board; some Sundays I go to church and spend the afternoons at Mr. Dougalls, playing checkers with him and other players on his lawn, which is a rendevous for the best players of Aston. Have given the job of cutting some of the hay on Oak Hill to Fetreault on halves; wild raspberries sell at 25cts. for 5 gallons. Helena Wakefield is on a visit at G's., she is a sensible, religiously inclined young lady, but alas, has red hair and a freckled face, which spoil the effect of a good figure and intellectual brow; have had a picnic and a few private parties for her benefit. I paid Mrs. Vincent to repair the rooms in father's house, as Mr. C. expects his wife to arrive shortly; have nearly finisned excavating the earth to a depth of 3 ft. out of our stable to make it have a height of 7 ft. Nicholas came out to see us with a friend, shot at targets, boxed, wrestled, played cricket and performed other athletic sports, such as lifting weights, throwing weights and movements on a horizontal bar; my aunt and Ethel passed, my aunt looked as astonished as if we were Earth men from Africa; this will give her fresh fuel to throw on her altar of gossip. "Cork, August '81. Dear Uncle Jonathan, I asked Uncle Timothy for information about Beaufort, but he never answered my letter. I have to give you a scolding for the nonsense you have thought of, and putting into Beauforts head such nonsense as those nice young men in Aston village, if I ever go to America it is for a home, not to be married; I thought you quite a different man, than to talk that trash, when I was on a visit with you and Aunt Sarah in London, you never spoke thus to me, nor will I or Angelica stand it, nature seldom changes with the climate. We never intended leading a life of celibacy while in Ireland but once we set our feet on American shore we will lead such; do not think for one instant I am in play, we do not care how fine your young Americans are for we do not want them, we will refuse to go if we hear any more disgusting low talk, perhaps if Beaufort was not married he would not be in such haste to marry now; it is for our health we should go out and not for our marriage, for I am far from being strong; we have chosen where we will love and have resolved to love our choice, uncle Jonathan; let me tell you that job has been taken off your hands; give us a solemn promise that you will never utter such trash again; love to Beaufort, Tom, Arthur and yourself, your affec. niece, Ethel M. Churchill. I am really ashamed that father did not exhibit better taste than to write thus to ladies who are old enough to be the average young man's mother; he once at least was a gentleman in manners but from constant vulgar associations during the last 20 years has greatly deteriorated. From Clifford: "The Elms, Aug. 23, '81. I only finished haying on the 5th; the first yr we got 20 loads off this place, last year 29 and this yr 58, off of 6½ acres of clover, the first cutting yielded 16 double loads and 2 single and the 2d cutting 9 double loads and yet there will be a good aftermath; we have put up 3 miles of fencing this year. President Garfield is, I read, in a very precarious condition. Hay is selling here for $10 a ton. Has your poetic muse been awakened lately if so please favor us with a copy. Mother, Flora, and I of her children have just left, Mabel and little Angelica are staying with me. From a letter to uncle Richard I have had an offer of $900 for Oak Hill from a reliable party who will pay half down, so if uncle Jerrold has decided to dispose of it he should not lose this good opportunity; we have just finished cutting some swamp grass which makes good fodder for cattle; some of our oats will be ready for harvesting in a few days." Received a postal card from Dr. Bacon and Mr. Meredith, church wardens for St. Mark's inviting us to a meeting to to be held in the church on church affairs; its members are $180 in arrears of their dues; the envelope system is not a success, it does not gratify human vanity as well as an open silver salver. We have to go twice a week to the village for bread as it gets mouldy if kept longer. Poor Dr. Oliver is dead, a man of brilliant talents, splendid education and capable of being an ornament to his profession had not his health and reputation been blasted by the use of opium and whiskey. The Meredith's have been invited to a high toned picnic of select French people at which Mr. Mignault, member from our county is to be present. We pay 15 cts a dozen for eggs; we rise every morning during haying at ½ past 4 and work till ½ past 7. The dramatic club of St. Andre cleared $75 at their last entertainment which is accounted for as it was in aid of the church and of course all the faithful attended. 16th Aug. the whole atmosphere is full of smoke a sign that forest fires are at work. Philip G. brought us some bear's meat which is as tender as chicken but to me had an unpleasant wild flavor. Roussin has had a beutiful fountain placed in his lawn, he is one of the most liberal and energetic French citizens in Aston In our spare time we are stumping our clearance. The English Lords and Commons cannot agree on the Irish Land Bill, but they will of course give way to the will of the Commons. The forest fires have run all over our clearance and done most valuable work by burning all the stumps out. Sarah is on a visit at Uncle Herbert's. How quick time flies, it seems but a short time ago all G. children and ourselves used to sit in the orchard in the cool air of a summer's evening and talk together about the great things we were going to accomplish. Childhood is truly a very happy period in one's life; joy and pleasure is less counteracted by the cares and vexations of life. Went to Brodeur's to borrow an ox yoke; we broke our own in pulling stumps; Louis was making rails for a hotel keeper of Aston. Mrs. B. Sr. tried to blow the dinner horn but failed; I pitied the sad look upon her face. Well do I remember years ago the strong, clear blast of that horn for three-fourths of a mile distance, when she used to call her poor old Antoine to dinner; but age has taken her teeth away leaving her a gray-headed, sad old woman. Broke Brodeur's yoke; this makes 3 ox yokes in 5 hours; all the ornamental trees we left in the clearance have been destroyed by fire. Daniel C. and I went to Davenport to a pic-nic; the grove in which it was held had too much brushwood for comfort; there were about 50 people in all, mostly of the middle class as could be seen from the ungramatical way they spoke. Old men talked agriculture and politics old matrons of gossip and "garden sass," the young men and girls amused themselves singing to the music of an old organ that ommitted the most heart-rending sounds as an ostentatious young girl, with as many grimaces as a French dancing master, played thereon, and looked around occasionally with that self consequential air that led one to believe that she actually thought we were all enraptured with the music. There were also several young children who appeared to derive great amusement from the numerous swings attached to the branches of the trees. I organized a set for croquet, and with Florence as my partner played a few games, but the afternoon passed in a most intolerable dull manner. In the evening there was music, singing and short orations in the church, and I must say I never heard such a great variety of miserable, squeaky voices. One clergyman, from Rawlings, was ungentlemanly enough to criticise a short speech Rev. L. C. W. made, but he being the meekest man I ever saw or expect to see, never uttered a word; the proceedings closed with "God Save the Queen." As all the apples are being stolen on Oak Hill I have sold them to Fetreault for $5. A comet is visible every evening in the vicinity of the "Great Bear." Read an old book called "Old Eritz," an historicnl novel of Germany. In reading books of life 250 years ago, one gets a good opinion of the increase of the morality of mankind. Fenians have had a fiendish plot to blow up English public buildings. Garfield it is thought will recover; his life has been one of noble self denial and heroic courage. Russia, through nihilism, is in a very unsettled state; France from a steady policy of international improvement has suddenly become the most aggressive nation of Europe. We are stumping every day; most of the stumps come out easily as the light, alluvial soil is nearly all burnt away from the roots; those that are difficult we pile the extracted stumps around them and burn them. Sold our oxen to a butcher for

$60 as they were getting old; Tom is private secretary and writes many of the love letters for the young Frenchmen in these parts; our blacksmith charges 25cts. for putting on a new shoe and 10cts for putting on an old horseshoe. Met poor Mr. Robert St. George; habitual intoxication has given him a fearfully wild and ghastly look; he is now really nothing better than a walking tempetence lecture. The fires that have raged in the woods the last 3 weeks have been almost extinguished by heavy showers. A Frenchman passed with a load of 85 bushels of charcoal for which he expects to get $10 from a tinsmith. 25th Aug. Have commenced harvesting the oats at Oak Hill; have hired Mike Murphy by the month; the G. boys make a great pet of Sarah's child that is on a visit at their place; it is a very old fashioned little thing; G. boys have changed work with us at harvesting. There are several picturesque roadways through Oak Hill, over-arched with grand old beech and maple trees. Lent G's our mare to draw bark, as one of their mares has had a foal. Our blacksmith does not temper the drills we send him properly, which causes us a great deal of inconvenience in drilling the rock in our well. Extract from a letter from uncle Jerrold to uncle Richard: "My dear Richard, enclosed is a letter of credit for the Howard lads; I wish the understanding to be always maintained that Tom and Arthur do nothing without your consent; If they do I will withdraw all assistance from them. Tell Arthur if he intends to speculate it must not be on hard earnings." I am certain that I never asked him for money to speculate, and that he made that offer himself. However, this ends it, I will take no more favors from either of them, and will go to some college as soon as possible. Received a letter from Florence; she will teach the school again this year. Uncle Richard writes that uncle Jerrold has decided to sell Oak Hill in London. While on a boating excursion on Richford river I was greatly surprised at the natural talent displayed by a young lad 6 years old who lives there, who can take good sketches of nearly everything on and about their farm. Clifford C. through a cramp was nearly drowned had not Philip G. rescued him. Uncle and aunt have returned from a visit to Davenport, where they say the yield of apples and plums will be enormous.

Father and G's have had another difference about the fence; I warded off a quarrel by repairing the fence. While driving to Aston with Mr. Churchill I was astonished to see him on one occasion gaze upward, and discovered he was engaged in prayer, although driving over an uninhabited road; I told him it was not a very suitable place for performing his devotions, and that he ought to bear in mind that wise injunction of St. Paul: "Let all things be done decently and in order." 30th of Aug; G. boys are changing time with us and are helping us to stump our clearance, which is very laborious; spent a pleasant evening at Meredith's; Nicholas and Mabel W. are great friends of late. Mabel wants him to give up smoking, and broke a cigar holder he had, for return for which he broke her bracelet. From appearances I believe that both their parents would be delighted to hear of an early engagement. Spent the evening at Vincent's; the filthiness of the conversation of the family and the numerous young people assembled there was disgusting. I can understand how a person can utter an oath or even vile language in a moment of fierce anger, but to do so day in and week out with a relish for it as if it was the most brilliant wit, makes it appear to me that filth and depravity must have taken a fearful hold on these peoples' hearts. Since Houde's have left Tom has commenced to spend an evening occasionally at Morean's, who has three charming daughters, one blonde and two brunettes; it is the great rendevous for all the young beaus of the range. Our oats in the back clearance has been fearfully trampled by bears and is extremely difficult to cut. Received the calender of Rawlings College; tuition for the Art course is only $20 a year and board and washing $2.70 a week. Wrote as follows: "Dear Uncles: From the recent letters I have lately received from you I plainly see that we can never agree as regards my 'modus operandi' of farming, therefore, taking this into consideration, with the great disadvantages here of vulgar and bad associations, I have decided to discontinue farming and study for some profession. I need hardly give you any reasons for my wishing to perfect my education, for you have both experienced the pleasure and benefit derived from it in your intercourse with the world. Perhaps you may reply, why not perfect your education and be a farmer still. I reply, this might be possible for a genius possessed of brilliant intellect and great physical endurance, who could handle the axe and plow all day and afterwards devote half the night to study; but even such as he would lose much time and suffer great inconvenience without the aid of experienced professors. As I have not the means to pay college expenses and carry on farming at the same time, I have decided if you both consent, to sell my half in Elmbrooke to Tom. I would not take an art course, but devote all my time to the obligatory subjects necessary for the profession of law. Do not think because I wished to change from farming to the army and now to law that I do not know my own mind, and will always keep changing about, which ruins all chance of success in life for those that do so. I only gave up the army when I was convinced of its impossibility on account of my age. The total cost for the 3 years course of lectures at the university and at lawyer's office will be $680; nearly double which amount I can get by disposing of my half in Elmbrooke, its stock, implements, etc. While at McNeill's at Richford he told me that he had money to loan at fair interest. I am afraid that no no such offer will be made to me when I part with my half of Elmbrooke, for no matter how honorable a man may be, matter of fact business men naturally dislike lending money even to their most intimate friends when they have nothing but their honor to offer as security. McNeill and his hotel have such a comfortable, genial appearance that they more resemble the English inn than the American hotel. I have been exceedingly busy of late finishing harvesting, packing up my personal effects, balancing our account books, and making a list of everything on Elmbrooke as regards stock, implements, household furniture, etc., and placing a fair valuation opposite each article. Tom reduced my valuation about half, and even then made objections to buy, I told him that it was immaterial to me, for although my uncles might prevent me from selling my half in the land they could not that of the moveables on it. Tom at last consented and gave me his note for them at half the price I valued them at. Wrote to the principal of Rawlings saying, that I should attend it as soon as it opened. Sept 7th; cut buckwheat at Oak Hill; in raking buckwheat it is best to do so while the dew is still on it as it shells less. "McLean St. George, Esq. Dear Sir: I have written to my uncles stating that you have no objection to being paid cash down for Oak Hill. Should I or my brother hear of anyone desiring to purchase land I shall mention to them the lots you referred to in you last. There are, as I suppose you have already noticed, two extremes into which farmers and land holders run; the first, a want of enterprise and lazy contentment on acquiring sufficient land to provide them with an humble living. In the second, an excess of enterprise in acquiring more land than they can properly manage or cultivate. Of the two, however, the first predominates in the Province of Quebec, whose farmers subdivide their land to such an extent that many of them occupy no better position than that of common laborers, which position they deserve as they disregard the advantages of education and have no ambition. Mike Murphy, our hired man, has cut his foot with an axe, while cutting the roots of stumps; I went to St. Marie to rent a house close to Meredith's, for Florence to teach school in, as some of the rate-payers have complained about Meredith's house not being in a sufficiently central position, the place has greatly changed within the last few yrs.; the splendid growth of primeval hardwood forest has almost disappeared, and been replaced by large clearances, but the village remains unchanged, is still one long straggling street; the enormous church appears to me far too costly for such a small place; apple and plum trees are loaded with fruit; the wheat crops in these parts is a fair average, but a small extent is under it, the wheat has nearly been destroyed in some countries in Europe, especially in England, where heavy rains during harvest did great damage to the crops; it will have to buy from India, Russia and the U. S., the latter country is one of the greatest exporters of agricultural products. In one orchard the ground is strewn with plums spoiled by mildew; all these windfalls the farmers feed to the pigs; this however is an extraordinary yield, which only occurs in 3 or 4 yrs.; some yrs. there are no plums at all when there are severe late frosts; the largest number of trees in an orchard seldom exceeds 50. Glowing descriptions of facts like these in rly. guide books etc. often give people in other countries a false idea of America; I have known emigrants who expected to have wild turkeys, peaches etc., for the mere trouble of shooting and collecting them; many Europeans appear to forget how vast a continent this is, and that all forms of climate are in it. A French peddler rode part the way home with us, he told me that he has peddled in this part of the country for the last 30 yrs., and that he has only just made enough to live on, which was all he cared for; I replied that if all people thought thus that this would be a wretched looking earth, that I thought it was every man's duty to acquire wealth, learning, and everything else that is useful and good, in as great a degree as is possible, as long as they are acquired by honorable means. Herbert C. who was with me said, father sing us a song, the term "father" is used by all French-Canadians to old men; he sang a song of his own composition, from which I saw that he possessed considerable education and natural talent; how sad it is to think that many men and women who might form the brightest human gems of this earth, remain all their lives in the mud at the bottom of the river of life; he also sang a revolutionary song of Papinean's time, "when a party of French-Canadians rebelled against English rule, and hoisted in several villages the tri-colored flag and cap of liberty, and a solemn oath was taken under it, to be faithful to the revolutionary principles of which they were emblematical;" he also sung a song about Father Chinguy, the great French-Canadian apostle of temperance in his early days, and now a reformed priest, who is doing great good by exposing the errors of Romanism, by lecturing all over the world. The *Witness*, the paper we take, is one of the best in Canada, has correspondents in England, France, Ireland and all the Canadian provinces. Tom gave me a note for $185, $100 of which was money I advanced the firm when we first entered partnership; the balance for my half of all the movables on Elmbrooke, it is ridiculously low, but of course I prefer selling even at half price to my brother, than to put him to any inconvenience. Received a letter from Uncle Richard, which in the first part says, he thinks I must be crazy, and in latter part that I may possibly succeed, but that I must not be rash, and acquire a thorough knowledge of Latin and French, by taking lessons from Rev. L. C. Willoughby, who is a good classical scholar, which is better than going to college; also reminded me than I would be nothing "better than a tramp if I sold my half of our fine estate." Paid Rev. L. C. my weekly subscription to date, $3.57; Tom and I pay towards the envelope system of St. Marks, 16cts. a Sunday; settled up all my business affairs preparatory to my departure for Rawlings college. Father showed me some relics of my dear mother's early life, paintings that she had taken of Alpine scenes, and a portrait of herself, when 18 yrs of age, by an Italian; as I gazed on that beautiful portrait, I could almost have wept when I thought of her leaving her luxurious home, to give her hand and affections to a man who, although he had magnificent prospects, as a civil engineer, lost them all through his want of energy and slothfulness, and at last became dependant on his wife's income for his support; a man who would take solemn vows upon himself to "cherish, honor, support and protect" a lady, and who through any fault of his failed to do so, does not deserve the name of man, let alone that of a gentleman, yet to my daily disgust do I see men who are in good standing in the Christian churches, break these solemn vows, as well as the hearts of the fair beings whose lives are sacrificed through their worthlessness. Father, who saw how dear the portrait was to me, kindly presented it to Tom and I. A phrenologist has made his appearance in Aston, and is reaping a bountiful harvest of 25cts. for examining the organs of people's heads, he has a chart showing the three great organs, intellect, feeling and propensity, with their numerous subdivisions, and where the organs are to be found in the human head; truly there are a great many ways of making money. On arriving at Rawlings, wrote to Uncle Richard. "Dear uncle; your letter recd. to day, from which I was sorry to hear that you had been suffering from pain in one of your eyes, also that my letter was written in such a decided manner, but how could I do otherwise, I merely wrote saying that I wished to study for a profession; you might merely think it was a foolish idea of mine, instead of being the fixed purpose of my life, and decide accordingly, whereas by your knowing that it is my unalterable decision, and that I am willing to devote yrs. of hard work to make it a success, you will be more likely to consent to my abandonment of farming for law, at which more favorable opportunities occur for associating with men of culture, which is of the greatest importance to a young man with his character, ideas, education, manners etc. yet to acquire; hence my hasty decision on a subject I should have decided yrs. ago, and which I must now accomplish with as little delay as possible, as in a few yrs. more it will be too late, as my character, manners and habits will be irretrievably formed and fixed; when I recd. your letter it was too late to follow your advice, of studying with Rev. L. C, W., as I had already written to the Principal of Rawlings college, saying that I would go there for the term ending Dec. 24th; I need not say how pleased I was to hear that you are not altogether opposed to my studying for law, and I will adopt the most inexpensive means for obtaining the object in view, as regards the balance we owe you, I will at farthest pay you in a few months, when I shall sell the produce of Oak Hill; the most important of what are to form my studies here will be Latin, Rhetoric, Logic, Philosophy, and mathematics. A lawyer here has offered to lend me his books and allow me to attend his office free of charge, he says in England they always charge for such a privelege, but not as a rule in Canada; I shall try and follow your advice by being "calm, steadfast and steady," not forgetting that a man's associations in a great measure form his ideas, habits and character for honor or dishonor, according to his choice of them; when I left home all the harvesting was finished, except a small field of oats not yet ripe, also a large tract of land, stumped and ready for sowing next Spring; your affee. nephew, A. N. Howard." I am quite astonished at the deserted and seedy appearance of this college, which has only two youthful professors who have not any college degree, and in fact are preparing for McGill university themselves, Prof. S. however is an M. A; I was greatly astonished and disgusted at the conversation at the dinner table and should not give it to the public even tho it was the conversation of so-called professors and a lady, to a criticism made by Mrs. S. on Prof. R's character, he replied. "Oh do not be too hard on me I know a nice little scene that occured one night to you; since writing the above have decided that the remainder of the conversation was not fit for publication. Next morning the conversation was even worse and decided to return home and study under Rev. L. C. W's tuition till I collect sufficient money to pay expenses at a college in Montreal; told principal S. that the college had been misrepresented to me in the calendar and that I considered myself justified in leaving it. On my return to Aston wrote to Uncle Richard: "dear uncle on arriving at Rawlings college I discovered that it had been greatly misrepresented with the one principal as the only professor in it qualified to give instruction and only 2 students, besides the language of all of them was so disgustingly vulgar and indecent that I could not stay there so I shall take lessons with Rev. L C. W, for a time when I hope you and uncle Jerrold will consent to my selling to Tom my half of Elmbrooke to pay college expenses in Montreal; I enclose you $50 out of which you can send me a Latin and French dictionary, the balance can go on what I owe you. While at Meredith's Florence told me of an amateur theatrical entertainment to be given at Durham and wanted me to take a part, told her that I greatly regretted that I could not do so; borrowed several histories in French from Florence; Mrs. M. told me their library was at my disposal for which I thanked her. Mr. and Mrs. Churchill arrived from Quebec this morning with a young nephew of his wife; Tom and Walter went to the exhibition at Montreal. Rev; L. C, W. charges $4 a month for 3 hrs tuition a week; Mabel is taking lessons in Latin with me. "Dear Arthur I rec'd the post office order for $50 for which I have given you credit; Clifford is coming out shortly to spend a few days with us, on his way back he will leave the books at Aston station; you write wildly in your letters but it is for want of knowledge on the subjects you write about; you do not want to go to college if you did you would be a dunce all your life; taking young men into college is one of the crying evils of this country and is the cause of the professions being crowded with young men that are not as well educated as tinkers apprentices in Europe. We have had a sick house here, Flora's 2 children are with us, the baby is very sick; Tom has just arrived, I asked him what books you had and you seem to be well supplied; I would advise you to stick to your farm and prepare yourself for your primary examination in your spare time, 4 branches will be enough for you to work yourself up in in one season, English, French, Latin and Geometry; next yr I will send you a paper of requisites for the primary examination; half an hour twice a week with Rev. L. C. W. will be sufficient for guidance and correction." "Dear Arthur patridge shooting is in full swing now I suppose; we have finished our harvesting and got 26 double loads of oats this yr where we got 21 last year; our crops this yr are about as follows, hay, oats and turnips, very good potatoes and buckwhat good, peas and barley half a crop, corn fair considering it was damaged by late frosts. President Garfield seems in a very precarious condition, one day the papers say he is in a fair way of recovery and the next that his life is despaired of; if it had not been for the wonderful strength of his constitution he would have been dead long ago; it would have been good if they had given Guiteau 20 or 20 lashes a day for 3 weeks and then hanged him, wretches like him do not care for hanging but rather like the notoriety of it. They have passed the Irish land bill in the House of Lords and now it remains to be seen whether the Irish can discover fresh grievgrievances. Had a discussion with Langevin he said Oh! what filthy blasphemy for your bishops and priests to have wives and at the same time say Saint mass, I replied that the celibacy of the clergy was only an ordinance of the church, that Christ never condemned it and would not have restored Peter's wife to him if he disapproved of his Apostles having wives, that St. Paul, one of the greatest of Apostles says, even in the Roman Catholic version of the bible, in the 3 chap. 2 verse of Timothy: "It behooveth a man to be blameless, the husband of one wife, sober, prudent and chaste." I study regularly 5 hrs a day mostly in the evening, continue working on the farm with Tom at stumping, plowing and ditching. 29th Sept. have commenced to dig our potatoes; had an argument with father, I argued that there cannot be a particle of a doubt that the U. S. with its thousands upon thousands of miles of inland navigation, its millions of acres of fertile soil, its vast forest and rich mines and its energetic educated inhabitants, will become in another 50 yrs the wealthiest and most powerful nation in existence. The G's have swamped all their bark, told them they could have their cows pasture on Oak Hill for the rest of the autumn; while at Vincent's Metz was shouting and cursing in a horrid manner but after a time fell down in a beastly state of intoxication; Louis B. was also drunk, I helped him back part of the way in search of a bag of provisions he lost. On arriving at Joe Vincent's found him and our hired boy dead drunk; 5 or 6 drunken men and boys were rolling about on the main road uttering obscene and blasphemous language, one of the boys that was drunk was a mere child only 10 yrs of age. I was disgusted to see Herbert and Clifford C. setting with the Vincent girls with their arms around their waists whispering the empty ideas of their idiotic brains into ears that were far too eager to listen to such sentimental trash; the girls I am sure had no charms to encourage love or even admiration but were brunettes frightfully pockmarked and one of them made such attempts to smile that it was positively painful to behold; Joe Vincent soon staggered around with a small demijohn full of whiskey treating the women as well as the men; I told the women that they ought to set a better example, that drinking intoxicants at best was only a useless habit to some and ruin and destruction to others, and that it was the duty of every true man and woman to avoid that which does not benefit themselves and is a source of destruction to others. Had a conversation with Murphy on Irish affairs, told me that he had seen Irish laborers sit down to a dinner of potatoes and buttermilk, that the potatoes were boiled in a large pot, and that the potatoes were thrown in heaps on a long table and eaten without the aid of any dishes or knives or forks; conversed with the G. boys on the Colvin Guernsey scandal; Mr. C. is an ardent admirer of bacchus and venus and hence the scandal between him and Miss G. Devlin offered Tom the chopping and drawing of cordwood 4 miles at $1.90 a cord. Mr. B. Mr. Churchill's relative came out to see us, he is a jolly rollicking young Irishman. Mr. and Mrs. C. are sight-seeing at Montreal; was invited with Mr. B. to Meredith's, had a delightful evening, Florence sang some of Arthur Sullivan's latest songs; Maud is in Montreal, it is feared her lungs are seriously affected, from a cold she caught while skating at Toronto, she is under the treatment of Dr. Hoadly, one of Montreal's most skillful physicians; yesterday we had the first snow storm, is considered a very early fall, as it is only the 5th of Oct., but it has all melted away; Mr. H. and I went ont riding, he is a superb rider; and no wonder having ridden after the hounds on his uncle's estate; attended an English ball at Aston school-house; there were many Richford and Aston people there; Mrs. Burnett of Richford has a fine physique but by no means of an etherial form', it however is well proportioned, and well set off by a close fitting black velvet dress; her husband gets $1,000 a yr. as manager of Sharps tannery, which he spends to the last cent "cutting quite a dash," Miss Moore wore a brown satin dress, has a fine figure, but her features are too angular, the length of her nose alone being sufficient to dispel in her heart any hopes of becoming the belle of Aston, although she has a heavy bank account; Miss La Rochelle is short in the extreme, has somewhat too stout a figure, weak looking eyes and an unpleasantly long face; Miss Vinberg is possessed of striking ugliness, her face is extraordinarily long and of a concave formation, with a nose in the center of the concave; like that which little boys put on snow men, her figure is gaunt and angular, but her eyes are the crowning point of hideousness, and glitter like those of a serpent; her escort Mr. Johnson, has legs like broom-sticks, square jaws, bony cheeks, and a nose that looks as if it had received a blow from a 12 lb. hammer; a receding forehead, and a mustache so waxed that the ends of them would pass through the eye of a needle, and seems to have lost all control of the risible muscles of his face, as it continually wears what cannot truthfully be called a smile; Mrs. Moore has an ordinary figure, oval face, and with a little more flesh on it and color in it, would make a fairly handsome woman; Miss McNeill has an apple dumpling figure, looks like a sack of flour bound tightly about the center, a short stubby nose and protruding teeth; there were of course many beautiful women but I would as soon attempt to describe some beautiful flower as them; there were 20 couple in all, the music consisted of violins, harps and pianos; the Harpers were Italians passing through the village; we all went to a grand supper at Waterloo hotel, on returning found that the Harpers had not tasted the supper that was sent to them, on being asked the reason why, they replied, gentlemen we nave played all over the world, in London, New York and Paris, and can truly say we have never been treated as rudely as we have been here, we have always been asked to take refreshments with the rest of the guests and a musician, allow me to inform you, is as respectable as any of the guests here this evening; some of the so-called ladies turned down the corner of their mouths and whispered, the idea! that such seedy individuals should be asked to supper with the other guests. I thought to myself, in the age of chivalry no musician would have been treated thus, but the matter of fact business people of the present day, laugh at the nations of former ages; during the rest of the evening I could not help looking occasionally towards the Harpers, a spirit of pride seemed to pervade their music that seemed to say, onr profession is honorable and wer'e not ashamed of it. "Dear Arthur; I recd. a few days ago a letter from your Uncle Jerrold for you which I herein enclose, I was very sorry to see by it that your letter had upset him very much, I was not at all surprised, when I thought of your sayings and doings for the past yr., I came to the conclusion that your mind had come a little off the balance, I trust it was only a temporary abberration and that you are all right again, this, in my opinion is the most charitable view in question, otherwise some of your acts were unpardonable, for instance, your abandoning your good brother as if he had no more claim on you than a rat; in your Uncle Jerrold's letter he says he would like to lease Oak Hill to your Uncle Herbert, if I will gnarantee the intetest at 6 per ct." "Sept. 27th. Dear Arthur, before you string together a few nonsensical sentences on the assumption that you are a man of genius, pray learn to write aud speak perfect English, also see whether your mighty genius can accomplish a thorough knowledge of the Latin grammar and syntax, this you ought to try before you begin to prophecy and launch out into ruin; do you think your health can stand close confinement? or do you think yourself capable, at all events try at home first, just as your Uncle Richard and I did in our younger days; as far as I can judge from the weak and washy style of your writing, that you are not the right sort either mentally or physically, to enter upon the hard and dangerous road of literary or professional competence, much less eminence, but certainly it is only right that you should try what you can do at home, nearly all, indeed all the great geniuses that have risen from lowly origin, have gained a certain amount of proficiency during the spare hrs. from labor and business; you have not given any sign, you are only the same Arthur that left your mother's tuition; see what you can accomplish first, and avoid your father's destructive fault, of being Jack of all trades and professions, and master of none, all to the loss of those that were foolish enough to help him, and to his own ruin; I have so much trouble and turmoil of my own that I must request you to cease writing to me as this ends our correspondence; your well wisher, J. R' Goldsmlth" from a letter to E. Howard; "Ireland with proper land laws could support a population twice as large as it has to-day, how much better would it be for England to have this larger population of contented patriotic subjects improving and increasing the productiveness of their small farms, instead of the small population it now contains, ⅔ of which are oppressed and discontented, with a few thousand lords and landlords with their mansions, parks, hounds and scores of servants, which do more harm to Gt. Britain than all the Land Leaguers combined; no one believes the boast of some of these great lords and landlords "that Englands greatness would be gone forever if they and their system was done away with," is not the producer, whether he be farmer, mechanic or laborer, of more actual benefit to the country than 20 lords or landlords who consume and waste the wealth of the country; for instance, like the Duke of Hamilton, in Scotland, who raised his tenants rents in some instances from £18 to £85 to meet the losses he incurred through horse racing and gambling; his only excuse for raising his tenants rent was, because they built comfortable houses on their holdings; is not injustice like this sufficient to paralyze the enterprise and energy of the best of tenants; there cannot be a doubt that the free-hold system would make Gt, Britain a greater and more prosperous nation, "Dear Clifford; Tom will accept your kind invatation to go "and have a good time shooting partridges with you" but not until a piece of fall ploughing is finished on Elmbrooke, where the fire burnt the earth to the depth of a foot on over 15 acres; we have nearly finished piling and burning the stumps and roots that remained; it has greatly improved the appearance of the place; the potatoe crop on Oak Hill was very good. 150 bushel; the expense was as follows; seed, 15 bushels $7.50, planting, 3 days work, $2, earthing them up $3.34, applying London purple and Paris green $2.20, manure $4, digging them out $10, The London *Times* asserts that the new land act is very nearly a direct confiscation of property by act of Parliament, the writer however appears to only think of landlords rights and utterly ignores tenants wrongs. One of the bells of Aston church weighs 2000 lbs. and cost $700. I now go more regularly to church. Florence is suffering from a severe cold and had her head all bandaged up which gave her a rather unpleasant appearance, if such a thing were possible; for she has such lovely eyes that were all her other features plain they alone would redeem the rest; let not the reader imagine that this is my own partial opinion for I have heard strangers say that they never saw such beautiful and expressive eyes. Have had wet weather, drizzling rain for several days; have had several boxing bouts with the G boys of late barehanded but I am no match for them as they are over 6 feet high and proportionally well developed; went to a bee of Andre La Rivere to clear land, his bill of fare at bees is considered the best given amongst the French: pork, beef, chicken, potatoes, soup, sauces, bread, butter, tea, sugar, milk, hot buns, apple and raisin pie; played a game called "bluff," which resembles the American game of "poker," in which game the player must never allow his face to be an index of what his hand contains; I have known a man with a pair of tens by having the nerve to raise the bet make his opponent who had a flush throw down his hand and allow his opponent to clear the table; this in French interpreted literally is called "eating a spruce;" while at Rev. L. C. W's I listened to Florence and Mabel play a few duets and sing, I thought at the time that if my dear mother had been preserved to me or that I had the gentle and civilizing society of sisters like these good and accomplished young ladies I would be much the better for it, but it is quite probable I would be no better than the majority of brothers and often treat them in a most unkind and ungentlemanly manner. The amateur dramatic troupe of Rawlings gave a performance in Aston town hall; Florence sang a song that received great applause; uncle Richard drove past our house with uncle Herbert and borrowed our lanterns; I saw him drive pass our gate with a sigh of regret for I know it is because he is displeased with me that he does not stop at our house as he used to do for he dislikes staying at uncle Herbert's who has married beneath him in Ireland to a woman belonging to the middle classes, who tho a respectable and good woman often uses vulgar language which sounds unpleasant in the refined ear; uncle Richard invited me to go up to uncle Herbert's and spend the evening there; uncle discussed Russia-phobia, landlordism, and told a most laughable anecdote about Jay Gold, illustrating the danger of having so much capital of the country in the hands of one man; next day he visited me and walked over the clearance on Elmbrooke and was greatly pleased at its improved appearance since we have stumped a large portion of the clearance; while at Wheeler's I heard father talking against Tom and I, saying that we should help him to work his place; told him afterwards that he had no right to run down his sons to the world and had no real cause or grievance to do so. The British empire has the largest empire in the world, 8,700,750 sq. miles; Russia, China, the U. S. and Brazil rank next in order. Maud Meredith has returned in perfect health. It has commenced to freeze hard during the nights; we will soon have finished our stumping. One thing I do not like about uncle Herbert's family is that they always try and get the lion's share from another in a bargain and always begin a couple of hours later than when we work for them. The traveling troupe called the Guy family have advertised for Aston again as a "highly moral entertainment;" by a proper use I think the stage could be made of immense benefit in educating the lower class of people by representing truly the beauty of virtue and the hideousness of crime. At a bee at Carmichael's there was quite a drunken row among the men, Joe Vincent flung a cat at another man but he missed him and struck me in the face, scratching my face in a most frightful manner, a fight ensued but we were separated by the rest; in the evening there was a dance and card playing, one half drunken scoundrel managed to get into a room where the girls and women's hats and shawls were, and threw them as well as every man's hat he could find into the well, which is 35 ft. deep; some hats and bonnets were borrowed from a neighbor and the rest had to go home bareheaded on a frosty night. "My dear Tom and Arthur I have been informed that there is $1200 worth of wood on Oak Hill, how would it do for you and Arthur to keep it and dispose of the wood, but I fear it would interfere with your other farm and that it would require capital to have the wood cut, should you think you can manage it and make money by it, you can consider the matter and I will write to your uncle Jerrold about it, but you must remember you only go into it as a speculation and will have to get rid of the land as soon as possible." Have just finished reading all the volumes of Rollins Ancient History. 2d Nov. it freezes at night but is bright and sunny during the day. Extract from letter from E. Howard: "I agree with you that Gt. Britain is suffering from the restraints imposed on agriculture by British laws; I care very little about military supremacy which is usually a temptation to a nation to do wrong as Gt. Britain has been doing lately in Afghanistan and Zululand and as France is now doing in Tunis; France has been more happy and prosperous during the last 10 yrs since her defeat by Prussia than before; Gt. Britain is now so strong that she does not care to conciliate Ireland by allowing the Irish to manage their own affairs; we ought to have a local parliament in Dublin as they have in the other colonies; remember that nearly all the news your hear and read in the newspapers about Ireland comes from London and is prejudiced; there has been quite as much excitement and disturbance in England at times of agitation for various reforms as we now have in Ireland but the English understanding their own affairs never thought it necessary to lock each other up without trial as they have at present locked up some 250 Irishmen. The U. S. have never been able to compete with Gt. Britain in selling manufactured goods in foreign countries, the cause I think that protection by raising the cost of wages as well as everything else has raised the price of all American manufacture so that England can undersell America nearly everywhere, high wages are of little use when the price of nearly everything you have to buy is also high; England by buying American corn and beef cheap without duty is able to manufacture goods more cheaply than America notwithstanding landlordism, which tends to raise the price of food in Gt. Britain; Americans do not seem to understand this bad effect of protection and they have gone on injuring themselves and other nations by it; American shipping has dwindled almost to nothing because it is cheaper to build ships in England and Canada; there is lots of coal and iron in the United States but the high cost of labor (the result of protection) keeps them from being used as they might be. While Louis Brodeur was working for us was surprised to discover that there can be such a thing as a "half holiday," that it is a sin to work in the forenoon but not in the afternoon, truly the priesthood are getting it down to a pretty fine point. Miss Guernsey tried to drown herself but her courage failed and she fell in a fit on Mr. Wheeler's veranda: 8th Nov. Tom and I have commenced plowing; have to clean the horses legs from mud and moisture every evening; carelessness in doing this gives horses sore legs; I finished collecting all the old corrrespondence at Father's, many letters and papers he would not give me, which I expect were full of criticisms on himself. 12th Nov , froze hard last night and has commenced to snow to-day; there is much dissension among the French people, some of them want to have the school-house moved closer to the East end of the range, which is more thickly inhabited; some of the R. C's. are trying to have our school fall into their hands, so we must be on our guard, and do all our business exactly up to the letter of the law; have heard from Mrs. Brodeur that Percile Vincent has my grandmother and mother's wedding ring, that Tom Somerset's father's hired boy stole from a wardrobe; I went to Vincents, and to avoid any unnecessary trouble I paid her $1 to give it up; one of Andre's calves came back to his farm with a dead cat tied to its tail, a very mean action for one neighbor to do to another; Fancher, an old lumberman says that shanty work does not pay, that a farmer is far better at home all winter, even if he only feeds his animals and works around his house, he says he will give up lumbering, which causes a great wear and tear on clothes, horses, harness, sleighs &c. As the afternoon was stormy, I classified my journal for the yrs. from '75 to '80; Tom and Clifford have just arrived from a political meeting held at Aston Town Hall. 16th Nov., the snow has disappeared, it froze so hard last night that we will not be able to plough to-day, but the weather is gloriously bright, clear and exhilarating. The outlook on my prospects of late are somewhat gloomy, both my uncles have ceased to write to me, but I feel confident that shortly I shall be independent of them all; have decided in my studies and reading never to pass a word or sentence until I fully comprehend its meaning, and to strive always to keep my footsteps in the path of duty, no matter how alluring may be the path of pleasure. "Elmbrooke, Dec. 26th '81. Dear uncle, we received your letter on Saturday, and wish to thank you for the unchanging interest you have always taken, and still take in our welfare, also for the Christmas present you so kindly sent us, Uncle Jerrold has not written either to Tom or myself for several months, from which I imagine he must be greatly displeased with me for having decided to study for a profession instead of remaining a farmer on Elmbrooke, which seems to have been his earnest wish as regards us both; I can-not tell you how much I regret having to act with apparent in-gratitude in not fulfilling his wishes by doing so, but in reality it would have been far more unwise and ungrateful of me to spend a life time among people and associations that have always had a degrading effect on the character of all those that were obliged to associate with them, and among whom not even a Christian gentleman could live for a number of yrs, without hav-ing his character and manners most unfavorably influenced by the vile associations with which he would be surrounded, how much more injurious must those associations be to a young man of an impressive age, with their characters but impartially formed and without the necessary safe guard of a good education, that they should escape deterioration, is nearly as great an impossi-bility as that of holding a cambric handkerchief in a smoky room without getting it discolored, no society at all, would be a great-er advantage to many people living in rural districts of this part of the country, than that which they have the misfortune to live in, the influence of which it is impossible to avoid unless one makes a hermit of himself, as life in the country is totally differ-ent from that in cities, where one can choose his own acquaintances from a greater variety of people, and avoid the acquaintance of even a neighbor without giving offence; in the country on the contrary, to avoid the acquaintance of a neighbor is about the surest way to make an enemy of him, and in most of the rural districts in this province there is really no good society at all to choose friends or acquaintances from, and the individual who at first would have preferred good society, generally from long acquaintance becomes accustomed to that which surrounds him, and in most cases gradually deteriorates, until he almost reaches the same level as that of his associates; however as I have not been able to act according to yours and Uncle Jerrold's wishes as regards Elmbrooke, I have decided not to trespass any further on the great generosity that my Uncle Jerrold has always shown to our family, and which if I did, would entitle me to the just contempt of my friends, for being so base as to receive money from a benefactor after I had lost his esteem and affection, therefore under the circumstances, and as so much of his money has been spent in Elmbrooke and intended for no other purpose than to make it a fine estate, I resign my half in Elmbrooke to you and Uncle Jerrold in equal shares, of which when you inform him you will greatly oblige me by expressing to him my sincere thanks for all the kindness he has shown us since our dear mother's death, and which I shall always think of with the deepest gratitude." All my expenses for labor, seed &c. on Oak Hill $81.36, and over $40 of this was permanent improvements, and my receipts too were $175, which left a fair profit. Extract from letter from Uncle Richard: "should you require any more books, send the name of any you may require, as I may have it in the house, I think there is nearly a cart load of educational books in my book case, if not I can get whatever you want at the book stores; do not be in too great a hurry to study, you have abundance of time for studying, if you had more your mind would get fatigued, you will get on much better as you are I know from experience, I hope you will use your judgment and only study essentials, I must congratulate you on your spelling, you hardly ever make a mistake in your letters, in fact few letters written, even by the average gentleman of the present day, will bear criticism." "22nd Dec. '81. Dear Mr.

Sherman, I am sorry that neither Tom or myself could avail ourselves of your kind invitation before this on account of our fall work, such as ploughing, stumping and preparing our winter's supply of wood, as well as having our grain threshed, on Oak Hill I raised 150 bushels of oats; I will certainly go and visit you by the first good sleighing, of which strange to say there has been none around here so far; the like of which has only occured once during the residence of one of our earliest settlers; I am not certain whether Tom told you in his last letter that I have decided to study for law, it will take me several yrs. as by my wishing to do so I have displeased my uncles, and of course can no longer honorably accept the income they have settled on Tom and I for life, so I have given up to them all my claims on Elmbrooke, and will in future depend on my own exertions alone; I was thinking that perhaps you would have the kindness to give me employment in your factory, I would not care what start it was to begin with, and later on you might find something better; reply at your earliest convenience, and oblige yours truly, A. N. Howard." "St. Liboire, Jan. 12th 1882. Dear Arthur, I should have answered your letter sooner but have been away at Montreal and Charlesburg on business; I would give you employment but it would be such as I would be ashamed to offer to you, such as firing the boiler' for which we pay $1 a day, and for easier work in the factory 80cts.; I could have given you the working of the pin at $1 50, but that is gone now; we hope to have the pleasure in a short time of seeing you both at St. Liboire; Mrs. Sherman joins me in love to you and wishing that the New Year may bring you every happiness, your sincere friend I. Sherman. P. S., tell Tom I wish he could sell my land next yours." 13th Jan.' embarked on the 10.35 train going East at Aston; Tom and Philip came into the car to bid me good-bye; I now start in life a second time with only $1.25cts. in my pocket, no matter how buoyant one's hopes may be, one can never leave old friends to seek new ones without a feeling of regret; for the last few weeks before leaving I cut cord-wood for Devlin, but he is to pay Tom for it; I left with Tom a photo of our dear mother, he has promised to send me a copy of it; on arriving at St. Andre found to my disgust that I was too late for the train that goes to Arlington, and that I would have to wait until Monday morning; put up at a first class French hotel for 75 cts. a day board and bed. The French here seem to put on more style than at Aston, handsome fur caps and overcoats are quite numerous; I was surprised to see what a number of well dressed young men assembled in "gents parlor" and had their drinks brought to them from the barroom, this seems to me an improvement to drinking it at the bar; there is also a "ladies parlor" where the young beaus of the village bring their sweethearts and treat them to wine, on Sunday especially when young beaus are returning from mass with their fair ladies; in the evening I sat in the barroom and listened to the conversation of its frequenters, which was chiefly on politics, horse racing, lumbering and reminiscences of old settlers; the French around here seem to be more respectable than at Aston; my bedroom was handsomely furnished and had a luxuriously soft bed; cannot imagine how they make ends meet at 75 cts. a day; the telegraph operator, who is English, tells me that there are only a few English families here; saw a whale pass thro on the cars for Montreal, about 50 ft. long and 8½ thick in the middle of the belly; I am informed that there is a superior court stationed at St. Simon 3 miles from here and that 12 lawyers reside there; had an interesting conversation with a Frenchman from old France, he says that when he first came to America he often threw the cup of water from him in disgust when he thought of the wine beverage in his own dear France; wine is to a Frenchman what beer is to a German a substitute for water; told me that a majority of Frenchmen in the cities and towns had no respect for religion, he spoke disparagingly of Manitoba, told him that I did not think that Senator Cochrane, the greatest farmer in Canada, would not spend thousands of dollars there if he did not have great expectations of the country, told him that St. Andre had been opened up for 50 yrs. whereas Winnipeg had its first settler only a fews yrs ago and has to-day 25,00 pop. while St. Andre has only 1,000 and that thousands were made every month by individuals who bought land there a few yrs ago, and that many young boys of to-day would live to see Winnipeg with a greater population than the city of

Quebec. After leaving St. Andre the country is cleared on both sides with stunted softwood here and there; the country is very flat (the conductor tells me that Mr. Milton was sent by Mr. Sherman with a horse and sleigh for to drive me from Arlington to factory village) softwood forest on either side; this train only carries 1 first class and 1 2d class car with only 3 first class and 10 second class passengers; it is only a short branch line from St. Andre to Charlesburg; still flat and uninteresting country covered with softwood forest averaging 30 ft. high; most of the stopping places are only composed of a few houses and are called "flag stations;" the country from Arlington to St. Andre is nearly all swamp, that is close to the track, farther back from the track the country improves I hear and is well settled, in some places pass peat bogs a mile or so in extent; arrive at Arlington which consists of 25 to 30 houses; had to walk 8 miles to Sherman's as my funds are reduced to 25 cts. passed over slightly rising ground in sight of Arlington covered with a fine sugar bush, the rest of the way passed thro slightly rolling uninviting country covered with stunted softwood forest with numerous clearances interspersed; on nearing St. Liboire the country becomes more hilly and picturesque; St. Liboire is a small village of whitewashed houses of one story, street with an unsightly whitewashed church which forms a striking contrast with the very handsome house of the priest who owns the best farm in the parish; from St. Liboire to the factory village is a mile and a half along a road on the edge of a bluff 50 ft. above the surface of St. Herbert river and a bluff above it 80 ft. high on the opposite side. Mrs. S. received me cordially and invited me to stay at their house till I could find a comfortable boarding place; their house is comfortably and tastefully furnished altho only a small villa, surrounded by a beautiful grove of pines; it appear to me to have more real comfort and home appearance than many stately marble faced mansions I have seen; it appears to me as if years of practical experience had been spent in concentrating to the greatest advantage everything necessary to beautify their charming little villa in as small a space as possible; no one in my opinion but a true artist can properly furnish a house to the greatest advantage no matter how much money they may possess; I spent the afternoon and evening in the drawing room in interesting conversation with Mrs. S. who is one of natures gentlewomen; much of the conversation was on past events and incidents in both our lives, she is in my opinion a model christian lady; had the nominal half hearted christianity of the present day more like her mankind would be the better and happier for it, yet this christian lady has such a high ideal of what a christian ought to be and such a great amount of christian humility that I confidently believe that she regards herself as one of the worst christians in christendom. The next day I commenced superintending the piling of cordwood until Mr. S. arrived. Clifford and I had commenced writing to each other in French before my departure from Aston; I give a specimen letter translated literally: "Dear Clifford I received your letter with great pleasure the day before yesterday and thought it would be good practice for us to write to each other in French language, a language that the English of this province should be acquainted with to render more easy their intercourse with the French Canadians; I am making fair progress with my studies but have been disappointed many times by Rev. L. C. W. not being at home; I assure you it is no light affair to walk 14 miles on a muddy road and then be disappointed; my father still lives at the old homestead and is greatly obliged for your good wishes; Churchill who I believe was "born tired" is going to Peterboro, Ontario, where his wife's brother lives; in my opinion we are blessed with an æsthetic in Aston named Miss Grant but I do not like her manners or conversation, there is too much of the "utterly beautiful" about it; this winter is certainly one of the strangest that the variable climate of this country has ever given us. "Jan. 13th, '82, dear Arthur, I rec'd your letter also the copy of the lot Oak Hill; in your letter you say you renounce all claim to Elmbrooke but you cannot do that, I hold the land in trust for you and Tom by the authority of your uncle Jerrold, and it was always understood, even before your dear mother's death, that this property was always to have been a home for Tom and yourself. Your uncle's motive for so arranging it was fearing that at any time either of you might be tempted to part with it. From your letters to me I have come to the conclusion that your mind is off the balance at present and has been for some time; I should advise you to avoid all excitement for a year or two; work steadily at your farm and make a comfortable homestead for yourself and while you are doing this learn to read and speak English and French correctly. You may say, look to your own son. I know it, but this is not my fault, I have given him every faculty for acquiring." When Mr. Sherman, he and Mrs. S. decided that firing was too hard and dirty work for me and gave me the job of superintending the piling of the hemlock bark into stacks as it is drawn here. From a letter from E. Howard: "Remember that the prosperity caused by protection is paid for in taxation by farmers. If protection is any good why not allow each Province of Canada to protect itself. And even the county of Bradford, should it not tax Montreal goods and set up factories for itself, and if Canada was annexed to the U. S. ought she not still to tax American manufactures or if not, why not? "Elmbrooke, dear Arthur, I have just received your letter and as I am confined to the house on account of a sprained ankle I take the opportunity of writing to you; I do not think you are acting wisely for the sake of 60 cts. a month to be at the trouble of buying provisions and having them cooked for you, if that French family live like ordinary mortals $3 per week is cheap enough; it seems to me that you did not get my uncle's letter by your saying that you would have nothing to do with Elmbrooke altho I enclosed it in mine; he wrote to me saying that he held the land in trust for us so that it is still yours; you allude to my having a fit of the blues, heaven knows I have reason enough. This has not been a good winter for teaming; I do not think my team will earn what I expected they would. After you left I started to get out those ties, and left Jerrold, our boy at home; when I came back I found that a great many of the potatoes were frozen on account of his not keeping the fire going, so I saw right off that I could not get along that way so I went and moved all father's things down here; he will sell his fodder to settle or help to settle his accounts. Montreal, Feb. 16th, 1882. "Dear Arthur: I send by book post to day, a French and German dictionary, $1.75; a Latin grammar, 25c. and a French grammar, 25c. There are translations of the classic poets published, but it would only be a waste of time studying over them;

take a Latin sentence and by the aid of your dictionary and
grammar work it out until you see the relation, bearing and sig-
nificance of every word. Your writing is bad, and never will be
better until yon begin from the beginning, just as if you were a
child commencing to write; adopt for a model a standard style,
Payson and Scribner's nation il system of penmanship is the best
and generally used in this country. A friend of mine, who is now
a judge, declared to me that it was owing to his being a good
writer that he got on the bench. I think you heard me tell of a
man named Murray who graduated with first class honors at
McGill college; at 32 he could neither read nor write and gained
his livelihood by mending shoes; in a few years he was gold
medalist in medicine and took the Shakspeare medal for English
literature and English composition. I can remember the day he
came into my surgery with a pair of shoes under his arm; he
was an untidy and unkempt specimen of humanity. I could
scarcely keep from laughing when he told me that he wanted to
be a doctor, for on examination he did not know his letters. I advised him to learn to read and write and then come and see me
again. On his return in a few months his progress was so great
that I could not help taking an interest in him. He could play a
little on the violin; I advised him to learn notes and take lessons
and learn the rudiments of music so as to be able to teach. He
had only taken a few lessons when he formed a class and was
learning and gaining money at the same time. He then got into
a French college on condition that he was to teach music, for
which he received board and instruction in French and Latin;
so that it was his music that was his actual stepping stone to
success. It is on the same ground that I advise you to become
a good penman; as a colateral accomplishment it may get you
into a lawyer's office and enable you to make as good wages as
what you are at and learn the practice of law at the same time.
Since I last wrote to you I went out to Aston and paid for Oak
Hill. I must now conclude; with love from all here, I remain,
your affectionate uncle, R. I. Goldsmith." In a letter before
leaving Aston, he says he believes that I am in love with one of
the young ladies in Aston, which caused you to be dissatisfied
with life in the backwoods. Elmbrooke, Jan. 2. "Dear Arthur,

I enclose you a letter from uncle Richard. From what he says you will perceive that things will not be as you said. He writes to me saying that he thinks uncle Jerrold has "dropped us," and it looks very much like it as he does not write to me either. You are all right by this time; I suppose you have got a good place, but it is different with me, and to say the least, my prospects are not promising. I also received a note from Clifford; he is to be out in a fortnight. Devlin has not yet paid for the wood you chopped. You might have boarded out and saved me the trouble of sending those blankets to you. Your affec. brother, T. G. Howard." From a letter from uncle Richard, dated 8th Feb. "With regard to the remarks I made to you in my last letter you must admit that your acts justified me, but as I probably have not been able to see the whole side of the question, I may not have been able to judge. Yourself and Tom were the only persons I have spoken to. Clifford may have read your uncle's letters, he made some remark to that effect, but I know he would never say to a stranger that he thought you crazy. Mr. Meredith dined here last Sunday; your name was not mentioned in my hearing. Your uncle Jerrold has directed me to lease Oak Hill to your uncle Herbert and send him the interest semi annually; you can guess what that will end in, your uncle Herbert will have the use of the lot and will have to pay the interest. I am glad to see that you have been so fortunate as to get such an excellent post, and I have no doubt but that it will lead to something better. Your cousin Flora is living in town and has a very fine house on Mackay st.; your aunt and Mabel have not been very well this winter, but I am happy to say are much better, they both unite in love to you. Since Clifford has come in town he looks very much paler, the town air does not agree with him; he returns to the Elms shortly Your affec. uncle, Richard." "Dear Tom, I received your letter, and thank you for being so prompt in sending the blankets. None of the French people in this little village are rich enough to furnish more than one bedroom, so I have to furnish it myself. Mrs. Gaudette, my landlady, charges me 40cts. a week for lodging and cooking; for washing I have to pay 25cts. and for provisions about $1.75. I have been very busy lately and sometimes have had to work till 11 o'clock, superintending men, covering bark piles; when I work till 11 it counts for a day and a half. This will only last a few weeks while the habitants are rushing in their bark. Some days as many as 320 loads of bark have been measured, besides cordwood, therefore you can see that my job of "walking boss" is very hard on the legs and throat; I have worn out a pair of boots and trousers since I have arrived and never have more than 5 hours sleep for the nights; the bark does not come in very late. I go to St. Liborie and take lessons in French from the notary there. As regards Elmbrooke I will have nothing more to do with it; of course it is rather hard for one to lose 5 years hard work on the place, but I prefer doing this than to be under a compliment to any one. I hope the Frenchmen who are indebted to me for farm produce paid you. I perceive by your letter that you have a fit of the blues, for which there is no occasion. Wishing you the greatest of success on Elmbrooke, I remain your affectionate brother, A. N. Howard." 6th Feb. 1882. "Dear Uncle, your letter received, by which I perceive that that the deeds of Elmbrooke are so made out that I cannot transfer my half in and of my own accord; this, however, does not affect my decision of transferring my half of it in equal shares to you and uncle Jerrold, on account of my inability to carry out your wishes and the many obligations I am under to you both, therefore, I would be greatly obliged to you both to do as you please with it and say no more to me about it. I would also deem it a great favor of you to discontinue making remarks by letter of your opinion of my mental equilibrium, which to say the least, are not gentlemanly. There are too many such foolish individuals at the present day, who, if a man goes out of the beaten track of the common herd of humanity say he is a crank, crazy or eccentric. Tom has, I suppose, told you of my coming to St. Liborie to work for Bently & Co. I now earn about $1.10 a day, but Mr. S. has promised me the post of pan man when the first vacancy occurs, for which $1.50 is paid for the easy occupation of sitting on a chair all day and testing the extract occasionally with a barkometer, and at which I shall be able to make great progress at my studies. At present I find time enough to take 3 lessons a week from a

French notary, I enclose $5 to buy me a French dictionary and grammar. I assure you I am grateful to you for your kind letters, which I could hardly expect after the ungracious manner I treated you and uncle Jerrold; however, what is passed can never be restored, but the present and the future may be preserved. Have the the kindness to continue your advice and criticisms and I shall do my utmost to show you that I appreciate them. If uncle Herbert is mean enough to take the use of Oak Hill and allow you to pay the interest, I shall make it good to you, but only for the first year, after which it can be sold or let to some Frenchman, who would be only too glad to get the use of the place for such a trifling sum; my hours of work are from 7 to 6. "St. Liboire, Feb. 10th. Dear Tom, yours recd. yesterday, was sorry to hear that you had sprained your wrist; the $54 that is due to me by the habitants, you can have the use of a yr. or so as, I do not require it at present; your note to me is to be paid in 2 yrs. in semi-annual instalments commencing from the 12th Sept. '81; it certainly looks unfavorable Uncle Jerrold not writing to you, but I am confident that he is too just to make you suffer because I displeased him, and I am certain that you and your children (if you ever get married) will get my half of the income as well as your own, as he told me when he was in Canada that if one of us displeased him the other would get the whole portion; I also feel confident that my uncles will not accept my half of Elmbrooke; if they offer to give it to you, I ask you as a favor to accept it without any compunctions of conscience, for I positively will have nothing more to do with the place, and you might as well have the benefit of my five yrs. hard labor as Uncle Herbert; for if my uncles do not take it it will be given to either you or Uncle Herbert; you ought not to be discouraged, for with the double income and that estate, you will be able to live like a country gentleman, and farming is rising every yr. in the estimation of the world, as a profession; even my short success on Oak Hill ought to convince you that money can be made at it; I read in the paper the other evening of a farmer near Montreal who made $80 clear profit from a single acre of land; few professions or manufacturing enterprises can equal that, so be not discouraged, let you and father live in harmony and help each other along; tell him for me to keep his valuable hardwood timber as long as he can, for that in 5 yrs. it will be worth 4 times as much as it is now, also to sow some of his land in potatoes, and not be afraid to plant 4 or 5 acres, as with Paris green and London purple the beetles can be easily kept from them, the beetles will frighten many farmers from sowing a large crop, and in consequence their price will be high; please, like a good fellow give up even a moderate use of spirituous liquors, even though you feel confident that you will never drink to excess, even a moderate use of them is a waste, for the most eminent of chemists and physicians have clearly demonstrated that the process of making spirituous liquors removes almost all the nutriment from them, and there is nothing in them to benefit man either physically or mentally, therefore as a useless habit it ought to be avoided, and still more so for the thousands of fellow-men it destroys." The factory village must look well in Summer when the long avenue of trees are in leaf; the factory is quite close to Mr. Sherman's house, on the river with a large chimney over 100 ft. high; both Mr. aud Mrs. S. treat me as an old friend; Mrs. S. showed me their house, it is the most compact and snug little villa I was ever in, although in the country it has all the appearance of a house in the city, with its chandeliers and supply of hot and cold water; the large open fireplaces in all the rooms has a most cheerful and homelike appearance; the furnace in the cellar keeps the house a warm and even temperature in even the coldest weather; it is surprising what beautiful homes can be had even in the country amongst farmers, if they only possessed more taste, and were not so indifferent to home comforts; Mrs. S. gave me a condensed history of her life, she has great conversational powers, and is an extraordinarily well read woman, and can converse on the latest scientific discovery with as much ease as on the ordinary chit chat of a drawing room; I cannot say how pleased I am to meet a lady who takes an interest in, and can converse inielligently on the leading subjects of the day, with how much more profit can a gentleman spend an evening in the society of such a lady as this, than with the average lady of the society of the present day, who waste much of their lives and

that of their gentleman acquaintances in conversing on light
vapory nothings, this I consider is much to her credit, as all her
life she has had very delicate health; there are large platforms
12 ft. wide and 10 ft. long to pile the bark on, the platform is to
prevent the loss of the small pieces of broken bark, and to keep
the bottom of the piles from getting wet it is piled in 3 rows on
the platform 15 ft. high; I have to make the farmers pile it 5 ft.
high with the white side of the bark down; the reader can imagine what an unpleasant task it is to run around amongst 150
farmers who are hurrying as fast as possible to unload, to persuade them to pile the bark properly and report to the cashier
the names of all those who do not fulfil their contract by piling
the bark properly when they unload it; after it is 12 ft. high I
have a number of men on top of the stack to receive and pile
the bark as it is thrown to them by the farmers, and although I
try to be as courteous and good natured as possible, many of
them swear at me in a most horrible manner; Mrs. S. says I ought
to follow a commercial life, and hinted of my keeping a store
for Bentley and Co. at a village where they have paper factories;
from 30 to 40 barrels of extract are turned out every 24 hrs; inside the factory there are employed 1 engineer, 1 pan man, 1 fire
man, 1 man to attend the leaches, 1 man to pitch the tan bark
out of the leaches, 1 "little pan man" to keep the liquor running
properly through long sloping boxes with ice in it; in running
through these the sediment is removed; 1 boy to fill the barrels
from the tanks, one wood drawer to draw wood to the furnaces,
1 bark drawer to haul the bark to the mills and 1 man to feed
the mills; 1 boss cooper to examine the barrels before leaving
the factory; 4 teamsters with double teams to draw the liquor to
Arlington station and 6 coopers to make barrels besides a hostler
for Mr. S., who carries the mail and does odd jobs for the factory
also 2 carpenters; Mr. Holden is the book keeper and cashier,
and Mr. Milton, the man who manages their bark shanties for
them, and goes about the country giving contracts for bark to
the farmers, and M. Alfred Young is the clerk who measures the bark and wood and aids Mr. Holden in shipping the
liquor; Mr. Holden's house is richly furnished, but most of the
paintings and portraits are out of proportion with the size of the

house, as they are legacies from his aunt in England who owned a large mansion; Mrs. Holden is a sister of Mr. Milton who has married a French girl; Holden has 3 children; Mr. Watts who manages the Co's. store has a wife and only one of his daughters living with him, Miss Kate Watts whose name I have already mentioned in my journal at Aston, so in all there are 4 English families; Mrs. S said she would have had me board at their house had not her health been so poorly, nothing can exceed the kind manner of Mr. and Mrs. Sherman since I have arrived here. Sent Florence a beautiful birth-day card on the 29th Jan. The factory uses about 30 cords of bark a day; on Sunday afternoons I take an occasional stroll out in the country towards St. Augustin, for part of the way is very hilly with steep ravines 150 ft deep; most of the farmers here derive great profit from the money paid out by the Co, for bark, cordwood, stovewood and labor; Mrs. S. invited me to dinner and to spend the evening at their house while Mrs. Bentley was there, a very handsome lady with a fine figure approaching embonpoint, has inherited all her mother's intellect, and is a lady of the highest culture with very graceful and unaffected manners; she gave me a nice description of Charlesboury and the different classes of society in it, that there are cn'y 500 English people there who are divided amongst 3 churches, Presbyterians, Episcopalians and Methodists; while I am writing this my landlady and her husband are saying their prayers at a terrible rate, some of them they repeat as often as 7 times, which seems to me absurd; I suppose they expect by constantly repeating them to tire out the patience of their God and make him consent; Mrs. S- says that we shall drive in their carriage to Charlesbourg next Summer which I shall greatly enjoy as I always take great pleasure in seeing new scenery and new faces. The other evening while Mr. G indette was praying some very long prayers that required much repetition, he indulged in an occasional remark in the conversation going on between his wife and myself, and then indulged in a joke which made us all laugh heartily, still at the same time I could not avoid thinking that such prayers as those were not in harmony with the precepts and commandments of the founder of Christianity, Christ; had a pleasant evening skating with Miss

Watt and Johnny Morrisson on the St. Norbert river; Johnny is a son of J. Y. Morrisson of Preston, whose wife died several yrs. ago. since which Mrs. S. has taken charge of him; Mr. S. had to act as a witness in a recent boiler explosion in which a mill proprietor sued a boiler Co. for damages thro the explosion of a new boiler bought from them which was guaranteed to stand a certain amount of lbs. of steam but failed to do so; I perfectly agree with Mrs. S. that Mr. Middleton and A. Young have associated so constantly and long with French Canadians that they have become completely Canadianized in their conversation and manners; Young often goes to see the French girls which Mrs. S. does not like; Mr. S. is so economical that he does not keep a watchman for the factory on Sunday but goes to see that all is right himself; the tan bark is carried by an endless chain from the mills into the leaches and after the juice is extracted the bark pitcher empties it thro a hole in the bottom of the leach on to another endless chain that carries it over the furnaces where there are holes in the brick work covered with iron covers which the fireman removes occasionally and shovels in tan bark which saves a great deal of fuel, but too much of this damp cannot be thrown in at one time for it would deaden the fires; Mr. S. has shown me his studio where he has a great number of paintings and water colors by himself, some of his English landscapes are really beautiful; some of his paints and colors cost as much as 60s, an ounce; Mrs. S. lends me all the English newspapers and magazines they take; I am especially interested in the "Truth," a fashionable radical journal; bread, potatoes, pork and tea is my usual fare; I sometimes drink koka but think it has a mawkish taste as compared with cocoa, chocolate, tea or coffee. The doctor of the village lives in a plain wooden house and his personal appearance is worse, he has a very red face and bloated figure altho not more than 30 yrs; his wife is very handsome but has a sad, careworn appearance in her face that is pitiable to behold; while at Dissett's store one of the loafers there made a vile remark on the doctor's character which brought a tell tale blush npon his face and he laughed uneasily to affect an indifference that I know he did not feel. Mr. Bentley has been here and said that the farmers who had taken contracts for drawing bark would have to be hurried up; have had some very cold weather lately as low as 30 deg. below zero. From a letter to Rev. L. C. W. please find enclosed my weekly subscription to St. Mark's church for the 2 months ending Feb. 1. From a letter to Tom, do not refuse my half of Elmbrooke if it is offered to you for nothing would give me greater pleasure than to see you in possession of the whole estate; you cannot now complain for want of snow for we have it now in abundance much to my disgust in the mornings when I have to get the men to shovel it off of platforms 1000 ft. long; I have had a very hard time of it for the last 2 weeks, the farmers in their hurry to get in their bark are very unreasonable, I have to keep on a brisk walk all day from 7 to 6 amongst 150 teamsters and never take more than 20 minutes to dine. I have been very poorly of late with a cough and pain in my chest; I need not inquire about fathers health as he has not had a days ill health in 5 yrs. Sunday 26 Feb. the average cost of my weekly board for the last 6 weeks has only averaged $1.30 a week. I had a fight with one of the farmers, he flung his bark on the ground any way without piling it, I asked him politely to come back and do so, he replied only with oaths and filthy names, I started for him and just as I got near his sleigh received from him a blow on the head with a stick out of the rack of his sleigh which almost stunned me and before I knew where I was we were engaged in a rough and tumble fight, I found to my disgust that I had caught a tartar, for the dirty brute caught hold of my ear with his teeth and had I not immediately placed my 2 thumbs on his wind pipe and choked him off I am confident he would have bitten off a piece of my ear, hostilities now ceased and I went to the office and told the cashier to deduct 25 cts. from the price of his load, which he did; 415 loads came in that day. Mrs. Bentley owns 18000 acres of land in her own name. The priest of this parish is the only one that is allowed to sell spirituous liquors; he only sells it in small quantities for medicinal purposes. From a letter to uncle Richard, as regards my leaving father and Tom the circumstonces I think justified my doing so, firstly because I believed I could succeed better elsewhere and secondly because you and I could never agree as to how we should conduct our business; from the picture you drew in your letter you must think I acted in a most heartless manner, you say I left an afflicted brother and helpless father to get on as best they could, if I did leave them it was in comfortable and easy circumstances; I left my brother with a fine farm all paid for, good buildings, stock, implements, plenty of fodder, grain, buckwheat and vegetables and $50 in money, and I myself, when I arrived at the end of my destination had only 25 cts. I must say if you consider me heartless in acting thus that you entertain a most false and unjust view of the case, and as regards leaving a helpless father, he has a $1000 farm, stock, fodder, implements, comfortable residence, etc. and only owed $18; I think if there was any one to pity that it is myself for having lost 5 yrs of my life in the backwoods without any benefit to myself; if I did take a note from Tom for my half of the stock, implements, furniture, library, etc., this surely was the least I should get after 5 yrs hard work, besides $100 of the note he gave me was money I advanced the firm when we first went into partnership 6 yrs ago, and this is all I have to pay whatever I owe you and make my first deposit towards college expenses; if however Tom is in need of it I shall give it to him; since I have arrived here nothing can exceed the kindness of Mr. and Mrs. S. Mr. S. has kindly p·omised to try and get me the position of bookkeeper in one of Bentley & Co's factories at a salary of 600 a yr. I enclose you $2 to get me "Havet's French Manual;" the week before last the factory here was flooded, the ice on the St. Herbert river being obstructed by rocks below the factory which flooded the village to a depth of 5 ft. I have still a bad cold caused by going thro the heavy masses of ice and water to one of the factory buildings to attach a rope to a fire engine to drag it ashore and to aid Mr. S. to stop the engines and let the steam out of the boilers before the water rose over them which kept me 2 hours in wet and icy clothes. Mr. S. is a very cool and brave man and was greatly disgusted at the cowardice of the French employees who were afraid to enter the factory but I must acknowledge I myself felt great fear but was ashamed to show it, when the huge masses of ice 20 ft. high piled one upon the other dashed against the wall of the factory, breaking the thick timbers as if they were so many straws, and causing loud explosions as the water rushed thro the red hot furnaces; the Co. will lose several thousand dollars. Aston, March

2d, "Dear Arthur, I was glad to receive a letter from you and I hope that you will succeed well, you are young and active and perseverance will tell in the end, especially where you recognize the eye of God over you; I am pleased to know that you still take an interest in our little church; your cousin Ethel Goldsmith is still spending a week at the parsonage with Mabel. Florence Meredith has not returned from her tour among her friends, Maud is improving slowly but has to be very careful; we are all well and join in kind regards to you, may God bless you, yours truly, L. C. Willoughby. "My dear Arthur I recd yours of the 21st ulto, and would have answered sooner but have been very much occupied lately in making an exchange for my farm the Elms with a French Canadian for some cottages in the city; you know what a tedious people they are to do business with; I get 4 cottages and a vacant lot for the Elms farm as it stands, land, houses, implements, stock, furniture, beds, bedding, crockery, cutlery, stoves, etc., reserving the library, pictures, guns, fishing tackle, and a young horse and I pay him $4,000; the purchaser, Mr. Baron, has a mighty soft thing of it, but since Clifford left it I found it an elephant on my hands and was glad to get rid of it. There is this difference in my present position; the cottages will bring in some return and the Elms cost me $600 a yr to run it; you say in your letter that I and your uncle could sell your half of Elmbrooke, I have no right or claim to do so, as your Uncle Jerrold is the only one that could sell it, and I am sure he never will nor intends to; for the last 30 yrs, he has been advancing money to your family, influenced only by motives of brotherly love to your dear mother, the same love and bounty he has contioned to your brother and yourself, and you abandoned the place and left your poor afflicted brother and helpless father, but now that Tom has possession of the place and has manfully determined to remain on it, should you ever be sick or the hand of affliction placed on you I have no doubt you would find a home and a welcome from him; Aston is one of the healthiest spots in the world, that is why I sent my dear son Richard there to recuperate his health, and that was one of the reasons your dear mother lived there; every one of your brothers and sisters died in London before your parents went to live there, and before you went there you were so frail and delicate that I did not think it possible for you to live; it was from congestion of the spine that Tom lost the use of his leg. And now that the pomps and vanities of this world have induced you to seek your fortune in pastures new and untrodden, may your Heavenly Father protect you is the sincere wish of your affectionate uncle, R. I. Goldsmith. P, S., your aunt and Mabel are well and unite in love." "Dear Tom, I recd. your letter yesterday and am greatly surprised with its contents, you ask me "to settle up like a man," a difference in my expenditures compared with yours while I lived on Elmbrooke; you say the accounts prove that I spend more on clothes than you did, what if I did, do you think I will pay you for some trifling extra amount I spent on clothes more than you did while I was pulling stumps, clearing land and digging ditches on the land that you are now having the use of for nothing, and will eventually posess as your own; I positively tell you that I never shall, for it would be a clear proof that one Howard was becoming a fool and the other a rogue; I can honestly say from my heart that I will in my straightened circumstances help you and father as much as I possibly can after having paid my just debts to Uncle Jerrold and Richard, for I never intend to die 1 cent in their debt, but to pay a cent for any of the clothes or food I used during the 7 yrs. I worked on Elmbrooke I never shall, but will appeal to my uncles, in whose justice I have great confidence, but were such a thing possible that they should decide against me, justice I can easily get elsewhere, exactly 7 yrs. ago I commenced working on Elmbrooke with $160 of my own, you commenced without a cent, to-day I have only your note for two hundred odd dollars, and you have the whole of your own and my labor as well as the half of the estate, and yet you are actually mean and foolish enough to think you can make me pay for clothes I wore out in clearing the land that you now own and cultivate free of cost; for those 7 yrs. I bore "the burden and heat of the day" and did more than a partners share of work, working harder than the average farmer in that part of the country, and am proud of those 7 yrs. of industry and economy, even though I reap no benefit, my brother will; I would never have mentioned this had not your meanness driven me to it, so now my dear Tom I think you can understand me on this subject; firstly that I have decided to pay all money obligations that I may owe my uncles, secondly that if they refuse to take my half of Elmbrooke I give it to you, and thirdly, that you will never mention this subject to me again." "Dear Mrs. Meredith, In a letter I recd. from Tom a few days ago he informed me that you were surprised at my leaving Aston without bidding you good-bye, which certainly I should have done, but I am willing to apoligize for this breach of etiquette and trust you will pardon it, I assure you it was not because I had forgotten the great kindness and friendship I have experienced from you, but merely because circumstances unavoidably prevented me, and caused me to commit this act of discourtesey to you, whom I have always considered as one of my best and truest friends, however, I entertain the hope that in a few yrs. I shall have the pleasure of spending many pleasant evenings with you and your family, until then I shall always think with gratitude of your generous hearted hospitality, that ever extended to me a cordial welcome to enjoy the society of your family and friends, wishing you and yours every success and happiness I remain, your affectionate friend, A. N. Howard," I have such a pain in my chest and a bad cold that Mr. S. excused me from work today; it is no wonder I have had a bad cough for the last 7 weeks after so much hardship and exposure, the Dr. agrees with Dr. R. of Quebec that my right lung is very weak and that I must be careful, avoiding sudden changes of temperature. On returning Mrs. Gaudette said the priest could have cured me better than the doctor, also told me that a priest can stop a fire or flood and can even if necessary bring to life a dead man; Mrs. Bobaire a neighbor of Mrs. G's. is a great gossip, her eldest son is only 13 yrs. of age, yet I never saw such a vicious looking young rascal in all my life, he has been accused of crimes that would even make a wicked man shudder, Mrs. S. very truly says that he has eyes like a serpent. 17th March, lovely weather, sun rather too hot for snow roads to last for any length of time; while at Mr. Sherman's house Mrs. Bentley told me that she had met Florence Meredith at a Calico ball that was given at Charlesbourg, Mrs. Holden also spent the evening there, but appears to be of the opinion that gravity and silence with affectation is the height of gentility, and formed a great contrast to the easy and graceful converation and deportment of Mrs. S. and Mrs. B., Mrs. B. kindly invited me to go and see her at Charlesbourg; how the curtain rises and falls, and the actors change their positions on this world's stage, exactly 14 yrs. ago this accomplished lady was the daughter of a settler in the backwoods, to-day in her own right and name she is worth $50,000, she dresses in the height of fashion and I must say has a fine appparance, her frank, benevolent features with sparkling intelligent eyes and the unaffected grace of her deportment, with her well cultivated conversational powers makes her society truly delightful. Dined at Mrs. Sherman's on Sunday, the dinner consisted of roast turkey, vegetables, sauces, jellies bread and butter, pastry, preserves, and tea; while spending an evening at Mr. Sherman's we had a lengthy conversation on political economy and religion, Mr. S. believes that rich people are perfectly justified in buying rich jewels, laces, pearls &c.; I affirmed that any gentleman or lady who would spend several thousand dollars to gratify their barborous vanity in wearing apparel were sinning against themselves, their fellowmen and future generations, that ideas that encouraged poor women to sacrifice their eye-sight and a whole life time over a few pieces of minature lace work were to say the least vain and selfish, and that all reasonable men ought to acknowledge that no man has a right to keep expensive shooting preserves, while his fellow-countrymen are leaving their native land for want of a piece of ground to call their own, I maintained that all those who spend their money or time extravagantly without first considering the most profitable and useful means of using it, were from a rational and even christian point of view, committing a sin by not using their talents and gifts to the best advantage; Mr. S. from his expressed opinion clearly shows that he does not believe in eternal punishment, as regards all the sorrow and sin tn the world, I said that some Christians argued that the existence of sorrow was necessary for joy, that repose is not fully appreciated until fatigue has been fully experienced, and that sorrow is as necessary to the world as are the darker shades to a perfect painting; in reference to gentlemen I said, that half the so-called gentlemen of society were not gentlemen at heart, that they only possessed the outer polish for social occasions, and that at other times they were actually selfish and even brutal, that a man who is only polite to ladies and who would not put himself to inconvenience to perform an act of courtesy to a poor woman, should no more be called a gentleman than gold plated ware should be called true metal, that another more worthy specimen of man is the thoroughly kind-hearted man who has all the natural qualities of a gentleman and that delicacy of feeling that prevents him from hurting the feeling of others, yet this man with all his delicacy of feeling and unselfishness of soul cannot be called a gentleman if he does not possess the necessary amount of education and outward polish. While the factory is stopped I am watchman so that I lose no time, I have to keep ten furnaces and 3 stoves going to keep the brick work and pipes from getting frozen; the water rose 9½ ft. in the factory. A great scandal has occurred here lately, Mrs. Defosa, daughter of Mrs. Gaudette, has left her husband and charges him with drunkenness, jealousy and laziness, the 3 greatest faults a husband could have; the priest came on Sunday and tried to persuade her to return but this she refused to do; said she would go to him during the week and confess to him all about it; she told him with tears in her eyes that if she was to be damned she might as well be so quietly alone than with her husband, for she said I can never fulfill my religious duties while I live with him; I advised Defosa to give up drink and try and win back the respect and affection of his wife and that I would persuade Mr. S. to give him the custom of the factory; he is a blacksmith by trade. Have played checkers French style with many of the best players in these parts. Mrs. S. has a choice selection of the works of all the leading poets, which she kindly lent to me. Mr. S. is quite indignant at the masons who do not want to build the brick work on what they call a "rotten foundation." Mr. S. says he will sacrifice good workmanship for the sake of getting extract to supply the Co's customers. In many points on the inconsistencies of the christian churches Mr. S. and I agree. Mrs. Gaudette was going to have her daughter sleep up stairs in a garret; I of course would not allow such an arrangement and said I would vacate my corner of the undivided room down stairs; I have in fact in some small houses seen as many as 4 beds in one undivided room which formed bed rooms, dining room, living room, kitchen and reception room. This neighborhood is divided into 2 parties, one takes Defosa's and the other his wife's part, the latter call Defosa a "sans cœur" for not leaving the country instead of trying to oblige his wife to return to him. 1 March, has rained hard all day, my gang of 20 men in the morning has diminished to 1 in the evening, and no wonder for flesh and blood does not relish the discomfort of being like a half drowned rat all day, still of course as the farmers continued to arrive with loads of bark we had to remain out in the rain to pile it. Dun and Martin, the 2 engineers, and myself have been removing the rust from the engines and machinery and oiling it; after the flood had subsided the bark contractors made a road across the river by chopping away the huge blocks of ice and pouring water on the broken places at night to have them freeze over. Mrs. S. is very sick. One of the factory hands has died from congestion of the lungs. Mr. S. says that a love for painting apart from the money gained by it is necessary to make a good artist. Mr. S. and I took a drive to Arlington by a new route, passed chiefly through low land covered with tamerac, balsam and spruce not over 30 ft. high, also a small collection of houses with a very handsome church of cut stone and over 3 streams that run into the Brisbois river, in which he says there are trout and proposes that I shall go fishing and boating with him next summer in his Indian canoe. This factory ships extract to many countries in Europe but chiefly to the U. S. and England; one of the partners is a Mr. Yankton of Boston. Its average expense for merely the bark and wood it buys and labor is $225 a day. 1 March, Davenport, dear Arthur, "I have been working here with my team drawing bark; I could have got $40 a month from the log shanties but the work would have been too hard; I make here $3.50 a day so that if good roads continue I shall clear a few dollars; uncle Richard and Clifford have been out since you left; the ties I sold to the rly Co. have not yet been culled or paid for; some weeks the roads are so bad that I can only team 3 days at a time. Montreal 28th March, from uncle Richard: "The money your uncle Jerrold advanced to you I do not think he will ever allow you to repay it, his only object was to aid you and Tom to make Elmbrooke a permanent home for you both; when I write to him I shall have much pleasure in doing as you advise. In a letter to uncle Richard I explained how Tom unjustly wanted me to pay for extra clothing I used while working on Elmbrooke. In a letter to Tom I said tell father that he ought to remember I am his son even tho I am not his eldest one, and that I feel hurt at the way he has neglected me, that I am not jealous but that I do not think it looks well for him to give you all his advise and counsel for the past 6 yrs. and take hardly any notice of me. In conversation one evening at Mr. Watts he said that this world would be better and happier if there never had been any form of religion in it, altho most religions have been the cause of great atrocities still we should be impartial enough to give them credit for whatever good they have done.'' Wrote a long letter to Angelica, my cousin in Salford, England, giving a brief review of the events that occurred to me during the past 9 months, and wrote as follows: "Mr. L. C. Willoughby's 2d wife is an American lady and not liked by some of his parishoners, however in my opinion she is an amiable lady and perfectly fitted for the difficult position she holds, that of being a poor clergyman's wife, his daughter is no longer a child but is an interesting and intelligent young lady and is apparently religiously inclined; I have only once had the pleasure of hearing Canon Baldwin preach and was much impressed by his earnestness which is a pleasing contrast to the formal and automatic sermons of a great portion of the Catholic and Episcopal clergy; many thanks for the photo of the beautiful park like landscape about your residence; the F Canadians will, I fear, admire the beauty of ornamental trees when it is too late, for their settlements have generally a bare and uninteresting appearance through their want of taste in destroying all the forest and not even planting an occasional ornamental tree to take its place." From a letter from Clifford April 3d: "I have owed you a letter for some time and have kept off answering it from one cause or another hence the delay; how do you like your present occupation; I suppose you wont be so busy now that the snow is gone; the weather is nice and mild here now and the snow is going fast and the street cars running on wheels; I am glad to hear that there is a probability of your becoming a bookkeeper for one of Bentley & Co's factories; I suppose this has been a bad winter for lumbering as there has been so little snow and the roads have been so much broken up by thaws; I go to the gymnasium here as often as I can to keep my muscle up; the Oxford crew has won the boat race by 6 lengths, this is the 3d yr they have beaten Cambridge in succession; there are a great many emigrants coming out from England to Manitoba this summer; they say that the prairies of the northwest are capable of supporting a population of 50 million; one batch of settlers have just left Liverpool, Eng. bringing £145,-000 with them; the opening of the northwest will be a grand thing for Montreal as most of its exports will flow thro this port. The Canadian Pacific Rly will be finished D. V. to the Rocky Mountains by next fall. Tom says seed oats sells at Aston for 45 cts. a bushel this spring. Mr. S. informed me that he intends to let me take Dun's place as engineer when he goes to St. Augustin to quarry a channel in the bank of the river for a pulp factory there; have conversed about religion with one of the brick layers in the factory, he believes in the persevering powers of the "scapular," which he says preserves men from drowning when they fall into water; I laughingly told him that according to statistics as many Catholics were drowned as Protestants; told him I was thoroughly disgusted to see that the followers of such a "perfect church" as his should believe in such absurdities; most religions have so much superstition and error that a great portion of the enlightened of mankind secretly despise them in their hearts; there cannot be a doubt that we are gradually approaching another great era of reform in the history of our earth. From a letter to Tom; "I am sorry to see that you still try to make me pay for the extra clothing wore on Elmbrooke; I do not think you will ever get riches or happiness by any such means as this, it is only the thoroughly honorable and upright man that can receive true enjoyment in after. yrs., from the fruit of honest industry; of late I have had a hard time working early and late sometimes until ½ 9 p. m., on account of the short time in which Mrs S. wishes me to have the factory working, so as to be able to fill their orders for Hemlock extract so as not to lose their customers; the factory has been worked by 5 boilers of late, while the furnaces of

the other 5 are being repaired, and only turns out a small quantity of extract; my cough is worse than it was so that I must
take more care of myself, I trust that you and f: ther have good
health and live happily together; this Co. only pays its men once
every two months; of late I have been trying a vegetable diet
and find it very much cheaper." "Staney Brae, Aston April 14th;
Dear Arthur, Maud and I wish to thank you for the beautiful
Easter cards you sent us, also for the Christmas cards which are
lovely; Mama received your note some time ago and says that
is all right, she will be glad to see you whenever you come back;
I have only returned from my visit to Charlesbourg, La Colle
and Montreal last week, I had a very pleasant time, and Maud
is now in Montreal where she will remain for a month or so,
hoping you will be successful in all that you undertake, I remain
yours truly, F. J. Meredith." I thank Heaven that with all my
faults I possess the ennobling influence of a pure and unchanging
love for this dear creature, one of the loveliest beings in God's
creation; never can I forget the gentle emotion that filled my
heart when I first saw her, even though I was yet a child; Dante
was a lover at 10 yrs. of age, but was unfortunate in his affections,
I trust that mine will not be the same but that I shall become
worthy of her, and succeed in winning her respect, admiration
and love; I am glad to say that since I have been here I have
honestly done my duty to my employers, and have made it a
rule to take as much interest and be as zealous as if I was working for myself; the snow is nearly all gone and the ice has left
the river, still the weather is very chilly; the masons have finished repairing the furnaces; there was a fire in a pile of tan bark
in the factory to-day, and I worked so hard in helping to extinguish it that on arriving in my room I fainted; what causes
me most uneasiness is the incessant cough I have with a pain
in my chest. The people here are nearly as low as those around
Elmbrooke, every day I hear foul and disgusting language; Mr.
S. has told me not to work in cold or damp places, also that
whenever I had time, to learn the running of the engines from
Dun; we cleared out the blacksmith shop, sorted the iron and
implements that were all washed together by the flood, also
cleaned aut the well by the river's edge, that supplies the fac-

tory with water. Mr. Iibideau, one of the pan men, and myself are making a boat, the cost of the lumber is only $1; a checker player in these parts made a checker board out of 482 pieces of wood and sold it for $50; in the latter part of March saw the strange occurrence of a snow storm and thunder. 28th April, my health has been steadily growing worse, have decided to go to Montreal to-morrow; have spent many evenings at Mr. Shermans, and played chess with Mrs. Sherman, have also read many interesting books, one by Everett the learned blacksmith entitled, "chips from many blocks," which contains much sound reason. On my arriving at Montreal my uncle told me there was nothing serious, that I merely had a bad cold. Received from Mrs. Bentley on my way back a very kind reception. she showed me her studio which is in the top of the house, and commands a magnificent view of Charlesbourg and the River St. Lawerance. Since my return I have worked at odd jobs around the factory. Elmbrooke May 2nd. "My dear Arthur, I have been wishing for a long time to write to you but I have even less leisure here than at the old place, and as I wanted to write you a long letter I kept putting it off, but I feel I can do so no longer; I am sorry to say I lost on the straw I bought from you, as it now sells in the French country for $1 a single load; Tom would not allow me to bring any of my fodder to his place, for fear of getting the "ox eye daisy" on Elmbrooke; you say in your letter to Tom that you have never been the "fair haired boy" with me, which I think is very unkind of you, if you will only reflect, you will see that I have done more for you than for him, as much as I could possibly do in my straightened circumstances with little or no resources, it therefore grieves me sorely to have you make such a remark, it must be either through jealously or your extreme impulsiveness; you are blind to the real facts of your dealings and conduct to others, why should you be jealous, I have never done so much to please him as to please you, (he never asked me,) and I only expressed my sympathy to him on account of his lameness; I do not blame you in the least for choosing another occupation, but for the abrupt and inconsiderate manner of doing so, I never expected you to remain a farmer, but for your intense ambition to gain notoriety, and impatience to make

a fortune before you knew how; we might have all been so much
better off and happier, and you still would have had good opportunities to study for law, which though I do not think much of
for a vocation, still I prefer it to the sea or army; if you had not
persuaded Tom to start for yourselves on Elmbrooke, aud sunk
so much money on so many buildings, and had remained with
me for 2or 3 yrs. longer, it would not only have been to my benefit
but to yours also; you shonld have helped me to make more improvements on my farm before moving to your own; it was your
duty to do so, and I could have kept you if I liked until you
were of age, but from the refractory way you went on and the
paper you so very cunningly got me to sign giving you power
to act, trade and buy for yourself, I saw that there was no use
in trying to do so, besides your disposition in aiming more after
quantity instead of quality of work, did not suit me, as I was
more acquainted and suited to the European style of farming,
than to the rough and ready way of bush farming; if I could get
you to see the sad effect of your erratic and impulsive character
of disposition, not only to others but to yourself, which must
cause you great difficulty in improving and developing the abilities that you have; you must remember that there are more
idols than those of wood and stone, most men have big or little
ones peculiar to themselves, honor, wealth, pleasure and fame,
are numbered amongst them, all of which we are told to beware
of; we must seek God's glory and not our own; God has the
most right to it, as being not only our Creator but our father,
who surrounds us with every blessing, but he has made those
blessings dependant on our own industry, for he put us into this
world in his own image and likeness, spiritually gifted with certain powers and abilities, and a certain amount of free will (wherein we resemble him) to be used in control of all things given into our power, which should be used to God's glory (not ours,)
and in so doing we are all bound to regard each as his children
and consequently brothers; in the Saviour's parable he compares
the Kingdom of Heaven to children playing in the market place,
and when he fulfilled the laws of a just and Divine Father in our
stead (whose eyes cannot behold unjustly) by his life example,
teachings, and ultimate suffering on the Cross, by the blind Jews

for exposing their pharasaic unrighteousness and degeneracy, he reduced the whole Mosaic commandments to 2: "to love God with all our hearts and our neighbors as ourselves;" love is the fulfilling of the law, love and charity are the same in effect, there are no extremes in either, therefore inordinate ambition is unlawful for it requires covetousness to help it on; covetousness is idolatry, our desire is to exalt ourselves above others, for notoriety is making an idol of fame; the man with the humble desire to do good, God always exalts in due time, and the proud he always abases sooner or later; besides inordinate desires lead to unscrupulous conduct towards others. You seem to think I do not care for you, but you little know how much you are in my thoughts day and night, and Tom well knows when your first letters arrived you seemed to make your case so plausible about what you spent for clothing on Elmbrooke that I pleaded with him for you, but when I came to get a full insight of how the case stood I decided that you only study your own gain. I was sorry to hear you had a bad cold, remember you have not a constitution that can stand wet clothes or excitement; do not follow those visionary ideas of vegetarianism, man's constitution requires bread meat and vegetables, but each in moderation to keep him in health and strength, do no be "penny wise and pound foolish;" you will perhaps think I have written severely to you, but I do it for your good and no one would more heartily rejoice at your success than I, but I fear you are too visionary to succeed in life without your uncle's advice and mine to check your impulsive spirit; be humble and patient, let honor not fame be your guiding star and you will succeed; your affec. father, J. E. Howard." Read this quietly and seriously; P. S. "I am in sympathy with you and wish you well, be true to God, your fellow men and yourself and you will become a prosperous and happy man." I have no food for my pigs, I was thinking of buying grue or moulie in Montreal, but Tom advises me to buy your buckwheat, I could only give 40cts. a bushel; I did not let my sugar bush this season being a poor one. In a letter from Tom he says: "potatoes are rising in price and I shall sell yours, I sold your oats for 32cts. a bushel; have you made up your mind as regards the extra clothes you wore while you lived on Elmbrooke, in reply I say, in a former letter you ask me if I am willing to lengthen the time of payment for your note, this I am perfectly willing to do although you have treated me in a most unbrotherly manner; as regards your unjust claim I have consulted Uncle Richard, he told me that it could not be legally collected and advised me not to pay it, he informed me that Uncle Jerrold or himself will never touch my half of Elmbrooke, and that you are to have the use of it for life and to your heirs at your death (if you have any;) he also tells me that Uncle Jerrold continues the income of $300 a yr. to you. From a letter to Angelica Fothergill: I have just returned from Montreal where I enjoyed a few days visiting at my Uncle Richard's; to all appearance Protection has been of immense benefit to Montreal, there is scarcely a factory closed in the city and very little unemployed labor. I was delighted to hear that you and Mr. Fothergill are going to visit Canada this Summer, what pleasure you will have in meeting all your old friends. Have of late been removing the huge masses of ice that broke in one side of the factory. "Dear father, I recd. your letter, and am thankful for your good advice, I regret that my remark in Tom's letter hurt your feelings, for I really do wish to do my duty towards you, for I can never forget how much my dear mother impressed the necessity of this duty on me, and though I have been somewhat wild and reckless I shall never forget the counsel and noble example she gave her children, not merely when they had arrived at the age of manhood, but from their earliest infancy she did her utmost for her children's spiritual and temporal welfare, by following up her precepts (by what is even more essential) a beautiful and holy example, of all the blessings I ever had I shall always feel most grateful for the gift of such a mother. When I first sat down to write you I am afraid my feelings overcame my reason, but the thought came into my mind, I must try as much as possible to write as my dear mother would have wished me to; so I smothered all my indignation and will try and write in as proper and respectful a style as possible and candidly tell you the cause of my displeasure. Your letters are written in such a way that one might imagine I was in danger of the gallows, or the vilest of the vile; you may not think so but I see it

in this light, an impartial stranger, from your letter would come
to the conclusion that I had scarcely any conscience or honor
in me, which is only a polite way of calling a man a rascal; for
the last 7 yrs. you have always industriously examined my business transactions and life, and could only find one tainted morsel,
which you seemed to take great delight in bringing under my
nostrils, in this business transaction I erred, not from a business
point of view but that of honor, by buying your hemlock bark
and making $25 profit on it, although you were going to sell it
to a stranger for less than I gave you, still I should not have
made that small profit on my father even though I did lose some
time in disposing of it, but since I have repaid you the amount
why did you write to my uncles about it, tell it to the Aston
people and be always casting it in my face; this surely is not acting a good father's part, and why say that I alone was the cause
of our moving to Elmbrooke. Was not Tom the first to leave
the homestead, and did I not do better to persuade him to come
back to Elmbrooke, than to accept that position as clerk in New
Brunswick by which he would have been separated from his
mother; but it seems to have been my fate, to be your scapegoat
ever since I was a child, you should remember however that I
have left Aston and those constant recriminations, therefore I
will hear no more of them, please never again use such an expression as "sympathize with you" for I am not in the position
to want the sympathy of any one; you think I am to be pitied
for giving away my half of Elmbrooke but I would not barter to
the best man living my liberty to think and act as I please for
the best estate or income in the world; if my uncle had allowed
me to use my own judgment in farming I would have made it a
success, and repaid in a few yrs. every cent of Uncle Jerrold's
income to us, it was an injurious kindness in them with their
want of knowledge in bush farming, to try and direct our system
of farming; I do not blame Uncle Jerrold for this, for he thought
Uncle Richard capable of advising and directing us, but the
cleverest men living cannot direct a business, army or any undertaking unless they are at the seat of action themselves; a
striking proof of this can be seen in the late American war, as long
as the movements of the army were directed by men in Wash-

ington it met with defeat, but the moment the independant spirit of Gen. Grant demanded absolute command victory was his reward; and I assure you that although my ambition and actions may not be "pur et sans reproche" like that of Bayard's, I trust at least to meet with tolerable success and accomplish some good for myself and fellow-men. As it is inconvenient for Mrs. Gaudette to give me board at her house, after I commence to run the engines for the night from 1 p. m. to 1. a. m. I shall board at Mr. Le Blanc's directly opposite the factory. Regulations I have written out for my guidance in running the engines: on Monday morning take packing out 3 glands on the small engine, and repack them with oiled hemp, this has to be done once a week as also all the many other glands on the engines; the gland on the liquor pump has to be packed whenever it leaks; the 4 glands on the air pump have to be packed every 4 weeks; the glands on the little and big engines have to be packed as much as the lengths of the bolts will allow, and care must be taken not to have the gland project so much that it would strike the piston where it enters the gland; see that the spout on the top of the dall and the valve below are in working order, if in packing the gland of the liquor pump the screw does got turn easily turn the fly wheel of the big engine; when the starting valve of the big engine leaks take it apart and put a new piece of rubber between the joint, take the cover off the condenser and remove any dirt that may have accumulated on the strainer; avoid letting the cover rub against the rubber band between the point of the condensor, also to have the well cleaned of any particles of dust that may have fallen on the point of the condenser as this would prevent the cover from being air-tight; great care must be taken while examining it, as it being situated in the cupola of the factory is in an out of the way place where the fire would not be noticed until it was too late; the oiling of machinery comes next, that of little and big engines and the shafts of the grinding mill, while the engineer is doing this he has to go out occasionally into the fire rooms and see that the fire man, bark grinder and leach man clean the ashes properly from off the grates and that the furnaces are filled with dry wood and lighted, also that the ashes are cleaned out beneath the boiler once every 2 weeks,

this and the cleaning of the grates is a terrible undertaking, the
men have to go into the hot brickwork of the furnaces on their
hands and knees, and so great is the heat that they can only remain a few minutes at a time, the engineer has also to see that
the leach man and bark man the oil machinery in their part
of the factory; the engineer now puts a wooden plug in the lower end of the big engine's exhaust pipe, as the accumulation of
water has all drained out of it by this time, and lets a small quantity of steam into the cylinders of the engines to warm them;
the big engine can be started with 40 lbs. of steam, and the little
one with 60; starting the big engine enough steam must be put
on at once to make the large fly wheel revolve slowly, for if
enough is not put on, it only partially moves the fly wheel and
gets the arm of the engine out of position, in which case it has
to be put in position again by using a small bar on the shaft of the
eccentric rod or large bar on the fly wheel, which causes a great
deal of unnecessary delay; care must be taken not to open the
valve too suddenly or too much, as this deranges the "governor";
the two escape valves at the end of the cylinder have to be
opened before starting to let the accumulated water escape; the
water glands of the pump have to be packed once a week, and
it has to be started, pumping immediately after starting the big
engine to see that it is in working or r; when steam escapes
from any of the glands tighten the screws with a wrench but
avoid making them too tight, which would break the piston;
also that the edges of the gland never touch the piston, which
through friction in a short time would wear it out; in starting
the water pump, the valves that convey the water into the boilers
farthest from the pump have to be opened first; in starting the
little engine or "air pump" the air valve has to be shut and the
starting valve turned 3 times around to the left, after which the
air valve has to be opened and closed alternately until the action
of the pump is felt, and then left shut while the pump is working and open when not; when the stream is high the boilers
should be filled with water, they should be more than ¾ full or
go lower than 3 inches in the glass gages; the gages indicating
the depth of water in the boilers should be emptied occasionally in
case of their being choked with dust; when the steam gets as high

as 60, the safety valve on top of the boilers should be carefully examined; if the steam does not escape through them, in stopping the engine leave the arms in good position, a quick movement of the eye and arm is neccessary to do this properly; before stopping the engines always open the "escape valves," after shutting off the steam from the little engine the exhaust pipe has to be opened; after the air pump is started throw a little water into the spout over the dall and make the pump go faster until the water appears, when a signal is made to the pan man of its appearance; whenever the water ceases to flow in the dall, open and close alternately the valve that lets water into the vacuum, oil the machinery once a day at 11 o'clock, before stopping the big engine ring to the grinder to cease throwing bark into the mills and allow them to become empty, for if the engine is stopped with bark in the mills they would get blocked; the signals from the pan man's room to the engineer are: 1 ring of the bell to stop or start the air pump, 2 rings, a little slower; 3 a little faster and 4 rings, close the exhaust valve the air vessel of the liquor pump has to have a cup of water poured into it to start it pumping; pump water into the extra big boiler at the same time as into the 10 other boilers, as it would force the pump too much to pump into it alone; the valve on the water pipe of the big boiler has to be opened only half a turn, the blow off valve of the big boiler when it is worked has to be opened every day to blow the sediment out of the bottom of the boiler, this has also to be done, with all the other boilers when the steam is high, so that when fresh water is pumped in, it will not lower the steam too much; commence filling the boilers at 10 o'clock so as to have them full when next engineers come to take charge; when the air valve of the water pump does not work unscrew it and place a bucket of water under it which makes the pump work, the same rule applies to the air pump of the pan; the big boiler should never have more than 40 lbs. of steam. I have a lazy fireman, I often go on the top of the furnaces and find him asleep and the "tan holes" in the top of the furnaces with all the tan bark burnt out of them, and the flames escaping from them which cools the furnaces and lowers the steam, explained to him that no matter how much wood he burns, as long as he allows these holes to burn open he would never be able to keep the steam high, he gave an impudent answer to do it myself, told him I was easier on him than Martin the other engineer was on his fireman, for I helped him to fill the furnaces occasionally, he gave me some more impudence at which I told him he was a fat, good for nothing lazy rascal and that he might go home, I then sent for the man whose business it is to replace these men who get sick or leave their work; the hot humid atmosphere of the factory is telling on my health; the pan man tells me that brandy, milk and eggs beaten together will cure my cough, another man presented me with some wild roots; gave Mr. Sherman notice that I could not work next week on account of my health, he says he will write to Charlesbourg for another engineer, and when I come back he will give me an easier position, but he advises me to become a farmer: nothing can equal their kindness to me since I have been here, Mrs S. sends me every day many delicacies from their table, but the oppressive, humid heat of the factory has completely taken away my appetite; last week made 115 barrels of extracts of liquor of 19½ degrees by the barkometer, which has been the best week during the past 5 months; there has been great rivalry between the 2 "shifts," the other "'shift" has taken advantage of ours by taking the strongest liquor to boil and leaving me the fires in a low condition, and very little water in the boilers, which obliges me to pump water into them on arriving, which as a matter of course lowers the steam and prevents my pan man from taking as much steam as he wants to boil the liquor, we are however 5 barrels ahead of them during the week, but burnt a few cords more wood than the other shift, Mrs. S. told me that I would soon get acquainted with the tricks of factory life, and that the only way I could bring the other engineer to his senses was to do the same as he did and boil down all the strongest liquor first, leaving him the weakest which would soon make him act square. From a letter to Tom: just think of it! I have to get up every Sunday night and run the engines from ½ past 11 until 1 o'clock the next Monday, and all the other days of the week have to run them from 1 in the night until 1 in the day, no joke I tell you, 13½ hours to be surrounded by steam, the smoke of kerosene lamps and the smell of oil &c., but I expect to get the job of book-keeper of the Pulp factory at St. Augustin when it is built; it appears to me that I could not live long in the damp hot air of this factory; I had to discontinue walking to the village to take lessons in French as it was too much for me, but I devote most of my spare moments to study by myself. I suppose you heard of Mr. Bentley's factory being burned, fortunately it was insured for 10,000, which will not however cover the loss; as it is now 7 p. m. I must go and take some rest, as I shall be awake at 11 p.m. to go to work; I shall try and hold out this week, but if my cough and appetite does not improve I shall go to Montreal; my honest opinion on agricultural and factory life is, that any man who owns 100 acres or even 50 of good land would be foolish to leave it to work in a factory, and that if he worked as regularly on his farm as factory men do, he would be just as well off, and what is still of more consequence, be a a healthy man. I trust that you are well advanced with your Spring work and that you will take an honest pride in trying to be the best farmer in your part of the country. From a letter to father: please tell Tom to pay Rev. L. C. W. what I owe him, also ask him if he received the amount I sent him. I hope Tom will continue a subscriber to the church, I think it is his duty, it being the nearest Protestant church to his place and also because our dear mother is buried there; the balance of the money he received for the produce of Oak Hill he and you will please spend in beautifying the spot where the object of our united love rests." June 3rd; for the last 2 weeks I have been holding out against an incessant cough and pain in my chest, for I am unwilling to give up being engineer, which gives me 50cts. more per day. One of the coopers has just returned from Norbert from a week's spree, as he could not buy liquor from the priest, he kept himself in a partial state of intoxication by drinking large quantities of Cambell's quinine wine, one day he drank as much as 6 large bottles. June 7th; Mr. Sherman's hostler drove me to Arlington; I write this in the waiting room waiting for the train; yesterday we burned 4 cords of wood and made 13 barrels of $19\frac{1}{2}$ deg. extract; the liquor too that we used for the first 3 barrels was very weak, as the leaches were 3 hours behind time through the breaking of the endless chain that carries the ground bark from the mills into the leaches; we also had great trouble with the pipe that supplies the factory well with water from the river; I had over 25 times in the night to go out with a boat into the middle of the river to remove the mud and bits of wood washed against the orifice of the pipe; the reader can well imagine that to leave the hot and steamy factory and go out into the cold night air had a most injurious effect on the bad cold I now have. Mr. S. has given me a leave of absense for 5 days; the train has arrived at last, bought a second class ticket for Dumas landing for 45cts.; Mrs. S. asked me to call and see Mrs. Bentley on my way to Montreal; the country after leaving Arlington is flat and uninteresting with a few small clearances; some nice looking farm houses on both sides, a thick second growth of soft wood on either side; pass a small "flag station," rly. ditches full of water; yrs. will pass before the land is reclaimed, as it has the disadvantage of being sandy as well as swampy; some nice clearances with ordinary houses on both sides; the ranges run at right angles with the rly"; St. Remi has a church and a large extent of clearance about it; its houses are mostly whitewashed; country cleared on either side with good looking farm houses; arrived at St. Heuri; the farms are divided into narrow strips and extend a great distance from the track; St. Gertetude is a compact village with a fine church and convent, also a friar's school; the houses are all of wood and whitewashed, which gives it a neat monotonous appearance; the soil is of a dark rich color and is celebrated for producing hay; pass by a beautifully picturesque little river and lake surrounded by handsome groves of hard-wood, the first I have seen on this line since leaving St. Andre, 70 miles from here, cleared country with numerous houses in the distance; the country becomes undulating and is more thickly settled; approach Dumas landing; Charlesbourg is to be seen across the river St. Lawerance and has quite an imposing appearance, being situated on rising ground; the train runs out into the river on a pier, at the end of which the passengers embark on a steam-boat; the most conspicuous objects in Charlesbourg as seen across the river are its cathedral, convent and seminary; Dumas Landing has a market, a church, and is a collection of whitewashed houses; bought a tweed suit for $8, a stiff felt hat for $2.40; received a cordial welcome from Mr. and Mrs. Bentley, and after lunch started for Montreal, rly. fare $2.80; the country has a flat, rich dark soil with the usual uninteresting French style of house; the remains of stumps in some fields, from which I conclude that it has not been cleared very many yrs. but this was only a small strip of country; the land is ploughed in long strips divided by deep furrows, ditches as well as fences divide the farms; river St. L. can be seen in the distance; a large sand bank runs parallel with the rly. on the right; I have been informed that this country yields quantities of hay but doubt it from the quality of the soil, which is very sandy land covered with a second growth of soft-wood; the appearance of the country is spoiled by the want of taste of French farmers and the numerous fences; many parts of the land is exhausted with moss and brush wood growing over it; quite a number of barns are thatched; the only animals I have seen so far are flocks of sheep; a trip through this part of the country would damp the ardor of many would-be farmers; the appearance of many of the houses around here are a disgrace to the fine country and the people, for it has been settled at least 200 yrs.; have passed numerous collections of houses but the train did not stop; it has just now stopped at St. Louis; a large village with more convents than factories, and more priests than school teachers; I hope the day will come when this superstitious people will become so enlightened that they will refuse to pay their hard earned money to these religious frauds to travel in luxurious first class cars, repeating so many dollars worth of prayers every five minutes they travel, for the repose of mothers, fathers and relatives of the poor French farmers; the blue summit of a range of hills can be seen on the right, and the river St. L. on the left; this line has fine passenger and drawing room cars; crossed a muddy little river, wonder of wonders! a factory chimney in sight; soil sandy; farm houses somewhat improving; a pretty view of a blue range of wood-lands seen over the top of woodlands on the right; clearances extend about a mile distant on either side; have passed a few small villages cultivated on small streams; range of hills becoming more visible on the right; rolling country, very sandy, growing up in soft wood in many places; houses and clearances again in sight; barren sand again which has not the strength to grow even brush-wood; mother nature here kindly tries to hide the poverty of the soil by a growth of stunted brush-wood; farms again; a rly. depot, what a phenomena, that they should exist in such a barren country; desolate country with a growth of tameracs and willows here and there; pass through a large peat bog, one end of it is cultivated; country rapidly improving; La Assomption, a small village surrounded by some rich fields; second growth is cut into cordwood in some places and piled along the line; another small village called Lavaltrie; the train hands on this line are great swells, dress in dark blue cloth, brass buttons, imitation diamonds and flashy neckties; pass a river on which large quantities of saw logs are floating; another small village; country steadily improving; arrive at Terre Bonne; most of the villages are back a distance from the rly., having been built before the rly. was; a muddy river; a mountain to the left; will arrive at Montreal at 4:50, making the distance of 90 miles in 4 hours; pass a quarry and a ledge of rocks, the first I have seen on this line; groves of hardwood which have a fine appearance; country begins to look picturesque with its hills, dales, streams and rivulets; St. Vincent de Paul has a large penitentiary, numerous maple groves give a fine appearance to the country; land could not be better than that which we now pass; the first branch rly. I have seen joins this line; pass several small villages, stony land; many stone walls, not enough stones to prevent ploughing; cross the river Ottawa; quarries for stone; Mount Royal in sight; land in fine state of cultivation; houses built of stone, enter Mile end; pay 5cts. fare in an omnibus to go at least 2 miles to the center of the city. Uncle Richard asked me if I liked my new occupation better than farming, said I did not, that I only looked on it as a stepping stone to something better; he said I was fortunate to get $1.50 a day, as few situations in the city commanded that price; uncle again examined my lungs but said as usual that I had only a bad cold; went to St. Georgie's Episcopal church, a very handsome stone building covered with variegated slate and beautifully finished inside, stained glass windows, pictures, etc. the church which will seat over 1000 was so full that chairs had to be placed in the aisles; Carmicheal preached a very eloquent sermon, his main argument was "that righteousness was necessary and profitable in this world; he also spoke on men overtaxing their energies both mental and physical, for what does wealth profit with a ruined constitution;" also gave some facts about the increasing amount of lunacy in Canada, he also eloquently and feelingly appealed to the congregation to turn their backs on unprofitable unrighteousness and follow their Saviour's example by which they would be happier in this world as well as the next; Clifford had an argument with Uncle Richard and myself about the French Canadians, who he said were inferior in intellectual power to the Saxons, we maintained that naturally they were not so, but that ignorance and superstition was the cause, also criticised the policy of "armed defense" of Christian nations which keeps millions of the best bone and muscle of this earth in a state of idleness, while millions of acres of land are waiting for the hand of man to convert them into fields of golden grain. Went to hear a New Orleans Minstrel troupe at Theatre Royal; the bayonet exercise and the singing of one of the men who imitated a female voice was all that was interesting, I left before it was half over; visited the water works; the present consumption of water is only 9,000,000 gallons every 24 hours, in Summer 13,000,000 on account of the streets having to be watered; in winter a great amount has to be used, as the water has to be kept running in some of the pipes to prevent freezing; uncle told me that he paid $30,000 for some property a few days ago to complete a block of buildings that he owns; my aunt says he ought to give himself rest from speculation and his practice, as he has sufficient to live in ease and luxury for the rest of his life; uncle told me that if I could acquire a thorough knowledge of French and the hardware business, he could get me a position that would command $1000 a yr. in this city, I visited the art gallery which every yr. is increasing its fine collection of paintings; I went to Aston and found Tom sowing oats on the homestead, helped him for a quarter of a day; before leaving, when I asked him to renew his note he told me to go to the d—l; sad were my thoughts as I heard these words and looked towards the old house and remembered how 9 yrs. ago our dearest mother was at the window smiling lovingly on us as we returned from our boyish labor, then we were young and innocent without the knowledge of the depravity of the people of this earth; we were then too young to see through the false gloss that hides the vileness of the lives of ⅔ of the nominal Christians of the present day; invited the G. boys to come down and spend the afternoon at Elmbrooke, conversed pleasantly with them all until 4 o'clock when they left; I consented to pay Tom for the claim he had for the extra clothing I wore while on Elmbrooke, and he renewed his note to me for $202, half payable in Feb. '83 and half in Feb. '84; father is so changeable, he now says to me, "Tom has treated you unjustly and I will leave all the home farm to you;" told him that I did not want it, that he might leave it to Tom and aid him as much as possible to become a successful farmer; while waiting next day for the train at Aston played checkers with Dr. Moore, a French-Canadian educated at McGill university and a very liberal man; saw a little bear in a cage at Aston station, it was very cross from the constant teasing the people gave it; on arriving at Montreal to convince myself of the soundness of my lungs I went to Dr. Howard, he lives in a stately mansion of cut stone, and his reception room is superbly furnished, drawing room with a richly furnished private office next to it; he is one of the cleverest and most popular Dr. in Montreal, he said "I detect a slight weakness of the right lung and advise you to give up the occupation you are now working at, if you do not the result will be serious, I would also advise you to move to a milder climate; paid him his fee $5, and he gave me a prescription on a drug store for a cough mixture; met Mrs. Meredith, had a long conversation while walking down Beaver Hall hill; told her that I intended never to return to farming, she informed me that the family would all move into Montreal this winter, and invited me to call on them when I came to the city; forgot to mention that while I was at Uncle Richard's I met Angelica whom I had not seen for 16 yrs., she is such a gentle and affectionate cousin, she conversed a long time with me about my dear mother and said that she had always acted towards her a mother's part, that whatever desire she had to be a true Christian was the result of my mother's advice and counsel, before parting she made me promise to continue my correspondence with her; met Mr. J. Y. Morrisson, he tells me that their factory in Pennsylvania turns out 100 barrels a week and employs only 11 men inside the factory. There is no leach pitcher, by opening a trap door the tan bark falls out of the leaches of itself and slides down an inclined plane over the furnaces; the valves are so centralized that one man is sufficient to run the pan and engines; Mr. M. says the country has a fine appearance, but that the soil is of an inferior quality; he is a free trader and believes that Canadians should be allowed to buy their goods wherever they can buy them the cheapest. While I was in Aston I was horrified at the terrible effect that the constant use of intoxicants is having on Mr. McDougal, he was once one of the handsomest and noblest looking men I ever saw, but now his face is fearfully flushed and bloated, and the once almost perfect symmetry of his physique is totally destroyed; I felt disgusted with the weakness and folly of nature when I saw how quickly the beauty of this man's figure and face were being destroyed, his intellectual powers becoming deadened, and a piece of God's most glorious workmanship being lost for all that is good and true on this side of the grave; paid a visit to a friend on Beaver Hall Hill, was quite astonished to meet his daughter, a beautiful and accomplished young lady, who when I met her 9 yrs. ago was a little child, and was agreeably surprised to find that she could converse intelligently on the leading subjects of the day, in fact she told me she had the most profound contempt for young gentleman who could converse on no other subject than society gossip; I am sorry to say however, that so far as my experience goes, such sensible young ladies as these are very scarce and not often met with. On my way to the Richliew Navigation Co's wharf I bought a very nice umbrella for 90cts. and paid a watch maker $1 for cleaning and putting a new glass into my watch; as I had 2 hours to spare went in the street cars to Hudon's cotton factory, but on account of being a stranger I could not get a pass to inspect the inside of the factory, it is 720 ft. long and 118 wide and 5 stories high, employs 1120 women

and manufactures 48,000 yds. of cotton per day; left Montreal on
board the Quebec, a good view of Victoria bridge, behind us St.
Helen's island rises high out of the river on the right with some
houses on it; Longueuil ferry is on our right; fine residences on
each bank of the river with shade trees around them; a church
on the left, no hills in sight. Montreal, situated as it is at the head
of navigation, and possessing such an enterprising class of citizens is certain to maintain its position as the commercial metropolis of Canada for yrs. to come. Fine houses, pretty groves and
gentle rolling country on either bank; Beloil mountains to be
seen on the right in the distance; Point Clair village on the left
with a few houses and churches; rising land on the left, shore
obstructs the view; houses on either bank at intervals of about
3 acres apart; a light-house, small village and convent to the
left; close to Pointe du Tremble; 2 light houses in view on the
left; passed between 2 small islands, also isles Vercheres and
Deloric; Charlesbourg is 90 miles from Montreal and the same
from Quebec; between Vercheres and Quebec there are 43 light-
houses; this steamer can accomodate 600 passengers with sleeping berths, is worth about $160,000; there is a bar room and
permanent book seller on board; the bill of fare covers 2 pages of
letter paper size and extra page for wines and liquors, only a few
hotels I have been in equal it; at Sutton the river Richelieu con-
nects Lake Champlain with the St. Lawerance; there is a rly.
from here to Aston; while waiting here I watched a steamboat
being loaded with pigs, calves, sheep and lambs, which recd.
very rough treatment; I also noticed fish on banks still alive
quivering with agony and dying a horrible and lingering death;
without doubt the great Creator is greatly displeased with this
sinful cruelty of his so called children; pretty houses with groves
about them on either bank; the soil is very fertile between here
and Berthier; many young ladies were out in boats upon the
river; there is an excellent English college here; some of the
islands are submerged and only the tops of bushes can be seen;
a gentleman on board has a boat he bought at Berthier made of
Spanish cedar, red cedar and English oak beautifully painted
and varnished with a patent contrivance that enables the rower
to feather his oars with the greatest ease, for which he paid $100;

arrived at Isle au Paix, which is 9 miles long and 4 wide, and contains a church and a whole parish which is formed of excellent farms and neat farm houses; ocean steamers can only pass in the channel on 1 side of the island; I almost imagine I am in Holland as we leave Berthier, land and water is so much mixed; the deck passengers of this boat are dirty miserable specimens of humanity; the river is divided into 2 channels by islands covered with stately elms, under which numerous cattle are grazing; I hear that many of them get drowned by venturing too far into the water; the outline of the shore on the right is indistinct in the far distance; we have entered Lake St. Peter; a thunder storm has just ceased and a beautiful rainbow is in view; pass a "light ship" permanently moored with a lantern in its mast head, also several bouys to direct the course of vessels into a safe channel, they are placed every Spring by the government along the course of the river and have to be removed every fall as the descending ice would carry them away; Lake St. Peter is 9 miles wide and 25 miles long; this steamer goes at about the rate of 12 miles an hour and burns 12 tons of coal each trip of 90 miles; its engine driver has $50 a month and board; the steamer has now stopped at the mouth of the St. Norbert river where there are 6 large steam saw mills; the country here although flat is interesting on account of the numerous groves; there is a French college in the village of Norbert 2 miles from here; there are some lovely little islands in the mouth of the river covered with willows which form a wall of green, rising perpendicularly from the water's edge; the steamer does not usually stop here but at Port St. David at the outlet of the St. David river; along the banks of the river there are no mountains, no grand primeval forest or stately residences to relieve the monotony of the scenery, still however the St. Lawrence is one of the grandest rivers in the world. Next morning I was awoke at the hotel by the sound of the martial music of the Christian idolaters of Charlesbourg, who on this day bow down and adore a piece of bread, to adore the sun or moon or even animals is bad enough, but in my estimation a piece of bread is about the most absurd God the dupes of priest-craft ever worshiped; on my way to Mr. Bentleys passed the "reposir" of which they

were taking a photograph and its numerous images; Mr. and
Mrs. B. introduced me to several of their Charlesbourg friends
also to Miss Bentley who is about as plain an English young
lady as I have ever seen, her features are long and angular and
her complexion is abominable, but she is well educated and
very much accomplished and a most agreeable companion; in
her opinion most of the wooden houses in Charlesbourg have a
temporary appearance as compared with those of Gt. Britain;
there are several large saw mills in this town owned by English
speaking people, which export millions of feet of lumber annually;
they are situated at the mouth of the St. Maurice river. I never
saw a lady or gentleman devote so much care in training their
children as Mr. and Mrs. Bentley; they do not seem satisfied
with leaving their instruction entirely in the h... of the teachers of a first class school, but supervise it themselves and act as
if they felt how much the future character of their children depended on their example and instruction. I now see how Mr.
B. accomplishes so much reading, he devotes all his spare time
to it and reads systematically only that which is useful, and skips
over all the trash. Mrs. S. favored us with some music and
singing, as well as Miss Bentley, the former has a very silvery
cultivated, though not powerful voice; Mr. B. also read for our
benefit choice selections of a most amusing character, out of all
Mark Twain's works; their sweet little son and daughter appeared to take as much pleasure in them as ourselves, and when I saw
this man full of business |cares and with very little time to call
his own, spend one hour in helping and encouraging his little
son to become acquainted as perfectly as possible with his lessons
for school to-morrow, and the mother do the same with the
daughter, I could not refrain from expressing my admiration,
when they told me that the duties of society or business were
not allowed to interfere with the hour they daily devoted thus
to their childrens welfare. Later on in the evening I had an interesting conversation with him on the manufacture of paper
and was told that there are 940 paper factories in the United
States, the largest of which turns out 4 tons a day. I am now
at work again running the engines, both Martin and myself find
it very diffcult to "keep up the steam" on account of the bad

wood we use; I only pay Le Blanc $2.00 a week for board. 21st June; the trees are all in leaf. Mr. and Mrs. Bentley have invited father and Tom on visit to their place; Le Blanc's little son, 9 yrs. of age, murders the Latin language every evening by repeating long prayers for the benefit of the family, in a sort of Latin jargon. In a circular published by E. Howard he says that "Irish bouroughs"have less than as many parliamentary voters in proportion to the population as English boroughs; Dublin, with a population of 267,000 in 1871 had only 13,590 voters for parliamentary purposes, and of municipal voters only 5000; in Leeds in '71, with a population of over 259,000 it had 49,000 parliamentary electors and over 50,000 municipal. Extract from a pamphlet by E. Howard entitled, "Irish grievances in 1882" with some remarks on Home rule; true liberty only exists where there is cheerful obedience to just and wise laws, (Bacon;) English land laws have been enforced in Ireland for centuries against the wish of the majority of the Irish people. Since Mar. 1st, 1881, every Irishman is liable to imprisonment without even a form of trial, merely on the secret sworn information of a policeman, and locked up during the pleasure of the Lord Lieutenant's secretary, who is an Englishman; over 500 persons are thus incarcerated in Her Majesty's jails in Ireland, amongst them 3 highly popular M. P's. No man is allowed to carry arms without a license, and in education although the Irish people have long desired a public system of education for their children, the British government have endeavored for the last 50 years to force on them a more or less purely secular education; also the pettiest acts of Parliament for local purposes bridges, canals or gasworks, must be squeezed by their promoters at a great cost of time and money through that lumbering, overworked machine the Imperial Parliament. In Gt. Britain owing to the partial prevalence of household suffrage 2 men ont of every 5 have votes, in Ireland where household suffrage is unknown only one man in 5 has a vote. The local government and finances of Irish counties are managed chiefly by grand juries appointed by the high sheriff of each county; the grand jurors are nearly all country gentlemen and either landlords or land agents, most of them being Protestants and Tories, while the rate payers whose money they expend are mostly Catholics and home rulers, except in Ulster; about 9 out of every 10 magistrates in Ireland who administer justice in the police courts and at the petty sessions are Protestants and Tories, while three fourths of the people to whom justice is administered are Catholics; magistrates and judges nearly all belong to the landlord class in sympathy and relationship. In Gt. Britain when a change of government takes place from Conservative to Liberal, the character of the Executive changes also in sympathy with the change of ministry. In Ireland the Executive is practically the staff of government officials at Dublin Castle who always are Tories of an advanced (backward) type. The police force in Ireland, instead of being controlled as in Gt. Britain by the local authorities in each town or county and unarmed except with truncheons, are under the control of the Tory officials at Dublin Castle, and armed with rifles, swords and bayonets and drilled like an army, and frequently act without regard to the wishes of the elected local authorities. As a result the Irish police, though not more effective in proportion to numbers than the British police in detecting crime, are most successfully employed in dispersing unarmed and peaceable public meetings, and in occasionally shooting or stabbing to death any riotously inclined peasant. Reforms of nearly all these grievances have been repeatedly asked for in Parliament by Irish members, but hitherto without avail. All bills intended to remove or lessen the evils mentioned have over and over again been introduced by Irish members and been supported in all cases by a majority of Irish members, but the votes of English and Scotch. members have invariably swamped the Irish vote. The coersion act of 1881 passed although 38 Irish members voted against it and only 16 in favor of it. On the other hand, Scotland practically enjoys home rule. Scotch affairs as a rule are arranged in Parliament in accordance to the wishes of the majority of the Scotch members, who meet unofficially before hand under the presidency of the Lord Advocate, who is himself a Scotch M. P., and arrange the main principles and chief details of Scotch legislation, which arrangements are generally but little interferred with by the House of Commons. Home Rule is proposed as a remedy for the present unsatisfactory state of affairs in Ireland; that Irishmen should manage their own local affairs as is done by the inhabitants of each State of the American Union. This would relieve the British Parliament of much trouble and annoyance which it at present incurs in endeavoring to manage the legislative business of a country of which it has but a very slight knowledge. In a letter from Tom, dated June 3rd, he says: I have now finished sowing father's farm. On Elmbrooke all I have sown as yet is 2 acres of wheat and 2 bushels of oats as the land is so wet, but I hope to finish all except the buckwheat next week. This Spring there were terrible bush fires; the fire burnt over the woodlands on every lot on our range for a distance of 7 miles; for 2 days and a night we had to battle with the fire; wood and tie contractors lost several thousand dollars worth of timber. I have sown 1½ acres of potatoes and 16 bushels of oats on father's place and have hired Perreault for 5 months. The supply of ice is getting low; Le Blanc is making a wooden drain to carry cold spring water to the factory; met the youngest Miss Watts who tells me Maud Meredith is to be married to Mr. Bacon of Toronto, but this I do not believe as he is too young, only 16 years of age. Sunday, 3d July; I told Thibideau and Le Blanc, both devout catholics, that their doctrine of the "real presence," appeared most disgustingly absurd to the great majority of Protestants. Le Blanc—"Did not Christ say; 'This is my body.'" Myself—"But he also said, 'I am the way, the truth and the life.' Yet no one would believe that Christ was a road, or believe that he was a vine because he said, 'I am the vine and ye are the branches.' He merely spoke figuratively as they have always done and still do in eastern countries." I also ridiculed the absurb nonsense of having holy water, prayers for the dead, penance, days of fasting, etc. Mr. S. came 3 times today to have me aid him to secure with ropes the wooden dam across the river to prevent it from being washed away; also said he could find no one else to help him do it. I felt it rather hard to be deprived of my Sunday's rest, but an employee might as well give up all hopes of gaining his employer's confidence and esteem if he does not determine to devote himself entirely to his employer's commands, and even have the keen perception to discern the meaning of even his slightest hint, and to anticipate as much as possible all his wishes. Young man, whoever you are, if you are working for an employer or a firm that is worthy of your esteem, never be satisfied with barely doing your duty, but let no effort of yours be spared to please them, and you will be certain to meet with success in life. A man should never be servile, yet at the same time, if he is determined never to put himself to inconvenience for the benefit and pleasure of his employers how can he ever expect them to take more than an ordinary interest in his welfare. Mr. S. has a very strong temper when it is aroused. A coachman left the leachroom windows open, and Mr. S. remarked that it would pay him to keep a man with a bayonet to make the idle vagabonds do their duty. A man has succeeded in getting a license to sell spirituous liquors in St. Liboire, much to the indignation of the priest, who will lose a handsome revenue by it; however, I think it would be more appropriate for him to deal out to the people his so called spiritual truths instead of spirituous liquor. Many of the French-women here tell me that they are glad a bar-room has been opened in the village, as their husbands, who must have liquor, were obliged to club together and buy 5 or 10 gallons at Norbert, 25 miles distance, which only caused them to drink harder. The bar-room will, I think, be injurious to the young men who have not yet acquired the habit and who would never think of spending several dollars at one time for whiskey. Rather unusual, dismal wet weather for the month of July, but Mr. Vennor, Canada's weather prophet predicted it and has gained considerable notoriety by his weather predictions. Mrs Defosa has been ordered by her parish priest to appear before "the Grande Vicarre;" he, however, does not deprive her of the rights of her church, even though she still refuses to return to her husband. I spend an occasional evening at Mr. Watts'; his two daughters and neice are more to be admired for their sociability than for their beauty; also spent an evening at Mr. Holden's whose neice is on a visit with him; one evening I was there he asked his wife to play a new piece, by Arthur Sullivan, which I thought she sang very nicely considering the few times she had sung it. When she began to re-sing the piece, Mr. H. remarked,

"Oh, pray do not inflict us with it a second time," which to say the least was a cruel and ungentlemanly remark to a woman who almost adores him. She flushed crimson and her eyes flashed indignantly as she replied: "Very well, my dear, but it was at your own request I sang it." While at Mr. Sherman's while Mr. and Mrs. B. were there, Mr. B. informed us that a 10 ton stone had been taken out of the river at Charlesbourg, to which I replied that the ancients almost performed as extraordinary feats in architectural science as are accomplished at the present day. The cordial reception I always receive at Mr. Sherman's and from Mr. and Mrs. Bentley fills me with admiration for ladies and gentlemen who are just as polite and gracious to me as to their most fashionable acquaintances, although I am reduced to the low positon of a common laborer. Whenever I converse with such ladies and gentlemen as these, I leave their presence with an ardent ambition and determination to rise above the adverse circumstances that have surrounded me since childhood. Read a life of Wellington; according to the author, he was one of the most exemplary heroes that ever existed. Have taken several boat excursions in my new boat with the Miss Watts' and their cousin, Miss Meklejohn; on one excursion down the river we disembarked and ascended a high plateau of land from which there was an extensive view in all directions, not even a single mountain or hill to relieve the monotony of the fringe of trees that surrounded the horizon; the view, however, up the river towards the factory is very nice. The precipitous banks of the river, covered alternately with trees, bushes and green grass, with cattle grazing here and there; the bright green islands in the river and the factory village in the distance peeping from amidst a grove of Elms and Pines; in walking through the village we saw several of the factory coopers staggering along the streets under the influence of intoxicants. Next day I hired a team and went to St. Augustin; passed some neat farm houses and excellent crops; the country, however, is very thinly settled as yet, and no wonder considering the tremendous strength and perseverance a man requires to clear up a farm of even 50 acres, on account of the dense growth of spruce and balsam whose stumps are so close together that a harrow cannto pass over the land, nor can it be sown as hardwood land until the stumps are removed, so that the timber has to be cut down and left thus a few years for the stumps and roots to partly decay to make them easier to extract. The average height of the trees does not exceed 40 ft.; what surprises me is that balsams grow here on high land as well as on low and the most of the high ground has no hardwood on it. The whole country from Arlington station to Hall's island in the Brisebois river, 25 miles apart, has only two slight elevations and in the whole distance there is not a mile of woodland that deserves the name of forest, and in the whole of those 25 miles hardly a load of stones could be gathered. but the soil is in most places sandy. The horse was a miserable old nag and I had to walk the greatest part of the way; the loneliness of this part of the country spoils its appearance. After dinner at Dun's house we went with him 1¼ miles to the falls on the river which are about 60 feet in height and about 1 acre wide and look very beautiful; the canal Dun is making in solid rock to convey the water from above the falls into the pulp factory, and when finished will form one of the finest water powers in the Province; the turbine wheel is of immense size, as also are the two stones to grind the wood to pulp. Mr. B's factory at Charlesbourg made 1 ton per day which was made from rags, a sort of grass that grows in the vicinity and from pulp. Had to walk the whole 15 mile driving back and left the old nag and teamster behind me and arrived just in time to begin work in the factory. Martin and Defosa are working in the pan at one of the drums which are of copper as well as the lining of the pan and all the pipes through which the liquor passes which makes them very expensive; also had the ashes swept off the bottom of the boilers so that when the flames and heat struck them would heat quicker. Mrs. Watts tells me that Sam Burnett is dead; he was was a talented, jolly, good-hearted fellow, but fast living killed him at 35. There was quite an imposing celebration of St. Jean Baptise at Norbert; it is the national holiday of the French Canadians. What between mosquitoes and bugs at LeBlanc's I cannot sleep at night, but with some carbolic acid I have exterminated the latter. In a conversation with Mrs. Bentley and Mrs. S. I said I was surprised to find Charlesbourg, one of the oldest towns in Canada, such a sleepy looking place; I was somewhat disappointed with the view from the steeple of the Cathedral which is 200 ft. high, a few ship's sails and the St. Lawrence river was all that I could see to relieve the monotony of the bare and level horizon; I was also surprised to see so few factories in such an old town which had such great natural advantages to start with, but the Saxon Protestant superiority of Montreal's English citizens triumphed over the natural advantages of Charlesbourg by deepening the river's channel and building magnificent stone quays they succeeded in making their city the commercial metropolis of Canada. Even still Charlesbourg has the great advantage of having sea going vessels laying at anchor in front of it all night on account of the difficulty of going through Lake St. Peter at night time, yet the citizens of Charlesbourg never took advantage of this or built quays for the vessels to stop at, if it had done this it might have become a great port; but no, its citizens mostly all belonged to a religion that has blighted the prosperity of greater cities than it is, and through which the suicidal sight is seen to day of shipping goods 90 miles past Charlesbourg and back again, all because its citizens have not the enterprize to make it what it ought to be—the commercial center of the country in which it is situated. This may yet be accomplished as it has a few hundred energetic English citizens who have successfully applied to Parliament for the deepening of the harbor. Although these few English only form one-sixteenth of the population, they take the lead in all its great works. Mrs. B told me that the small, plain church I had seen near the cathedral was one of the oldest in Canada; said I was against the increasing expensiveness of christian churches, and referred to St. George's church as an example; the church itself cost over $500,000 and its pastor gets $6,000 a year; some of the members pay as much as $500 a year to the church alone not including the great amount they give in charity and to the mission fund; in my opinion some of the money spent on costly churches and expensive stained glass windows might be more profitably expended in supporting a superior class of free schools that would be able to compete with the convent schools of the French, which would have greater effect in removing the credulity and superstition of their fellow countrymen the French and Irish Catholics. Also discussed the want of taste exhibited in most of the Catholic churches in the Province, all their interiors being in most cases too flashy and gaudy, and that the interior of the majority of their country churches were monstrously square and plain. Mrs. B. tells me that Mr. B has studied book keeping and French since he has commenced business, not having studied it enough while at Woolich military college; he also takes the leading leather paper and scientific journals and has lost most of his English reserve since he has come in contact with the free and familiar business men of America. From Tom, dated July 16th. "Was glad to hear your cough is better; I have earthed up my potatoes 3 times and finished sowing buckwheat, now I am getting ready for haying, which I am glad to say in spite of all the bad weather. is a fair crop." Ibideau, the pan man has gone to do mason work for Mr. B. at Port Neuf. I presuaded Mr. S. to give poor Defosa the charge of the pan; he used to have it formerly, but was discharged for drunkness. Defosa belongs to the Society of St. Joseph, and has great confidence in the efficacy of the prayers of its members and informed me that at his death he will have a certain amount of prayers said for the repose of his soul free of charge. Defosa says he is too wicked to pray to God alone and therefore requires the intercession of saints to aid his prayers. I ridiculed such prayers as useless. The Isot's have been barbarous enough to try and get some strangers to keep their daughter who is dying of consumption at their house till she is dead. Mr. W. is in Montreal buying goods for Bentley's store. On my way from the village met Defosa; he noticed that I had a bottle of whiskey in my po ket which Mr. LeBlanc had commissioned me to get for him; he asked me to let him see the bottle for a moment and before I could prevent him one-fourth of the contents of the bottle was down his throat; he returned it to me with a look of shame on his face, for he knew that he had done an act uuusual even to drunkards, but what will a man not do when constant gratification of his appetite has almost extinguished all honor and self-respect I often go out rowing in my boat, but have to use a pole in ascending the rapids; we are having occasional showers during July with bright, warm weather, but not at all sultry; Defosa makes a very bad pan man. Dun, the engineer says if Mr S does not allow him to work at St. Augustin he will go to Lake Superior where there is a great demand for miners and good mechanics Spent a Sunday afternoon with Mr. S. in gathering beautiful ferns for Mrs. S. Mr. S. showed me a painting he is engaged on which is 4x3; it is of a range of mountains, the summits of which are surrounded by fleecy clouds through which the moon is shining dimly; there are two cataracts with a canoe load of hunters below them; the sides of the mountains are covered with dense forests, and when finished will, I have no doubt, form a fine painting. LeBlanc's brother-in-law, Mr. Chutie called to see him with his son who is studying for medicine at Laval university; they are both Liberals in politics and religion, which is an unusual occurrence among the French Canadians. LeBlanc said that he would never vote before asking his confessor's advice and defended his position by quoting, "Whatever ye shall bind on earth shall be bound in heaven;" which Chutie and myself ridiculed. Three batches of liquor are made by each "shift" and strained and passed through boxes in which the sediment settles, and the 3 batches are all boiled together in the last part of the 12 hours shift; I am beginning to get tired of the sameness of the diet at Le Blanc's, for the last 3 days the same little piece of pork has been placed on the table before me with watery rice soup of a mawkish taste, which is served out to us twice a day; on Sunday we have beef or mutton. While Martin was at Quebec I ran the factory 32 hours without a rest, kept myself awake by reading a histor of James the II and 40 yrs in Turkey, from the first I derived a very unfavorable opinion of James with his vacillating character, from the second, a good idea of the habits and customs of the Turks, Bulgarians, Albanians, Greeks and Armeans In running the afternoon shift it is necessary to see that the leach pitcher does not allow too much tan to go on top of the furnaces, as it gives great trouble in covering the orifices in the furnaces, through which the tan falls on the fires; also that enough damp tan is left over the furnaces to prevent it from catching fire; a sharp lookout must be kept to pump enough water into the boilers to "blow them off," and have enough in them to commence on Monday morning; when the liquor is finished boiling by 12 o'clock the valves of the pan have to be opened and the valve that allows water to go to the condensor has to be partially closed; after sufficient water has been pumped into the boilers the dampers of the chimney must be raised their full height and the doors of the furnaces opened to draw the heat out of them, also the red hot coals stirred to make them burn quicker; the men fill several barrels of water in different parts of the factory in case of fire, the men then go to sleep and the engineer awakes them at 3 o'clock, and sees that they haul out the hot ashes out of the furnaces with hoes with long handles; the engineer then takes a tour of inspection throughout the factory to see that there is no danger of fire, and that all the doors and windows are locked. I explained to Mr. Comeault at his request the state of affairs between England, France and Egypt; explained how France and England were interested in Egypt on account of the money their subjects had invested in the country, that Europeans had been massacred at Alexandria, and that they wanted to have a more honest administration of the country's revenue, so that there might be some possibility of their subjects getting back the money they had lent in Egypt, also explained the importance of the Suez canal to England as a short route to India. An Episcopal clergyman who holds services fortnightly at St. Andre, calls here on his way to Charlesbourg and holds services here, he is one of the oldest Protestant missionaries in the province, he preaches a very good sermon from the text "Let your light so shine before men that they may see your good works and glorify your Father which is in Heaven," after the service he baptised Mrs. Holden's little infant Had a conversation with the minister on the probabilities of the French-Canadians preserving their language and instititutions; he has a gloomy opinion of the prospects for the future success of Protestantism and English predominance in this province; I predicted that 2½ millions of Frenchmen could not preserve their language surrounded as they were by 55 million English speaking people, that they might preserve it for a time but that constant association with Americans and the English people of Canada would cause it to become nearly extinct ere another century had elapsed; also that Romanism was making mighty efforts to become all powerful in the Western Hemisphere. In speaking of Leyard's book on antiquity, to my surprise Mr. S. said that that Scriptural passage about "eating locusts and wild honey" really meant locusts instead of the locust bean as I had always imagined, also that the Ancients used the same means of transit that is used to-day, for moving a heavy weight, a gang of men with ropes in front and a fulcrum behind; by an allusion to St. Anne de Beaupre the conversation turned on miracles; Mr. S. and the minister said the age of miracles was past, I replied that from a Christian point of view miracles were just as possible to-day as in the earlier days of Christianity; in the minister alluding to the sun standing still in the reign of Hezekiah Mrs S. smiled incredulously, and remarked that his sundial must have been out of order; he does not think that a Supreme Creator was unable to stop the earth's motion, but that he did not and would not reverse the order of his unalterable laws to remove the sinful unbelief of a semi-barborous king. the more I see of such unbelief as this amongst the followers of religion the more I am convinced that Christianity will be purified more and more each year of the supernatural superstitions that have descended to us from our barborous ancestors, or that if Christianity refuses to be purified of these, ere a few more centuries have elapsed there will be another reformation almost as great as that of Luther's; let us hope that it will do as much good in removing the cobwebs of ecclesiastical lies from the eyes of mankind as was accomplished by the glorious Protestant reformation. On leaving they came into the garden with me to admire the brilliant auroro borealis, which they say some suppose to be the reflection of light from large tracts of ice. Have of late been reading a work by Butler; newspapers take different views of it, some imagine it to be a defense of Christianity, others "a covert attack upon it;" in many ways I agree with the author that "truth must be maintained in religion as well as everything else;" why should any doctrine be forced on mankind if it is hard to believe and contrary to human reason, even though the priesthood declare that it has been especially revealed by God; God is not so inconsistant as to make great laws and then reveal doctrines that are entirely contradictory to them. The Roman Catholic church tried to keep science and scientific men under its control, and even imprisoned men and roasted them to death for giving to the world scientific truths that were contradictory to their absurd teachings, but it was of no avail, not even to the mighty tyrannical church of Rome could resist the grand progress of science and modern civilization, and to-day it acknowledges as scientific truths what it once declared to be heretical and false; thus the progress of truth, civilization and science goes on year after year independent of all the religions of the earth and any church that refuses to bring itself in harmony with them will be crushed beneath them and destroyed, and as the ages roll on every religion, belief and doctrine that are contrary to science and human reason will be swept from the face of the earth. Oh what a beautiful world this would be if the followers of all religions would cast away their absurd and imaginary Gods and only believe in one Supreme Creator and teach their future generations how to become noble men and women, by giving them a perfect knowledge of the practical truths of life, instead of long and useless prayers to saints, pages of Catechism etc., how quickly then would peace and happiness appear and hatred and discord vanish if man had been taught to be guided only by his reason and better sentiments, instead of by a tyrannical and fanatical priesthood, there never would have been those religious persecutions and atrocities that even the "ungodly infidels" are ashamed of. The pilgrimage to St. Anne de Beaupre came off, 1,500 people went, but out of all the pilgrims not one was cured, which Le Blanc informed me was for want of faith; on the contrary I believe they have too much credulity. Rev. E. Chillingworth and Miss Mavor have arrived on a visit at Sherman's, the latter I have met when a little child. Rev. E. C. is over 6 ft. high, has black hair, whiskers and mustache, and has a frank and pleasing countenance; Miss M. has a light olive complexion, a pretty physique and a sweetly melodious voice, which are somewhat counteracted by a slight squint and her nose (from an accident, is somewhat bent to one side; had services on Sunday;

Miss M's voice is very rich and powerful and can ascend to the highest note without any apparent effort. Mr. C. preached extemporaneously on the life and character of St. Peter and exaggerated his virtues and talents to a most absurd degree, I doubt if even an R. C. priest would have preached more nonsense; one would imagine from his sermon that St. Peter was a being of superior creation to the rest of mankind; I thought to myself at the close of the sermon when some ladies quietly remarked to each other "what a beautiful character St. Peter had," that if that Saint could be brought back and introduced to them that they would be greatly disappointed; I however admired the apparent sincerity of the Rev. C. C. and feel confident that he imagined that every word he said was truth. I thought to myself what a wonderful creature is man, he can be trained to be one of the noblest beings of all creation or one of the most despicable, and in most cases it depends upon his parents and instructors whether he is to be a degraded heathen, a superstitious Catholic, a half enlightened Protestant or a grand noble being, who allows none of the fraudulent revelations or commands of ecclesiastical tyrants, either ancient or modern, to dictate or interfere with his reasoning powers or freedom of thought. The more I see of the present state of christianity the more I am convinced that the most enlightened portion of mankind are rapidly advancing towards another period of reformation which will completely remove the bogus revelations and absurd superstitions that remained after the most outrageous of them had been removed by Luther's reformation. Mrs. S. invited me to dinner; Miss M. told me that Herbert Carmichael acted like a regular spooney and actually had the cheek to propose to a lady friend of hers. In the evening read in a book on New England life by Mrs. H. B. Stowe. Mr. S. amused us considerably by his perfect imitation of Scotch, Irish and Dutch brouge. Rev. C. C. and Miss M. are to be married next week; they have been intimate friends since childhood; as they passed Le Blanc's he appeared horrified that a priest of God should desecrate himself by marriage, I replied that even from the Catholic translation of the bible nothing could be found in favor of the celibacy of the clergy for in Timothy 3 chap. 2d verse of their bible Paul says: "It behooveth therefore a bishop to be blameless, the husband of one wife," also said that the celibacy of the clergy was only ordained of the church and was not scriptural, that if a young minister felt he could do more good and preach the gospel with greater ease by remaining unmarried he had a perfect right to do so, but if he felt influenced by one of the noblest sentiments that a Supreme Creator gave to man and loved a good young lady why should he not marry her and by their good and holy life set a bright example to their parishoners, and who would be more fitted in visiting their parishoners to take the hand of a sister in trouble or disgrace than the wife of the minister and with good advice and loving words plead with that sister and bring her back to a noble and useful life; I also maintained from a Protestant point of view that the heads of the church had no right to make ordinances contrary to scripture which the church itself had given to the world as a book divinely inspired; I do not hesitate to say that the Saints take a logical view of this text and can defend themselves against any other christian sect in controversy on it. The Catholics inconsistently acknowledge that St. Paul was divinely inspired and yet at the same time their clergy refuse to obey his command by living a life of celibacy, which from a scriptural point of view is far more contradictory to its teaching than the interpretation the Saints give it namely, "that a bishop should be the husband of at least one wife." The human race however will as it gets more civilized cast away with disgust and indignation all the fraudulent, barbarous and blasphemous so called revelatio s of our savage ancestors, but to accomplish this all men with the interests of humanity at heart must fearlessly and perseveringly raise their voices in favor of truth, liberty and reason, and not through the cowardly fear of being unpopular and unfashionable hide from their fellow men their honest contempt for a religion that asserts that God created the atrocious laws of war, divorce and slavery that are found in the 4 books of Moses; some christian apologists say that those laws were created for the savage people of those days which is as much as to say that God winked at their wickedness and tolerated laws in former days that all civilized men now regard as brutal and unjust. Let the liberal reader study thoroughly the so-called laws of God revealed to Moses and compare them fearlessly and impartially with the civilized laws of the present day and in 9 cases out of 10 the better sentiments of his nature will revolt against the diabolical savage brutality of laws that set a price on the head of slaves and reduced the fairest, purest and gentlest sex to a state of slavery and helpless dependancy on her husband; even in the new and improved dispensation of Christ women do not get perfect justice for in Ephesians 6th chap. and 22d verse it says: "wives submit yourselves unto your husbands as unto the Lord, for the husband is head of the wife even as Christ is head of the church, is subject unto Christ so that the wives be subject unto their husbands in everything," and in the next verse it only says to the husband "love your wives." Thus through all the ages of christian history woman has been regarded as an inferior creature dependant on man and has not been allowed to speak in churches or occupy the position she is entitled to, that of being a man's partner and perfect equal. It is a well known fact that until quite recently the women of Christianity never received as good an education as the men and merely occupied the positions of housekeepers and drawingroom ornaments in their husbands homes. Dun is coming back next week and I cannot say that I am sorry as the damp hot atmosphere of the factory is unhealthy for me and I still have a most irritating cough; I have also some trouble as regards my eating arrangements, Mrs. Le Blanc washes her children, handles the baby and then cuts bread for our dinner without washing her hands; also saw her eldest boy who washes the dishes pick his nose while putting some dishes in the cupboard. Mr. Ihibideau is an expert fisherman and has caught several masklonge that weighed 2½ to 3 ½ lbs. each. Sherman's have had several lady and gentlemen guests of late, among them Miss Crandal, a young lady of plain but pleasing features and a poor physique; also a Miss Miller, formerly a Miss Mavor, who against her will received the attentions of Walter Crandal, she, however, was indifferent to him; he then in desperation flirted with several other ladies to try and make her jealous, but without success; after which he became deeply enamored with Mabel Willoughby; she, however, only received his attentions with a sisterly, friendly contempt; he in disgust and dispair married a Miss Price, whose amiability is unbounded, but whose physical beauty is utterly bankrupt, having a chubby, flabby face frightfully marked with the smallpox and a short, stout physique. Have read many of Charles Dicken's works of late, and give my humble opinion that he is the king of character describers. During the last few weeks we have been repairing the factory; there has been two boiler makers from Pt. Levi to repair the boilers, some of which leaked; have collected an immense amount of reliable facts and statistics for my history of the world, especially from Australian newspapers which I take and those of Gt. Britain and Canada. Mr. LeBlanc has given me a Jules Verne description of a trial of Socialists in Europe which says, "that the culprit struck his two cuff buttons together saying, 'thus shall perish all who resist our efforts to liberate the oppressed people,' and that he and the whole court was blown to atoms." Although explosives are being improved yearly I ridiculed the idea of their being so powerful as this, and told him that the miserable little French paper that his wife reads to him was guilty of gross exaggeration; Clutie, his brother-in-law is in sympathy with the republican party in France, which is a rarity among French Canadians; he says the crops are splendid at St. Monique and invited me there. Miss Kate Watts told me that I was a regular hermit for not coming to see them oftner; I replied that after working 12 hours out of the 24 I had very little time left for sleep, study and visiting. Mrs. S. informed me that several of Mr. B's fashionable relatives from England were on a visit a his house, and that unfortunately Mrs. B. was suffering from Canadian cholera as well as several other people in Charlesbourg; Mrs. S. takes great interest in reading about the faith cures. Received a letter from Mr. Hogarth saying that he was coming to America I answered giving him all the information he required, asking him for a description of life in Germany. The Stratford *Herald*, Ontario, says: "We let even the Indians govern themselves, and yet some people have doubts whether the Irish are fit to govern themselves. Let them try and if they do not do it well they alone will have to bear the consequences." I reply that the writer of the above cannot have the interest of our empire at heart. The idea! "Let them try, they alone will have to bear the consequences." In the first place, Gt. Britain has not enough territory around the center of its vitality and power. The constant emmigration from Gt. Britain is a proof of this. Is she then to part with a quarter of the whole united kingdom? and have only 99,325 sq. miles of territory instead of 121,138, a loss of 32,513 sq. miles, capable of sustaining 10,000,-000 inhabitants. Is this a small item to a nation that has been the first rate power of the earth for many years, but through a mad colonial policy can have little hope to continue so much longer; her legislators have been indifferent to the preservation of the mightiest empire that ever existed; they lost the grand opportunity of allowing the greatest colony, the U. S. to be represented in the Imperial Parliament. Those days are, however, past and the Englishmen of the present day are determined not to allow the Irish to become a free and independent nation, for the very reason that they could not be trusted in event of a war and what is still worse Ireland in all probability would form a stepping stone and recruiting field for the enemies of the British Empire, besides Britain herself would lose Ireland as a recruiting field from which she gets some of the best of her soldiers. Ireland, however, as well as England is in need of just laws to do away with the feudal evil of landlordism. I have been paid by the company for the last 9 weeks and sent $70 to uncle Richard to put in the bank for me; during the last 9 weeks I only spent $1; I am proud of my economy. Poor Defosa still drinks heavily, and one morning in a fit of the blues said, I have a great mind to clear off to the States. I told him he should have taken my advice and not try and force his w..e to live with him through the influence of the priest and Grand Vicaire, that he should first live a better life which was the only way to win back his wife's affection and respect; when she would say to herself my husband has acted nobly and conquered his faults, I now see I have wronged him; I should not have left him alone in temptation and despair, I should have remained with him and with unceasing love, gentleness and good advise have tried to aid him to reform; I tell you Defosa, you have both acted wrong, and the one that first redresses their faults acts the most noble part, regains the admiration and respect of their fellow-men; but even supposing all the wrong was on your wife's part, you should as her husband use your utmost efforts to reform her, but this you well know is not the case, though she has her faults and has been foolishly influenced by your stepmother, she still loves you, and if you only act a manly noble part, you will be able to correct her faults as well as your own, and live a happy life with a wife that you should be proud of instead of doing what you now propose to do, travel about the world a discontented miserable man; perhaps you may think it strange for me to advise you and take notice of your greatest fault, but if you do you should bear in mind that if only perfect men reproved the faults of others, faults would remain forever unreproved; a man who would injure a fellow man's character by speaking of his faults deserves the contempt of all honorable men, but any man that reproves his brother's faults in private and persuades him to abandon them, is a friend of humanity, and the sympathy and advice he extends to his fellow-man elevates his own character as well as his friends; to illustrate more clearly I shall suppose that you are extravagant, and by false generosity are certain to end your days in poverty, and that I am avaricious and miserly, we are friends and often meet, it is your duty to keep constantly bringing to my notice that I am guilty of false economy, and foolishly depriving myself of the comforts of life, thus by blending our two extreme opinions together, in a friendly manner we persuade each other that we have strayed too far from that grand word, moderation. Read a book called ' John Inglesant," which gives a good portrayal of the events and characters of the Cromwelian period in English history. Letter from Uncle Richard, dated Oct. 1st. "Dear Arthur, enclosed is a receipt in full for the payment of the money you owed me, and the balance of the amount you sent me, $46.37 I deposited at 3 per ct interest, when you make the sum a little larger I will invest it for you at 6 per ct., I could get 7 or 8 but not on such security as I could recommend; Tom has just gone home, he came in to see me about the wages of the men he has hired which amounts to $50; it grieved me to see him look so wan and anxious, I know his debts are a grievous burden to him; the dear fellow, when he spoke of the necessity of a man on account of his lameness, I could see a tear in his eye which made my heart ache, $26 a month for hired help and nothing coming in is a serious state of affairs; may the Lord strengthen and comifort him and put it into his friends hearts to assist him; kind sympathy is a good thing but you know it will not make the pot boil, in the mean time I have advanced him sufficient money to pay his most pressing debts. I propose to you that if yon will forgive him the debt he owes you I will also forgive him what he owes me, by so doing we will take a great load off his shoulders; please God I shall not be in such tight circu nstances in a yr. or so as at present most of my money is invested in property; as regards your claim on your brother, you can never collect it as the property is so held by your Uncle Jerrold and I that if you sued him you could not touch the land, besides if all your friends know that you refused to help your brother they would condemn you; I tell you that if you refuse to aid your brother you will be hooted out of the society of your friends, and their doors closed in your face as if you were a venomous viper; I know my dear Arthur that none of these remarks can or will be applied to you, I am merely showing you the other side of the question, and you I am certain will grant my request and send me his note to you for $265 and I shall send it to him with a receipt for what he owes me, after all it will only be an investment, for if either of us were sick or sore we would be sure of a home and a welcome with Tom; I am glad to see that you have been able to make a good beginning with regard to saving money; after a little time after it accumulates it will make you independant of your situation; there is no money so valuable as that made by your own honest industry. The exhibition was not as good as usual; we have some friends from New York city staying with us just now; I hope during the winter you will be able to pay us a visit; we expect Mabel home next month from England; your aunt and Clifford unite in love; believe me to remain dear Arthur, your loving uncle, Richard Goldsmith." From a letter in reply: "I was extremely sorry to hear of Tom's difficulties and I assure you I never would have asked him to give me a note for my half of the movables on Elmbrooke, had I not thought that Tom and father, with what they possessed, and Tom's income from England, could live in a most comfortable manner until I got a start in the world, but it seems I have been mistaken, so I consent with pleasure to your generous proposition; truly mine would be the deepest of ingratitude did I hesitate a moment to consent, even if I had lost all sense of my duty and affection to my father and brother, the influence alone of your life's example should have made me readily consent but I am happy to say I love my brother and wish to do my duty towards my father." From a letter from Tom. "I am not progressing as fast as I wish with harvesting as it has not stopped raining for some time past, I have the barley, buckwheat and 2 acres of oats out yet and ripe for these 2 weeks past; I have been working a granary in the shed and lined the corners with tin to prevent rats and mice from entering; I have had poor health of late, lost 20 lbs. in weight during the summer; only weigh 120 pounds." In a letter to Mr. Hogarth, told him that the grand primeval forests around Aston had almost disappeared, and tangled trunks of trees heaped in confusion one on another had taken their place, and in many places in a charred and blackened state, and advised him to settle in Manitoba. Mrs Fairburn has returned from England, a long journey for Mrs. Sherman's mother who is over 80; told Le Blanc that from my point of view not all the prayers of all the saints and priests that ever existed could better the condition of man in the other world, and that all the excommunications of all the religions of the earth could lessen the happiness of a good man's hereafter, even though he ridiculed their supernatural lies, also that I was greatly disgusted while at the parish church to see lazy vagabonds, drunkards, blasphemers, slanderers and men living in open sin, go and kneel with the most devout and pure and eat what they believed to be the real flesh of a merciful and loving God, that if these men were filled with sincere contrition and desire to lead a better life the sight would not be so disgusting, but that they had not, for I had seen many of them that came from that table with the taste of the flesh yet in their mouths begin to laugh and utter stinking jokes, that would do credit to the vilest scoundrel on the face of the earth, and that same evening get beastly drunk, and yet the priest knowingly allows the body of his God to be thus defiled, told him that the priesthood of his church preferred to possess power, wealth and influence for their church even though they sacrificed purity and the approbation of a Supreme Creator. While at service at Sherman's the singing was very feeble, Mr. S. passed around a plate to collect money for the Bishop of Algoma's yacht, which he is to use for mission purposes on the great lakes, when the plate reached Mrs. Watts she had no money and to make matters worse she said "I have no money but will bring you some to-morrow." I felt both admiration and pity for poor Miss Kate W. who blushed to the roots of her hair at the stupidity of her mother, and she must have blushed in earnest for me to have noticed it, for her complexion is a dark olive. In a conversation with Mr. Holden he said he was disgusted when a child at being confirmed against his wishes, and with the evident hypocrisy of many of those who professed to be Christians, and from his remarks I saw that he is inclined towards Deism, but at the same time he acknowledges that Protestantism is the purest, noblest and most elevated religion on the face of the earth; and says he will have his children taught that religion for their mother's sake and their own, on account of the great prejudice that exists at the present day against those who do not belong to some special religion or church. From a letter to Tom; "Oct. 13th '82. I was sorry to hear that you are unwell, now do not kill yourself with work, remember that if you manage well the income and property you have, you will be in independant circumstances in a few yrs; physical strength is a mere "bagetelle" when compared to those mental qualities that have raised thousands of men from poverty to affluence; if you could only resolve to spend money for what is absolutely useful and necessary and make no improvements on your land that did not give 5 per ct. with the outlay, you would be certain to succeed. Recd a letter from Uncle Richard saying that you were rather short of capital, and generously proposing to cancel your debt if I would do the same with your note, which I did with the greatest of pleasure, although you may think I should have given it to you of my own accord, and that I was rather close in my transactions with you, but I assure you no one takes a greater interest in your welfare than I do, and this is perfectly natural seeing that besides myself you are the only one in our family

this country to preserve the honor and reputa-
mily, this I trust my dear Tom you will accom-
ing an energetic and prosperous farmer, and liv-
a perfect gentleman; you have vile surroundings
break away from their contaminating influence
you down to their own level; if you wish to live a
orable life, avoid the low and vulgar society of
s, always dress neatly, go to St. Mark's church
ccount of the good society you will meet there,
ice a week some of the most refined and agree-
Aston, and try and improve your manners and
powers so as to make your society agreeable to
ink you have succeeded until your conversation
re equally interesting to feeble. So, and to, "sweet
this systematically devote 2 hours a day to read-
perfect yourself in the practical knowledge requir-
ssion of agriculture, so that you can follow it with
)eak intelligently about it in society, then keep
rounded on the leading subjects of the day, giving
ous consideration whenever you can do so, instead
)ut silly "chit chat" let your thoughts dwell on
ul subjects, on your way to or from market, or at
even at work on your farm; employ your thoughts
ir opinion on the great events and questions of the
h and justice as your guides; of course while you
u should never allow your thoughts to injure the
r work, such as making crooked furrows, &c., but
l, professional or laboring man who can do a per-
c at his profession or trade and, at the same time
urs serious thought on worthy subjects, has add-
lis life; some men by systematically doing this add
yrs. to their lives; above all things in conversation
ir begin to speak on a subject before you have
if you do it will not be considered interesting and
d afterwards; my life still runs in the same groove,
, 6 hours sleep and 6 hours for taking meals and
occasional evening at Mr. Sherman's or Watts;
going to send him money shortly; also that I re-

quest him to attend St. Marks church, which deserves to be encouraged in the good work it is doing, for although we cannot agree with all it teaches, it is perfectly justifiable to encourage it for the great amount of good it accomplishes. Went to a husking party at Mr. Cluties at St. Monigue with Le Blanc and several others, drove through a level country in a North-westerly direction, in which there was considerable amount of second growth and wood land interspersed until we reached Cluties farm, prettily situated on the edge of a deep ravine surrounded by a grove of pines, in which grew an enormous vine with its branches spreading through the branches of the trees, it bears very small grapes. Arrived at the house singing a gay French song; the husking was going on in the back kitchen, there were about 30 persons chiefly young people; most of the young girls were dressed in calico, looking very neat with pieces of lace and ribbon adorning their costumes; Mrs. Clutie conducted me into the living room and took my gloves, hat and overcoat; had she had any daughters sufficiently old they would have performed this duty, on returning she introduced me to Miss Le Blanc; a very sociable little "brunette," with whom I soon commenced an animated conversation; she shortly after introduced me to her 2 sisters who wore merino dresses and were dressed with great taste, having even dainty little gold watches, they could speak English better than French, and appear to be greatly benefited by their long residence in the New England states; yet as is usual with factory girls they spend all their money on dress; it somewhat amused me to think that these girls at home live on buckwheat cakes and fat pork, and then appear at a husking party (much to the chagrin of rival belles) dressed like ladies; the conversation as is usual with young Canadian people was not general, each young man conversed only to his companion, in an undertone with only an occasional remark to those sitting near him; the conversation was better than is usual among the Canadian people, in fact there were only a few dozen or so improper remarks, and these were only a few degrees below decency; the evening might have passed thus had there not been in the company a young man whom the girls regarded as a "polisson," some of the girls would not sit by him, he revenged himself by grossly insulting them by the use of horribly indecent language, at which one of the young men, whose companion he insulted, challenged him out to fight, which however Chutie prevented; some of the couples worked industriously at husking corn, but many others passed most of the time in whispering sentimental nonsense to each other; after the husking had been finished, boiled corn and salt were passed around, after which there was dancing until one o'clock; went to church next morning with the family, country slightly undulating; the valley through which the Norbert river runs is about 150 below the surrounding country and half a mile wide, country sandy in some places and dry in others; a few well cultivated farms and many deserted and ill kept; St. Morigue having no rly. or market to infuse life into it is a very stagnant little village with an enormous church, the inside especially is very tastefully finished. I also imagined I was in a Greek temple when I gazed on the large Corinthian pillars, the whole height of the interior of the church and painted so well that one might almost imagine them to be marble; the service as I have previously remarked resembled an uninteresting pantomime; there was no sermon, the priest made a few remarks against certain people, who left before the service was over and said it was wrong for the followers of the true church to show Protestants and barbarians such a bad example, he also read a "bull" from the Pope to which many of the poor deluded creatures listened as if the words were from God himself; he also published 2 banns for marriage; the paintings were of a somewhat superior sort and nearly life size of Saints, Apostles, etc., with gorgeous gilt frames; a minature of St. Peter's Church at Rome in gilt extends nearly the whole length of the church behind the altar and cost I was informed several thousand dollars; there was a good choir and a fine organ; in going out of the church I was somewhat amused to see the coarse figures of the rough farmers which a few minutes before had removed a quid of filthy tobacco from their mouth, dip down into a dirty looking stone basin into holy water and make a sign of the cross and immediately after the white and dainty fingers of a lady go through the same operation. The reader can imagine how holy and clean that water was after the fingers of 400 people had been dipped into it; there were very few men dressed in homespun or with beefskin moccasins which most French farmers went to church in a few yrs ago; in all the congregation I only saw one beaver hat which was worn by the lawyer of the village, soft felt and cloth caps being mostly worn; many of the women wore flaming shawls and the old fashioned bonnet, all the young belles of course dressed in the latest style and the young beaus in dark dress suits with enormous rings and watch chains and their hair saturated with hair oil; the majority of the men lit their briar and clay pipes on coming out of the church. Called at the postoffice which was also a store, it was full of people who had come a distance from the country, who were buying groceries and other articles; stopped at LeBlanc's house which his Americanized daughters have made look very neat with a $125 organ, rag carpet and numerous nick nacks of their own construction; they sang to my surprise several English songs. On my way back a very large and savage dog rushed out from a house and kept jumping at us behind the wagon and was only rendered more furious by several blows of the whip, finally I made them stop the wagon and I jumped out on the road with my overcoat on my arm, the dog for a moment appeared astonished but kept running towards me, I then ran quickly forward and threw the heavy overcoat over him beneath which he struggled several moments before he could get it off; it was comical to see the puzzled undecided look he had then on him, when however I rushed forward at him yelling in a horrible manner, the last vestige of his brute courage disappeared and he ran for his life in the somewhat similar manner that Mark Twain's "yaller dog" sneaked into Noah's Ark. The overcoat idea I derived from a friend who told me "he would not be afraid to face the fiercest dog with a good heavy overcoat." On arriving at factory village spent the evening at Sherman's; Mrs. S. Mrs. B. and myself conversed about the strange anecdotes that are looked on by many as authentic of which I give this sample. "The wife of a sea captain on Monday evening saw a white object flit thro the room and said to her friends my husband is drowned, when true enough the news arrives that he was drowned on the same day, same hour and same minute, that his wife saw the white object which some people imagine was the spirit of the

dead man; they seem to be of the opinion that the
beings have power to influence the thoughts of t[
have a great many thoughts in common with(
versed with Mrs. B. of how difficult it is for a la(
model hostess; she kindly invited me to pass Chris
bourg. Went to a horse race at St. Liboire; th(
horses that could be called good trotters; the hi
$25; the entrance fee for spectators on foot 10 ct
the judges stand was of rough lumber; there was
ring back the uneven and false starts; there were
people in their best costume and wagons; towarc
was no such thing as order or any possibility
course clear of the excited people who were very
by the men who raced on horseback. H. Miltoi
him for a while because he objected to her going
she turned Protestant to get him and now has
think it served him right. I think if I loved a w
marry her that I would also love her enough to
ligious convictions. Letter from Clifford: "My de
tells me that he wrote to you some time ago and
as they are not always regular at a country posto
that either you did not get the letter or that you
and overlooked it; father tells me that he offered
what Tom owes him if you would do the same; :
ing you as I have done for so many yrs and alwa
you of a kind and hospitable disposition, that you
ed since then and that you will do as father prop(
start free of debt there is reasonable prospects of
to make the farm pay expenses; we have been
weather here lately; I suppose you have been h
I rec'd a beautiful $60 double barrel shotgun fro1
21st birthday; I should like to visit you but fea
time." England seems to have got complete co1
and France and the other powers are left in the c
certainly deserve. There has been competition·
P. R, and the G. T. R. between here and Ott
advertize 2 fast daily express trains which is a
the public. Tom received the full income from

In a second letter to uncle Richard sent a receipt for Tom's debt to me and said the first letter must have gone astray." The excavation of a channel through a ledge of rock to divert a part of the current of the Brisbois river over a precipice cost $3,000, but it will form a magnificent water power with a fall of 45 ft. steam is considered too expensive to be used in the manufacture of pulp; there is an excellent market for extract which enables this company to dispose of it as fast as it is made. The country around here is level and uninteresting, in most places a sandy loam with an occasional patch of clay or rich alluvial soil; the highest elevation does not deserve the name of hill, from it one can gaze to the 4 points of the compass without seeing a single break in the forest that extends around the horizon; the valley through which the Norbert river runs has a fine appearance which greatly relieves the flatness of the surrounding country, on an average is 60 ft. below the surface of the adjoining country; the rivers current is very swift in dry seasons, its volume is ⅔ less than in spring and fall; maskinonge, pickerel, white fish, and trout are caught but not in great numbers; duck shooting is a favorite sport. Of late I have had a fine opportunity to improve the fluency and correctness of my knowledge of French, as a student from Laval who is studying medicine with a doctor in the village is boarding at the same house I do, he speaks to me in English and I to him in French and we have made it a rule to correct each others mistakes; I was surprised at the superior class of books he has, mostly from Paris; French literature yet occupies the same position amongst the French of this province as English Literature does amongst us. It is truly wonderful how education dispels superstition and bigotry from a naturally liberal mind. The chief drawback to the enlightenment of the French Canadians is their blind unquestioning belief in the doctrines and customs of their forefathers, imagining them to be perfection, which belief is encouraged by the clergy as it destroys all spirit of enquiry which a tyrannical priesthood so much dread; the members of the little community here are far from being unanimous in their religious beliefs, 1 of them ridicules everything of a religious nature, the rest are composed of 4 members of the chruch of

England, a Presbyterian, 2 Congregationalists and 1 Methodist; 2 of the Protestants are married to R. C's., and 2 more are Deists at heart, through the influence of a book called "the fair haven" by a Mr. Butler of London. From a letter to Clifford. "I greatly regret that you are unable to join our party to hunt caribon, though a rather fatiguing and uncertain sport, the game and excitement more than compensates for the fatigue." The comet caused quite a sensation amongst the most ignorant portion of the French here, who declared that it was a certain sign of war, ana would not believe me when I told them that astronomers could predict their appearance; strange how some people will believe in nonsense and not in science! Also said that every yr. or so there was always some war in progress on the earth and that comets appeared frequently, but that there was no connection whatever between them; but even among English people there are ladies and gentlemen who are somewhat superstitious, some time ago an English lady in Charlesbourg astonished me by saying that she believed that a departing spirit could communicate with a person it loved, and that even living spirits can influence each others thoughts, as an instance she told me, that she had a very dear friend in Germany that she had totally forgotten, but suddenly thought of him a few days ago and received a letter a few days after saying he was coming to America to see her. Mr. Yankton, son of a partner of this firm, who has travelled all over Europe is staying here at present, although a graduate of Harvard I do not like his manners or style of conversation, he is what I should call an 'upstart American," and speaks as if all mankind were fools except the American people; good American society I imagine would not tolerate him in its midst, for the rules that govern it are almost the same as those that govern the society of Europe. A few weeks ago the R. C's. had a great revival here which lasted a week, the preaching was done by two Jesuits on different subjects, such as communion, confession, prayers to saints &c., they devoted 3 afternoons to preach, the first afternoon to old people, 2nd to middle aged and 3rd to young people. Le Blanc the firm's carpenter told Mr. S. that he had worked a long time for his body and must now work a while for his soul, so Mr. S. gave him a week's leave of absense; the church was crowded, farmers left their grain that had been cut all the week; the Jesuits told them, "take care of your soul and God will take care of your grain;" during the week 1,500 men, women and children feasted on the flesh of their God; only 2 farmers in the whole parish who did not partake of "Le bon dieu;" and for whom I have a hearty respect; they incurred the displeasure of the priest by not paying to him the customary tithing from their farms, which is 1 bushel out of every 26. From a letter from Tom. "I have been busy stumping all week, have been all right again as regards my health, and have gained 4 lbs. since this Summer; Uncle Richard told you the truth when he told you that I was short of capital, I had Perreault for 5 months which came to $130, then in haying I had another man for 5 weeks, and I had a bill for wagon reapairs for $30; I expect to be able to commence lumbering next week and earn something; I expect to sell some potatoes, I grew 80 bags; the old barn is full of hay and half the new one of hay and grain; I have done some fail ploughing in the land you stumped; I am very much obliged to you for being so good as so cancel my note, father unites with me in love to you; ever your affec. brother I. G. Howard." From a letter from Clifford, dated Oct. 25th '82. "You are right about American society, one can scarcely distinguish the American gentleman who mixes in the best society from an English gentleman; there may be some slight differance of accent or otherwise but it is hardly noticeable; the same rules govern them both; that abominable class of Americans who are continually boasting of their money and how they made it &c. are perfectly insufferable, and are not tolerated in the best society of the U. S; the weather has been lovely here of late; I see there is a rebellion in the South of Egypt, and their leader claiming to be a prophet is marching with a large force on Cairo, when he meets the British troops he will order a "right about face," "quick march." "26th Oct. Dear Arthur, I was much pleased to receive your talented and well written letter, and with it also your generous assistance enclosed. I shall write to Tom telling him he is relieved of the debt; I am happy to say your Uncle Jerrold is going to give him your half of the income. I believe as that lady does of whom you mention in Clifford's letter, and will demonstrate to you my views on the subject when next you come to see us; in haste I remain your affec. uncle, R. I. Goldsmith." Last week the factory underwent repairs, the masons repaired the brick work around the furnace doors and made 2 new furnaces, the carpenters put in new flooring in some places, repaired the liquor tanks, leaches and water drains; 2 boiler makers took 2½ days to put a 20 rivet patch on one of the boilers that leaked; the 2 engineers, Mr. S. and myself worked at repairing pipes and valves, and examined all the machinery; I of course acted as an assistant; the inside of the pan that boils the liquor is over 10 ft. in diameter; in some places the excrescense on the bottom of the boilers was 3 inches thick; this week I have to "chink" the new coopers shop with flax straw, which I first thresh and then drive in between the logs with a wooden wedge and mallet; in the night time I occasionally "pitched" 2 leaches, a leach is a tank 8 ft. deep and 14 in diameter full of steaming tan bark; only 75cts. is paid to throw the tan out of it, it takes a man of good physical endurance to throw 2 of them out in the hot, steamy atmosphere. I buy my provisions for my own use now and have them cooked which cost me $1.40 a week, and 40 cts. for cooking them and lodging. On October 2nd '82 a non-religious system of education was adopted throughout the whole of France; under it images of St. Mary, crucifixes etc. are removed from the schools, and scholars are not permitted to make the sign of the cross, which must be a great hardship to ignorant and devout people who are of the opinion that the nation will go to destruction if religion, politics and education are not under the control of the priesthood. Surely there is enough bigotry and and lack of brotherly love in the world without trying to increase it by separating the children of the same nationality and sending them to sectarian schools to be taught to believe that all men are to be damned who refuse to believe in the doctrines of one particular sect; what in the name of reason is the use of having priests, nuns and monks if they cannot teach religion without forcing themselves into the schools with the crafty desire to so educate the rising generations that they can exercise an almost unlimited power in temporal as well as spiritual affairs; France is acting nobly in deciding that all her children are to be educated together and that the public money is not to be paid to teach her subjects to hate each other or to learn the absurd and useless prayers of a bloody and fanatical religion. If France can carry out this system she will become a happier and grander nation, by teaching her children that patriotism, virtue and liberty are to be preferred to bigotry, superstition and credulity. And yet I have met Protestants who were foolish enough to prefer having a false and absurd religion taught than no religion at all, but I feel confident that the day is not far distant when the tide of public opinion will ebb the other way, and all mankind will acknowledge that this earth contains such a great number of self-evident truths that man is only wasting his time to pay any attention to the imaginary revealed truths of the bogus religions of the earth. "Dear Uncle, I was pleased to hear that Uncle Jerrold intends to continue the full income to Tom, as it will enable him to continue farming without having to undergo those difficulties that beset all farmers, that of farming without capital, but in reality the success of the most successful farmers is mainly due to this cause, as from necessity they quickly learn one of the most valuable lessons of life, that of producing the greatest effect from the least amount of means. If man gave this subject more thought there would be less of that unfortunate class of people who attribute their want of success in life to the will of Providence when in reality the cause is mismanagement or idleness. I have seen some extreme cases here, two Canadians who told me that their Cure told them that their Savior begged his bread on earth as an example to poor people to be content with their lot. This of course to a certain extent is the duty of all men, but the great fault of most Christians is that they do not conscientiously draw the line of distinction between what is "God's will" and man's neglect. I have often been amused when a Canadian would say to me in a tone of self-satisfied, pious resignation, "If I am poor and miserable in this world I shall have all the more enjoyment in the next, and the wicked rich man will have to endure the torments of purgatory." I only send you $25 this time as my wages are 40cts. a day less than when I ran the engines, also my board is $2.50 a week. From a letter to Clifford: "As regards Egyptian affairs I have not had much time to study the question. It appears to me, however, that the use the Gladstone government made of the island of Cyprus shows that his criticism on its acquisition by the Beaconsfield government was unjust; also some of his speeches on the note of credit for the Egyptian war shows great inconsistency to his opinions when a leader of the opposition." Read in the paper that Florence and Maud Meredith attended a fox hunt in Montreal. In another letter Clifford says, "A slate quarry has been discovered near your place. I have bought a property at the corner of Craig street, from father for $10 000; I have paid $3,500 cash, the balance I pay in 5 years at 6 per ct The property brings in $1,000 a year; he sold it to me for what he gave for it." We have had a few slight falls of snow lately which has made pretty fair sleighing on roads that are free from stones and ruts; I have helped LeBlanc to make a new endless chain to draw the tan from the leaches over the furnace. Had service on Dec. 1st; 11 attended; I was struck with what intense interest old age listens to the preacher's voice. I discussed with the clergyman the absurdity of singing such prayers as "Lord have mercy on us and incline our hearts to keep this law." That even from a Christian point of view singing was more adapted for praise than for prayer. Mr. Yankton can play chess with both Mrs. S. and myself at the same time on two different boards and win every game; he is also a crack shot and can shoot a bottle every time it is thrown up into the air. The factory is stopped for want of bark; I am in charge of the factory and keep small fires burning and open the valves occasionally to let steam into the pipes throughout the factory to prevent them from freezing. It snowed two inches last night and the weather is quite mild. Extracts from a book written by a French bishop; entitled, Criticisms on Protestantism. "Protestantism is an easy religion for life but not for death.". I do not believe that the average Protestant dies a more wretched death than a Catholic. "When a Catholic turns Protestant it is apostacy, but when a Protestant turns Catholic it is a conversion. Protestantism is not a religion but a combination of sects; it is not an institution but a revolt. Protestantism and Protestants are not the same God, and the church loves Protestants like other men, but hates Protestantism as it is a revolt. The following is all that is necessary to believe to be a good Protestant: Luther created our religion and established it in the world. A Protestant is one who has been baptised or not baptised, it is all the same, he believes what he likes and does what he likes. The mark of a Protestant is a horror for a cross, a hatred for Saint Mary, the Pope and the saints, as well as a forgetfulness for the poor saints in purgatory; this is the true doctrine of Protestantism. The salvation of a Protestant in errror is possible, but that of one in heresy is impossible, for he revolts against God and the church. No Catholic turns Protestant from christian motives or does so from conscience. Catholicism receives through conversion some of the most enlightened Protestants, the most learned and distingushed for their morality; whereas Prot stantism only receives the weeds thrown from the garden of the Catholic church. The majority of those that leave the Catholic church do so for wicked and unlawful purposes. During the last 25 years the flower of the English nobility have abjured their heresy." He says "the poor Protestants in France have left the church for worldy gain." How about Cardinal Manning in England, he truly has had a rise in the world since he became a Catholic. "A Protestant can never declare what his belief is. Our church nses Latin because it is apostolique and never changing in her doctrines. The language is dead and does not change and is marvelously adapted for a church that never changes. If our church had adopted French instead of Latin it would have had to change the sacrament of baptism over 250 times. Protestants have grand houses but their churches are nude and bare; everything must be extremely simple in their religion; would it not be more simple still if there was neither religion or temple. It is no use for Protestants to say God does not require pomp and grandeur, did not God demand it and accept it in the temple of Solomon and did he not accept incense and myrrh at Bethleham. A perfect sign that the Catholic church is the true one is that is always attacked by Turks, Pagans, Protestants aud Revolutionists, but this we expect for Christ said, 'You will be hated of all men.' It is also impossible that God would choose such vile characters as Luther, Calvin or Henry the VIII to reform His church.

Protestants have no respect for God, they preach in theatres, hotels and other unconsecrated buildings. The Protestant sects all acknowledge that all that is necessary for salvation is found in the Catholic church, therefore they act in direct contradiction to their principles in trying to tear away souls from the Catholic church. When the Catholic church converts a Protestant from Protestantism it saves a soul that the church believes would be otherwise lost, and makes the convert believe more than he used to, whereas the Protestants instead of adding to their convert's faith, make it less. The Apostolique Roman church, founded by Christ and governed in his name by St. Peter and the Soverign Pontiffs and their successors, have preserved the doctrines of the church unchanged for the last 1800 years. The Popes and councils of the church have labored without ceasing to improve the discipline of the church and change it when needed, partictularly the council of Trent, which effectually reformed the discipline of the church. Luther and his followers pretended to reform the tenants of the faith, but instead of a reform they made a revolution which deformed everything and carried all faith away. Catholics are often divided on minor points, but never on the doctrine of their church, for all good Catholics bring any doubtful doctrine to the tribunal of the Pope and bishops, a tribunal always living and always assisted by God, and in particular on the interpretation of the scriptures. The Protestants on the contrary without this rule of faith, are as St. Paul says, 'Carried about by every wind of doctrine,' and notwithstanding the Bible which is in their hands believe to day what they reject to-morrow; whereas the Catholic's rule of faith is for all Christians and is an institution divine that cannot be rejected on the pain of losing one's soul. The Bible is truly the word of God, but cannot become our rule of faith as the Protestants use it. For Jesus Christ did not say to his apostles, go colport the Bible, but 'go and teach all nations;' also, 'to those that listen to you I will listen.' The Bible cannot be a rule of faith because its religious teachings are not clear and complete; the whole book is only an account presented for the edification of the faithful the Bible can never be a rule of faith for it contains a multitude of difficult passages that from their Divine depth cannot be interpreted by even the most profound of intellects; the word of God cannot be the rule of faith for if it was, ignorant people that cannot read would be without the means of salvation; the Protestants do not know for a certainty that the Bible is inspired, whereas the Catholics know it is for the church tells them so. In speaking to Le Blanc about the book I said, if by credulity your church means faith, and by servility obediance, then let them be swept away the sooner the better. In a letter to Clifford. Protestantism is the moral pressure that is and is gradually straightening out the crooked barbarism of all the supernatural religions of the earth. Received leave of absense from Mr. S. for a few days at New Years and started for Montreal; met Rev. J. C. P. our priest of St. Liboire in conversation he said religious education was necessary in the schools for the welfare of a nation, also that there was more crime in Protestant Upper Canada than in the Catholic province of Quebec, which statement I have since discovered to be incorrect. On arriving at Aston found it somewhat changed, and many of my old acquaintances gone away, hired a horse and sleigh for $1; father, Tom and Philip G. were at Elmbrooke and gave me a warm welcome; father appears as young as ever; visited Uncle Herbert's family, and I spent a few hours pleasantly there; Tom showed me a letter in which Uncle Jerrold sent his love to me; left next morning for Montreal at 3.30 a. m. and arrived at 6; drove to the Richlieu hotel, it is on the European plan and charges from $1 to $2 a day for rooms; it is a very fine building with handsome tesselated floors, a barbers shop, telegraph and telephone office, billiard room, a lunch bar, superbly furnished parlors and a beautiful garden on the roof, full of the choicest flowers roofed in with glass, from which a fine view can be had of the city; its bill of fare for dinner consisted of several sorts of soup, meat, vegetables, fowl, fish, pastry and dessert, which consisted of apples, oranges, pears, grapes nuts etc.; as I viewed the city from the garden of the hotel and considered that it is 600 miles from the sea and reached by a channel partially artificial, and has a harbor that is ice locked for almost half the year and that notwithstanding these disadvantages is one of the greatest shipping ports on the continent, with 7 lines of transatlantic steamers; and maintains competition with cities of larger population and greater natural advantages; I was filled with admiration for its English citizens who deepened the St. Lawerance river, built handsome stone quays, and own all the great manufacturing industries of the city. Father gave me a letter when I left as he did not have time to tell me all his complaints. "Dear Arthur, I intended to write to you a long time ago, and I am sorry to say I will not be able to pay you what I owe you this yr.; I have had to sell my pigs to help to pay my debts and only killed one Spring pig for ourselves; we might have had 4 or 5 had Tom done as I wished; I raised a nice little piece of corn by my own industry as well as clearing up the ground for it, and some blue buckwheat about an acre in all, but the buckwheat was too late as he would not give me my half and I had to superintend his hired boy, who attends to the animals; I wanted to have some pasture for my pigs in the Summer, but he made me shut them up and I had to get feed at the store all Summer and sold the pigs at a loss in the fall; he sent my sheep to pasture at Goldsmith's, through which I lost one of the lambs; he had a fine crop of oats and potatoes off my place though he pretends not, and yet he wants me to sell my horse to pay the balance of my debts, which was incurred through his neglect; I am not well of late, yet he expects me to see that the hired boy does his work properly; I have told him that if things do not change I shall take a situation in Montreal; I refused to sell the cut of the ties on my lot and gave them to him; he wanted me to raise money on my place of which there was no necessity as he gets regularly from England $300 a yr.; and now that I know that you and your Uncle Richard have cancelled his debts to you, I shall certainly in my will leave the Home farm to you, for I consider you have been treated with the greatest injustice, to get no compensation for your 5 yrs. hard work; I was very mnch pleased with your letter and advice to Tom he is getting so vulgar of late, and I told him it was no wonder you did not agree together on the differance in your accounts; I told him that he associated more with the French than you did." Bought a fine dress suit for $16.50, the merchant asked $20 but on my saying it was too high and leaving the store he called me back and commenced reducing his price, until he came down to

the price I paid for it; paid $5 for a very fine pair of French
calf shoes. The troupe of actresses and actors of Emma Abbot
are stopping at this hotel; I drove from the hotel to the theatre
in an omnibus with them and heard some of the wildest and
most reckless conversation imaginable; in justice however I
must say that many of them were dignified and lady like; Emma
Abbot has a wonderfully sweet voice but not quite as powerful
as that of Patti, it rose however high enough to fill the theatre
with melody and then died away, until I almost believed that no
human voice could sound so sweet and so low; I tried to find Mr.
Meredith's house but could not find the name in the directory;
went to Uncle Richard's where I recd. a cordial reception, and
remained for dinner; they told me they admired my independent
spirit and hoped I would succeed; I informed the n that the firm
of B. and Co. was in a shaky condition and that I intended to go
to Manitoba shortly; uncle said he would give me letters of introduction to friends of his in Winnipeg. On my way back to
St. Liboire I saw doubtful characters in the car, but what surprised me most was that the railway conductor (who ought to be
a gentleman) sat down beside them and conversed in the loudest
and most disgusting manner possible, without any regard for the
presence of the other ladies and gentlemen in the car; had I had
any lady friends with me at the time I should have threatened
to report his conduct to the superintendant of the railway at the
next station; paid 75cts. to be driven 8 miles from Arlington to
the factory village; Mr. Milton has received a leave of absense
from Mr. S. to hunt Caribou; I measure bark in his place; when
the bark is at all mildewed and curled up like stove pipes, I deduct ⅓ the bulk and often ½ to make allowance for the holes in
the load; the Frenchmen only swear at me and call me vile names
for doing this, but some hot blooded Irishmen threatened to
"thrash me within an inch of my life," in fact one fellow tried to
do it and succeeded in giving me a black eye and bruised face;
I had the satisfaction however of drawing his claret by the time
Mr. S. arrived and separated us; Mr. S. said he did not want to
buy mildewed and curled up bark and that if he was not satisfied with the measure he would go and sell it, if he could to the
Yankee buyers. The parish priest told me that "Protestants were

united on one subject alone, that of hatred of the Catholic church;" Mr. S, one evening showed his disrespect for Scriptural truths by saying of a captain that sat on a safety valve of a Mississippi steam boat while racing with another steamboat, that he went up like Elijah, for which Mrs. S. gravely reproved him; Miss Kate Watts is trying to form a little literary society among the 11 English people here; had a warm discussion with Le Blanc; he was terribly indignant because I said I saw nothing wrong or contrary to the spirit of Christianity in Luther's marriage to a nun. From a letter to Clifford. "I am at present superintending the piling of the bark in huge stacks as the farmers draw it in, to see that the couple of hundred teamsters pile their bark properly, and that the 30 bark pilers do not "loaf" too much; if you intend to hunt Caribon with me come here as soon as possible as the season closes in a few weeks." The weather here is very severe; one night I had to sleep in my overcoat although I had two blankets, a quilt and a buffalo robe; my landlady is so stingy that she does not keep a fire burning at night. I heard the poor little children crying from the cold in the other room. On getting up in the morning at 4 o'clock I found the thermometer in my room 25 degrees below zero; it was only 35 outside. French Canadian girls and women in the country districts are almost utterly devoid of that beautiful delicacy that is to be so much admired in English ladies; I hear language every day since I have associated with them that clearly confirms my belief that the majority of the French women of this Province are vastly inferior to English women in delicacy. The bishop of this diocese in a sermon in the parish church said, "The Catholic who acts upon, speaks or writes his own opinion regarding anything that effects the doctrines of the church ceases by that fact to be a good Catholic." From a letter to Tom: "There is a great excitement here at present; this is such a Conservative stronghold that two Conservative members ran opposition to each other instead of a Liberal and Conservative, but the chances of the success of one of them is small, for 20 years ago he had the misfortune to be a member of the Free Mason lodge, and most of the French are so superstitous and bigoted that they entertain the opinion that whoever becomes a Free Mason sells himself to the devil. In fact, his opponent said publically, "A man that enters a wicked society in opposition to his church is not worthy to represent in parliament the faithful and devout Catholics of this parish." This remark was received by cheers from some and in silence by others. The other candidate replied, with tears in his eyes, that he acknowledged his sin of having once been a Free Mason, but that he had sincerly repented of it and was now a good and dutiful son of the church, in proof of which he read a certificate from his parish priest of his having performed his religious duties faithfully for the past 10 years. Approving cheers from his partisans greeted this remark. Although the priest's candidate is very unpopular with many of the people for having voted for the sale of a Canadian government railway to a syndicate. I am confident he will be elected as the priests are quietly working in his favor; they cannot, however, openly curse the rouge party as they used to do, since the Pope sent them an order forbidding them to enterfere in elections." Feb. 3. Went to Cluties at St. Monique; our sleigh nearly went through the ice several times in driving across the Norbert river. The people were in a great state of festivity and had any quantity of gin, whiskey and wine, "pour le Jour gras" for "the days of feasting" before Lent; conversed with an intelligent young French girl who is a Protestant at heart on account of the beneficial influence she derived from associating with Protestant girls for 8 years in the United States; she has been educated at a convent and said that no Protestant who valued the truths of his religion should send his child to be educated at a convent, for that she her self had seen the mother superior encourage and persuade Protestant girls to attend the Catholic services, and even teach little Protestant girls Catholic prayers, although she had solemnly promised the child's parents not to interfere with the child's religion; conversed about the priests' political candidate for this parish who voted in favor of selling a government railway to Senecal, a second Boss Tweed, who pocketed $1\frac{1}{4}$ million dollars at the expense of the Province through the transaction; card playing, singing songs and relating smutty stories was the order of the evening; some of these stories would have made even

Cleopatra or Lady Hamilton blush to the roots of their hair, yet the French maidens of even sweet sixteen, seemed to thoroughly enjoy them, with all their superstition and ignorance. I take great pleasure in spending an evening occasionally in studying the bright and dark characteristics of this gay and hospitable people. Have spent many pleasant evenings at Mr. Sherman's, where Mr. and Miss Morrison are on a visit; in a discussion with our "occasional minister," he told me that confession was of great benefit to the Province of Quebec and that it would not be inhabitable without the sin restraining power of the confessional. I replied that it was a barbarous and degrading system, and that modern freedom and liberty were more suitable for civilized men than a debased and servile christianity; also in a further discussion of the rapidly increasing power of the church of Rome on this continent; I remarked that if the rate of decrease in native born American children continues, by the year 1982 there will not be a single infant remaining among the families of the better class of Americans; and that on this by no means slender basis, the church of Rome rests its arrogant boast of possessing the entire control of this continent in another century; and that it was the duty of every enemy of priest-craft and spiritual tyranny to prevent this grand Continent of ever becoming the home of a race of servile and credulous slaves. From a letter to Clifford: "I regret that you are unable to come and see me as you would have a good time hunting caribon, snowshoeing and skating; a caribon has been killed here by a farmer; it had become entangled in a number of upturned trees; since I last wrote to you a lady from New York has been on a visit at Mr. Sherman's; I was greatly pleased with her manners, they were such a contrast to those of Mr. Yankton, who seemed to be suffering from anglophobia. Last Sunday, I with a party of young men went a 25 mile race to St. Norbert on snowshoes; I arrived the first, in 5½ hours time; I did not see any grand primeval *forest; most of the way I followed a range that is named "Le petit Saint Esprit;" this road is called "the little holy ghost," as there is another road a few miles west of it that is called "the big holy ghost;" for such a devout and reverent people I think that such names are improper. The country looks very uninteresting, it is very flat and covered with a second growth of willows, balsams, spruces and pines here and there between the clearances; the farm houses are all of the same size and appearance and give an unfavorable opinion of the taste of their owners. On approaching Norbert, however, the appearance of the farm houses and country improves; the country becomes quite undulating and the farm houses larger and less plain; only saw two brick houses in the whole distance; in one house I entered there was a grandfather only 39 years of age; most of the houses were filled with children. St. Norbert College is 300 ft. long and 5 stories high and had 300 students last year, 40 of whom were Irish-Americans. The kitchen was one of the dingiest I ever entered; the only ornaments I saw on the bare walls were caricatures of God, St. Mary and Saints, and absurd pictures of the heart of God with the blood trickling from it; I did not have time to enter the chapel library or museum. The tin covered roof of this college can be seen from lake St. Peter on the St. Lawrence. Norbert has only 7 stores, 1 of them wholesale and retail, and 5 saw mills which, as is usually the case, are run by English capital; its market is open 3 times a week; it has a few shabby hotels, a church and a population of 3,000; a very small newspaper is published in the old college building which is 100 years old; the present college has been established 60 years, and a student tells me that they often have to eat rancid butter and badly cured meat. The crust on the snow was so hard as to almost allow one to walk on it without snow shoes. The election came off, and, although Mr. Hilbert's election was annulled by the courts last year on account of corruption, the devout people have re-elected him in preference to his opponent, "who once committed the horrid crime of being a Free Mason." The poor ex-Free Mason went so far as to get a document from his parish priest containing the following clause: "Since Mr. Danseran has solemnly renounced Free Masonry and declared in public that no good Catholic can belong to it or any other secret society; and has publicly fulfilled his religious duties for the past 10 yrs. and conducted himself like a man sincerely attached to the Catholic faith, he ought to be considered as having recovered his good reputation among the faithful." Yet notwithstanding this, Mr. Baron, Vicar General of the diocese said in a sermon on the Sunday preceding the day of the election. "The fear I have of the influence of free mason lodges on any man that has even once belonged to them is a sufficient reason for me to refuse my vote to any such man." I was perfectly disgusted during the election campaign at the manner in which religion and politics were mixed and at the outrageous way they slandered that honorable and useful society of free masons. Much to lumberers regret Mr. Venner's prediction of a thaw in February has been verified. I went up St. Norbert river some time ago and received 1500 saw logs for Bentley & Co; the country consists of a somewhat cleared pleateau cut up at distances of 2 miles with precipitous ravines over 100 ft. deep and heavily wooded which looked very picturesque: in one place I could see the blue outline of hills in the distance beyond St. Andre; saw a few comfortable farm houses but the majority were miserable log shanties; on arriving at the shanty in the midst of a dense forest I dined with the shanty men on pea soup, pork, potatoes, bread and green tea, the usual diet of lumbermen; 6 men came with us and shoveled off the snow from the rollways while the contractor and myself measured the logs at the smallest place and strictly adhered to the letter of the contract, a copy of which I had with me, stating that no logs would be accepted from the head of the trees which would be knotty for the purpose the company wanted the lumber. From a letter from Clifford, March '83: "Dear Arthur, I have just been shoveling snow to get my muscle up, so you must excuse my hand if it is shaky; I was much pleased to get your letter with the interesting description of your snow shoe tramp; I agree with you in deploring the dense ignorance of the French Canadians; the only remedy I see is government or public schools over which the clergy could have no control, and I believe that this can only be brought about by the people themselves when they get their eyes opened by going to other countries, reading, etc.; they are about 200 yrs behind the French in old France and the English people of Canada. Let us hope that there are brighter days in store for them. Bright made speeches all over England saying that force is no remedy for Ireland, well, they tried this plan and what was the result, in a few months the country was in a fearful condition, worse than it has been since '48, outrages in all directions; then force was tried as a remedy and in a short time the country was comparatively quiet. Law and order must be preserved in any country if it wishes to enjoy prosperity. When a country is in revolution the turbulent spirits get the upper hand and they are not the ones that conduce to a country's prosperity. I myself agree with father that the law of entail ought to be abolished and that there ought to be some law to discourage a man from owning more than 1000 acres, when the owner died the property of course to be left to his children and soon become divided up. It is of course a very difficult problem and all kinds of suggestions have been made on the subject; one thing certain is that they cannot take the land from the present owners without paying them for it." From a letter to uncle Richard: "The millions of £ that England spends annually on strong drink would be better employed in building pyramids for the money spent on them altho a waste, would not fill the kingdom with murderers, wife beaters, paupers and idiots, as the money spent on spirituous liquor does. How very foolish for a so called civilized and christian nation to have thousands of paupers in its midst and have to buy grain from foreign countries and yet at the same time legalize by legislation the pernicious waste of grain by manufacturing beverages, that the most eminent chemists and physicians have proved to be injurious to the human race; England has to have wheat shipped to her thousands of miles across land and water all because its "highly civilized people" drink an unhealthy beverage of their own brewing in preference to water, the purest, cheapest and healthiest beverage in existence. Unforseen business difficulties made it no longer advisable that I should remain in the service of Bentley & Co. so I bid farewell to my kind friends Mr. and Mrs. Sherman and departed for the great Northwest, which offers greater advantages to young men than the Province of Quebec. The reader and I must now part for we have arrived at the end of "Six Year's Life and Travel in the Province of Quebec," but I shall again have the pleasure to appear to the public in a few months to solicit their patronage for another work entitled "Four Years in the Great Northwest."

CITY OF QUEBEC

AGRICULTURAL STATISTICS OF THE PROVINCE OF QUEBEC.

	1721.	1760.	1792.	1827.	1831.	1844.	1852.	1861.	1880.	1882.
Fall Wheat				2,931,000	3,404,756		3,075,000	636,000		
Spring Wheat						942,835		2,588,000		
Oats	64,000			2,341,000	3,142,000	7,238,000	8,967,000	17,551,000		
Potatoes				6,790,000	7,357,000	9,918,000	450,000	12,770,000		
Corn	72,000			333,150	339,663	141,000	400,000	334,000		
Barley	4,500			363,117	393,000	1,195,000	665,000	2,281,000		
Rye				217,543	234,000	333,446	341,000	844,000		
Flax, Hemp lbs.	56,000							975,000		
Peas	57,000						1,205,000	2,648,000		
Mangolds								207,000		
Turnips							369,000	892,000		
Carrots								293,000		
Other roots							186,000	689,000		
Hay, tons							965,000	20,384		
Beans								1,250,000		
Buckwheat				121,395	106,050	374,809	530,000	33,934		
Timothy, Clover										
Cattle	59,000	50,300					586,000	488,000		
Horses		12,757					236,000	248,000		
Sheep		27,064					629,000	682,000		
Swine		28,900					256,000	286,000		
Milch Cows								328,000		
Acres Cultivated			1,570,000					4,804,000		
Tobacco, lbs.	4,800									
Butter, lbs.							9,537,000	15,906,000		50,000,000
Cheese, lbs.							511,000	686,000		
Wool, lbs.								1,967,000		
Gals. Cider								21,000		
Pork, lbs.								3,930,000		

STATISTICS OF POPULATION AND NATIONALITY OF QUEBEC AND CANADA.

	1640.	1663.	1701.	1775.	1814.	1844.	1860.	1870.	1883.	1882.
Beef, lbs.								12,410,000		
Maple Sugar								9,325,000		
Occupants land								105,671		
Acres per inh. under cultivator						4		4 acres 1 rood		
Agricultural products Land under grain 62,000 and vegetables 12,000								$21,912,000		
Land under grass 12,000									$18,738,000	
Export of Animals									$2,395,000	
Exports of Agriculture								315,000 acres		
Amt. land sold								115,000,000		
Wild lands								210,020		
Area Quebec sq m.								24,853,300		
Acres Surveyed to date										
Population of Canada	200	2,500	11,000	90,000	350,000	667,000	3,187,883	3,670,435	4,350,922	
Population Quebec	200	2,500	11,000	80,000		1,106,148		1,358,469	1,274,000	
Fr. Canadian pop. Quebec				75,000						
British pop. of Canada				15,000						
Foreign Born						57,715	706,781			
Population of Montreal			3,000				101,102			
Natives of England							4,293			
Natives of Ireland							14,199			
Natives of Scotland							2,196			
Anglo-Canadians & Foreigners							22,226			
French Canadians							43,509			
Population Quebec							57,109			
Natives of England							2,177			

Natives of Ireland	
Natives of Scotland	7,773
French Canadians	28,000
Anglo-Canadians & Foreigners	11,346
Inhabited houses, Quebec Pro.	
Inh. Canada per sq. Kilometre	9,722
Pop. of O. & Q. per sq. mile	65
Revenue per inh. of O. & Q.	840
Expenditure " " "	$3.30
Debt " " "	$3.86
Imports " " "	$20.59
Exports " " "	$16.50
Duty " " "	$15.03
Residents of Cities and Towns of C	$1.85
Negroes in C	450,000
Indians in C	18,143
Immigration to C	15,200
Emigration from C	28,217
Families in Province Quebec	183,174

STATISTICS OF RELIGION OF CANADA.

	1763.	1844.	1860.	1880.	1882.
Protestants	500		1,906,562		
Protestant Churches			2,111		
Protestant Ministers			2,666	36,550	47,000
Catholics	78,000	578,000	1,460,000		
Catholic Churches			716		
R. C. Priests			1,086		
Non-Religionists			35,828		582,963
Methodists			448,000		8,630
French Protestants					

EXPORTS, IMPORTS, SHIPPING TRADE AND COMMERCE OF QUEBEC AND CANADA.

Q. P. stands for Port of Quebec; M. P. for Montreal Port; Q. stands for Province of Quebec.

	1764.	1792.	1832.	1852.	1863.	1870.	1880.	1882.
Exports of C			$7,200,000	$13,434,000	$33,596,000	$123,161,000	$87,958,000	Q $41,141,000
Imports of C			$9,202,000	$21,204,000	$48,600,000		$71,182,000	Q $31,000,000
Inward vessels at C ports			10,009		13,894			
Their tonnage			1,198,000		2,386,000		3,487,000	
Ships built in C			209		697			
Their tonnage			34,700		157,000			
Value of vessels sold in C					$2,287,000		$11,000,000	$12,000,000
Exports of C to Manitoba								831,000
Flour imports of C bbls					3,309,000		6,971,000	8,102,000
Inland vessels tonnage								6,775,000
Wheat imports of C bush								928,000
Wheat Exports								
Ships entered at Port of M		53	64	211	439		612	698
Their tonnage		9,127	13,156	46,100	195,000		509,000	
Ships entered Q P		114	941	1,351	1,661			
Their tonnage	54,090	150,000	240,000	570,000	807,000			
Ships owned by C					700			
Inland vessels M P					142			
Their tonnage					10,730			
Dutiable imports of C								$50,000,000
C's export of live stock								$3,500,000

Export of Mines		$871,649		
Export of Fisheries		$789,000		
Export of Forest		$13,543,000		
Export of C grain		$21,584,000		
Imports of grain		$8,231,000		
Exports of Q P	$5,891,000	$11,887,000		
Imports of Q P	$2,745,000	$4,984,000		
Exports of M P	$7,182,000	$8,500,000	$30,244,000	$26,334,000
Imports of M P	$1,854,000	$18,607,000	$37,103,000	$49,742,000
Ships built at Q P	14	88		
Their tonnage	909	54,700		
Duty Collected at Q P	$484,000	$588,000		
Duty Collected at M P	$1,030,000	$,990,000	$7,692,000	$8,396,000
Ships built at M P		23		
Their tonnage	5,598	3,000		
C's imports to the U.S	$10,820,000	$18,816,000		
C's exports from U.S	$2,888,000	$23,109,000	$28,106,000	
Exports of wheat of Q	1,000,000			
Imports of wheat of Q		3,000,000		
Imports from Gt.Britain to C		$18,636,000	$45,814,000	
Imports from U.S	$1,400,000	$3,840,000	$2,934,6000	
Vessels employed in C	1292	2187		
Their tonnage	345,000	922,000		
Produce of Fisheries Q	$144,000	$730,000		922,000	

STATISTICS OF MANUFACTURING INDUSTRIES OF QUEBEC.

	1861.	1880.	1882.
Woolen Goods, yds	3,827,008		
Cotton Factories		7	21
Oat Mills	12		
Flour and Grist Mills	450		
Saw Mills	810		
Carding and Fulling Mills	88		
Woolen Factories	47		
Distilleries	5	19	
Tanneries	214		
Foundries	60		
Breweries	16		
Edge Tool Factories	7		
Cabinet Factories	25		
Carriage Factories	66		
Agricultural Implement Factories	14		
Miscellaneous Factories	352		
Button Factories			47
Cheese Factories			278
Tobacco Factories		39	
Tobacco Manufactured, lbs		759,000	
Export of Manufactures		84,484,000	
Distilled Spirits, gals		2,996,000	

SELECTED ITEMS OF INTEREST ON AGRICULTURE.

In 1664 wheat was sown in Canada for the first time; farmers carried arms to defend themselves from savages. It was not until 1854 that the feudal system was abolished; under this system the farms were burdened with enormous taxes. Total number of fields in '54 was 2,220, possessed by 110 Leigneurs and about 72,000 renters; the area occupied was 12,828,000 acres, half of which was rented. Number of acres under cultivation in '61 was 13,128,000. In 1852, Quebec had 244,000 under wheat; 955,000 under oats; 75,000 under buckwheat; 139,000 under barley; 83,000 under rye; 15,000 under corn; 118,000 under potatoes. Nationality: The French Canadian gain in Montreal has increased from 53 to 56 per cent.; if they rule the city its rapid progress will end. Manufactures: A St. John tomato canning factory put up 23,000 cans in 1882. The capital of Quebec's cotton factories in 1882 was $2,000,000. In a woolen factory at Sherbrooke, the output of cloth is 800,000 yds per year; in it 600 hands are employed and over 800,'00 lbs. of wool is used. The wool is all imported; Canadian wool being too long to make nice cloth or neat, smooth finish necessary; for popular goods Cape wool is used, which diminishes half in cleaning and working. Sherbrooke has also a flannel mill, employing 55 hands, with an output of 360,000 yds. The largest knitting factory in Canada is at Chaticock, it turns out 400 dozen shirts and drawers per week. Since the recent extension of Valleyfield cotton factory,

STATISTICS.   361

1,200 hands are employed; the new section will be devoted to the manufacture of colored and dyed goods, hitherto not made in Canada. A Canadian cheese factory received 1,450,000 lbs. of milk and made 140,000 lbs. of cheese; average amount of milk to make a pound of cheese, 10-33 lbs. In Canada 2,000,000 ft. of lumber is annually manufactured. Miscellaneous products, statistics and facts from the year 1817 to 1844.—Canada's exports of fur ranked next to those of timber; the fur consisted of bear, stag, elk, deer, fox, martin, wild cat, mink, a great variety of the weazel species, beaver and otter. The aggregate value of the trade was 150,000 pounds sterling, annually according to the caprice of fashion. Another article of export for that period was pot and pear ash., 1,000,000 lbs. turkey is frozen annually in Canada and Maine for New York markets. Many bee keepers in Canada feed their bees for a part of the winter on sugar. Review of Canada's wars and rebellions.—In 1607 war between the French and Indians; in 1629 Quebec surrendered to the English; in 1632 England renounces all claims to New France; in 1646 Indians destroy many French settlements; French military force in 1687, 2,000; in 1699 the Indians destroy Montreal; same year the French and their Indian allies destroy many English settlements and villages; in 1690 Sir W. Philipps and fleet attacked Quebec and lost 1,000 men. The English and French at this time paid the savages high premiums for the scalps of Frenchmen and Englishmen; same year the French defeated 700 English before Montreal; Bostonians commence the subjugation of Acadia; The French armed force on the St. Lawrence river now numbered 4.800; the English sent a fleet and 4,000 infantry against them, but a storm destroyed a part of the fleet; the French had 100 cannons on the ramparts of Quebec. In 1726 the English and French fortified strategic places on the lake frontier of Canada; in 1745 a war broke out between England and France; the French and savages of Canada in 3 years made 27 raids on English settlements. In 1756 Marquis Montcalm arrived in Canada with 1,400 men and 1,300,000 in specie; the whole French army numbered 12,000; in 1759 additional forces were sent from France; in all the early engagements the French were successful; in 1758, the 5th year of the war, the forts Fontenac, Duquense and others surrendred to the English, as a whole, however, the French were superior to them in military glory. Towards the close of the war the French forces numbered 15,000, the English 30,000; the French were defeated, the Governor and 3,000 French people returned to France, the remainder became British subjects. During the American revolution. Quebec was unsuccessfully attacked by the 'Americans; from 1812 to 1814 there was desultory warfare along the American and Canadian borders, in which the Americans were generally the losers. From 1832 to 1837 portions of Canada were in a state of rebellion; in the most serious engagement 100 men were killed and 370 wounded. A cartridge factory has been started at Quebec by the Dominion Government which manufactures 50,000 cartridges a day. In 1864, British North America possessed 500,000 men capable of bearing arms, but had only at that period 30,000 militia, on account of the apathy of the government and people to keep a militia organization in a proper condition. Revenue, Debt, Expenditure and Financial Review of Canada.—In 1832 revenue $2,003,000, expenditure $2,058,-000; in 1862 revenue $12,293,000, expenditure $13,290,000, debt $70,935,000; rev. in '80, $33,300,000, exp. $27,000,000. Quebec crown lands in '82, $1,000,000 The Dominion subsidy to the Quebec government under the B. N. A. act is $969,000. Quebec's debt in '82, $15,000,000, chiefly incurred in rly enterprise. Since the debris of the crash of '75 has been cleared away, there has been a super abundance of capital seeking investment in Canada. The great increase in wealth as indicated,

46

by bank deposits was the outcome of the economy forced upon the peop'^ by the depression of 1875 to 1878, and the bountiful harvests of 1879-80 81; but the store of capital has been drawn upon in the establishment of new enterprises, extension of foreign and home trade, land investments and railway construction. A comparison of the banks in Canada in Sept. 1881 and 1882 will show the occasion of the advance in the rate of interest: Due by banks in Canada to banks in the U. S. Sept. 1881, $90,082; in 1882, $62,422. Due banks in the United Kingdom in 1881, $1,447,174; in 1882, $2,205,208. Circulation in 1881, $27,481,-000; in 1882, $31,458,000. Quebec dep--its in 1881, $83,418,000; in 1882, $99,-734,000. Specie in 1881, $6,205,000; in 1882, $7,621,000. Dominion notes in 1881, $10,540,000; in 1882, 11,545,000. Due from banks in Canada in 1881, $7,-621,000; in 1882, 99,430,000. Due from banks in the U. S. in 1881, $19,388,000; in 1882, $14,371,000. Due from banks in the United Kingdom in 1881, $4,285,-000; in 1882, $1,144,000. Advances on stocks and bonds in 1881, $10,205,000; in 1882, $15,031,000. Commercial discounts in 1881, $10,205,000; in 1882, $152,-680,000. The cash reserves of the banks including specie, dominion notes and balance due from other banks in 1882 was $44,511,000; in 1881, $47,967,000. In the foreign exchanges in 1881 the balance in favor of Canada was $22,188,000; in 1882 only $13,344,000; on the other hand loans have rapidly increased, the discounts of '82 exceeding those of '81 by the large sum of $20,555,000. A free trade paper says, the old Canadian tariff in '81 would have yielded enough to meet the ordinary expenses of the Dominion government. The large surplus of over $6,000 for '82 represents so much over taxation. The capital of 13 leading Canadian banks amounts to $41,570,000; discounts, $1,113,000; liabilities of directors, $6.638,000. From egistered letter department in 1871, the Canadian government received $367,000, and in '81, $841,000. The deposits in Montreal District Savings Bank in Dec. '82 amounted to $6,000,000 deposited by 26,000 depositors. The first year protection was in force the Canadian receipts only amounted to $23,307,000 against an expenditure of $24,850,000, which the Liberals noticed with great jubilation, but the years '80-'81 placed a different face on the matter, the receipts running up to $29,635,000 against an expenditure of $25,502,000. It gives Canadians satisfaction to see a decrease of $61,000 in the imports of Montreal Port in Dec. '81. Canadian revenue for Nov. '82: Customs, $1,820,000; excise $654,000; postoffice 107,000; public works, including rlys., 34,-800; miscellaneous 166,000, total $3,099,000. The following is a statement of the value of goods that entered the Dominion for consumption for the month of Oct. '82, exclusive of British Columbia: total dutiable goods $7,648,000; free goods 2,055,000; coin and bullion except as coin $6,161. Statement of the banks of Canada for Nov. '82: capital paid up $60,930,000; Dominion government deposit $8,801,000; provincial government deposits $2,160,000; deposits to secure contracts $152,000; public deposits $97,052,000; loans from other banks 1,367,000; due banks in Canada $1,267.000; due banks in the U. S. 162,404; due banks in the United Kingdom 1,992,000; other liabilities $551,374; assets, specie $6,648,000; Dominion notes 11,025,000; notes from other banks $6,893,000; due from banks in other countries 12,09,000; due from banks in the United Kingdom 2,834,000; government debentures 1,021,000; foreign securities 1,479,000; loans to government 1,639,000; loans on stocks and bonds 15,834,000; loans to municipal corporations 2,154,000; loans to other corporations 11,162,000; loans to other banks 559,000; discounts current 445,696,000; discounts over due unsecured 1,-448,000; discounts over due, secured,$1,728,000; real estate 1,398.000; mortgage on estate sold 746,000; bank premises 3,102,000; other assets $2,251,000; total

STATISTICS. 363

$233,203,000; directors liabilities 9,354; expenditures for Quebec government for '81: public debt 828,000; legislation $237,134; civil government $170,000; administration of justice $380,000; police officials, Quebec and Montreal, 15,000; reformatories 44,000; inspection of public offices, travelling expenses, etc.,9,800; education 342,000; special Roman Catholic educational fund for schools of art and sciences 500; literary and scientific institutions 13,500; boards of art and manufactures. 10,000; agriculture 97,000; immigration and repropriation 14,600; colonization 8,240; public works and buildings 1,212,63; charities 298,299; miscellaneous 27,- 199; pension fund 8,385; municipalities fund 144,000; Crown land department 162,126; Quebec official gazette 13,776; stamps, licenses, etc,, 2,724; special police revenue purposes 4,146; marriage licenses 6,000; loan to Papist fathers 10,- 000; payment of revenue officers out of collections made by them 16,300; Quebec, Ottawa, Montreal and accidental rly. expenses, traffic, etc., 763,000; repayments of temporary loans 871,000; consolidated rly. fund 911,000; deduct warrants outstanding 3,082, balance $379,000. In '83 the debt of the Dominion was $200,000,- 000; some papers say that Eastern Canadians are looking up too much capital in the North-West and that it may bring on a financial crisis. The Dominion government spent on government bonds in '82 $511,852. The Canadian Indian fund held in trust for Indians amounts to $3,147,000. Canada's total imports for 1883, $91,611,000; of which $36,704,000 was from the U. S., in 1880 Canada had 311 banks, in '68 Canada had 81 postoffices; saving banks, in '81,304 with $4,175,; 000; deposits in 1880 had 5,600 postoffices. Canada's exports in June '83, $10,- 173,526; imports 9,090,000; Internal revenue $504,228; Eastern receipts 368,181.: Excise Dominion of Canada, statement of tobacco manufactures and duties occurring on them in 1880; amount paid in licenses $6,500; cigar duty 174,391; snuff duty 21,784; duty collected on manufactory 268,780; duty on goods warehoused 1,528,000; tobacco duty $1,549,182; total duty 1,766,000. The payments of the Canadian government in '80 were 53,284,000. Revenue of Canada for the month of August '82: from spirits $219,000, seizures 22,490; spirits from barley 55," ; malt 22,179; tobacco 173,000; coal oil inspection 1,957; products of manufacture 2,762. other receipts 1,909; canals 53,504; lumber inspection 9,478; rent of hydraulic and other powers $692; public works of least importance $209; inspection of weights and measures 1,731; inspection of gas 375. In '77 the receipts of Canada's registry postal department was $367,438; in '81 $841,497, The new Parliament House in Quebec is to cost $300,000. Quebec's postoffice revenue in '80 $448,351; expenditure $559,412. Labor, land and produce market of Canada; the price of cereals in '81: Fall wheat 81cts. a bushel to $1.35; Spring wheat $1.34; barley 90cts., peas 75, oats 42. In 1882 wheat was $1,15,· Spring wheat $1.20, barley 75, peas 75, oats 35. The decline of price in barley and wheat made a loss of $11,000, to the farmers of Ontario. A raft of pine timber 350,000 ft. in Quebec in '82 sold for $100,700; 17,622 square ft. on Sherbrooke st. Montreal sold for 87cts. a foot; a corner store on Bonaventure st. Montreal, for $4,000. The following are the salaries of Montreal's fire brigade; to the chief 1,800, to sub-chiefs $1,300; engineers 700, fireman $550. The demand in '83 for skilled labor is such that it cannot be supplied at home, hence employers are obliged to advertise in English papers. Stock in store in Montreal on Dec. 6th '82; wheat 223,705 bushels; corn 8,000, peas 21,934, oats 68,744, barley 5,594, rye 2,182, flour, barrels 57,844, oat meal 265 barrels· A Quebec cheese factory sold its cheese in '82 at, from 11 to 15cts. a lb.; Tommy cods in Montreal in '83 at $1 a barrel; in '59, 134,000 acres were sold in Quebec for $76,960; in '63· 279,993 acres for $154,983. The Quebec public lands are sold under three designs.

STATISTICS.

nations brown, clergy and school lands. Exports of the dominion of Canada for 1880, $87,911,451. Value of goods entered for consumption $71,782,349. And trade, commerce, shipping etc.—from the yrs. 1817 to '40 the aggregate exports of Canada, including the freight of a portion of the lumber exported in Canadian built vessels, amounted to $4,000,000 annually, and in the same period Canada imported from Gt. Britain a supply of manufactured and Asiatic products to the amount of $7,000,000 annually; from May to August '85 Allan steamers took 4,499 oxen, to 4 horses and 3,445 sheep from Montreal to England; during 3 months ending Sept. '82 there were 166 failures in Canada with liabilities amounting to $1,715,000 against 130 last yr. same period with $787,000 liabilities. Total receipts of flour in Canada from 1st Jan. '82 to 4th of Oct. '82—590,470 brls. Same period in '81—613,051 brls. Apple shipments from Montreal for the season of '82—45,981 brls. Eastern Canada in '82 shipped to Winnipeg $2,000,000 worth of goods; groceries 1,500,000; liquor 3,000; settlers effects 608,400; machinery and implements $1,000,000; manufactures of leather 200,000; hardware 2,000,000; miscellaneous goods 4,500,000, comprising lumber, ready made houses, breadstuff, furniture, animals. When nature formed Lachine rapids she decreed that Montreal should torn the head of navigation. Quebec's lumber trade for '82, 12,005,- 240 ft.; in '81, 11,333,960 ft.; in '80, 27,196,760 ft.; in '79, 7,708,240 ft.; in '78,- 11,999,760 ft. In '82, 227,040 was of ash, 213,680 of birch, 1,959,760 oak, 778,- 360 elm, square timber, white pine, wancy, 912,160; red pine 1,024,,680 ft. In '82 Quebec received in rafts, 5,935,977 standard of pine; in '81, 6,973,529; in '80, 9,023,393: in '79, 7,054,719 standard of pine and spruce; in '78, 3,692,996 of pine alone. Before the establishment of the reciprocity treaty in 1854 the average transactions between Canada and the U. S. were $14,000,000 per annum. The 2nd year after reciprocity was in force, the trade between the two countries to over $40,000,000, and the year before the abrogation of the treaty they were $84,670,955. The Canadian people have adopted retalitory measures, but the fact that during the existence of the treaty the people of Canada bought from the U. S. $346,180,364, and the U. S. purchased from Canada, $325,726,200, which was a great proof in favor of reciprocity. The amount of grain shipped from Montreal in '82 has been 8,600,099 bushels; in '81, 13,001,000, and the average for the past 10 years, 13,000,000; of the amount of '81, 6,352,538 was wheat and 3,334,078 of corn. Amount of goods entered at Port Montreal in '81, $35,918,935; duty collected, $7,627,139; in '82, $40,644,581. Receipts of Quebec government in '81, $5,263,273 as follows: Balance in banks in June, '81, Dominion of Canada subsidy and interest on trust funds, $1,014,712; Province of Ontario, interest on common school fund, $25,000; Crown land department, $300,473; Department of justice, $233.715; Public officers, $9,084; License hotels, ships, etc., $244,016; Legislation, $9,734; Lunatic asylums, $2,967; Quebec Official Gazette, $20,988; Public works, buildings, rents, etc., $966; Casual revenue, $1,418; Superannuated teachers, $18,483; Quebec city fire loan, $1,160; Municipal loan fund of Lower Canada, $554,146; Trust funds, 6,784; Repayments Beaufort asylum proprietors, $6,000; St. Jean de Dieu asylum interest, 6,C00; refunds, $6,823; Quebec, Montreal, Ottawa and Occidental railway revenue, $1,- 024,994; Temporary loans from the Bank of Montreal, 600,000; from Quebec Central railway, returned subsidy and guarantee deposit, 606,849; Canadian debentures advanced in 4 years 12 per cent. The receipts of the Richelieu and Ontario Navigation Company for '82 were $504,226; its disbursements, $18,420. The company paid 2 dividends in the year of 3 per cent. Total value of furs sold by the Hudson Bay Company since organization, $120,000,000, In '83' Canada exported $25,000,000 worth of lumber; in 1859 Canada exported 2,635,000 bushels of oats, 1,766,000 of rye, 690,863 of peas, nearly 12,000,000 of wheat and 427,007 bbls. flour. The following is the value of the exportation and importation of the Canadian Province since their confederation in '68: Exports in '69, $66,474,700; imports, $70,415,000; Custom receipts, $8,298,000; in '70, exports $73,573,000; imports, $123,070,000; Custom receipts, $15,361,000; in '81, exports $98,290,000; imports, $105,330,840; Custom receipts, $18,700,000. Exports of the Port of Quebec in '80, $6,448,097, its imports $6,242,775. Hospitals, disease, mortality, etc.—Notre Dame hospital during '81, treated 876 patients, 468 males and 408 females; at the general dispensary attached to the hospital, 3,084 patients were treated, and at the eye and ear dispensary, 778; total, 4,791. The number of beds occupied in the Montreal general hospital averages 150. At the Montreal dispensary 10,000 patients are treated annually; the expenditure for the last quarter of '83 was $10,335; number of patients remaining in the hospital from last quarter of '83, 121; numbers admitted during the quarter, 501; number of patients discharged, 452; deaths 32; number cured during the quarter, 484; number outdoor consultations during last quarter 1542 males, 1145 females; eye and ear consultations, 1,336. There were 40 cases of typhoid fever during the quarter, 3 fatal. In '61, 379 were admitted and 336 discharged from the Lunatic Asylums of Canada, East and West. In Canada $7,750,000 is paid annually to Fire Insurance companies; rate of insurance 110; in France it is only 010; in the U. S. 090; ratio of population insured, 30 in Canada, 15 in U. S. and 75 in France. Canada's loss by fire annually, $41,000; loss annually per inh. $230; in the U. S. $105. Some of Canada's national sports.—Lacrosse is one of Canada's national sports; it is an Indian game; an Irish Montreal team are the champions of the world; Canada has a chess association. At Montreal carnival in 1883, tobagganing, curling, skating on immense rinks on the St. Lawrence; an ice palace costing $2,000, lit with electric light; snowshoeing, a steeple chase, torch light processions, trotting races, lacrosse matches, excursions on the ice railway and other novelties were the order of the day. The close season for all sorts of deer in the Province of Quebec is from Jan. 1st to Sept. 1st; partridge, from Jan. 1st to Sept 15th; close season for wild ducks and geese, from 1st of May and 15th of Sept. to 15th of April and 1st Sept; close season for insectivorous and all other birds excepting eagles, hawks, wild pigeons, crows ravens, wax wings and shrike, from 1st of March and 1st of May to 1st of March and 1st Sept. To slide down a hill over unbeaten snow a tobaggon is a decided success, but on a well beaten track it figures like a scow with a shell boat placed alongside of the "American Bob." The department of fisheries in '82 decided to bring in use a fish ladder to be used in salmon streams which will do away with the necessity of maintaining hatcheries. After many poor years the Canadian fisheries produced in '82 $14,504.000 worth of fish. Religion.—Francis I of France justly rebelled against the Pope for giving to Spain the whole Continent of America. The intestine wars which existed between the Catholics and Hugenots in France gave rise to the proscription of Protestants in the French colonies of America. De Monts, a Calvinist and a favorite of Henry the IV, was allowed the free exercise his religion for himself and his followers, on condition that he should establish the Catholic religion among the natives. In 1600, the ecclesiastical authorities in France endowed a number of conventional institutions in Canada. The island of Montreal was granted religious orders, who erected numerous convents on it. The Viceroy of Canada having entered the holy orders, his chief aim was to convert the natives; for this purpose he sent 3

STATISTICS.

jesuits and 2 lay brothers to join the 4 Recollects at Quebec; these 9 were the only priests then in Canada. Cardinal Richelieu now revoked the privileges of the Hugenots and ordered that all emigrants to Canada should be native Frenchmen and Roman Catholics. and that no stranger or heretic should be introduced into Canada. In 1644 the French missionaries began to combine with their religious efforts political objects and employed all their influence in furthering French power. In 1662 the governor and bishop had a dispute which resulted in the recall of the former. In 1680 Quebec was constituted a bishopric and in the Governor, Intendant, Bishop and military officers were centered all power legislative, executive and judicial. The bishop and the clergy were all powerful and the power of the Ecclesiastial court was not unfrequently employed in regulating and controlling the civil tribunals. Canada was constituted an apostonic vicarte in 1657 and became an Episcopal See in 1674. In 1659 the Catholic clergy passed from the hands of the Jesuits into those of the secular priesthood; 1-26 of the products of the soil was ordered to be paid to the clergy which is still the case in '82. The most complete religious liberty was granted the French after their conquest by England. During the American revolution the Catholic bishop of Canada addressed a cyclical letter to his Canadian people exhorting them to be true to British rule and repel the American invaders. The Canadian constitution of 1774 confirmed French civil procedure, guaranteed the free exercise of the Roman Catholic religion and sanctioned the payment of tithes. In 1799 an English Protestant bishop was stationed at Quebec. In 1804 Canada had 140 priests. In Quebec in 1860 there were 580,000 Catholics. Methodist church of Canada has one general Conference for the Dominion, composed of ministers and laymen in equal numbers, which meet once in 4 years for legislative purposes only. There are 6 Conferences which meet in the Dominion annually for the general review of pastoral work, but are incapable of any legislative act and are composed of ministers only, every ordained minister being a member of some one of them. Every minister must change his pastoral charge in 3 years. These exchanges are arranged by a committee composed of ministers only, 2 from each district called the stationing committee. The children of deceased or superanuated Methodist ministers receive $20 a year till 18 years of age. In '82 the Methodist church of Canada spent $184,203 for Indian, French and foreign missions, and $52,000 on home missions. There are 4 Methodist bodies in Canada: Methodist church of Canada 582,902; Episcopal Methodists 103,372; Bible Christians 27,236; Primitive Methodists 25,680. The idea of an organic union of the 4 Methodist churches of Canada had been steadily growing and there has been proposed concessions by each of the bodies. In 1743 in Montreal a French soldier for disrespect to a crucifix was led through the streets with a halter around his neck and made kneel before the door of a church and humbly confess his profanity of holy things, utter which he was sentenced to 3 years hard labor on the kings galleys. The militia of the Pope in '82 had many of Montreal's citizens in its ranks. The receipts and expenditures of the Angolican church of Canada in '82 about balanced. Recepts from Montreal subscriptions $4,463; county subscriptions $2,433; from the society for the propogation of the gospel in foreign parts $4,490; miscellaneous $550; interest on sustentation fund $2,762; clergy trust $1,154. Amongst its expenditures it paid $9,520 to pensioners and to missionaries $4,413. By a Canon of Synod in '82 Deacons are to receive $500, Priests under 10 years study $600. The revenue of the Fabrigue of Montreal is steadily decreasing. The bishop published the following in '82: "To remove the Fabrigues debt the Holy name of God is invoked; we have ruled, enacted and ordered as follows: Each family in our parishes will pay annually for the extinction of the debt of the Fabrigue of Notre Dame the sum of $2; every Catholic of 18 years and over earning a salary or providing for his own maintenance will pay for the same purpose $1. The Presbyterian church of Canada has 42 ordained missionaries amongst the French of Quebec; 41 mission day school teachers; 11 colporteurs; 4 Bible women; total number emp'oyed in mission work 113. The work is carried on at 90 preaching stations having a church membership of 3,180, and an average artendance of 6,401; it has also 48 Sabbath schools with 1,930 scholars; 23 institutes and day schools with 827 pupils, 31 of which are theological students. In '82 Ottawa and Montreal Bible societies distributed 3,095 bibles. A Protestant missionary says: "The Protestant churches of Canada have a common interest and should combine in one Congress so as to fulfill as one body the grand commission of the church universal. Another writer maintains that the divided front of Protestantism does not retard christian conquest in foreign lands so long as the human mind is constituted as it is there is real necessity for diverse centers of religious thought." Another writer said, "Better the clear and emphatic declarations of belief at present extant than the mute and meaningless attitude of the proposed organic union." Some of the Fench papers in Quebec hope that if the French monarchy is restored the Pope will regain his temporal power. Form of government. politics, legislation, taxation, national usages, etc. In early times Canada was divided in 3 districts, Montreal, Quebec and Three rivers, and a governor located in each. In 1651 a judge was appointed over all matters in the colony called a "grand seneschel." In consequence of abuse of power this system was remodelled and a sovereign council appointed, which consisted of governor general, intendent, bishop, attorney general, and 5 councillors, afterwards 12. Various courts were constituted. In 1717 an admiralty court was established; this system was continued till 1760. Till 1653 the governor had exercised in person and without control all the functions of the government but Louis created Canada into a royal government with a council and intendant, to whom should be intrusted the mighty affairs of justice, police, finance and marine. Under the royal jurisdiction the governor, a kings commissioner, an apostolic vicar and 4 other gentlemen, were formed into a sovereign council, to these were confined the powers of cognizance in all cases civil or criminal, to judge in the last resort according to the laws and manners of France. Its governors on state occasions were surrounded by a body guard, valets and pages. In 1721 mails were conveyed between Quebec and Montreal. The French were so gratified with the change they experienced in coming under British rule, that when George II. died all the French in Canada of any distinction went into mourning. At the time of its conquest the French government owed the Canadian people 41,000,000 francs, little of which was ever paid. The Canadians submitted to the stamp and other duties of the British government. In the year 1775 a code of laws was promulgated in Canada which combined, with the same modifications the Civil code of France and the criminal laws of England. After the Popes Bull of 1773 expelling the Jesuits from France and other countries the English appropriated the present estates in Canada to other uses. The Canadian government has frequent changes since its conquest, martial law first, second, military sway, civil absolution, 3rd and 4th an elective system; under the latter system in 1792 the House of Assemblage in Canada East numbered 16 members and that of Canada West 16; while the Legislative council of the latter. numbered 7, that of the former 15. Under Lord Dochester Canada was divided into 2 provinces, Upper and Lower Canada, and a legislature was established in each. The first Provincial Parliament met in Quebec in 1792 in which the French were in a large majority. In 1840 Upper and Lower Canada were united, and its legislature consisted of the governor general and two Houses; the Legislative council and Legislative assembly. In '60 the qualification for voters in point of fact almost amounts to universal suffrage, as 1 out of 6 in the province has the power to vote from paying $50 annual rental on owning a free-hold of $10 yrly. value. In 1840 the revenue of Upper and Lower Canada was £184,000, and expenditure £143,000. In 1841 Upper Canada had 465,375 inhabitants; in '51 952,061; in '44 Lower Canada had 690,782; in '51 800,261. The indemnity of Quebec members was reduced to 500 in '78, and raised in '82 to 800. The Liberal party of Quebec have debased themselves by asking a testimonial of harmlessness from the Pope to prevent the clergy from interfering in the elections, and received the defeat they deserved. The Quebec government decided in '82 to tax business corporations. A Quebec city newspaper says: "our tradesmen are ruined, our rly. we sold to our adversaries, and our city kept in the claws of a clique of manipulators." The equilibrium between the revenue and expenditure of Quebec should be restored before its politicians should subsidize all kinds of enterprises from its treasury, for its debt is rapidly increasing with annual deficits. The new Insolvency act of Canada has had the effect of enabling merchants and tradesmen, some of them dishonest, to settle with their creditors for 50 and even 25cts. on the dollar, and then sell those goods in competition against honest merchants who pay cent for cent. The national policy of protection in '82 is doing good work as a stimulant to immigration. The amount of fine derived from the Scott act attest that it is still in force and violated, but drinking is robbed of its respectability; the politicians of Quebec in '82 want a larger income but are afraid to raise it by direct taxation, and have imposed a tax of $500 on all life insurance companies in the Province, $100 for all insurance offices in Montreal and Quebec, and $500 for all others elsewhere. Use of flags by governors and colonies; 1st, the Royal standard shall be flown from the Government house on the Queen's birthday, and on the days of Her Majesty's ascension and coronation; 2nd, the union flag shall be flown without the badge of the colony, at the Government house from sun rise to sun set on other days; 3rd, the union flag with the approved arms or badge of the colony emblazoned in the center thereof, surrounded by a green garland, shall be used by governors or officers administering the government of the colonies, or dependencies when embarked in boats or other vessels; 4th, the British blue ensign with the badge of the colony emblazoned thereon; the fly and the pendant shall be flown by all armed vessels in the employment of the government of a colony; 5th, the ensign described in the preceding section but without the pendant shall be flown by vessels which belong to, or are in the service of a government of a colony but are not armed; 6th, all other vessels registered as belonging to one of Her Majest'/s colonies or dependencies will fly the red ensign without any badge. Thus there are 2 distinct publi nsigns; for forts, public buildings or merchant vessels, there is no Canadian flag and we do not want one but we are proud of the privelege to use in common with our fellow-subjects the world over the sacred emblem of the indivisible and ever glorious British empire. The leader of the Quebec opposition says in '83: "that there is a clause in the confederation bargain that is exceedingly unfair to Quebec; the clause fixing our Dominion subsidy at 80cts. per head perpetually on the basis of the population in '61, while all the other provinces except Ontario were entitled to an increase of their subsidies on the increase of their population, at such decennial census. In consequence of a long term of corrupt administration of Quebec's government, the condition of the finances of the province are serious, not for its creditors but its people, who are quite able and willing to pay its debts. The Quebec assembly in '83 is composed of 16 lawyers, 13 farmers, 13 merchants, 7 physicians, 7 notaries, 3 manufacturers, 2 journalists and 3 who belong to no particular profession. English Quebec papers praise the government's policy of introducing the wedge of direct taxation by making muncipalities support their own prisoners, it makes every man in the muncipality interested in the morals of his neighbors. The Dominion government is going to assimilate the electoral franchise in the different provinces. The highest Canadian duty in '80 was 35 per ct. ad valorem, lowest 5 per ct. ad val., and many classes of goods were admitted free. Canada has 88 foreign consuls and 200 from the U. S.; in '82 Canada had 6,171 postoffices; number of miles of route 48,037; letters sent by post 56,200,000; postal cards 113,000,000; registered letters 2,450,000; free letters 2,390,000; newspapers for 11 months of '82 11,005,000; circulars, patterns, miscellaneous articles 7,186,000; parcels by parcel post 304,000. In 1851 Canada had 601 postoffices and 7,595; number of letters by post per annum 2,135,000; total revenue $230,629; total expenditure $276,191. In '63, number of postoffices 15,327; number of letters 11,000,000; total revenue $749,475; total expenditure 753,057. Area, physical features, climate etc. of Canada and Quebec; total area of Quebec government lands 120,000,000, of which in 1875 10,078000 were in seignories; 10,153,090 in clergy lands; 29,386,240 acres leased under licenses to cut timber, leaving over 60,000,000 acres in wooded lands. The province of Quebec occupies the river St. Lawerance from the Ottawa river to the gulf of St. Lawerance, is very cold in winter and has a hot dry summer. The valley of the St. Lawrence is exceedingly fertile, but the north bank east of the Sagheney, owing to the severity of the climate is almost incapable of cultivation. Quebec's area in square miles 193,325; frost sets in about the middle of October, the sun continuing to render the days mild and agreeable for 3 or 4 weeks, when snow storms set in which continue about 1 month with variable and hazy atmosphere, until the middle or end of December, when the whole country is covered with an average depth of from 3 to 4 ft. of snow; an unvariable season now commences, an uninteruptedly clear sky for about 20 weeks; the thermometer ranging for the most part of the time from 20 to 30 below zero, when the frost suddenly breaks in the course of a few days, about the end of April or 1st of May the snow suddenly disappears and in the short space of a month the most luxurious verdure and vegetation spreads all over the land; the thermometer sometimes in June ranging from 90 to 100 deg; through the Summer from 75 to 80. The advantage of Winter is that a horse can draw twice the weight 3 times the distance on a snow road than it could draw on the best constructed road; without snow timber could not be removed from the rough uneven forests. On Dec. 18th '82 the first team crossed the ice on the river St. Lawrence near the mouth of the Nicolet river. Feb. 10th '83 a snow blockade delayed the mails in the province of Quebec. The winter of '83 was favorable to the Canadian farmer, snow being abundant, which protected the roots of the grass from frost, snow is also a great fertilizer. Mean temperature in Montreal in '61, Jan. 18th, 0 degrees above zero; Feb. 16th, 8 degrees; Mar. 8th, 95 degrees; April, '41, 4 degrees; May, '56, 12 degrees; June, '69, 97 degrees; July, '71, 36 degrees; Aug. '71, 4 degrees. Sept. '58, 56 degrees. Oct. '44, 50 degrees. Nov. '32, 26 degs. Dec. 18th, 50 deg. The area of Canada, including Newfoundland, is 3,476,742 sq. miles. Sir H. Allen, one of Canada's great men, died in '82: in 1831 he commenced to give his attention to the shipping trade; in 1856 he contracted with the Canadian government to establish a fortnightly service to and from Gt. Britain via the St. Lawrence when it was open, and monthly to and from Portland during the winter. In 1857 weekly service was commenced. In addition to the mail from Liverpool he established a line from Glasgow; besides these lines of steamships he and his friends owned a large fleet of sailing vessels. The Allen line grew until it became the largest steamship company in the world. In '74 he received the honor of knighthood; he was president of 22 business companies during his life. Statistics of Montreal: In 1857 its population was 50,000; revenue of its skating rink in '81, $8,134; it has a ladies educational association. During a week in '81 there were 60 deaths, 60 Catholics and 0 Protestants. Montreal grocers that sell liquors pay a license of $200 a year, and wholesale druggists pay $100. Montreal's population in '81 was 140,652, an increase in 10 years of 33,457; Montreal's parish church seats 12,000; it has a ladies benevolent society; 54 persons were admitted in its home in '82; total number in the home, 150; the cost of each inmate for the year was $45.17. The custom receipts for Montreal for the quarter ending Sept. '82 amounted to $2,595,000. There are over 30 Protestant churches in Montreal; it has a grocers' association, a ladies female emigration society and a French society for the preservation of the architectural antiquities of that people. It has an assessed property of $66,000,000; it does not offer bonuses to manufacturing firms, it has greater advantages to offer, that of being a commercial center, cheap labor, large market, railway and water communication with every part of the country, and low rates of freight for the raw material and the manufactured articles. A Montrealer says that there is too much credit given in Montreal and that some of its wealthiest citizens are the worse payers. Total amount of merchandise entered for consumption at the port of Montreal for the month of Dec. 1882 was as follows: Dutiable goods, $1,628,320; coin and bullion, excepting American silver, $1,901; free goods $468,031, making a total of $2,098,312, on which duty was collected to the amount of $406,564. The principal items were manufactures, woolen, $126,613; leather, 65,763; iron and steel, 204,612; cottons, 201,482; flour and meal, 48,390; grain, 23,518; books, pamphlets, etc., 32,320; total amount of goods that entered Montreal in '82, $40,644,518; duty collected, $8,395,768. In 1881 the amount of goods entered was $31,118.985; duty collected, $7,672,137. The average amount of postoffice orders issued per week in Montreal in '82 amounted to $183,161; revenue of Montreal postoffice for '82, $172,822. Mr. Grenshields of Montreal, after providing for his heirs, left the following amounts: To the poor of St. Paul's church, $1,000; Montreal Thistle Curling Club, $500; St. Andrew's Society, $1,000; Mackay's Deaf and Dumb Institute, $1,000; Protestant Orphan Asylum, $500; Ladies Benevolent Society, $500; Harvey's Institute, $500; Trefalgar Institute, $500; Boys' Home, 500; Widow's and Orphan's Fund of the Presbyterian church, 500; Young Men's Christian Association, 500; Young Women's Christian Association, 250; Working Girl's Association, 250; Montreal Sailor's Institute, 1,000; Art Association, 500; McGill University, 40,000; Montreal General Hospital, 4.000; Morrin College, Quebec, 5,000; Queen's University, Kingston, 5,000; Home Mission Fund of the Presbyterian church of Canada, 10,000. The city District Saving Bank of Montreal gave in '82, $10,000 to charitable societies. There is a law in Montreal that forbids the building of wooden houses within the city limits. Montreal's Catholic Deaf and Dumb Institute receives aid from the Government, the Protestant one does not. In '82 there were 775 licensed vehicles in Montreal. A Montreal auctioneer sold in 9 days, $150,000 worth of property. In '82, 5,000,000 people travelled in the street cars of Montreal; in Montreal the names of the streets are printed on the glasses of the corner lamps; in '80 Montreal had 11,665 qualified voters; in '61 Montreal's population consisted of 65,806 Roman Catholics and 22,504 Protestants; Montreal's population in 1618 was 3,000. 24 newspapers and periodicals are published in Montreal. Statistics of Quebec: In '81 it had 62,447 inhabitants, an increase of over 2,000 in 10 years. Revenue of its postoffice in '82 $35,969; the whole water supply of Quebec is conducted through one main pipe, hence so many destructive fires; Montreal's is conducted through 3 pipes. Quebec's population in 1781 was 7,000; it is 400 miles from the mouth of the St. Lawrence. The tide extends 90 miles above it to Three Rivers; it is built on a promontory formed by the confluence of the St. Charles river and St. Lawrence; Cape Diamond, at the lower end of which the city stands, is a bold promontory, 350 ft. above the river; its fortifications cover 40 acres. The city is divided into two parts, upper and lower; the former includes the citadel and fortifications; the latter is the seat of commerce. Most of the houses are of stone founded on rock, environed as to the most important parts by walls and gates and defended at every point by numerous and heavy cannons. Its spacious harbor contains, during 6 months of the year, fleets of foreign merchantmen. Its streets are narrow, populous and winding up and down almost mountainous declivities. Its wharf accomodations is extensive and timber coves are numerous and spacious. The mountains north and east of Quebec are the most beautiful amphitheaters to be seen in North America: mountain and plain, narrow ravine wide retreating hollow, rocky escarpment and lofty hills almost assuming the magnitude of mountains. Among its public structures are Laval University, Parliament House, Anglican and R. C. Cathedrals. 20 churches, 2 colleges, a normal school, Wolfe and Montcalm monuments, Post Office, Custom House, Marine Hospital and Markets. In '61, Quebec had 41,477 R. C's. and 9,224 Protestants. In '51, Three River's population was 4,500; in '61. 6,058, though, situated at the outlet of the St. Maurice river and in front of immense lumbering forests, with navigable outlets and a great extent of arable land, it has made very little progress. Sherbrooke is 91 miles by railway below Montreal; it lies on both sides of the St. Francis river; in '51 it had 3,000 inhabitants, in '61, 5,889; the same year it had 2 colleges, 1 R. C. and 1 Protestant; 1 Protestant academy, 1 convent, 1 public library and 2 newspapers. St. Hyacinthe in '60 had 4,000, inhabitants, a college, convent and a few factories. In '82 the Province of Quebec had 19 towns, Point Levis being the largest with a population of 7,937; Terrebonne being the smallest with 1,308. In '51 Quebec had 5 towns with a population of 4,936. The increase in population in 30 years in Quebec's towns and cities amounted to 167,066; that of its counties and villages, 300,242. Extracts from newspapers, press opinions, etc.—A French newspaper says: "The annexation of Canada to the U.S. would effect the absorbing of the French Canadian race among the numerous nationalities of the U. S. and therefore it is better that Canada should remain separate." Circulation of the "Witness," one of Montreal's largest papers, daily 13,334; weekly 26,700. "Aurore," a French Protestant paper, circulation 1,276. A leading Canadian writer says: "It is not impossible that the day will come when Canada will demand and have an effective representation in the British Parliament, and be able to have a hand in directing the acts of the Imperial Government. This is more likely to occur than annexation to the U. S. Canadians are not likely to relinquish privileges and power as British subjects, but are more likely to make the greater use of those rights and extend their power and privilege to the utmost. As to their contemplating any change in future it would be more likely to be independence than annexation;

If Canada can have all the practical benefits of independence without the name they will not hurry to get it." The Pall Mall Gazette of England has the following: "Canada is a tie for England. How its annexation to the U. S. would tighten the bond of friendship between it and England. There is one consideration in connection with the probable absorption of Canada by the U. S. This consideration is the importance of an Americanized Canada as a link between ourselves and the U. S. as a bond of friendship to unite even more closely the two great divisions of the English speaking people. It is probable that at the present time sympathy between England and America runs higher than at any other previous period; still the manner the U. S. originally separated from England has left on the part of the Americans a feeling which we indeed have for many years ceased to share, but which is naturally kept alive by historical associations on the other side of the Atlantic until the war of the secession; the one salient event in American annals was the revolutionary struggle. Now if Canada's 5,000,000 inhabitants became quietly and peaceably of their own free will citizens of the U. S. as well as well wishers to England, the value to the latter country would be incalcuable. Every Canadian who settled in the U. S. would become a center for dissemination of phil Brittannic ideas among born Americans around him; another danger which this would counteract is that the Irishmen who have settled in Canada have become loyal subjects of England, and their influence would moderate and counteract the hatred of thousands of their fellow countrymen that have settled in the U. S. who still retain and show it by their political influence that they would injure as much as they could the imperial government that drove them from their native land by misgovernment in the past. These considerations for securing the friendship of the only other great industrial non-military nation in the world are surely as well worth our attention as any other impossible schemes for governing a universe from Downing street by telegraph; another reason is that a great part of the division line between the two countries is only imaginary and also that the river St. Lawrence is the natural outlet of a great portion of American commerce. The Manitoba legislature tried to pass a rly act allowing rly connection with the American system to tap the Canadian Pacific rly, which would have diverted the trade of Manitoba to Chicago and St. Paul, but the Dominion government preserved the Manitoba markets for the merchants and manufacturers of Canada, which is just beginning to enjoy the fruits of its enterprise. Canada, including the bonus to the C. P. rly has spent $45,000,000 to develop the Canadian northwest. Montreal "Witness" says a flood of indecency has flowed in upon society both in literature and art. Montreal dealers sell undraped figures including a large proportion of vulgarly realistic works of French artists. Quebec "Gazette" was published in French and partly in English in 1767. Rivers, harbors, railways, canals. etc, In 1882 the commissioner of Quebec government rlys affected economies to the amount of $20,000 in the pay rolls. In '82 there was a 25 foot channel from Montreal to Quebec, while the natural channel is only 10 ft. 6 in. In 1850 the flats of Lake St. Peter allowed navigation to the depth of 11 ft.; two years later 16 ft. had been secured; in '78 22 ft; $5,000,000 have been spent on this channel and Montreal harbor in the last 10 years. The Grand Trunk railway controls considerably over 3,000 miles of road. The Earth Shore railway from Quebec to Montreal is a paying line. Formerly the price of Canadian stocks moved submissively with the American railway department now the Canadian market on the contrary asserts a will of its own. The Canadian securities refuse to sympathise and have even been buoyant when American stocks are falling.

The action of New York at:te imposes on the Canadian government the same duty. The government is confronted by the alternative to abolish the tolls on Canadian canals or render inoperative the $40,000,000 that has been spent on Canadian canals up to '82. Of the freight paying tolls of the Welland canal in '81 no less than 629,347 tons out of a total traffic of 700,478 tons were derived from the United States over half of which was United States merchandise passing down the St. Lawrence to Canadian ports for export to Europe. The Quebec government sale of the North Shore railway to the Grand Trunk railway is detrimental to the interests of Quebec. Now there will be little if any of the produce of the Northwest shipped from Quebec, which would have been the terminus of the Canadian Pacific railway. In 1879 the mileage of Canadian rlys was 6,265 miles; in '81 7,230. Canada shows the largest rly increase of all the British colonies except India; 5000 cars are coming and going between Montreal and Toronto in '82, loaded with freight and an equally large amount on the Eastern division; 25 miles of the Canadian Pacific rly was built in a week in July '82, which is without parallel in the history of rly construction; at that date 728 miles of track had been constructed west of Winnipeg. By the completion of the Ontario and Quebec rly a thro connection has been established between the Eastern seaports and the Rocky Mountains. In 1880 $316,538 worth of tolls were collected on the Welland, St. Lawrence, Chambly, Burlington Bay, Ottawa and Newcastle canals. Nominal capital raised for the railways of Canada: ordinary share capital, $119,000,000; preference share capital, $70,450,000; bonded debt, $80,661,000; government and municipal aid, $100,435,000; total capital, $371,051,000; total number of passengers carried on Canadian rlys in '82, 4,811,582; tons of freight, 8,045,678; yield of passenger traffic, $7,076,339; freight traffic, $15,506,935; mails and express freight, $851,222; other sources, $102,075; total annual receipts of rlys, $23,561,477; their expenses were for maintenance of line buildings, etc., $3,068,376; working and repairs of engines, $5,170,193; working and repairs of cars, $1,629,247; general operating expense, $6,253,728; total expenses, $16,840,705. During the month of Aug. '82, the Canadian Pacific Ra'lwy Co, paid out $2,200,000. The Dominion government before it sold the Pacific rly to the syndicate spent on it $4,175,000. In '82 it spent on telegraph and cable lines, $53,635. In '63 there were in Ontario and Quebec 3,130 miles of telegraph and 4,045 miles of wire; 146 stations open to the public; 208 instruments in use and 332,770 messages sent in the year. The cost of road and equipments of all Ontario's and Quebec's rly in '60, $92,283,495; net income of all their rlvs in '60, $1,033,033; total length of rly in Canada in '60, 1,907 miles; gross earnings of the Grand Trunk railway in '61, $,517,829; that of the Great Western, $2,266,684. Schools, colleges, education, etc. In '82 McGill University was 50 yrs old. A branch of Laval University of Quebec was started in Montreal in '82. In '81 166 students attended McGill University, 56 from Quebec, 16 from U. S. and the remainder from other Canadian provinces; $133 in 4 yrs has to be paid by each student for lectures; $5 for matriculation fee; $4 for reregistration each session; for degree $20, reregistration of degree $1; hospital fees for medical students $12; good board from $15 to 20 a month; 12 French Canadians and 13 English passed at McGill for the degree of B. L. A. in '79; 57 students have taken and are taking the degree of L. L. B.; Since 1844 720 have passed as doctors of medicine, 88 as M. A's, 2 as masters of engineering and applied science, as bachelors of civil law 600; 32 as bachelors of applied science; in mining and assaying 7; in practical chemistry 1; in civil engineering 16. A leading Canadian paper says some Canadian male students object to the coeducation of ladies in medical colleges because it involves the suppression of coarseness. Many of the ladies also take the highest scholarships. The land occupied by schools in Montreal cost $121,308. The buildings $192,222, and the furniture of them $17,685; number of teachers 99; number of scholars 3,676. The Polytechnic school of Montreal cost $72,050, each graduate from the school costs the government $1775. In '84 Canada had 860,000 schools. Quebec Seminary, now Laval University, was founded in 1714; 75 students attended it; in '60 300. In '62 Canada had 3,676 schools with 188,335 scholars; 3 normal and model schools with 200 pupils; 4 special schools 135 scholars; academies for boys 41 with 3,976 pupils; academies for girls 84 with 15,564 pupils; colleges 7 with 247 students; classical colleges 13 with 2,688 students; industrial colleges, 14 with 2,300 pupils; universities, 3 with 371 students. In '62 Canada's people paid $379,675 for school purposes and its government $187,195. McGill university is Protestant, but is free to all denominations; it is 350 ft. wide. In '58 it had 711 students; 30 in law, 90 in medicine, 35 in arts; its high school contained 244, its normal school 70, and model school 230; in '63 it had 937 students. Quebec gov. in '60 had appropriated 2,125,179 acres of land in aid of its collegiate institutions. Quebec had in '80, 4 universities, 1 English and 2 French. Minerals, mines, their products, etc. $6,000,000 were invested in phosphate mines in Canada in '82; deposits of iron discovered in '82 at East Sherbrooke. No hard soil mines have as yet been discovered in Quebec; petroleum has been discovered at Port Neuf. In '61 Acton copper mines produced 3,203 tons of ore valued at $150 a ton; in '63 the amount of copper exported from Canada amounted to $92,080; in 1880 the export of mines were $293,650; in '61 Champlain county produced 17,877 tons of iron valued at $5,390; in '59, 7000 tons of copper were shipped from Lake Superior mines; in '61, 1,011 tons of copper, worth $328,581 were raised in Canada; west petroleum, naptha and asphalt were found in Canada. The oil region covers 7000 square miles; silver has been discovered in small quantities; gold also in similar quantities. Quebec is one of the poorest provinces of Canada in minerals. Laws, crime, prisons, lunacy, pauperism etc.—A Quebec justice of peace was fined $50 and 24 hours imprisonment for tampering with a jury-man. "The Prisoners aid society" of Quebec has appealed to the government for a better classification of Protestant prisoners. The general council of the bar of Quebec held a session in '83 and discussed reforms in direction of cheaper and more expeditious legal procedure. Annual report of Montreal jail for '71—There were 2,350 commitments; 438 wer females and 628 were of foreign birth; 1,522 were R. C's; of these criminals 27 were under 14; 308 between 14 and 20; 745 between 20 and 30; 338 between 30 and 40; 99 of them were sailors, and only 1 professional man. Church wardens are liable for obligations conrracted purely in their official capacity.